Paul and the Self

Paul and the Self

Apostolic Teaching for Personal Wholeness

J. Knox Chamblin

Baker Books

A Division of Baker Book House Co
Grand Rapids, Michigan 49516

© 1993 by J. Knox Chamblin
Published by Baker Books
a division of Baker Book House Company
P.O. Box 6287, Grand Rapids, MI 49516-6287

Printed in the United States of America

Library of Congress Cataloging-in-Publication Data

Chamblin, J. Knox
    Paul and the Self: apostolic teaching for personal wholeness/J. Knox Chamblin.
      p. cm.
    Includes index.
    ISBN 0-8010-2572-9
    1. Bible. N.T. Epistles of Paul—Criticism, interpretation, etc. 2. Bible. N.T.
Epistles of Paul—Theology. 3. Spiritual life—Christianity—Biblical teaching I. Title.
BS2655.S62C43 1992
227'.06—dc20   92-19885

Unless otherwise noted, Scripture translations are the author's own.

Cover art: Rembrandt van Rijn
            Dutch, 1606–1669
            The Apostle Paul, Date: probably 1657, Canvas
            1.29 × 1.02 (50 3/4 × 40 1/8 in.)
            National Gallery of Art, Washington
            Widener Collection

To Ginger,
my wife, my sister, my friend,
who strengthens
and encourages
and consoles me
(1 Corinthians 14:3)

Contents

Abbreviations

BAGD	Walter Bauer, W. F. Arndt, F. W. Gingrich, and F. W. Danker, *A Greek-English Lexicon of the New Testament*, 2d ed.
BDB	Brown, Francis, S. R. Driver, and C. A. Briggs, *Hebrew and English Lexicon of the Old Testament*
EDT	*Evangelical Dictionary of Theology*, ed. Walter Elwell
ExpT	*Expository Times*
FFB	F. F. Bruce, *The Letters of Paul: an Expanded Paraphrase*
JSNT	*Journal for the Study of the New Testament*
JTS	*Journal of Theological Studies*
KJV	King James Version
LXX	Septuagint, Greek translation of the Hebrew OT
MT	Massoretic Text of the Hebrew OT
NASB	New American Standard Bible
NEB	New English Bible
NIDNTT	*New International Dictionary of New Testament Theology*, ed. Colin Brown
NIV	New International Version
NKJV	New King James Version
NRSV	New Revised Standard Version
NT	New Testament
NTS	*New Testament Studies*
OT	Old Testament
Phillips	J. B. Phillips, *The New Testament in Modern English*

RSV	Revised Standard Version
s.v.	*sub voce* ("under the word," of a lexical entry)
TC	Bruce M. Metzger, *A Textual Commentary on the Greek New Testament*
TDNT	*Theological Dictionary of the New Testament*
TDOT	*Theological Dictionary of the Old Testament*
WTJ	*Westminster Theological Journal*
ZNW	*Zeitschrift für die neutestamentliche Wissenschaft*

Preface

Each of us is made for three relationships—to oneself, to other people, and to God.[1] These three are distinguishable from one another, but inseparable. Moreover, each of the three is affected by the relationship that exists between God and other people. To illustrate:

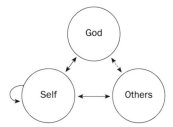

In seeking to maintain and to develop these relationships, we discover that each entails a struggle; and that (in keeping with the relationships themselves) these are not three struggles but one, each aspect of which can be understood only in relation to the other two.

We also discover to our dismay that the threefold struggle persists; that despite our longings we cannot enter into peace and rest. The struggle to end the struggle, in any or all of its dimensions, invariably fails. Indeed, it sometimes seems that the harder we strive against our problems, the more tenacious they become.

I write these words at the age of fifty-five. During the past ten or twelve years, I have often—and with greater seriousness than ever before—reflected upon the course of my life. Certain patterns of thought and atti-

---

1. These are "the three parts of morality" discussed in C. S. Lewis, *Mere Christianity* (New York: Macmillan, 1943), 55–59. He likens persons to a fleet of ships. The voyage succeeds when (1) each ship is seaworthy and running properly, (2) the ships do not collide or get in each other's way, and (3) the ships together stay on course and reach their appointed destination.

tude and conduct have come to light, some of them quite disturbing. I look back upon repeated failures in my efforts to subdue inner conflicts and fears, to combat immaturity and self-centeredness, to build genuine and enriching relationships with other people, to conquer besetting sins, and to grow in holiness and in communion with God. I now see that every period of my life has been marked by this threefold struggle. But the persistence of the failures, together with a growing understanding of the past, has made the struggles of recent years exceptionally intense and painful.

An integral part of this pilgrimage has been the personal and professional study of the Bible, especially the life and letters of the apostle Paul. My first venture into publishing was to co-author a preacher's commentary on Romans.[2] The subject of my doctoral dissertation was "Gospel according to Paul."[3] Throughout my teaching career, first at Belhaven College and then at Reformed Theological Seminary, I have concentrated on the Pauline Epistles.

I have found Paul to be a daunting presence. I suspect that many of us who chat warmly about blessings we have received from Paul's writings would find it more than a little unsettling to engage him in personal conversation.[4] But I have also found in Paul a fellow struggler. His very acknowledgment of a personal *agōn* (e.g., Phil. 1:30)—"conflict" or "struggle" or "agony"—has helped me to bear my own burden (cf. Gal. 6:2). I have discovered, furthermore, that my three areas of conflict were his as well; and that for him, as for me, the three are inextricably bound together.

A reading of his thirteen letters leaves us in no doubt that Paul agrees with M. Scott Peck: "Life is difficult."[5] But the apostle does more than witness to the reality and the magnitude of his struggles. While we might find some solace in knowing that Paul experienced hardships and could thus empathize with ours, this is hardly sufficient reason to consult him. Paul helps us by the way he interprets and responds to his struggles. In the course of pondering and teaching Paul, I have been astonished to see how often his mighty theological affirmations directly address the psychological, emotional, social, and spiritual problems with which I have wrestled. Paul has been both my pastor and my doctor, my teacher and my therapist. In my struggle toward maturity and authenticity, nothing under God has helped me so much as Paul's letters. No other source has brought such conviction and rebuke or offered such consolation and hope.

2. John R. Richardson and J. Knox Chamblin, *Proclaiming the New Testament: Romans* (Grand Rapids: Baker, 1963).

3. Ann Arbor: University Microfilms, 1979.

4. What a critic once said of Hugh Walpole, some might wish to say of Paul: "You are glad he lived, but very grateful that you didn't know him" (quoted by George F. Will, *Newsweek* [2 July 1990]: 62). Who of us would not want a Van Gogh original on the wall? Who of us would not be nervous at the prospect of sitting down to a meal with him?

5. Thus Peck begins his book *The Road Less Traveled* (New York: Simon and Schuster, 1978), 15.

In a real sense, this book is about "me and Paul" (to borrow the phrase that Dizzy Dean used of himself and his brother, both major-league pitchers). But I hope that it is not individualistic—which would violate one of Paul's great teachings. The book is written in the hope that the lessons I have learned from Paul may benefit readers as well.

For I have related Paul not merely to my personal struggle, but also to what I have seen going on around me, both within and beyond the Christian church. There are more than a few aspects of contemporary thought and life which, when viewed in the light of the Pauline Epistles, are deeply disturbing—and in some cases exceedingly dangerous. By the same token, these are matters that Paul directly addresses and concerning which he challenges us "to be made new in the spirit of [our] minds" (Eph. 4:23).

It has been exceptionally unsettling to find non- or even anti-Pauline patterns of thought and life within the precincts of the church, where persons would be expected to adhere faithfully to the apostle's way. Here too there is evidence of our doing the very thing against which Paul warns—being, or staying, "conformed to this world" (Rom. 12:2a).[6] In the face of this, he summons us, under the impact of his own teachings, to "be transformed by the renewing of [our] minds" (12:2b).

There are many books on the theology of Paul. And a growing number of books address personal problems from a Christian perspective. This book does not aspire to be a comprehensive study of Pauline theology; nor does it attempt to encompass the range of subjects that one might expect to find in a Christian counselor's handbook. I do seek, however, to bring these two areas together. The book is written in the firm conviction that Paul's teaching, including its most profound aspects, is eminently practical. When we wed the "groom" of Paul and his teachings to the "bride" of the self in its threefold struggle, a very fruitful marriage can result. It is a great pity that many excellent studies of Paul's theology fail to apply his profound insights to the deep and persistent struggles that ordinary people experience.[7] It is equally regrettable when books that seek to combat various human problems with ammunition from the Bible pluck assorted principles and promises from Paul's Epistles without attentiveness to his teaching as a whole or to the person who wrote the letters.

6. On various respects in which contemporary Christian thought and life fashion themselves according to the standards of the secular culture, see Stephen D. Eyre, *Defeating the Dragons of the World* (Downers Grove: InterVarsity, 1987). The classic treatment of a complex subject is H. Richard Niebuhr, *Christ and Culture* (New York: Harper and Brothers, 1951).

7. Lawrence J. Crabb, Jr., *Understanding People* (Grand Rapids: Zondervan, 1987), argues strongly that the Bible "provides a basis for understanding *every essential issue* with which counselors struggle" (44, with 46–73). He therefore bemoans the tendency for exegetes to address fellow scholars "while worried parents, hurt spouses, stubborn depressives, and self-hating bulimics turn in vain to Bible teachers for answers to their urgent, personal questions" (ibid., 19).

This book is an attempt to overcome, if only to a small degree, this twin deficiency. The work itself will of course be deficient: "For we know in part and we prophesy in part" (1 Cor. 13:9). Nonetheless I hope that readers may hereby encounter anew the person and work of Paul, and be directed by this means to the God who dominated his life and thought.

Acknowledgments

Many persons have contributed to the conception, progress, and completion of this book. I want to express special thanks to

those who have preached and taught the Pauline Epistles to me from my childhood, including my parents, various pastors, and my teachers at Wheaton College and Columbia Theological Seminary;

the supervisors of my doctoral studies in Paul, C. F. D. Moule of Cambridge University and Paul J. Achtemeier of Union Theological Seminary in Virginia; and to fellow doctoral candidates in both institutions;

students at Belhaven College and Reformed Theological Seminary for their attentiveness to the Scriptures and for their insights into Paul; and especially to Tom Whetstone, Tom Baird, Richard Konieczny, Greg Grigsby, and Steve Frieswick, my student assistants during the writing of the book, and to John Farrar and Janie Pillow for financial support;

churches in which some of this material was presented in the form of sermons or Sunday school lessons—especially the Trinity Presbyterian Church of Jackson, Mississippi, and the Presbyterian churches of Fayette, Rosedale, Shelby, and Union Church, Mississippi;

the board and administration of Reformed Theological Seminary for their encouragement and the provision of a sabbatical;

colleagues at Belhaven College and Reformed Theological Seminary for their camaraderie and stimulus; and especially to Ralph Davis, who challenged me to write a book on Paul before I died, and to Richard Pratt, whose approach to biblical interpretation has influenced my own;

Baker Book House, for their willingness to publish an unknown author, and especially to Jim Weaver and Linda Triemstra for all their help;

the members of my family and to all other friends who have evidenced interest in the work and have prayed for me; and especially to my wife,

Ginger, for her manifold love, her unfailing loyalty, and her constant encouragement;

Paul himself, for all that he has taught me about the gospel of salvation, and about the outworkings of God's good and acceptable and perfect will in human life and history; and to the many whose writings on Paul have helped me better to understand him;

my sovereign God and heavenly Father, for the disclosure of the glory of his Son (2 Cor. 4:6), for the wonders of his grace, for the constancy of his faithfulness, and for the enlightenment of his Holy Spirit. "Not that we are sufficient of ourselves to consider anything as from ourselves; on the contrary, our sufficiency is from God" (2 Cor. 3:5). *Soli Deo Gloria.*

1

Learning to Read Paul

If Paul is to help us, we must learn to read him. This means paying close attention to *Paul himself*, to his *writings*, and to his *readers*, and joining the three in the closest way.

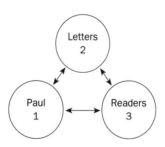

Paul and his writings are inseparable (1–2). The letters are not dispassionate but deeply personal; what Paul teaches, he has experienced. The letters in turn exert an ongoing influence upon him. And these are indeed letters, addressed to particular persons with known needs (2–3). The letters evoke responses, whether positive or negative. Given the nature of the writings, Paul and the readers encounter each other (3–1). We will consider these three in turn, recognizing all the while that they are inextricably bound together.

The Writer

This discussion rests on two convictions. The first is that Paul's experience and Paul's theology are inseparable. "I consider everything a loss compared to the surpassing greatness of knowing Christ Jesus my Lord, for whose sake I have lost all things. I consider them rubbish, that I may gain Christ and be found in him, not having a righteousness of my own that comes from the law, but that which is through faith in Christ—the righteousness that comes from God and is by faith" (Phil. 3:8–9 NIV). To detach theology from experience in that statement would be like trying to separate the color red from the color yellow in the color orange.[1] Out of his experience, Paul writes his theology, which in turn interprets the experiences of the past and shapes those of the future. So it was from the time of his conversion: Here, encountered by the risen Christ, he experiences grace that is both shattering and restorative; and he comes to recognize the truth of the early Christians' theological claims about Jesus.[2] Moreover, what Paul teaches, he embodies; his beliefs become incarnate in his life: "Put into practice the things you learned and received and heard from me, and saw in me" (Phil. 4:9). It would be illegitimate to employ Pauline doctrine merely as an aid to psychoanalyzing Paul himself, and equally illegitimate to ignore his religious experience when interpreting his theology.[3]

In the second place, eisegetes must strive to become exegetes. In seeking to encounter and to identify with Paul, we do well to be aware of the constant temptation to read our personalities and experiences *into* Paul (*eisegesis*) and refashion him in our image, rather than to let our picture of Paul arise *out of* the text (*exegesis*).[4] Yet let us not, in an effort to avoid that pitfall, focus exclusively on Pauline theology. Sound exegesis calls for being alert to insights the letters provide into Paul's person and experiences.

1. Moisés Silva, *Philippians* (Chicago: Moody, 1988), 178, says of Phil. 3:7–11, "Profoundly theological yet intensely personal, these verses ban any attempts to characterize the gospel as *either* doctrine or life."

2. See J. Knox Chamblin, "Revelation and Tradition in the Pauline *Euangelion,*" *WTJ* 48 (1986): 6–10. The complementary emphases are represented in the titles of two books stressing the cruciality of the revelation on the Damascus road: J. Gresham Machen, *The Origin of Paul's Religion* (Grand Rapids: Eerdmans, 1947); and Seyoon Kim, *The Origin of Paul's Gospel* (Grand Rapids: Eerdmans, 1982).

3. "For Paul, theology and religion are inseparable," writes George E. Ladd, *A Theology of the New Testament* (Grand Rapids: Eerdmans, 1974), 377. Cf. James D. G. Dunn, *Jesus and the Spirit* (Philadelphia: Westminster, 1975), 199–342.

4. David E. Aune, *The New Testament in Its Literary Environment* (Philadelphia: Westminster, 1987), 28, says of ancient biography: "Today it is assumed that human behavior can only be adequately understood in psychological terms. . . . In the ancient world . . . individuals were defined by the groups to which they belonged. Psychological factors were insignificant as explanations of human behavior." This is a salutary word of caution. Yet we are dealing with Paul's own writings, not those of a biographer (as in Acts); and according to these writings Paul's behavior was partly, though of course not solely, influenced by psychological factors. Ernst Käsemann, "On Paul's Anthropology," in *Perspectives on Paul*, trans. Margaret Kohl (Philadelphia: Fortress, 1971), 1–31, affirms that Paul assigns importance to the individual, but always in relation to the world to which one belongs.

A Threefold Disclosure

Paul writes as a whole person whose reason, emotion, and will constantly interact with each other as he writes.[5]

We illustrate from two letters. Of his mission to Corinth Paul says, "I came to you in weakness and in fear and with much trembling" (1 Cor. 2:3, emotional). One reason for these feelings is his sense of responsibility as the bearer of a mighty and holy message, "Jesus Christ and him crucified" (2:2, rational). His emotions also result from his obedience to Christ's commission (1:17, volitional). Had he refused to preach, he might have been spared such fear, only to be seized by one far worse (9:16–17).

In Romans, Paul calls his message "the power of God for salvation to everyone who believes" (1:16b, rational). Of this message Paul is "not ashamed" (1:16a), words expressive of a deep emotion (strictly, of a passion that issues in an emotion),[6] one that does not override but coexists with those described in 1 Corinthians 2:3. The feeling rests directly on the fact that the gospel is a saving power (note the "because"), and indirectly upon the declaration of Jesus in Mark 8:34–38.[7] Allied to both the rational and the emotional is the volitional—Paul's faithfulness to his commission (Rom. 1:1–15).

Later in Romans, Paul confesses, "I have great sorrow and unceasing anguish in my heart" (9:2, emotional). For most of his fellow Jews have

5. For a discussion of these three dimensions of the self, see Lawrence J. Crabb, Jr., *Understanding People* (Grand Rapids: Zondervan, 1987), 122–89. The idea of approaching Paul in terms of the triads *writer-letter-reader*, *rational-emotional-volitional*, and (correspondingly) *informative-affective-directive* was suggested by my friend and colleague Richard L. Pratt, Jr. He has employed such an approach in *He Gave Us Stories: The Bible Student's Guide to Interpreting Old Testament Narrative* (Brentwood, Tenn.: Wolgemuth and Hyatt, 1990).

6. "Emotion-dispositions are concerns, and concerns of a special type which can be called passions constitute our character, our inmost self. Passions differ from other concerns in determining a person's actions and emotions over relatively long stretches of his life, and roughly by being 'higher' in the order of his cares. . . . But all passions are emotion-dispositions, and the disposition issues in an emotion when the individual construes his circumstances as impinging upon the object of his passion" (Robert C. Roberts, *Spirituality and Human Emotion* [Grand Rapids: Eerdmans, 1982], 19, well expressing what lies behind Rom. 1:16).

7. For the dependence of Rom. 1:16 on Mark 8:34–38 (including the words *If anyone is ashamed of me*), see C. K. Barrett, "I am not Ashamed of the Gospel," in *New Testament Essays* (London: SPCK, 1972), 116–43. We must not, however, divest the expression of its psychological dimension (cf. ibid., 116–17).

rejected God's covenantal gifts, especially the Messiah (9:3–5, rational). The knowledge and the emotion together impel Paul to evangelize not Jews but Gentiles (11:13–14, volitional); for he also knows that Israel's salvation awaits the ingathering of the Gentiles (11:11–32). Thus in the end, Paul both bows before God's unsearchable judgments and celebrates God's revelation of Israel's coming deliverance (11:25–36). The doxology of 11:33–36 reverses 9:2. Both passages are deeply emotional; but Paul's anguish over the Israelites' alienation is now superseded by joy over their coming salvation.

Apostolic Struggle

Paul experienced *agōn*—"conflict" or "struggle"—in relation to himself, to other people, and to God.[8] As with everyone, his is a threefold struggle, each aspect of which is intelligible only in relation to the other two. Moreover, each was affected by what happened between God and other people.

We illustrate from several epistles, beginning with Galatians. "When Peter came to Antioch, I opposed him to his face" (2:11). This conflict between Paul and Peter is inseparable from the struggle to define "the truth of the gospel" (2:14); in other words, to discern the mind of God, the author of the gospel (1:6–16). What makes the conflict so intense, both within Paul and between Paul and Peter, is the question about Gentile believers' relationship to God. Paul does not dwell on his or Peter's internal struggle on this occasion. But we do know that Peter capitulated to fear (2:12), and that Paul stood fearlessly, each in the face of tremendous pressure.

Paul's love for Christ and the Philippians presents him with a dilemma that racks him to the depths of his being: "Yet what shall I choose? I do not know! I am torn between the two: I desire to depart and be with Christ, which is better by far; but it is more necessary for you that I remain in the body" (1:22–24 NIV), "necessary" because the readers have much growing to do in their relationship to God (Phil., *passim*).

Again in 1 Thessalonians, Paul's inner struggle is acute but not self-explanatory. The reason for his "intense longing" is his love for the believers (2:17–20). The restlessness that impels him to send Timothy (3:1–5), with the repeated "when we [I] could stand it no longer"), is rooted in his concern for the Thessalonians' spiritual state amid persecution and satanic assault.

Second Corinthians voices Paul's *agōn* with special poignancy. Of one episode he writes, "I had no rest in my spirit. . . . Our flesh had no rest, but

---

8. The noun *agōn* occurs only five times in Paul, the verb *agōnizomai* only six. But expressions of Paul's struggle are by no means limited to these terms. For a full treatment of the theme, see V. C. Pfitzner, *Paul, the Agon Motif* (Leiden: Brill, 1967).

we were afflicted in every way—conflicts without, fears within" (2:13; 7:5). The latter passage resumes the former; the psychosomatic character of the struggle witnesses to its intensity. Again it is other people who account for Paul's condition. He is desperate to find Titus (2:13) and to gain news of the Corinthians. His apostolic calling explains his fear of personal rejection (7:7). As the one appointed to be their spiritual father (1 Cor. 4:15), he agonizes over his children's waywardness (2 Cor. 12:19–21). His greatest dread is that the Corinthians will be "led astray from sincere and pure devotion to Christ" (11:3). "I am under daily pressure, because of my anxiety for all the churches," he testifies (11:28 NRSV), climaxing a long list of hardships.

Such passages reveal that Paul's greatest anguish was prompted by the state of things between the people under his care and the God who had commissioned him. To put the matter another way: Paul's personal *agōn* belongs to his apostolic *agōn*. It is his determined proclamation of the gospel in the face of human obduracy and antagonism both within and beyond the church that makes his personal struggle intelligible. Two further texts underscore the point: "My little children, for whom I am again in the pains of childbirth until Christ is formed in you" (Gal. 4:19). "We proclaim him . . . so that we may present everyone perfect in Christ. To this end I labor, struggling (*agōnizomenos*) with all his energy, which so powerfully works in me. I want you to know how much I am struggling (*agōn*) for you . . ." (Col. 1:28–2:1 NIV).

Suffering is central to Paul's *agōn*. "I die every day," he says (1 Cor. 15:31), as confirmed in 2 Corinthians 11:23–29. While his suffering is acutely personal, it is not individualistic but deeply relational. By this means he identifies with Christ's own suffering. "We always carry around in our body the dying of Jesus" (2 Cor. 4:10). Paul does not merely endure pain; he aspires to "the fellowship of [Christ's] suffering" (Phil. 3:10), and considers such suffering a gracious gift from God (Phil. 1:29). Identification with "Christ crucified" in turn defines the whole character of his apostolic ministry (1 Cor. 1:18–2:5). "I was appointed a herald and an apostle and a teacher" of the gospel. "That is why I suffer as I do" (2 Tim. 1:11–12). All the perils and deprivations named in 2 Corinthians 11:23–28, including the floggings and stoning and other threats to his life, are offered as evidence that he is a "servant of Christ." This is the sole explanation for his imprisonments: "I am in chains for Christ" (Phil. 1:13).[9] As with his *agōn* generally, the main explanation for Paul's suffering, as for Christ's, is believers' relation to God: "So death is at work in us, but life in you" (2 Cor. 4:12). "I fill

---

9. As a herald of the gospel, Paul becomes "an ambassador in chains" (Eph. 6:19–20). "To talk of an ambassador in chains is to employ an oxymoron. Normally an ambassador had diplomatic immunity and could not be imprisoned by those to whom he was sent, but prison chains now become the appropriate insignia for representing the gospel, the mark of the suffering apostle" (Andrew T. Lincoln, *Ephesians* [Dallas: Word, 1990], 454).

up in my flesh what is lacking in Christ's afflictions, for the sake of his body, which is the church" (Col. 1:24).[10]

Apostolic Joy

Amidst his struggle (*agōn*), Paul experiences joy (*chara*): "sorrowful, yet always rejoicing" (2 Cor. 6:10). He asks the same for others: "May you be strengthened with all power . . . for all endurance and patience with joy" (Col. 1:11 RSV). The struggle without the joy is inconceivable, given Paul's understanding of Christ and the gospel. The joy without the struggle loses its very raison d'être. As sin causes grace to go into action (Rom. 5:20–21), so suffering causes joy to spring to life.[11] As with the *agōn*, Paul's *chara* marks his relationships to himself, to other people, and to God; flows from each relationship into the other two; and finds its greatest stimulus in what happens between God and other selves.

Paul's joy over the Philippians ("my beloved . . . my joy and crown," 4:1) is simultaneously a rejoicing in the God who accomplishes his purpose in them ("I rejoice greatly in the Lord," 4:10; cf. 1:3–6). Paul rejoices over their gifts, not because of personal need, but because he knows God will bless them for their generosity (4:10–19). The joy both presupposes struggle— the threat of suffering (1:12–30), relational tensions (2:1–18; 4:2–4), and financial needs (4:10–19)—and fortifies Paul and his readers for ongoing struggle (1:6–30; 3:7–4:1). First Thessalonians is similar. "*You* are . . . *our joy*" (2:20)—which finds expression in prayer: "For what thanks can we render to God for you, for all the joy with which we rejoice for your sake before our God" (3:9 NKJV). Paul is especially glad to learn that the Thessalonians are growing in their faith and "standing firm in the Lord" (3:7–8).

The acute *agōn* of 2 Corinthians highlights the answering *chara*. Corresponding to the depths of his anxiety over Titus's mission (2:13; 7:5), Paul's jubilation over Titus's report reaches the heights. One reason is the news of the Corinthians' love for him (7:7). But he is even happier over their repentance toward God, of which their renewed love for Paul is a sign (7:8–13; cf. 13:9). Moreover, this letter eloquently demonstrates that to Paul's mind joy does not await the resolution of conflict or the end of struggle; instead, it arises precisely amidst the conflict and the struggle. "In all our troubles my joy knows no bounds" (7:4). "I delight in weaknesses, in insults, in hardships, in persecutions, in difficulties" (12:10 NIV).

In that light we look more closely at the apostle himself.

---

10. Paul's participation in Christ's death does not in the least compromise the uniqueness of Christ's atoning work.

11. "Joy is not something we can pursue directly. It is an efflorescence, a by-product of the passion/ Passion that is the only thing that can be its occasion" (Robert Farrar Capon, *Health, Money and Love* [Grand Rapids: Eerdmans, 1990], 129).

Paul's View of Himself

How closely does Paul inspect, and how seriously does he reflect upon, himself? What does he think and feel about himself? What is his self-concept?

In 2 Corinthians Paul writes with discomfort and embarrassment about his "visions and revelations from the Lord" (12:1, 11); he even refers to himself in the third person, as "a man in Christ" (12:2–5). Yet elsewhere he says that his achievements surpass those of other apostles (1 Cor. 15:10), and that readers should emulate his conduct (1 Cor. 11:1; Phil. 4:9).

Paul experienced deep, sometimes turbulent, personal struggles. Yet the evidence does not permit us to say that he was a deeply introspective individual who constantly examined and brooded over his psychological or spiritual state.[12] Paul speaks genuinely of himself, but not as a self-intoxicated navel-gazer. His talk about himself is remarkably disinterested. He "boasts" not of himself but of Christ (1 Cor. 1:29–31) and other people (1 Thess. 2:19–20). God's activity in the lives of his spiritual children evokes his greatest joy. The letters in fact reveal a person who is learning to be humble, free from himself and preoccupied with other persons and with God. Paul's talk about his struggles and attainments betrays neither self-centeredness nor self-pity nor self-glorification.[13] But it does raise another question.

Struggle and Sin

We have seen evidence that Paul agonized over the sins of his spiritual children. How does he view his own sin, and what does this contribute to his struggle? In seeking to answer this question, we consider three stages of his spiritual pilgrimage.

Paul the Pharisee was, and considered himself to be, genuinely righteous (Phil. 3:4–6).[14] It would be wrong to depict Paul during those years as an ancient counterpart to Martin Luther engulfed in despair over his manifold iniquity and longing to find a merciful God.[15] Yet in Romans 7:7–13

---

12. Nor may we say that Paul was *not* deeply introspective. The evidence is insufficient for us to dogmatize in either direction.

13. Barbara Hall, "All Things to All People: A Study of 1 Corinthians 9:19–23," in *The Conversation Continues*, ed. R. T. Fortna and B. R. Gaventa (Nashville: Abingdon, 1990), 157, writes that "Paul is a prime example of someone who had the freedom to forget self.... Having forgotten himself, because his self is guaranteed in Christ, he can use himself all the time to make whatever point he believes is needed. None of us would dare to do the same."

14. Richard N. Longenecker, *Paul, Apostle of Liberty* (New York: Harper and Row, 1964), 78, distinguishes between an "acting legalism" and a "reacting nomism" in the Pharisaism of Paul's day, and rightly places Paul in the latter category. The former means "an ordering of one's life in external and formal arrangement according to the Law in order to gain righteousness and/or appear righteous"; the latter, "the molding of one's life in all its varying relations according to the Law in response to the love and grace of God."

15. This view ascribes to Paul a degree of introspection for which there is insufficient evidence in his letters. The point is well made in Krister Stendahl, "The Apostle Paul and the Introspective Conscience of the West," reprinted in *Paul among Jews and Gentiles* (Philadelphia: Fortress, 1976), 78–80.

Paul recalls his experience of sin as a youth, beginning with the sin of covetousness, and his own murder at the hands of sin by the agency of the law. Even as Paul maintained a life of scrupulous fidelity to the commandments, he was committing sins in his heart.[16] Paul the Pharisee was, and knew himself to be, both genuinely sinful and genuinely righteous.

Paul viewed his attacks on the church as an offering pleasing to God. The letters offer no evidence that Paul's persecuting zeal was either an outlet for deep spiritual conflict or an effort to suppress suspicions that Christianity might be true. I believe that Jesus' words in Acts 26:14—"Saul, Saul, why are you persecuting me? It is hard for you to kick against the goads"— describe not Paul's struggle against conscience or suppression of truth but the futility of his opposition to Christ.[17] Nonetheless, these actions seriously affect *him*: "It is hard for *you*." While Paul believes himself to be championing God's cause (Gal. 1:13–14), and acts in ignorance of what he is really doing (1 Tim. 1:13), he is in fact persecuting the church of God (1 Cor. 15:9), which is tantamount to persecuting Jesus himself (Acts 26:14). Paul's opposition to God sets Paul in opposition to himself, even if Paul does not know what is happening to him.

The second stage is Paul's perception, as a Christian, of his preconversion state. "I was once a blasphemer and a persecutor and a man of violence," the worst of sinners, he recalls in 1 Timothy 1:13–16. It is now some thirty years since his conversion; yet he writes, "I am (*eimi egō*) the worst" of sinners, still dependent on Jesus' "mercy" and "unlimited patience" (1:15–16).

Similar but more revealing is an earlier confession: "For I am the least of the apostles and do not even deserve to be called an apostle, because I persecuted the church of God. But by the grace of God I am what I am, and his grace to me was not without effect. No, I worked harder than all of them— yet not I, but the grace of God that was with me" (1 Cor. 15:9–10 NIV). Verse 9 is written by a man still broken under the weight of his past sin: "I am [*egō eimi*, as in 1 Tim. 1:15] the least . . . and *do* not deserve. . . ." Vital to Paul's effectiveness as an apostle is that he never forget his days as a persecutor. Yet it could hardly be said that the memory leaves him paralyzed. On the contrary, 15:10 testifies to his superlative achievements. The explanation lies in God's grace, by which Paul has been liberated from the guilt of his sins and energized for apostolic service. An ongoing awareness of grace

16. On the autobiographical dimension of Rom. 7:7–13, and its compatibility with Phil. 3:4–6, see Robert H. Gundry, "The Moral Frustration of Paul before His Conversion: Sexual Lust in Romans 7:7–25," in *Pauline Studies*, ed. Donald A. Hagner and Murray J. Harris (Grand Rapids: Eerdmans, 1980), 228–45.

17. See Longenecker, *Paul*, 98–101. F. F. Bruce, *The Book of the Acts* (Grand Rapids: Eerdmans, 1954), 491, believes that Paul is trying to "stifle the conviction" that Christianity is true. I. Howard Marshall, *The Acts of the Apostles* (Grand Rapids: Eerdmans, 1980), 395, thinks a struggle against destiny (rather than conscience) is probably in view.

reminds Paul of the appalling sin from which he has been delivered; an ongoing awareness of the sin keeps him dependent on grace.[18]

Paul the Christian concludes not that his "righteousness under the law" was spurious, but that his confidence in that righteousness was the gravest of sins (Phil. 3:3–7). But again, he is far from despairing. Solidarity with Christ and other believers renews his zeal (3:9–14) and releases his joy (Phil., *passim*). Paul "forgets what is behind" (3:13), not by being unable to remember it (3:5–6 recalls his past in some detail) but by abandoning it (3:7–8).[19] There is a struggle (3:12–14), but not over Paul's preconversion sin. He can hardly be said to strive over something he has flung away in disgust.

We turn to Paul's Christian experience. The main subject of 1 Corinthians 9:27—"I beat and enslave my body"—is not Paul's rights (as in 9:1–18), but his battle against personal sin.[20] Yet the act does not signal self-absorption or self-reproach or self-destruction. Paul's focus is outward. His overriding motive is not personal moral triumph but the fulfillment of his apostolic commission and the victory of the gospel (9:14–23), which in turn explains his striving for moral excellence.[21]

Romans also speaks of Paul's ongoing struggle against sin: "I have the desire to do what is good, but I cannot carry it out. For what I do is not the good I want to do; no, the evil I do not want to do—this I keep on doing" (7:18–19 NIV). Yet in this very condition, Paul experiences "life and peace" (8:6), and "joy in the Holy Spirit" (14:17). Even as the war persists, battles are won. Paul has received God's saving verdict (8:1, 30–33); through the power of Christ and the Spirit he knows what it is to achieve real, though partial, victory over the "sinful flesh" (8:2–17 RSV).[22]

With respect to his sin, as in other respects, Paul is not preoccupied with himself. He does not often talk about his sins. What evidence we have indicates that Paul is by no means indifferent to his sins. He recognizes their enormity and their tenacity. The sins of his Jewish past he views with horror. An integral part of his struggle as a Christian is an ongoing battle against personal sin.[23] At the same time, Paul is not obsessed with his sins.

---

18. Paul places himself both beneath the other apostles (v. 9) and above them (v. 10; cf. vv. 3–8). In both cases he states what for him are matters of fact; neither statement is self-serving. Only a genuinely humble person could honestly make both statements, and speak as disinterestedly in the one as in the other.

19. I believe that Paul "forgets" (3:13) both his credentials as a Jew (3:4–8) and his experiences as a Christian (3:7–12). See also Gerald F. Hawthorne, *Philippians* (Waco: Word, 1983), 153.

20. 9:27b pertains not to rights but to Paul's fidelity to his message. Cf. Rom. 6:13, 19; and C. K. Barrett, *The First Epistle to the Corinthians* (New York: Harper and Row, 1968), 218.

21. Well emphasized by Pfitzner, *Agon Motif*, 190–95.

22. On Rom. 7:14–25 and 8:1–17 as two views of the Christian struggle, see chap. 7.

23. Thus too David Wenham, "The Christian Life: A Life of Tension? A Consideration of the Nature of Christian Experience in Paul," in *Pauline Studies*, 80–94. Stendahl, "The Apostle Paul," in his zeal to distance Paul from the "introspective conscience of the west," minimizes the Epistles' witness to Paul's struggle against personal sin. See the critique of Stendahl by Ernst Käsemann, "Justification and Salvation History in the Epistle to the Romans," in *Perspectives on Paul*, 60–78.

His experience of sin's utter sinfulness (Rom. 7:13) does not leave him frozen in despair or paralyzed by guilt. On the contrary, joined to his self-awareness as a sinner is an astonishing freedom of spirit and zest for work. The explanation lies in his ongoing experience of God's grace and the Spirit's power. He remains conscious of past sins but has ceased to struggle over them. Against present sins he continues to fight, but amid the battle he experiences victory and joy.

The Writings

The thirteen epistles are an essential bridge between Paul and the Christians under his care.[24] How are we to view these documents?

The Declarative and the Hortatory

Paul declares the gospel of salvation through Jesus Christ, and exhorts his readers to live accordingly.[25] The declarative and the hortatory are inseparable, but they are distinguishable too. The *euangelion* is pure indicative; its purpose is to proclaim saving events, not to prescribe a pattern of conduct. To be sure, the message of salvation calls for a certain kind of behavior; all the gospel's indicatives are veiled imperatives. Still, believers' good works are the effects of the gospel rather than its basis or its content (Eph. 2:8–10).[26]

For addressing the struggles of the self, both the declarative and the hortatory are vital. But we must begin with Paul's great indicatives about the person and work of Christ. Only on this basis are his ethical exhortations intelligible and workable. We may begin with a theme of the *euangelion* such as the cross, and then make further inquiry of Paul: What are the implications of Jesus' death for each dimension of the human struggle? and what are the ethical consequences of belonging to Christ crucified? Or we may start at the other end of the spectrum, with, for example, our difficulties in getting along with other people, and in that light explore Paul's teaching about such a subject as the end of history, asking how the prospect of those events can influence conduct toward others.

24. For a defense of the Pauline authorship of all thirteen letters, see Donald Guthrie, *New Testament Introduction*, 4th ed. (Downers Grove: InterVarsity, 1990). While the Book of Acts is an eminently trustworthy source for the life and preaching of Paul, the present study concentrates on Paul's own writings.

25. The terms *declarative* and *hortatory* apply to the content itself, not to the mode of presentation; either may be proclaimed (*kēryssein*) or taught (*didaskein*).

26. The structure of the letters illustrates this distinction and order, e.g., Col. 1–2 with 3–4, and Eph. 1–3 with 4–6. Victor Paul Furnish, *Theology and Ethics in Paul* (Nashville: Abingdon, 1968), in stressing the inseparability of the indicative and the imperative in Paul, obscures the proper distinction between them. Cf. the critique in J. Knox Chamblin, *Gospel according to Paul* (Ann Arbor: University Microfilms, 1979), 509–25. "With Paul, the 'imperative' of God's demand is never absorbed by the 'indicative' of the communication of salvation. Otherwise, the 'indicative' would itself become law" (Hans Conzelmann, "Current Problems in Pauline Research," *Interpretation* 22 [1968]: 181).

The Word of Truth

Paul testifies that he is, by God's appointment, an apostle (*apostolos*) of Christ. His autobiographical statements are offered in the service of his apostolic calling and message.[27] The teaching he imparts, whether to non-believers or to believers, whether to Jews or to Gentiles, whether by letter or by oral presentation, has its origin in the holy Trinity. Both elements of his teaching, the hortatory no less than the declarative, are invested with divine authority. He is Christ's ambassador, duty bound to deliver what Christ has entrusted to him (2 Cor. 5:20). He proclaims God's Word, not man's (1 Thess. 2:13). He has been tutored not by human wisdom but by God's Spirit (1 Cor. 2:13).[28] He therefore identifies his teaching as *alētheia*—the true as opposed to the false, the real as opposed to the spurious, the reliable as opposed to the deceptive.[29]

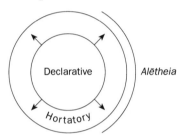

The church was quick to recognize the unique authority and divine origin of the Pauline Epistles. That nearly half of the writings in the New Testament canon (thirteen out of twenty-seven) come from Paul's pen testifies to the immense weight that the early Christians attached to his teachings.[30]

27. Writes George Lyons, *Pauline Autobiography: Toward a New Understanding* (Atlanta: Scholars, 1985), 225, 226, "As in the ancient philosophical lives, Paul's autobiographical remarks are closely bound to his profession, i.e., his vocation as an apostle of Jesus Christ, and his 'philosophy,' the gospel which he proclaims and under the authority of which he himself lives. . . . He highlights his 'autobiography' in the interests of this gospel and his readers." On Paul's use of *apostolos*, see K. H. Rengstorf, *TDNT* 1:437–43; Dietrich Müller, *NIDNTT* 1:128–35.

28. On the Godhead as the source of Paul's teaching, and the consequent authority of all its parts in all its modes, see also Rom. 1:1–17; 15:16–19; 1 Cor. 1:17–2:16; 7:25, 40; 9:1–23; 14:37; 15:1–4; 2 Cor. 10:8; 13:10; Gal. 1:1–16; 1 Thess. 4:2, 15; 2 Thess. 2:15; 1 Tim. 2:7; 2 Tim. 1:10–11; Chamblin, *Gospel*, 94–165; ibid., "Revelation and Tradition in the Pauline *Euangelion*," 1–16; F. F. Bruce, *Tradition Old and New* (Grand Rapids: Zondervan, 1970), 29–38; Ladd, *Theology*, 380–94.

29. See the excellent treatment of Paul's understanding of "truth" (*alētheia*) by Anthony C. Thiselton, in *NIDNTT* 3:884–88. *Alētheia* refers expressly to the declarative (*euangelion*) in some passages (2 Cor. 4:2–5; 6:7; Gal. 2:5, 14; Eph. 1:13; Col. 1:5; 2 Thess. 2:13–14); in others it embraces the hortatory as well (more likely so in 1 Tim. 2:4; 3:15; 4:3; 6:5; 2 Tim. 2:15, 25; Titus 1:1; less likely so in 2 Cor. 6:7; 11:10; 13:8).

30. See 2 Pet. 3:15–16. Bruce Chilton, *Beginning New Testament Study* (Grand Rapids: Eerdmans, 1987), 51, calls Paul "the most influential writer in the New Testament . . . [and] a religious event in his own right." On the criteria for canonicity, and the process by which Paul's letters came to be included in the canon, see Bruce M. Metzger, *The Canon of the New Testament* (Oxford: Clarendon, 1987), 251–62. For a popular appreciation of Paul's impact on the course of history to the present day, see Gerald Parshall, "The Momentous Mission of the Apostle Paul," *U. S. News and World Report* [22 April 1991]: 54–55.

It indicates too that God has chosen Paul's Epistles as a principal means for addressing human beings. Given the nature of the letters, it is ultimately the triune God, not Paul, who confronts the readers.

The *euangelion* entrusted to Paul, besides being a witness to saving events (Rom. 1:1–4; 1 Cor. 15:1–4), is itself an expression of saving power, the channel along which God's saving righteousness is imparted (Rom. 1:16–17; 1 Cor. 1:18). It is no bare word but one laden with the Spirit's power (1 Cor. 2:4–5; 1 Thess. 1:5). By this very means God works in those who believe (1 Thess. 2:13).[31] In other words, Paul's teachings are not an alternative to therapy but are themselves a source of therapy. By the agency of the Pauline gospel, together with the hortatory teachings built upon it, God transforms readers and invites them into wholeness of life. This is to be strongly and urgently proclaimed in the face of assorted therapies on today's market that encourage us to find healing not in God (whose very existence may be denied) but in ourselves; not by encounter with objective reality but through clarifying the values that lie deep within our own psyches; not by the reception of revealed truth but by commitment to truth as we ourselves define it.[32] According to Paul, being made whole entails an encounter with the triune God; and this occurs, by God's own design, through God's revealed Word. We gain access to the *alētheia* that is in Jesus (Eph. 4:21) through the *alētheia* of the Word (Eph. 1:13), which, like its subject, is true, real, and reliable. We encounter the Christ who is "the power (*dynamis*) of God and the wisdom (*sophia*) of God" (1 Cor. 1:24) through the *dynamis* and *sophia* of the Word, which witnesses to him (Rom. 1:16; Col. 3:16).

In the last of his preserved writings, Paul exhorts Timothy: "Proclaim the Word" (2 Tim. 4:2). The Word in question is "the word of God" (2:9) and so "the word of truth" (2:15). It includes both the Old Testament (3:15–17; "All Scripture is God-breathed," v. 16) and the apostolic message (1:8–14); it embraces both the declarative and the hortatory: "All Scripture is . . . beneficial for teaching, for reproof, for correction, for training in righteousness" (3:16–17); "reprove, rebuke, encourage, with great patience in teaching" (4:2). Paul's appeal is urgent, for false teaching threatens to turn believers "away from the truth" and thus from God (4:3–5). If the Christians under Timothy's care are to be sound (in every sense of the word), let them give heed to "sound doctrine" (4:3).[33]

---

31. On the gospel as a power, see Chamblin, *Gospel*, 53–71.

32. See the passionate assault on the academy's advocacy of the relativity and subjectivity of truth in Allan Bloom, *The Closing of the American Mind* (New York: Simon and Schuster, 1987). George F. Will writes concerning "a Sixties disorder" that "the cult of self-validating expression contributed to the debasement of education, which came to be considered a process of letting something out of students rather than of putting something into them," *Newsweek* (25 March 1991): 65.

33. Behind "sound" lies *hygiainousēs*, from *hygiainō*, "be in good health, be healthy or sound" (BAGD, *s.v.*), hence our word *hygiene*.

The word of truth is able to renew and transform the mind (Eph. 4:22–24; Rom. 12:2), in the face of a host of teachings that ignore or assault or contradict sound doctrine, or employ Paul's writings in a highly selective manner, or mingle his healthy teachings with those that are injurious. This book is written in the belief that "Paul has remained unsurpassed in his insight into the mind of Christ,"[34] and that his letters are a message from the Great Physician delivered by a person who had experienced to an extraordinary degree the divine surgery. Paul is one patient telling other patients where to find healing. So let us be both vigilant and expectant as we begin this study. To reapply some of Paul's words, "everything that was written in the past was written to teach us, so that through endurance and the encouragement of the Scriptures we might have hope" (Rom. 15:4 NIV).

The Readers

Paul does not write dispassionately or theoretically. He is not producing term papers or articles for an encyclopedia. He writes as a pastor to real persons, and he writes as a whole person to whole persons. Moreover, out of his own threefold struggle he addresses that of the Christians under his care.

To be sure, as we move from Paul's day and his first readers to our own day and a new set of readers, certain adjustments must be made.[35] Yet the meaning of persons remains essentially the same throughout history, and the human condition is fundamentally the same in our day as in Paul's, which helps to explain why people today read (and argue about) Paul as avidly as ever. We approach the apostle in the confidence that he speaks from the depths of his own person to the depths of ours.

Addressing the Whole Person

Just as Paul writes by the united exercise of his reason, emotions, and will, so the informative, affective, and directive are woven together in his letters. Correspondingly, the recipient is called upon to respond as a whole person whose reason, emotions, and will constantly affect each other.[36] None is a freewheeling entity capable of operating independently of the other two. The effects therefore are manifold. For example, the informative addresses not only the reason but also the emotions and the will, and the

---

34. F. F. Bruce, *Paul, Apostle of the Heart Set Free* (Grand Rapids: Eerdmans, 1977), 474.

35. Cf. Anthony C. Thiselton, *The Two Horizons* (Grand Rapids: Eerdmans, 1980); and Pratt, *He Gave Us Stories*, pt. 3.

36. Says Crabb, *Understanding People*, 69, "The Scriptures will never come fully alive until we bring all of who we are to its truth."

directive can influence the emotions and the reason as well as the will.[37] A reader may be moved to tears or to action by being informed of Jesus' death; Paul's own tears or actions may affect the reader's reason, and so on.

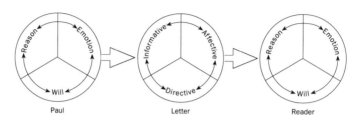

We may illustrate from several epistles. Romans 12:1–2 is primarily directive: "Therefore, I urge you, brothers, in view of God's mercy, to offer your bodies as living sacrifices, holy and pleasing to God. . . . Do not conform any longer to the pattern of this world, but be transformed by the renewing of your mind" (NIV). The directive is founded upon both the affective (the doxology that immediately precedes) and the informative ("God's mercy," an apt summary of the preceding chapters, to which the opening "therefore" points). The person who obeys the directive discovers God's will, which is *"good, acceptable, and perfect"* (12:26b) and therefore affects the emotions as surely as the intellect and will.

Philippians 4:4—"Rejoice in the Lord always; again I will say: Rejoice!"—is an emphatic appeal to the will, as indicated by the repeated imperative *rejoice* and the adverb *always*. Paul also calls the reader's reason into action. The very study of the verse requires the use of the mind; and the presence of the phrase *in the Lord* demonstrates that joy is inseparable from the right understanding of Christ. Yet a reader has not fully obeyed the command until he or she experiences the emotion of joy. The emotion does not occur to the exclusion of the reason and the will; but a joy that excludes the emotional is no joy at all.

Paul's teaching about love is likewise to be understood. For example, in Ephesians 5:2 the command to "walk in love" (directive) is based on the fact of Christ's sacrifice, "just as Christ loved us and gave himself up for us" (informative). And the directive of 1 Corinthians 14:1, "Pursue love," rests upon the preceding portrait of love, including the statement that

37. J. I. Packer, *Knowing God* (Downers Grove: InterVarsity, 1973), 236, says of Paul's pastoral purpose in Rom. 8: "Think of what you know of God through the gospel, says Paul, and apply it. Think against your feelings; argue yourself out of the gloom they have spread; unmask the unbelief they have nourished; take yourself in hand, talk to yourself, make yourself look up from your problems to the God of the gospel; let *evangelical* thinking correct *emotional* thinking." Yet true "evangelical thinking" embraces and moves the emotions; the book just quoted has this effect. On the influence of actions on emotions, and on emotions as "setting one's mind" on what one believes, see Roberts, *Spirituality*, 21–24.

"love . . . rejoices in the truth," 13:6 (both informative, "the truth," and affective, "rejoices").

Such passages warn us against interpreting Paul atomistically. He is not a purely emotional being whose sole responsibility is to make us feel good about ourselves. "Paul does not suspect the emotions per se or wish them suppressed in the Christian life . . .; but he is all too aware of their unreliability and volatility in themselves,"[38] that is, when severed from the cognitive and the volitional. And while Paul's theology is intellectually overwhelming, it is not addressed exclusively to the reason: he decries a knowledge (so-called) that is divorced from love (1 Cor. 8:1–3; 13:1–13). Nor can his directives be obeyed by the bare exercise of will power: let us recall that Paul was not only obliged to preach in Rome, but also eager to do so (Rom. 1:14–15). An atomistic approach would fragment both writer and reader.[39]

Addressing the Person in Relationship

Paul's threefold address to the reader encompasses all three relationships and the struggle that each entails.

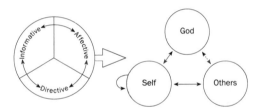

We start with readers' relationship to themselves. Second Corinthians 13:5 (NIV) begins with the directive ("Examine yourselves to see whether you are in the faith; test yourselves"); then speaks informatively of the factual basis for the test ("Do you not realize that Christ Jesus is in you?"); and concludes by showing how closely linked these two elements are ("unless, of course, you fail the test"). The affective element is present too, both underscoring the directive and resting on the informative, in the preceding threat of judgment (13:2–4, for arousing readers' proper fear) and in the following promises of apostolic intercession (13:7, 9) and gentleness (13:10, for encouraging fearful readers).

38. James D. G. Dunn, *Romans* (Dallas: Word, 1988), 364.

39. Richard F. Lovelace, *Dynamics of Spiritual Life* (Downers Grove: InterVarsity, 1979), 250, speaks of three "false pieties" that arose within evangelicalism owing to ignorance of Jonathan Edwards's teaching about the unity of understanding, will, and emotion: "one based on emotional tastes divorced from works and theological depth, another based on will power and works, and a third consisting of notional orthodoxy."

Relationships to other persons may be illustrated from Philippians. The directives of 2:2–5 ("Make my joy complete by being like-minded. . . . Do nothing from selfish ambition or vain conceit, but in humility consider others better than yourselves") are founded on 2:1, both its informative elements (union with Christ, experience of his love, fellowship in the Spirit) and its affective ("encouragement . . . comfort . . . affection and compassion").[40] Moreover, the directive is interlaced with the informative and the affective in 2:2–5 ("by being like-minded [*phronēte*] . . . in humility consider . . . your attitude [*phroneite*] should be . . ."),[41] and further sustained by the informative in the hymn of 2:6–11. On this basis the directives are resumed in 2:12–17 ("*Therefore* . . . work out your salvation," etc.), they being again buttressed by both the informative ("as you have always obeyed," "it is God who works in you") and the affective ("with fear and trembling," "I am glad and rejoice with all of you").

Consider readers' relationship to God according to 2 Thessalonians 2. The informative of verses 13–14 ("brothers beloved by the Lord . . . God chose you to be saved [and] called you through our gospel") leads to the directive of verse 15 ("So then, brothers, stand firm and hold fast to the traditions"), both of which prepare for the affective of verses 16–17 ("encouragement and good hope," the effect of God's love, and a spur to obedience).

Finally, we illustrate the inseparability of the reader's three relationships by turning to Colossians 3.

God and the self. "The peace of Christ" (3:15) speaks concisely of the manifold liberation and restoration that his work achieves (3:1–14). "The word of Christ" (3:16), embracing both the declarative and the hortatory, is the means by which the peace of Christ is imparted. Verse 17 affirms Christ's sovereignty over every aspect of the person's life: "Whatever you do, in word or deed, do all things in the name of the Lord Jesus."

The self. The "rule" of the peace of Christ establishes stability and order at the very center of one's being ("in your hearts," 3:15).[42] By the Word of Christ the self is devastated: "Put to death . . . , rid yourselves . . . , you have taken off the old man . . ." (3:5–9). By the same Word the self is restored: "you have been raised with Christ . . . , have put on the new man, which is being renewed . . . Let the Word of Christ dwell in you *richly*" (3:1–4, 10–16). By self-abandonment, whether through utterances of praise to God or in acts of service to other people (3:16b–17), the self finds fulfillment.

---

40. Here in Phil. 2, the affective provides a basis for Paul's directive, whereas in Rom. 12:1–2 (considered earlier) the affective is a consequence of the directive.

41. The verb *phroneō* embraces both thought and feeling, and implies a course of action on which one has "set the mind."

42. For more on the heart as the center of the person as a rational, emotional, and volitional being, see chap. 2.

The self and other selves. The peace of Christ is no private possession. The self experiences peace in relationship both to God and to other people: "As members of the one body you were called to peace" (3:15). Offered in place of destructive relationships (3:5–9) are those that heal wounds and bind persons together (3:10–14). Paul calls us to far more than simply "affirming one another" with "a word of encouragement": what imparts the peace and renews the person is nothing less than "the word of Christ."[43] What each individual has experienced of the peace of Christ, and learned about the Word of Christ, is to be imparted to other members of the church: "teach and admonish one another with all wisdom" (3:16b). Others are built up as they hear us voice praise and gratitude to God (3:16c).[44]

Embracing Paul

Correctly reading the Pauline Epistles requires more than detached analysis. Paul writes, as he says, "to persuade men" (2 Cor. 5:11). He clearly considers that until readers positively respond to his manifold appeal they have not properly read him.

To embrace Paul requires two steps. The first is to make him and his writings rather than ourselves the center of gravity. That is, rather than to allow our preunderstanding to govern our exposition, or to employ Paul to help us clarify our existing values and struggles, we must make an effort to enter into his world and discern his perspective on reality.[45]

But a further step is necessary, and that is to share Paul's experience of reality. Until this happens, we have not fully understood him. He writes out of faith to secure a response of faith (Rom. 1:16–17), which includes both an encounter with the person of Christ and the acceptance of the apostolic teaching about him.[46] Only thus can persons perceive the spiritual realities of which Paul speaks (1 Cor. 2:6–16). Only when a person has been (in Paul's language) "justified by [Christ's] blood" (Rom. 5:9), "saved . . . through the bath of rebirth and renewal by the Holy Spirit" (Titus 3:5),

43. Eph. 4:29, "Do not let any unwholesome talk come out of your mouths, but only what is helpful for building others up according to their needs, that it may benefit those who listen" (NIV) must be read in light of 4:15, "speaking the truth in love," where "the truth" is "the word of truth, the gospel of your salvation" (1:13).

44. Doubtless a principal reason for the joy expressed in these "psalms, hymns and spiritual songs" is the experience of rescue from the destructive conduct of 3:5–9 and of entry into relations marked by the qualities of 3:10–14.

45. Bloom, *Closing*, 374, observes, "There is an enormous difference between saying, as teachers once did, 'You must learn to see the world as Homer and Shakespeare did,' and saying, as teachers now do, 'Homer and Shakespeare had some of the same concerns you do and can enrich your vision of the world.' In the former approach students are challenged to discover new experiences and reassess old; in the latter, they are free to use the books in any way they please" ("The Student and the University," 336–82, is most illuminating). The same applies, *mutatis mutandis*, to the reading of Paul.

46. Chamblin, "Revelation and Tradition," 1–16.

"baptized into Christ Jesus" (Rom. 6:3), and endowed with "the mind of Christ" (1 Cor. 2:16), can he or she understand and appropriate Paul aright.

"By setting forth the truth (*alētheia*) plainly," says Paul, "we commend ourselves to every person's conscience in the sight of God" (2 Cor. 4:2). The right response to *alētheia* entails much more than an intellectual grasp of Pauline doctrine (as the presence of the term *conscience* already indicates). According to Paul, until my life bears the marks of *alētheia*—until I, like *alētheia* itself, become real and genuine—I cannot be said to have understood it. The sure sign of knowledge is love for God and neighbor (1 Cor. 8:1–3; 13:1–13).[47] "Knowledge of the truth . . . leads to godliness" (Titus 1:2 NIV).

The Already and the Not Yet

Paul's *agōn*, and that of his readers, is deeply personal and relational; but it is not explicable in these terms exclusively. The Christian *agōn* is part of a larger *agōn*, one which spans the whole of history and in which the entire creation participates. To be more exact: Paul's struggle is intelligible only in the context of his eschatology, his teaching about the last things.[48]

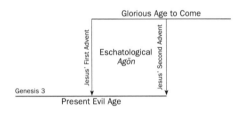

The coming of Christ inaugurated the last days (Gal. 4:4). The gifts promised in the Old Testament are now being bestowed: Messiah, the Holy Spirit, God's saving righteousness, the gospel, even faith (Gal. 3:23). The powers of the glorious age to come are being loosed against the powers of the "present evil age" (1 Cor. 10:11; Gal. 1:4). By his death and resurrection Christ achieved a decisive victory over Sin and all the agencies at its command.[49]

But God's final rule thus inaugurated is not yet consummated. The decisive battle has been fought and won, but the war continues; final victory is assured but not yet attained. The cosmic struggle which commenced with the incarnation of God's Son will persist till the powers of the "present evil age" are completely vanquished upon Christ's return to execute final judgment.

47. On this point, see Thiselton, *NIDNTT* 3:885–88.
48. To be especially commended for their treatment of this subject are Herman Ridderbos, *Paul: An Outline of His Theology*, trans. John R. DeWitt (Grand Rapids: Eerdmans, 1975); Geerhardus Vos, *The Pauline Eschatology* (Grand Rapids: Eerdmans, 1961); and Ladd, *Theology*.
49. For development of these points, see chaps. 2, 3.

By his personal struggle Paul participates in the cosmic struggle. His life illustrates the tension between the "already" and the "not yet" of Christ's saving work (Rom. 7:14–25). His ministry becomes an arena in which Christ and Sin wage war against each other. The *euangelion* is itself an eschatological phenomenon, one that dominates history between the advents of Christ, and by means of which God's saving purpose advances towards its consummation. It is therefore not at all surprising that the bearers of the *euangelion* encounter the fiercest resistance from the entrenched powers of darkness (Eph. 6:10–20; 1 Thess. 2:18).[50] Yet so certain is Paul of ultimate victory that he endures in hope. The *agōn* of the present both foretells the future glory and helps to usher it in (Rom. 8:18–25). Because of what he has already experienced of God's saving righteousness (Phil. 3:7–12), Paul both confidently awaits the consummation and remains faithful to his present task (3:11–14, 20–21).

Paul summons his readers to the same "endurance inspired by hope" (1 Thess. 1:3). "I consider that the sufferings of this present time are not worth comparing with the glory about to be revealed to us" (Rom. 8:18 NRSV). Moreover, personal afflictions (8:35) are here joined to those of all creation; the very universe shares believers' agonized longing for the consummation of God's saving purpose (8:22–23).

Paul does more than identify the Christian life as a struggle: that might be interesting (though hardly enlightening) but would offer no hope. Paul explains the nature and the causes of the struggle. He affirms that it will last, and indeed intensify, until Christ returns. Such realism is itself a safeguard against false expectations and disillusionment.[51] But just as realistic, given the reality of Christ and the Spirit, is Paul's expectation of victory amid the conflict. Of hardships and perils generated by forces both human and demonic, he says: "in all these things we are more than conquerors through him who loved us" (Rom. 8:37).

Through Paul's Epistles God calls us away from conformity to the standards of "the present evil age," into being "conformed to the image of his Son" (Rom. 8:29; 12:2); away from a craving for self-actualization, into thralldom to Christ the Lord (2 Cor. 5:14–15); away from being "well-adjusted" citizens, into unity with Christ crucified (1 Cor. 1:18–31).[52] To

50. On the *euangelion* as an eschatological reality and a dominant mark of the time between the advents, see Chamblin, *Gospel*, 24–53, especially 46–53. The consequent apostolic struggle is well depicted by Pfitzner, *Agon Motif*, 82–129.

51. A merit of Lawrence J. Crabb, Jr.'s book *Inside Out* (Colorado Springs: NavPress, 1988) is that it respects the "already" and "not yet" of Pauline eschatology.

52. Christ's people are to be no better "adjusted" to society than he was. Christ "was not at all like the psychologist's picture of the integrated, balanced, adjusted, happily married, employed, popular citizen. You can't really be very well 'adjusted' to your world if it says you 'have a devil' and ends by nailing you up naked to a stake of wood" (C. S. Lewis, *The Four Loves* [New York: Harcourt Brace Jovanovich, 1960], 81).

become like Christ is to be made whole in the fullest sense. In this hope let us begin.

> *O God, who, through the preaching of the blessed Apostle Saint Paul, hast caused the light of the Gospel to shine throughout the world; Grant, we beseech thee, that we, having his wonderful conversion in remembrance, may show forth our thankfulness unto thee for the same, by following the holy doctrine which he taught; through Jesus Christ our Lord. Amen.*[53]

53. *Book of Common Prayer*, Collect for January 25, "The Conversion of Saint Paul."

2

God, the Self, and Sin

"Without knowledge of self there is no knowledge of God." "Without knowledge of God there is no knowledge of self." Thus does John Calvin open his *Institutes of the Christian Religion*.[1] To these statements we may add a third: Without knowledge of God and knowledge of self, there is no knowledge of other selves.

That threefold belief is deeply rooted in the letters of Paul. But what does Paul mean by "knowledge," and how is it acquired and experienced? In this chapter, with this question before us, we begin to explore his teachings about God and about the self as God's creation. We shall also take account of Paul's concept of sin. For almost everything he says about "knowledge" presupposes the tyranny of sin and its threat to true knowledge of every kind.

The God-Centered Apostle

Rudolf Bultmann discusses Pauline theology under two major headings: "Man Prior to the Revelation of Faith," and "Man under Faith."[2] He explains his choice of language: "Pauline theology . . . deals with God not as He is in Himself but only with God as He is significant for man, for man's responsibility and man's salvation. Correspondingly, it does not

---

1. Ed. John T. McNeill, trans. Ford Lewis Battles (Philadelphia: Westminster, 1960), 35, 37.
2. *Theology of the New Testament*, trans. Kendrick Grobel (New York: Scribners, 1951), 1:190–352.

deal with the world and man as they are in themselves, but constantly sees the world and man in their relation to God."[3]

Thus far Bultmann sounds like Calvin. But he goes on to say: "Every assertion about God is simultaneously an assertion about man and vice versa. For this reason and in this sense Paul's theology is, at the same time, anthropology."[4] Bultmann rightly cautions us against separating Paul's teaching about God from his teaching about man. Yet Paul's theology and anthropology are by no means equivalent. We begin with theology, for only in this light can Paul's anthropology be understood.

"Paul was a God-intoxicated man"; God stands at the very heart of his teaching.[5] The noun *Theos* (God) occurs in his thirteen letters no fewer than 548 times. For Paul, God is utterly sovereign in every respect: "For from him and through him and unto him are all things. To him be glory forever. Amen" (Rom. 11:36). All that Paul says about humankind, he says on this basis. If a human being knows God, it is because God has already chosen to know him or her (Rom. 8:29; Gal. 4:9).

The Triune God

Paul is a monotheist; never does he abandon his Jewish belief in one God. He is "the eternal God . . . the only wise God" (Rom. 16:26–27). "For us there is one God" (1 Cor. 8:6).[6] He is "the living and true God" (1 Thess. 1:9). But Paul's understanding of God has been radically affected by his encounter with Jesus Christ and his experience of the Holy Spirit.

Paul often speaks of God (*Theos*) as the Father of Jesus Christ, and of Christ as the Son of God (*Huios Theou*).[7] But there is, in all probability, only one passage where Paul identifies Jesus as *Theos:* "our great God and Savior, Jesus Christ" (Titus 2:13 NIV). The rarity of such an ascription is understandable: for Paul, *Theos* applies to the Father; Jesus is "the Son of God."[8] Moreover, Jesus' sonship is unique. He is God's "own Son" (Rom. 8:3), God's "beloved Son" (Col. 1:13). Human beings may indeed become "sons

3. Ibid., 190–91.

4. Ibid., 191.

5. Leon Morris, *New Testament Theology* (Grand Rapids: Zondervan, 1986), 25. The first chapter of Morris's treatment of Paul is titled "God at the Center," 25–38. James D. G. Dunn, *Romans* (Dallas: Word, 1988), 363, speaks of "the sustained theocentricity of Paul's soteriology."

6. Cf. Deut. 6:4; Rom. 3:30; Gal. 3:20; 1 Tim. 1:17. 1 Cor. 8:4–6 denies the divinity, not the existence, of the "so-called gods." These are in fact demonic powers whom some treat as though they were divine (cf. 10:20–21).

7. E.g., Rom. 1:3–4, 9; 8:3, 29, 32; 1 Cor. 1:9; 2 Cor. 1:3, 19; Gal. 1:16; 2:20; 4:4, 6; Eph. 1:3; 4:13; Col. 1:3, 13; 1 Thess. 1:10.

8. Phil. 2:6 affirms that Jesus Christ was "in the form of God" and "equal with God," thus distinguishing him from God (*Theos*). Given Paul's dominant usage of *Theos*, and the ascription of Rom. 1:25, the best translation of Rom. 9:5b is "Christ. God who is over all be forever praised! Amen" (NIV mg.).

and daughters of God" (Rom. 8:14; 9:26; 2 Cor. 6:18). But Jesus is already the Son of God when he becomes a man (Rom. 1:3; Gal. 4:4).[9]

In twelve of the thirteen letters (all but Titus), Jesus Christ is expressly called "Lord" (*Kyrios*).[10] The full designation "Lord Jesus Christ" occurs in the salutation of eleven letters. Only rarely does Paul apply *Kyrios* to God the Father.[11] If *Theos* denotes a distinction of person between Jesus and God, *Kyrios* points to their identity of being and character. Paul speaks of Jesus as the source of spiritual realities that the Old Testament attributes to Yahweh (LXX, *Kyrios*) alone. Joel's promise, that "everyone who calls on the name of Yahweh will be saved" (Joel 2:32), is fulfilled in those who confess that "Jesus Christ is Lord" (Rom. 10:9–13; 1 Cor. 1:2). The very "glory of Yahweh," which Moses glimpsed at Sinai (Exod. 33:18–23), is beheld "when one turns to the Lord" Jesus Christ (2 Cor. 3:14–16; 4:4–6).[12] Christ "has become . . . our righteousness and holiness and redemption [for kindred ascriptions to Yahweh, see Exod. 31:13; Ps. 19:14; Jer. 23:6], so that as it is written [about Yahweh in Jer. 9:24]: 'Let the one who boasts, boast in the Lord'" (1 Cor. 1:30–31)—that is, in "our Lord Jesus Christ" (1:2; cf. Phil. 3:3). To have "the mind of Christ" (1 Cor. 2:16b) is to be given, by the Spirit's agency (2:15), insight into "the mind of Yahweh" (2:16a, quoting Isa. 40:13). Jesus Christ receives Yahweh's universal acclaim (Phil. 2:9–11, quoting Isa. 45:23). The coming "Day of Yahweh" (Isa. 13:6; Amos 5:18; Zeph. 1:14) is the "Day of the Lord Jesus."[13]

Corresponding to their unity of being and character, God the Father and Christ the Lord are united in their activity. Both bestow grace and peace (1 Cor. 1:4; Phil. 4:7; Col. 3:15; and the salutations and closing benedictions of most letters). It is in Christ that one receives the righteousness of God (Rom. 3:21–26; 2 Cor. 5:21). Both are objects of faith (Rom. 4:3–5, 24; Gal. 2:16; 3:22; Phil. 1:29; 1 Thess. 1:8) and of worship.[14] God exercises kingship by the agency of his Son (Eph. 5:5; Col. 1:13; 1 Thess. 2:12). To be

9. See Donald Guthrie, *New Testament Theology* (Downers Grove: Inter-Varsity, 1981), 317–19; and George E. Ladd, *A Theology of the New Testament* (Grand Rapids: Eerdmans, 1974), 417–21. It is only through union with Jesus the Son of God that others can become sons and daughters of God (Gal. 3:26; 4:4–7).

10. E.g., Rom. 1:4, 7; 1 Cor. 1:2–3, 7–10; 8:6; 2 Cor. 1:2–3, 14; Gal. 1:3; 6:14, 18; Eph. 1:2–3; 6:23–24; Phil. 1:2; 2:11; 4:23; Col. 1:3; 2:6; 1 Thess. 1:1, 3; 2:15; 2 Thess. 1:1, 2, 7, 8; 1 Tim. 1:2, 12; 6:14; 2 Tim. 1:2; Philem. 3, 25. Vincent Taylor, *The Person of Christ in New Testament Teaching* (London: Macmillan, 1958), 42, judges that "the conception of Christ as 'Lord' is the dominating idea in the Pauline theology."

11. See 2 Cor. 6:16–18; Rom. 9:29; 12:19 (all of which contain quotations from the OT); 1 Tim. 6:15. Not so likely are 1 Cor. 10:9 and 2 Tim. 1:18 (but see *TDNT* 3:1087). Paul never uses the title *the Lord, [our] God* (Luke 1:16, 32, 68).

12. The work of Christ brings glory to God (Rom. 15:6–9; Phil. 1:11). Where Christ is honored, God is glorified (2 Cor. 4:14–15; 9:13; Phil. 2:9–11). God glorifies believers by calling them into the glory already possessed by his Son (Rom. 8:29–30; Eph. 1:3–14; 2 Thess. 2:13–14).

13. E.g., 1 Cor. 1:8; Phil. 1:6, 10; 1 Thess. 4:13–5:2. The "judgment seat of God" (Rom. 14:10) is the "judgment seat of Christ" (2 Cor. 5:10). God judges by the agency of Christ (Rom. 2:16).

14. Paul usually speaks of offering prayers to God the Father through, or in the name of, Jesus Christ. But prayer may also be directed to Christ (2 Cor. 12:8–10; 1 Tim. 1:12).

under the lordship of Christ is to be under the rule of God.[15] The church belongs to both God and Christ (Rom. 16:16; 1 Cor. 1:2; 11:16; 2 Cor. 1:1; 1 Thess. 1:1; 2 Thess. 1:1). The Christian is slave to both (Rom. 1:1; 6:22; Phil. 1:1; Titus 1:1), although a slave by definition can belong to only one master.[16]

"The Spirit (*Pneuma*) of God" is for that reason "the Holy Spirit" (1 Thess. 1:5–6). Through the Spirit God bestows his love (Rom. 5:5) and his power (Rom. 8:11). Moreover, "the Spirit of God" is "the Spirit of Jesus Christ" (Gal. 4:6; Rom. 8:9–11). Christ baptizes believers with the Spirit (1 Cor. 12:13). Yet the Spirit is no mere influence; he is himself a person. Like God and Christ, he loves people (Rom. 15:30). He imparts to them life (Rom. 8:2) and power (Rom. 15:13, 19; 1 Cor. 2:4) and the capacity to pray (Rom. 8:15, 26). He cultivates in them "the fruit of the Spirit," supremely love, and grants to them "the gifts of the Spirit" (1 Cor. 12:1–13; Gal. 5:22–23).

Paul does not systematically expound "the doctrine of the Trinity." Yet he unites the Father, the Son, and the Spirit to one another in a way that "cannot be regarded as accidental."[17] Through the Spirit, God discloses his "hidden wisdom" as embodied in "Christ crucified" (1 Cor. 1:18–2:16). The three together accomplish salvation: "God sent forth his Son . . . to redeem. . . . God sent forth the Spirit of his Son into our hearts" (Gal. 4:4–6; cf. Eph. 1:3–14). Paul speaks of "brothers beloved by the Lord, [whom] God chose . . . for salvation through sanctification by the Spirit" (2 Thess. 2:13–14; cf. Titus 3:4–6). "For the law of the Spirit of life in Christ Jesus set you free from the law of sin and death. . . . God [sent] his own Son" (Rom. 8:2–3). By the activity of all three the church is enlivened and empowered. "There is one body and one Spirit . . . one Lord . . . one God and Father of all" (Eph. 4:4–6). Recipients of the *charismata* are indebted to all three: "Now there are varieties of gifts, but the same Spirit; and there are varieties of services, but the same Lord; and there are varieties of activities, but it is the same God who activates all of them in everyone," (1 Cor. 12:4–6 NRSV). The people of God are dependent on all three: "May the grace of the Lord Jesus Christ and the love of God and the fellowship of the Holy Spirit be with you all"

15. In the language of 1 Cor. 15:20–28, the messianic rule prepares for the full realization of the kingdom of God. See chap. 11.

16. On such matters as are summarized here, see Walter Elwell, "The Deity of Christ in the Writings of Paul," in *Current Issues in Biblical and Patristic Interpretation*, ed. G. F. Hawthorne (Grand Rapids: Eerdmans, 1975), 297–308.

17. Guthrie, *Theology*, 113; see further 111–13. Frances Young and David F. Ford, *Meaning and Truth in 2 Corinthians* (Grand Rapids: Eerdmans, 1987), 256–57, hold that Paul speaks correctly about the Trinity without knowing the "grammatical rules" associated with later Trinitarian formulations, and that Paul's talk about God "might be called the 'deep structure' of the Trinity." Cf. the thoughtful remarks by C. F. D. Moule, "The New Testament and the Doctrine of the Trinity: a short report on an old theme," *ExpT* 88 (1976–77): 16–20.

(2 Cor. 13:14). Believers offer prayers to God the Father through Christ the Lord by the Spirit's agency (Rom. 8:26–27; Eph. 2:18; 6:18).

That whole process is nothing less than "new creation" (2 Cor. 5:17). God the Savior "calls things which have no existence into existence" (Rom. 4:17)—just as he did at the beginning.[18]

Humanity, the Crown of God's Creation

"God . . . created all things" (Eph. 3:9) through a mediator. "For us there is one God, the Father, from whom are all things and for whom we exist, and one Lord, Jesus Christ, through whom are all things and through whom we exist" (1 Cor. 8:6 NRSV). Christ is "the firstborn over all creation," through whom and for whom God created all things, and in whom all things cohere and endure (Col. 1:15–17).[19] By means of Christ the Lord, God both creates and upholds the universe.[20] Therefore Paul identifies the world, even in its fallen state, as the handiwork and the gift of God. God "gives life to all things" (1 Tim. 6:13). "The earth is the Lord's and all that is in it" (1 Cor. 10:26, quoting Ps. 24:1). "Nothing is unclean in itself," for it comes from God through Christ (Rom. 14:14; 1 Cor. 8:4–6). "Everything God created is good" and is to be "received with thanksgiving," even in a time of great evil and error (1 Tim. 4:1–4; cf. 1 Cor. 10:27–30).

Integral to God's good creation, and to be received with special thanksgiving, is man (*anthrōpos*) as male (*anēr*) and female (*gynē*). This is indeed the Creator's crowning achievement, the sole creature that God fashions in his own image. Thus Paul affirms with Genesis 1.[21] Yet he says very little about humanity in its prefallen state: he chiefly views the self as the slave of Sin and of Christ respectively. But we know that Paul views the human creation with particular respect, from his teaching about Christ as the Savior of fallen humanity and the inaugurator of a new humanity within a restored universe. An attempt to identify the character of the self before the fall will help us better to understand the impact of Sin and of Christ respectively.

18. This translation of Rom. 4:17 comes from Dunn, *Romans*, 218, who stresses the close connection between God's saving righteousness and creative power.

19. As the "firstborn" (*prōtotokos*), 1:15, Christ is both prior to and sovereign over the whole creation; note the fourfold "all things" in 1:16–17. See P. T. O'Brien, *Colossians, Philemon* (Waco: Word, 1982), 44–45. Behind NIV's "hold together" (1:17b) is *synistēmi*, here both "consist" and "endure" (BAGD).

20. Paul's portrait of Christ both as mediator of creation and as "the wisdom of God," recalls the description of wisdom in Prov. 8 as "the craftsman" beside Yahweh at creation. Yet it would be wrong to claim that the wisdom of Prov. 8 *is* the pre-existent Christ: see F. F. Bruce, *Colossians, Philemon and Ephesians* (Grand Rapids: Eerdmans, 1984), 60. Furthermore, it is in the context of salvation, or *new* creation, that Paul expressly calls Christ "the wisdom of God" (1 Cor. 1:24, 30; cf. Col. 2:2–3).

21. The whole of 1 Cor. 11:2–16 rests on Gen. 1:26–27. Gal. 3:28 contains the very phrase of Gen. 1:27 LXX—*arsen kai thēlu*, "male and female."

Paul views the person in a variety of ways. In doing so, he employs a cluster of terms that are joined to one another in various ways, some of which have various meanings, and several of which may be used synonymously.[22] Paul's anthropology is in fact one of the most difficult aspects of his thought to fathom—itself a witness to the complexity and mystery of God's human creation. But this subject is of utmost importance for our study, so we must clarify what we can.

The Self's Diversity in Unity

We consider this matter in the awareness that Paul principally looks upon the self as an integrated whole (see the next section, "The Self's Unity in Diversity," pp. 44–46).

In accord with both Hebrew and Greek antecedents, Paul views the person as both corporeal and incorporeal.[23] His favorite word for the former is "body" (*sōma*).[24] He also uses "flesh" (*sarx*) in this sense: "always carrying around in the body [*sōma*] the dying of Jesus . . . that the life of Jesus may be manifested in our mortal flesh [*sarx*]" (2 Cor. 4:10–11). Being "absent in body" (1 Cor. 5:3) is the same as being "absent in flesh" (Col. 2:5; cf. Col. 1:22, "the body of his flesh"). The "weakness of the flesh" (Gal. 4:13–15) and the "thorn in the flesh" (2 Cor. 12:7) are (the same?) physical infirmities.

Paul describes incorporeal activity by various terms, whose meanings overlap considerably.[25] There is no significant difference of meaning between presence "in spirit" (*pneuma*, 1 Cor. 5:3) and presence "in heart" (*kardia*, 1 Thess. 2:17). One reasons and understands with "the mind" (*nous*, 1 Cor. 14:14–16), but the heart (*kardia*) may likewise be "enlightened" (2 Cor. 4:6; Eph. 1:18), and "the spirit (*pneuma*) of the man" understands "the things of a man" (1 Cor. 2:11 NKJV; cf. Eph. 4:23, "the spirit [*pneuma*] of the mind [*nous*]").[26] In 2 Corinthians 6:11–12, *kardia* and *splagchna* (NIV, "affection") are synonymous expressions of love. Obeying "from the heart" (*kardia*, Rom. 6:17; 1 Tim. 1:5) is the same as obeying

22. See Robert Jewett, *Paul's Anthropological Terms* (Leiden: Brill, 1971), 9–10, 447. Jewett seeks to show that variety in Paul's usage of the terms is directly related to the variety of needs addressed in the letters.

23. According to Robert H. Gundry, *Sōma in Biblical Theology, with Emphasis on Pauline Anthropology* (Cambridge: Cambridge University Press, 1976), 79, 83, "anthropological duality," not "monadic unity," best describes Paul's view. John W. Cooper, *Body, Soul, and Life Everlasting* (Grand Rapids: Eerdmans, 1989), 50, 179, uses the terms *functional holism* (as opposed to "ontological holism") and *holistic dualism* (as opposed to "holistic monism") for Paul and the Bible generally. I find their arguments convincing.

24. *Sōma* occurs ninety-one times in Paul's letters, not always in the present sense.

25. Gundry, *Sōma*, 156.

26. Gordon D. Fee, *The First Epistle to the Corinthians* (Grand Rapids: Eerdmans, 1987), 112, n. 60, comments on 1 Cor. 2:11, "It seems clear in this case that the word *pneuma* is another expression for *nous*. Cf. v. 16, where to have the Spirit of God is the same as to have the *nous* of Christ."

"from the soul" (*psychē,* Eph. 6:6, Col. 3:23; NIV, "heart"), and serving "with my spirit" (*pneuma,* Rom. 1:9; NIV, "whole heart"). To stand "in one spirit" (*pneuma*) is to struggle "with one soul" (*psychē,* Phil. 1:27), though Paul's concern here is not personal psychology but believer's harmony of purpose.

Paul distinguishes the incorporeal from the corporeal in several ways. He speaks of being "devoted in both body (*sōma*) and spirit (*pneuma*)" (1 Cor. 7:34); of "being absent in body but present in spirit" (1 Cor. 5:3), and of being separated "in person not in heart" (*kardia,* 1 Thess. 2:17). He exhorts readers to purify themselves "from every defilement of flesh (*sarx*) and of spirit (*pneuma*)" (2 Cor. 7:1).

To the above must be joined Paul's distinction between the internal and the external. True circumcision is not "outward" but "inward," not "in the flesh" but "of the heart" (Rom. 2:28–29). Man's spirit is "in him" (1 Cor. 2:11). Certain persons "boast in outward appearance and not in the heart" (2 Cor. 5:12 NRSV). The corporeal dimension obviously embraces the internal as well as the external, the hidden organs as well as the visible ones. Moreover, Paul describes certain incorporeal functions with terms that could also denote bodily organs—for example, the literal *kardia* (heart) or *splagchna* (variously the intestines, the liver, the kidneys, the lungs, or the heart).[27] In this light, two points call for equal emphasis. (1) Paul never confines an incorporeal function to a particular bodily organ. In the verses cited above, *kardia* stands not for the literal heart, but for "the whole of the inner being of man in contrast to his external side."[28] In 2 Corinthians 3:3 "fleshly hearts" is no more literal than the Spirit's handwriting. Paul's interest in *splagchna* is not physiological. This is "the most expressive term available to indicate the source of human emotion"; by metonymy, Paul focuses on the emotion itself. [29] (2) Paul never dissociates the internal-incorporeal from the internal-corporeal. "An essential part of the original [i.e., literal] meaning has been retained to the degree that *splagchna* concerns and expresses the total personality at the deepest level."[30] *Kardia* likewise stands for "the whole of the inner being" in both its corporeal and incorporeal dimensions. Thus fear or anger or excitement may cause the heart to beat rapidly.

27. For the literal usage in Greek and Hebrew antecedents of Paul, see *TDNT* 3:606–11 (*kardia*); 7:548–53 (*splagchna*).

28. Johannes Behm, *TDNT* 3: 612.

29. Moisés Silva, *Philippians* (Chicago: Moody, 1988), 55. Metonymy is using one name for a closely associated name, as when Paul calls the Jews "the circumcision" (Gal. 2: 7–9). The *splagchna* of Philem. 12 may be translated "heart" or "love" (BAGD, *s.v.*).

30. Helmut Köster, *TDNT* 7:555.

The Self's Unity in Diversity

The self's diversity in unity must be kept in view as we proceed. But there is far greater emphasis in Paul's letters upon the self as an integrated whole.

In keeping with the usage of *kardia* just noted, the heart is "the integrating center of man as a rational, emotional, volitional being."[31] Thus the heart may be enlightened (Eph. 1:18); it may experience anguish (2 Cor. 2:4); and it is from the heart that one obeys (Rom. 6:17).

Paul frequently speaks of the whole self by means of terms that in other contexts designate an aspect of the self. In doing so, he is not contradicting the other usage, or confusing the part with the whole. Rather, by the literary device known as synecdoche, he is viewing the whole self from a particular standpoint, or stressing the contribution of a particular aspect of the self to the functioning of the whole.[32]

The crown of God's creation is by nature a bodily being; the body (*sōma*) is essential to being truly and fully human. To offer "your bodies [*sōmata*] as living sacrifices" (Rom. 12:1), or to offer "your members" (6:13a, 19; NIV, "the parts of your body"), is to offer "yourselves" (6:13b, 16). In Romans 12:1, *sōma* denotes "the person in his corporeality, in his concrete relationships within this world; it is because he is body that man can experience the world and relate to others."[33] Yet the *sōma* is not equated with the whole person, for the mind and the will are active in the offering of the body (12:1–2).

Similarly, we learn from some instances of *sarx* that human beings are by nature creaturely, limited, and weak (Rom. 6:19; "flesh and blood," 1 Cor. 15:50; Gal. 1:16; Eph. 6:12); devise and adhere to certain standards ("not many wise according to the flesh," 1 Cor. 1:26); belong to a physical lineage (e.g., Rom. 1:3; 4:1; 9:3); and stand in relationship both to other human beings and to God (Philem. 16, "both in the flesh and in the Lord"; Rom. 3:20).[34]

Psychē ("soul" in earlier examples) may likewise denote one's whole life or, by metonymy, the whole person. "So deeply did we care for you, that we were willing to share with you not only the gospel of God but our own lives (*psychai*) as well" (1 Thess. 2:8; for "lives," NRSV has "selves"). Epaphroditus "nearly died for the work of Christ, risking his life" (*psychē*, Phil.

---

31. Dunn, *Romans*, 100; cf. Behm, *TDNT* 3:612; Ladd, *Theology*, 475; Jewett, *Anthropological Terms*, 447–48.

32. Synecdoche is the use of a part for the whole, or a less inclusive term for a more inclusive (and vice versa). For biblical examples, see G. B. Caird, *The Language and Imagery of the Bible* (Philadelphia: Westminster, 1980), 135–36.

33. Dunn, *Romans*, 709. Cf. Ladd, *Theology*, 464.

34. In none of these passages is the *sarx* depicted as inherently sinful (but see below). Cf. Anthony C. Thiselton, *NIDNTT* 2: 674–75.

2:30): his whole earthly or natural life was in danger, not just his "soul."[35]
Like *sōma*, *psychē* designates the person from a particular point of view:
"man as a thinking, working, and feeling person"; "the ego, person, or personality . . . the whole man, with all that he believes, hopes and strives
for."[36] Similarly, *nous* can mean "the whole thinking man, man as a creature capable of understanding."[37] In setting "the law of my mind" (*nous*)
over against "the law of sin which is in my members" (Rom. 7:23), Paul is
not describing warfare between two segments of the self. Rather (to anticipate later discussion), "my mind" designates the whole person as
renewed by Christ and the Spirit, and "my members" the whole person as
threatened by slavery to sin (cf. 7:25).

While the corporeal and the incorporeal are distinguished, the dynamic
activity between them witnesses to the unity of the person. The distinction
between *sōma* and *psychē* is strictly anthropological, not ethical: the body is
not intrinsically evil (for it is integral to God's good creation); and the soul
is not a "higher self" that is by nature protected from temptation and sin.
Moreover, within creation, the soul, far from being destined to overrule or
escape the body, fulfills its purpose precisely in relation to the body. The
"life" denoted by *psychē* is a bodily existence, which helps to explain why
psychē can be employed by synecdoche for the whole person.[38]

Much the same can be said of body and spirit. Paul does not view the
pneuma "as a divine spark (the real 'I') incarcerated in the physical, 'the
ghost in the machine.'"[39] The self which, as spirit, experiences communion
with God, is a bodily being. At the very moment Paul distinguishes the
sōma from the *pneuma*, he unites them in devotion to Christ (1 Cor. 7:34).
Salvation embraces both body (1 Cor. 6:12–20; 15) and spirit (1 Cor 5:5).
Similarly, the offering of the body entails the renewal of the mind (Rom.
12:1–2).

Paul likewise unites the flesh (*sarx* as a synonym of *sōma*) to the spirit.
Both must be purified if the person is to become holy (2 Cor. 7:1). It is
instructive to juxtapose two texts: "I had no rest (*anesin*) in my spirit (*pneu-*

---

35. See also Rom. 2:9; 11:3; 13:1; 16:4; 2 Cor. 1:23. Such usage is thoroughly Hebraic. In the OT *nephesh*
(translated *psychē* in LXX) is "the usual term for a man's total nature, for what he is and not just what he
has" (Edmond Jacob, *TDNT* 9:620). The classic text is Gen. 2:7, "Man became a living *nephesh* [LXX,
psychē]"—not "a living soul" (KJV), but "a living being" (NKJV).

36. The respective quotations are from Ladd, *Theology*, 460, and Günther Harder, *NIDNTT* 3:683. Cf.
Jewett, *Anthropological Terms*, 448.

37. Guthrie, *Theology*, 169. Cf. Ladd, *Theology*, 476.

38. *Psychē* is the person's vitality "from the point of view of his body and flesh" (Ladd, *Theology*, 460),
as often is the case with *nephesh* in the OT (Jacob, *TDNT* 9:620). "Paul never links [*psychē* and *sōma*] in a
description of a person, since either covers both, i.e., the whole person" (Guthrie, *Theology*, 165). "[B]ecause
of their interpenetration the soul *is* the animation of the body and the body *is* the incarnation of the soul.
The soul *has* a body and the body *has* a soul and man as a whole *is* both, a psychophysical unity . . ." (Gundry, *Sōma*, 121).

39. Dunn, *NIDNTT* 3:694. Cf. Bultmann, *Theology*, 1:206.

mati), because I did not find my brother Titus there" (2 Cor. 2:13). "For when we came into Macedonia, our flesh (*sarx*) had no rest (*anesin*), but we were afflicted in every way—conflicts without, fears within" (7:5). "Spirit" and "flesh" are not interchangeable: the turbulence "within" (*pneuma*) affects the "outside" (*sarx*).[40] Yet Paul describes one experience; his anxiety over Titus and the Corinthians affects his whole being.

First Thessalonians 5:23, with its triad "spirit (*pneuma*), soul (*psychē*), and body (*sōma*)," appears to divide the person into three segments. But Paul's intention is just the opposite: "May God . . . sanctify you *wholly* (*holoteleis*). May your *whole* (*holoklēron*) spirit, soul and body be kept blameless" at Christ's return. Far from dissecting the person, Paul expresses the hope that believers may, by God's sanctifying work, be saved from disintegration and preserved as whole (*holos*) beings. He joins the three terms together (here only in his letters) "for emphasis rather than for definition."[41]

The Self's Experience of Knowledge

As creatures made in the divine image, human beings have a unique capacity for knowing God. We begin by observing a distinction well expressed by two French verbs. *Savoir* is descriptive knowledge about reality; *connaître* is intimate knowledge of reality. *Savoir* may state factual truth about love in a propositional way, whereas *connaître* is the experience of loving. The distinction may also be illustrated from Paul's usage of the Greek verbs *oida* (corresponding to *savoir*) and *ginōskō* (corresponding to *connaître*): "We had already suffered and been insulted at Philippi, as you know" (*oida*, 1 Thess. 2:2). "But now that you have come to know (*ginōskō*) God—or rather to be known (*ginōskō*) by God . . ." (Gal. 4:9). To be sure, Paul's usage does not consistently reflect this distinction.[42] Yet the distinction itself is important. For Paul *connaître* is by far the more significant kind of knowledge. Yet he never divorces it from *savoir*; from the very beginning, knowledge about reality is essential for knowledge of reality. Knowing about (*savoir*) God's "eternal power and divine nature" is integral to "knowing (*connaître*) God" (Rom. 1:18–21). Abraham's being right with

40. In these two texts "Paul carefully chooses his terms after the pattern of an anthropological duality of flesh as body and spirit as the incorporeal part of man" (Gundry, *Sōma*, 144).

41. Guthrie, *Theology*, 165. Cf. the intelligent remarks of Ernest Best, *The First and Second Epistles to the Thessalonians* (New York: Harper and Row, 1972), 243–44. For clusters of anthropological terms to accentuate the commitment of the whole person, see Deut. 6:5; Matt. 22:37. For the Bible's consistent presentation of the self as a "psychosomatic unity," see Anthony A. Hoekema, *Created in God's Image* (Grand Rapids: Eerdmans, 1986), 203–26.

42. The *oida* of Gal. 4:8 matches the *ginōskō* of 4:9; in 2 Cor. 5:16 the verbs are synonymous. See Heinrich Seesemann, *TDNT* 5:116–18.

God himself (*connaître*) is inseparable from understanding and trusting his promises (Rom. 4:3, 20–21).

Knowledge entails the exercise of the mind (*nous*). "My mind" knows that the law is good and desires to obey it (Rom. 7:14–23). Decisions about special days call for rational deliberations: "Let each one be fully convinced in his own mind" (*nous*, Rom. 14:5). The heart (*kardia*) too has intellectual capacities. The Israelites' "minds (*noēmata*) were made dull. . . . Indeed to this day a veil covers their hearts" (*kardia*, 2 Cor. 3:14–15); Paul describes not the effects of one organ on another, but the blunting of the heart's own cognitive powers.[43] Conversely, if truth about God is to be grasped, the *kardia* must be enlightened (2 Cor. 4:1–6; Eph. 1:17–19). Moreover the conscience (*syneidēsis*) makes rational judgments when appraising the actions of the self (Rom. 2:15).[44]

Yet knowing is not purely cognitive. In Paul the *nous* is a place of moral judgments; its deliberations always affect the will.[45] The renewal of the *nous* is requisite for knowing and doing God's will (Rom. 12:1–2). Being "convinced in one's own mind (*nous*)" affects behavior (Rom. 14:1–8). Renewal of the *nous* issues in a life of holiness (Eph. 4:20–32). Similarly, the verb *phroneō* denotes an "attitude of mind" that finds expression in the will.[46] Once the Philippians' "attitude" is like Christ's (2:2, 5 where *phroneō* occurs three times), they too will become obedient (2:6–11). When the Colossians "set their minds" on things above (3:2, *phroneō*), their conduct will become holy (3:5–17). The mind-set (*phronēma*) of the "flesh" or the "Spirit" (Rom. 8:6–7) determines a whole way of life (8:1–17). Insights of the *kardia* are likewise wed to conduct: Gentiles demonstrate "the work of the law in their hearts" by doing what the law requires (Rom. 2:14–15); "Let each one give what he has determined in his heart to give" (2 Cor. 9:7). Fidelity to apostolic teaching arises "from the heart" (Rom. 6:17).

Pneuma designates the self's capacity for three kinds of knowledge.

Knowledge of self. "For what man knows the things of a man except the spirit (*pneuma*) of the man which is in him?" (1 Cor. 2:11 NKJV). Within the one question, *pneuma* represents both the whole self (what his spirit knows, the man knows) and the internal or incorporeal dimension of the self ("the spirit . . . which is in him").

43. Thus too Ralph P. Martin, *2 Corinthians* (Waco: Word, 1986), 69. *Kardiai* and *noēmata* are again closely parallel in Phil. 4:7.

44. For Paul the conscience is not a legislative faculty: "it does not make the law; it recognizes it and judges conduct by it. . . . The 'law of nature' is not a different law [from the Mosaic law], but only a less precise and complete revelation of the same eternal law of right and wrong" (C. H. Dodd, *Romans* [London: Hodder and Stoughton, 1932], 36).

45. In Paul *nous* can denote "moral attitude," or "the moral consciousness as it concretely determines will and action"; both "understanding" and "judgment, resolve" (Johannes Behm, *TDNT* 4:958–59). Cf. Ladd, *Theology*, 476.

46. Bultmann, *Theology*, 1:214.

Knowledge of other selves. "For though absent in body (*sōma*) I am present in spirit (*pneuma*). . . . When you are assembled, and my spirit (*pneuma*) is present" (1 Cor. 5:3–4 NRSV). While distinguishing the corporeal from the incorporeal, Paul says that he himself will actually participate in the church's life; his *pneuma* is present and active by the agency of the divine *Pneuma*, who works through the letter Paul is writing.[47]

Knowledge of God. Galatians 6:18, "The grace of our Lord Jesus Christ be *with your spirit*, brothers," is just as comprehensive as 1 Thessalonians 5:28, "The grace of our Lord Jesus Christ be *with you.*"[48] Or, as we may also put it, the *pneuma* is that dimension of the self through which the whole person communes with God: "The Spirit (*pneuma*) testifies with our spirit (*pneuma*) that we are God's children"; through the Spirit's agency "we cry, '*Abba*, Father'" (Rom. 8:16,15). First Corinthians 5:5b ("and his spirit [*pneuma*] saved") speaks not of the incorporeal to the exclusion of the corporeal (see 1 Cor. 15!), but of the whole person as oriented toward God.

There is a kind of knowledge that is distinct from the cognitive. "For if I pray in a tongue, my spirit (*pneuma*) prays, but my mind (*nous*) is unfruitful" (1 Cor. 14:14 NIV). Such a prayer is unintelligible to the reason (whose activity is temporarily suspended), but the person is in genuine communion with God ("If *you* are praising [God] with the spirit," 14:16) and is thus edified (14:2, 4). Again speaking of prayer, Paul affirms that "the peace of God, which surpasses all understanding (*nous*), will stand guard over your hearts (*kardiai*) and your minds (*noēmata*) in Christ Jesus" (Phil. 4:7). Such a person gains not descriptive knowledge about "the peace of God" (the faculties of the *nous* are superseded), but intimate knowledge of that reality (the peace of God is experienced in the heart). Most strikingly of all, Paul prays that Christians "may know (*ginōskō*) the love of Christ, that surpasses knowledge (*gnōsis*)" (Eph. 3:19): to experience Christ's love is to know him (*connaître*). Loving God is the evidence that one is known by God (1 Cor. 8:3). This understanding of knowledge is deeply rooted in the Old Testament, where *yada'* ("know" in Heb.) is expressive of intimate personal communion based on mutual love and loyalty.[49] Such evidence does not suggest that the human reason is contradicted or eradicated. Paul knows and writes about (*savoir*) the knowledge that surpasses knowledge (*connaître*). It is possible to know (*savoir*) that one's capacity for knowledge (*savoir*) has been transcended.

---

47. According to Fee, *First Corinthians*, 204, Paul understands himself "actually to be present 'in spirit/ Spirit' in the gathered community."

48. Likewise, the "refreshment of the spirit" (1 Cor. 16:18; 2 Cor. 7:13) affects the whole person.

49. The supreme example is Yahweh's relation to Israel, which is best illustrated in the marital bond. See Walther Eichrodt, *Theology of the Old Testament*, trans. J. A. Baker (Philadelphia: Westminster, 1967), 2:291–93.

We conclude that the experience of knowledge in the full sense requires the active involvement of the entire person. It is the self as a united whole who knows. Such knowledge begins with concerted activity within the incorporeal or the internal dimension of the self, as especially to be seen in Paul's references to the heart. But that experience is not complete until the corporeal dimension is activated, as is especially evident in Paul's language about the body (Rom. 12:1–2). Until the whole person is affected, true knowledge has not occurred—whether one is speaking of knowing oneself, knowing other people, or knowing God.[50]

Thralldom to Sin

Thus far we have concentrated upon the self as the unspoiled creation of God. Yet as noted early in the chapter, almost everything Paul says about knowledge presupposes the tyranny of sin and its threat to true knowledge of every kind.

The Master and the Slaves

Sin is a ruthless tyrant that entered the world and established its rule through the transgression of Adam and Eve (Rom. 5:12–21), and has henceforth held the whole of humanity in terrible bondage (Rom. 3:9; Gal. 3:22). Christians used to be "slaves to sin" (Rom. 6:20).[51] When speaking of *hamartia* as a power, I shall use the capitalized *Sin*.

The slaves of Sin obey the master by committing sins (Rom. 3:23; 6:12–19). This happens for two reasons: their racial solidarity with Adam and their personal bondage to Sin. "Death spread to all men, because (*eph' hō*) all sinned (*hēmarton*)" (Rom. 5:12), both in or with Adam and like Adam. The rest of the passage witnesses to both aspects. (1) Solidarity with Adam: "the many died by the trespass of the one man"; "the judgment followed one sin"; "by the trespass of the one man, death reigned through that one man"; "the result of one trespass was condemnation for all men"; "as through the disobedience of the one man the many were made sinners" (5:15–19 NIV). The counterpart is believers' solidarity with Christ in his

---

50. In Paul, as in the OT, "knowledge is not thought of in terms of the possession of information. It is possessed only in its exercise or actualisation" (Rudolf Bultmann, *TDNT* 1:698).

51. Of the forty-eight instances of *hamartia* in Rom., forty-five are singular, which already suggests "a trans-subjective power" (Hans Conzelmann, *An Outline of the Theology of the New Testament*, trans. John Bowden [London: SCM, 1969], 194). Rom. 5:12 ("sin entered the world through one man") portrays Sin as "a mighty force of evil which used Adam as its instrument" (Leon Morris, *The Epistle to the Romans* [Grand Rapids: Eerdmans, 1988], 229). Sin "is armed like a leader of mercenary troops and pays off its subordinates with death [Rom. 6:23]. . . . This way of speaking of sin shows that 'sin' is more than just a collective term for various sinful acts . . ." (Günther Bornkamm, *Paul*, trans. D. M. G. Stalker [New York: Harper and Row, 1971], 133). "Paul never speculates on the origin of sin; he simply assumes its reality as a power in human experience" (Dunn, *Romans*, 383).

death and resurrection (see the second half of each verse just quoted): "For as in Adam all die, so also in Christ will all be made alive" (1 Cor. 15:22).[52] (2) Personal slavery to Sin: immediately after 5:12d Paul writes, "for before the law, Sin was in the world. . . . Death reigned from Adam to Moses, even over those who did not sin in the likeness of Adam's transgression" (5:13–14). The Sin that found a point of entry through Adam's trespass exerted its power over all of Adam's offspring. They all fell under its tyranny, as demonstrated by the fact that they "all sinned" (*pantes hēmarton*, 5:12); as Paul said in 3:23, "all have sinned" (*pantes . . . hēmarton*), where the actual sins of Jews and Gentiles are clearly in view (cf. 3:9–20; 2:12). That they all sinned personally (albeit not by transgressing a specific command, as had Adam) is shown by the fact that death reigned from Adam to Moses. That whole period reveals that death indeed "spread to all men"—pervaded the whole of humanity—"because all sinned" (5:12), actively so, as had their father Adam. The spread of death testifies to the spread of sin.[53]

In exerting its rule, Sin employs several agencies.

Bondage to the Self

Sin's objective is to win the undivided allegiance of the whole person, to which end it capitalizes on the self's unity in diversity.[54]

We return to Paul's anthropological terms, beginning with "flesh" (*sarx*). In Paul, as in the Old Testament, *sarx* denotes creaturely weakness (as we saw earlier). But Paul also employs *sarx* in a sense not found in the Old Testament, namely, "man's being and attitude *as opposed to and in contradiction to God and God's Spirit*."[55] The *sarx* has sworn its allegiance to another: "By means of the flesh I am enslaved to the law of Sin" (Rom. 7:25). The *sarx* of every person from Adam onward, Jesus alone excepted (Rom. 8:3), has been Sin's habitation and slave.

52. For arguments favoring this reading of Rom. 5:12d, see, e.g., Herman Ridderbos, *Paul: An Outline of His Theology*, trans. John R. DeWitt (Grand Rapids: Eerdmans, 1975), 95–100; F. F. Bruce, *The Epistle of Paul to the Romans* (Downers Grove: Inter-Varsity, 1963), 129–30; John Murray, *The Epistle to the Romans* (Grand Rapids: Eerdmans, 1968), 180–87; Morris, *Romans*, 228–32. Awareness of Paul's stress on sinners' racial solidarity with Adam is increased when we recognize that the "just as" of Rom. 5:12a has no answering "so also" in 5:12 (an instance of *anacoluthon*), and is only resumed in 5:18 ("just as . . . so also").

53. For this reading of Rom. 5:12d, see, e.g., A. J. M. Wedderburn, "The Theological Structure of Romans V.12," *NTS* 19 (April 1973): 339–54; William Hendriksen, *Romans* (Grand Rapids: Baker, 1981), 178–79; Guthrie, *Theology*, 209–12. Dunn, *Romans*, 271–75, 290, well recognizes the unbreakable connection in this passage between Adam's trespass and the sins of his offspring—the power of Sin arising from without and from within respectively. For the various views on a much-debated verse, see C. E. B. Cranfield, *The Epistle to the Romans* (Edinburgh: T. & T. Clark, 1975), 274–81.

54. As we have seen, human reason, emotions, and will always act in concert, the emotions no less than the others. So while one may speak theoretically of the neutrality of emotions such as anger or fear, in actual practice emotions come to expression within a context of fallenness (slavery to Sin) or of salvation (slavery to Christ).

55. Bornkamm, *Paul*, 133. Cf. Eduard Schweizer, *TDNT* 7:132; Thiselton, *NIDNTT* 1:675–76.

By means of the flesh, Sin subjugates the whole person. In the garden Sin's main appeal, through the serpent, was not to physical desire but to human reason and pride (Gen. 3:1–6); Eve was deceived by the serpent's cunning (2 Cor. 11:3; 1 Tim. 2:14). So too, while "the works of the flesh" (*sarx*, Gal. 5:19–21) include what we would call fleshly sins such as sexual immorality and drunkenness, the catalog is dominated by sins of the mind and spirit: "hatred, discord, jealousy, fits of rage, selfish ambition, dissensions, factions and envy" (NIV). Again by synecdoche, Paul uses a term for a part of the self (*sarx*) to designate the whole person viewed in a certain way, namely, in rebellion against God and in thrall to the powers of "the present evil age" (Gal. 1:4), the chief of which is Sin.

Accordingly, neither the *pneuma* nor the *nous* nor the *kardia* escapes Sin's clutches. Believers must purify themselves "from every defilement of flesh (*sarx*) and spirit (*pneuma*)" (2 Cor. 7:1)—that is, both corporeally and incorporeally. Where *sarx* wars against *pneuma*, it is invariably the human *sarx*, including its spiritual dimension, versus the divine *pneuma*: "he who sows to *his own* flesh (*sarx*) will from the flesh reap corruption; but he who sows to *the* Spirit (*pneuma*) will from the Spirit reap eternal life" (Gal. 6:8 RSV; cf. Rom. 8:1–17; Gal. 5:16–26). The human *pneuma*, far from offering salvation, itself needs to be saved (1 Cor. 5:5).

Paul speaks of "the mind (*nous*) of the flesh (*sarx*)" (Col. 2:18), that is, the mind as the possession or organ of the flesh as the tool of Sin. The moral standing of the *nous* "is determined by what is dominating it, either the Spirit of God or the flesh."[56] When ruled by the devil, "we lived in the passions of our flesh (*sarx*), fulfilling the desires of the flesh (*sarx*) and of the thoughts (*dianoia*)" (Eph. 2:2–3a). I think it likely that in this text the second *sarx* and *dianoia* represent two ways "the passions of the flesh" find expression—sensually and intellectually.[57]

God judged those who "suppress the truth" by accelerating their descent into error: "their thinking became futile and their foolish hearts (*kardia*) were darkened"; "since they did not think it worthwhile to retain the knowledge of God, he gave them over to a depraved mind (*nous*)" (Rom. 1:18–21, 28 NIV). By the darkening of "their foolish (*asynetos*) heart" (Rom. 1:21), Paul means "not merely a chance lack of knowledge . . . [but] a sign that a man in his deepest being rejects God. . . . [The] lack of insight must be regarded as culpable behavior."[58] The effect of the "hardening of the heart" toward God is culpable "ignorance" (*agnoia*), a "darkened understanding" (*dianoia*) and "futility of mind" (*nous*), Ephesians 4:17–18.

---

56. Guthrie, *Theology*, 169.
57. Cf. Eph. 5:3–5 (akin to Gal. 5:22–23); 2 Cor. 7:1; Col. 1:21 (where the enmity of the *dianoia* is joined to "evil behavior"); Johannes Behm, *TDNT* 4:966–67.
58. Jürgen Goetzmann, *NIDNTT* 3:132.

Similarly, while in Romans 1:14 the *anoētoi* ("foolish") are "the simple and uneducated whose power of thought is undeveloped," elsewhere in Paul (Gal. 3:1, 3; 1 Tim. 6:9; Titus 2:3) the term denotes "adverse religious and moral judgment."[59] The sense of right and wrong is therefore blunted: "Both their [the nonbelievers'] minds (*nous*) and consciences (*syneidēsis*) are defiled" (Titus 1:15; cf. 1 Tim. 4:2).

In keeping with the unity of mind and will noted earlier, a depraved *nous* and a foolish *kardia* produce "every kind of wickedness" (Rom. 1:18–32). "Hostility of mind" toward God is joined to "evil works" (Col. 1:21); those whose hearts are hardened and whose understanding is darkened, predictably "practice every kind of impurity" (Eph. 4:18–19). Talk among persons who are "corrupt of mind (*nous*) and bereft of truth" inevitably leads to envy, avarice, and the like (1 Tim. 6:3–5; cf. 2 Tim. 3:8).

In Paul's usage, the *sōma* (body) never belongs to itself but always to a master.[60] By virtue of creation, the body belongs to God; but in consequence of the fall it becomes the subject of Sin. "The body of sin" is the body under Sin's dominion (Rom. 5:12; 6:6). Such a person habitually offers the members of his body (*sōma*) to Sin, as instruments of wickedness (6:13). The deeds of the body that need to be destroyed are those committed by persons who live "according to the flesh" (Rom. 8:13). "The body is not meant for sexual immorality," but this is exactly how it behaves as Sin's slave (1 Cor. 6:12–20).

Psychē still designates "natural life," but now it is such life in its fallen state. The "natural man" (*psychikos anthrōpos*) is unable to understand spiritual realities (1 Cor. 2:6–16); and the "natural body" (*sōma psychikon*) is destined to perish (1 Cor. 15:42–55).

Slavery to Sin offers no escape from personal responsibility. The self does not resist but readily submits to Sin's assaults. It is by the mind's own suppression of truth and the heart's willful disobedience that Sin establishes and maintains its mastery. The body readily gives itself ("yields its members") to Sin's servitude (Rom. 6:13; 7:23). The sinner cannot say, "Sin made me do it," as though thought and conduct were beyond one's own control. Those who are "under Sin" are nonetheless "held accountable to God" for their decisions and "deserving of death" for their actions (Rom. 1:32; 3:9, 19).[61]

---

59. Behm, *TDNT* 4:962.

60. Bornkamm, *Paul*, 131.

61. On the personal responsibility of Sin's slaves, see Ladd, *Theology*, 405; Ridderbos, *Paul*, 118–19. On the phrase *sin living in me* (Rom. 7:17), Dunn comments, "The ambivalence of the imagery reflects the ambivalence of the experience of sin—always as a power exercising great compulsion on the individual, but sometimes more easily conceptualized as a force bearing upon one from without (social pressures, constraints of tradition, etc.), at others as a force rising up from within (psychological addiction of ingrained habit, hereditary traits, etc.)" (*Romans*, 390).

Bondage to the Law

"The law is holy, and the commandment is holy and just and good" (Rom. 7:12); for it is God's law (7:22, 25), declaring what is right and wrong in his sight. Yet once the law demonstrates to human beings what sin is, there is produced in them not so much an abhorrence of sin as a desire to sin. The knowledge of sin that the law brings is both cognitive and experiential. "If it had not been for the law," writes Paul, "I would not have known (*ginōskō*) sin. I would not have known (*oida*) what it is to covet if the law had not said, 'You shall not covet'" (Rom. 7:7 NRSV). It is not merely that his mind is enlightened (note the verb *oida*); rather, the enlightenment aroused in him the very desires which the law prohibited.[62]

Yet it is Sin, not the law, that is to blame: "But Sin, seizing its opportunity through the commandment, produced in me every kind of covetousness" (Rom. 7:8). God's righteous commandment is the very means that Sin employs to bring its victims into intimate personal acquaintance with itself: through the law one has "*known* (*ginōskō*) sin" (7:7). So it was in the Garden. The divine command was the very means the serpent used to seduce Adam and Eve: through Adam's transgression Sin entered the world.[63] While the law rightly demands that its hearers be holy, righteous, and good, it cannot bestow the life it prescribes (Gal. 3:21b). Instead, it affords the "opportunity" for Sin to produce the sort of conduct the law prohibits. "For apart from law, sin is dead . . . but when the commandment came, sin [not righteousness] sprang to life and I died" (Rom. 7:8b–9 NIV; cf. 1 Cor. 15:56). In short, to be "under law" is to be "under Sin"; conversely, being a slave to Sin excludes the possibility of being anything but a slave to the law as well.[64] Such is the power of Sin over the individual that he or she inevitably falls far short of fulfilling the law's commands (Rom. 3:9–20, 23). This, combined with the persistent demand that the law must be kept on pain of death (Gal. 3:10; 5:3), makes one's condition hopeless.[65]

---

62. "The law is not simply a reagent by which the presence of sin may be detected; it is a catalyst which aids or even initiates the action of sin upon man" (C. K. Barrett, *The Epistle to the Romans* [New York: Harper and Row, 1957], 141). Both kinds of knowledge are in view in Rom. 3:20, "through the law comes the knowledge [*epignōsis*] of sin" (NRSV); NIV's "through the law we become conscious of sin" is inadequate.

63. Adam's *cognitive* knowledge of sin came at Gen. 2:16–17, his experiential knowledge at 3:6–7. Adam's act was *parabasis* and *paraptōma* (both of which mean "transgression" or "trespass"), and *parakoē* (disobedience); the law was later added to make existent wrongdoing a legal offense (Rom. 5:13–19; 4:15; Gal. 3:19).

64. Rom. 6:14 ("under law"); 7:6 (the law "once bound us"); Gal. 3:21–25 (where *hypo hamartian*, "under sin," v. 22, is parallel to *hypo nomon*, "under law," v. 23). "The law of sin" (Rom. 7:23; cf. 8:2b) is God's Law as used by Sin (7:7–13); thus also Dunn, *Romans*, 394–96, 416–19.

65. See Günther Bornkamm, "Sin, Law and Death (Romans 7)," in *Early Christian Experience*, trans. Paul L. Hammer (New York: Harper and Row, 1969), 87–104; Walter Gutbrod, *TDNT* 4:1069–75; and Ladd, *Theology*, 495–506.

Bondage to the Spirits

Paul explains demonology by reference to Sin, rather than the reverse. The demons may be considered the first creatures to fall under Sin's dominion.[66] Now, as Sin's henchmen, they preside over "the present evil age" (Gal. 1:4) under the headship of Satan, "the god of this age" (2 Cor. 4:4), "the ruler of the realm of the air" (Eph. 2:2).

In fidelity to Sin and to his own nature, Satan ("the Adversary"), together with the powers at his command, blinds human beings to the truth of God (2 Cor. 4:4); propagates untruth masquerading as truth (2 Cor. 11:3–4, 13–15; Col. 2:8; 2 Thess. 2:9); seeks to supplant "the Lord's table" with "the table of demons" (1 Cor. 10:20–21); and tries to thwart the heralds of the gospel (1 Thess. 2:18). For the same reason Satan seeks to ruin personal relationships, by encouraging anger (Eph. 4:27), marital infidelity (1 Cor. 7:5), slander (1 Tim. 5:14–15; the devil is the *diabolos*, "the slanderer"), and coldness of heart (2 Cor. 2:11).

The demonic powers employ the law as a means of driving persons away from God and holding them in bondage to themselves and other human beings (Gal. 4:1–11; Col. 2:16–23). The Old Testament laws concerning the Sabbath, for example, were meant to beget joy rather than misery (Isa. 58:13–14); but in the hands of the "elemental spirits" such laws become enslaving.[67] Human beings' violation of the law serves the same purpose. The "hand-written document" (*cheirographon*) that "was against us and opposed to us" (Col. 2:14) is not the law itself but a "certificate of indebtedness" to God for failure to keep the law; it is not a highway code, but a traffic ticket. This state of guilt becomes a weapon in the hands of the "powers and authorities." They shake the document in their victims' faces, so to speak, to remind them that they stand guilty and condemned before God.[68]

Bondage to Death

It is to Sin that death owes its entry into the world (Rom. 5:12). As though repaying a debt, death becomes Sin's vicegerent, exercising domin-

---

66. Cf. 2 Cor. 11:3, 14; and D. E. H. Whiteley, *The Theology of St. Paul* (Oxford: Blackwell, 1964), 23.

67. Cf. Col. 2:16 ("a Sabbath day"); Gal. 4:10 ("You are observing special days . . ."). I believe that the *stoicheia* (Gal. 4:3, 9; Col. 2:8, 20) are "elemental spirits," otherwise called "powers and authorities" (Col. 2:15), who victimize people both by propagating "hollow and deceptive philosophy" (Col. 2:8) and by misusing the divine law. For this understanding of *stoicheia*, see O'Brien, *Colossians, Philemon*, 129–32. "Paul is not condemning the use of sacred days or seasons as such; it is the wrong motive involved when the observance of these days is bound up with the recognition of the elemental spirits" (ibid., 139, on Col. 2:16).

68. For this interpretation of *cheirographon*, see O'Brien, *Colossians, Philemon*, 125–26; Bruce, *Colossians, Philemon, Ephesians*, 109–10. Jesus, by nailing the certificate to the cross, forgives the sins and disarms the powers (2:13–15).

ion over all human beings and terrorizing them on Sin's behalf.[69] As bondage to Sin produces sinful behavior, so servitude to death brings with it the experience of death. Slavery to Sin inevitably "leads to death" (Rom. 6:16); death is a "wage" that Sin dutifully pays for services rendered (6:23). Sin inflicts death upon its victims both through the flesh (Rom. 8:6; Gal. 6:8) and through the law (Rom. 7:9–11; 8:2; 1 Cor. 15:56). Nor is it at the end of natural life that one first comes under the rule of death. A person who is enslaved to Sin and estranged from the life-giving God is on both accounts already "dead."[70] As the slave of Sin, the *sōma* is by nature mortal (Rom. 6:12; 8:11; *sarx* is used in the same sense in 2 Cor. 4:11). The slave's sinful behavior inevitably produces more of the same, which being by nature corruptive, eventually destroys him.[71]

As the ally of Sin, death destroys God's handiwork. The end of natural life is the disintegration of the self (2 Cor. 5:1–10). The magnificent unity in diversity that God achieved in creation, is now undone. Despite his assurance that "to be away from the body [is to be] at home with the Lord" (5:6–8), Paul dreads the experience of death; for death will usher him into a state of bodiless existence (5:3–4). In flagrant violation of the inseparability of soul and body in the creation, death sunders the one from the other. "Without a body, man ceases to be truly and properly man. . . . At death the soul is separated from the body, and man's integral nature is disrupted."[72]

The Effects on the Three Relationships

It was stated at the opening of the chapter that knowing God, knowing oneself, and knowing other selves are inseparable experiences. Through bondage to Sin we lose knowledge both as *savoir* and as *connaître*, in all three relationships.

---

69. Rom. 5:14, 17 ("death reigned"), 21 ("sin established its reign by way of death," NEB); 7:5 ("we bore fruit for death"). Whereas Sin "comes into (*eiserchomai*) the world," death "goes through" (*dierchomai*) all humanity (5:12). The theme of Rom. 5:12–21 is "original *death* more than original *sin*" (Dunn, *Romans*, 273).

70. Rom. 7:10–13, 24; Bornkamm, *Paul*, 134. Cf. Gen. 2:17 ("in the day that you eat of it you shall die," RSV); 3:23–24.

71. Rom. 5:12; 6:16–23; 7:5, 9, 13, 23–24; 8:6, 10, 13; Gal. 6:7–8.

72. Philip Edgcumbe Hughes, *Paul's Second Epistle to the Corinthians* (Grand Rapids: Eerdmans, 1962), 171. The same view is ably defended by Gundry, *Sōma*, 149–54; Cooper, *Body, Soul, and Life Everlasting*, 155–63; and Andrew T. Lincoln, *Paradise Now and Not Yet* (Cambridge: Cambridge University Press, 1981), 60–71. As Lincoln observes (ibid., 70), "what is to be seen here . . . is not an ultimate anthropological dualism but rather a temporary duality brought about by sin and death, which until the consummation of salvation continue to mar the wholeness of human existence." The abnormality of the state helps to explain why Paul nowhere expressly speaks of the existence of a bodiless *psychē* (soul) between death and resurrection. He focuses upon the disintegration that death causes and especially upon the self's reintegration at Christ's return (see chap. 11).

Relating to God

The first effect is loss of knowledge, in both senses. The heathen, says Paul, "do not know God" (1 Thess. 4:5; cf. Gal. 4:8; 2 Thess. 1:8). "The world through its wisdom did not know God" (1 Cor. 1:19–21; cf. Col. 2:8). The Gentiles outside of Christ are "without hope and without God in the world" (Eph. 2:12), "darkened in understanding, alienated from the life of God" (4:18). Prior to his conversion, Paul knew Christ "according to the flesh" (*kata sarka*, 2 Cor. 5:16)—that is, in an utterly erroneous way owing to his bondage to Sin through the flesh. This loss of knowledge occurs by the creature's own design; fallen humanity willfully "suppresses the truth" about God, deliberately choosing not "to retain the knowledge of God" (Rom. 1:18–20, 28). "Once you were alienated from God and were [his] enemies in your minds" (Col. 1:21 NIV). Men of "depraved minds" do not merely abandon the truth, they actively "oppose" it (2 Tim. 3:8). It is therefore Paul's mission to demolish "every proud obstacle that is raised against the knowledge of God" (2 Cor. 10:5).

The second effect proceeds from the first. "The wrath of God is being revealed from heaven against all ungodliness and unrighteousness of men who by their unrighteousness suppress the truth" (Rom. 1:18). Persons who are "dead in transgressions and sins" are therefore "objects of [God's] wrath" (Eph. 2:1–3). God's wrath is neither arbitrary nor capricious; it is his personal, holy and settled opposition to human evil.[73] He exercises wrath by "giving over" the ungodly to further and graver wickedness, with the result that the wicked destroy themselves (Rom. 1:24–32).[74] Thus the death that results from bondage to Sin is at the same time the effect of the divine wrath. When the present is viewed from the standpoint of "the day of wrath, when God's righteous judgment is revealed," sinners are seen to be "storing up wrath" against themselves (Rom. 2:5), and to deserve no less than misery and death for having distorted God's truth and violated the demands of his righteousness (Rom. 1:32; 2:8–9; 9:22).

"As Rom[ans] 1:18–32 shows, God's wrath means a process willed by God—the outworking of the destructive consequences of sin, destructive for the wholeness of man, in his relationships."[75] It is every relationship that is affected. The slave of Sin and the object of wrath is for both reasons under sentence of death, and destined for eternal separation from the life-

---

73. Wrath is "a strong and settled opposition to all that is evil arising out of God's very nature" (Leon Morris, *The Apostolic Preaching of the Cross*, 3d ed. [Grand Rapids: Eerdmans, 1965], 180). For the wrath of God in OT and NT respectively, see ibid., 147–54, 179–84; cf. Whiteley, *Paul*, 61–69.

74. Especially 1:24, 26, 28 (the repeated "God gave them over"); and 27 ("received in themselves the due penalty for their perversion"). Cf. Gal. 6:7–8; Gustav Stählin, *TDNT* 5:441–44; Bultmann, *Theology*, 1:288.

75. James D. G. Dunn, "Paul's Understanding of the Death of Jesus," *Reconciliation and Hope*, ed. Robert Banks (Grand Rapids: Eerdmans, 1974), 139.

giving God. Moreover, rebellion against God pits man against himself and against other people.

Relating to Oneself

As we have seen, one means by which Sin establishes its mastery over the person is by enslaving the self to the self. The self is therefore both master and slave.

In the first place, the self deifies itself, and enthrones itself as king in its own universe. Whatever form it takes, and whether it is embraced by Jews or by Gentiles, the "wisdom of this age" is a human creation designed to supplant the "wisdom of God" and to glorify man rather than God (1 Cor. 1:18–31; 3:18–21; 2 Cor. 10:5, "every proud obstacle that is raised against the knowledge of God"). Adam's sin was to aspire to God's throne (Gen. 3:5, "you will be like God"). The man of lawlessness "who proclaims himself to be God" (2 Thess. 2:3–4) typifies and magnifies a mentality that pervades fallen humanity. The love that was meant to be directed toward God is now self-directed: "People will be lovers of themselves . . . lovers of pleasure rather than lovers of God" (2 Tim. 3:2, 4).[76] Why did human beings, both Jews and Gentiles, become idolaters (Rom. 1:23)? For one thing, idolatry puts the idolater in charge. He can now dictate what shall be required of him. He can create a religion that tolerates or even sanctions the sins he wants to commit.[77]

But the self that is enthroned is simultaneously the self that is enslaved—enslaved to Sin, and enslaved to itself. Sin effectively maintains its rule by convincing its victims that they are autonomous, self-determining beings. "Man is always servant, never more so than when he thinks he is master."[78] This helps to explain why human pride is often joined to the gravest self-doubt, and why determined efforts toward self-actualization are joined by equally strenuous acts of self-destruction.[79] Nor can the self as slave escape the self as king; deliverance must come from outside the self.

---

76. "The Protestant theologian Dean Fitch reminds us in his stunning book *Odyssey of the Self-Centered Self* that civilization has moved through several stages, and that we have recently entered upon the most acutely degenerate of them: The Age of Love of Self. For a period we loved God; then we loved rationalism; then we loved humanity; then science; now we love ourselves, and in that concupiscent love all else has ceased to exist" (William F. Buckley, Jr., *Cruising Speed*, paper ed. [New York: Bantam, 1972], 164).

77. Truth about God is suppressed, because for the proud, self-deified individual, the true God poses the greatest threat of all. See further chap. 5.

78. Dunn, *Romans*, 366.

79. Insecurity can generate a compensatory egotism. Conversely, the exertions of self-admiration can mask deep self-loathing. Cf. Richard F. Lovelace, *Dynamics of Spiritual Life* (Downers Grove: InterVarsity, 1979), 90. Writes Dan O. Via, Jr., *Self-Deception and Wholeness in Paul and Matthew* (Minneapolis: Fortress, 1990), 1, "Self-deception is the act and state of actually holding a belief about or an image of oneself, or a vision of one's situation in reality, while at the same time knowing that the belief, image or vision is not true. In self-deception the person is simultaneously the victimizer who lies and the victim who is lied to."

Until that happens, the self is radically different from what God the Creator intended.[80] The self was never meant to be its own ruler or its own slave. The human being remains God's crowning achievement, the sole creature that God fashions in his own image; and there remain qualities that even a person under Sin's rule may rightly esteem in himself or herself. But as the image was to manifest itself precisely in the self's communion with God and submission to God, and as the self has become its own master and slave, the reflection of the divine original in the mirror of humanity has been horribly distorted.[81] The image can be restored only by the reconciliation of the fallen self to God; attempts to cultivate self-esteem by any other means are doomed to failure.[82]

Relating to Other People

The effect of alienation from God and from oneself is alienation from other human beings. Human solidarity under God the Creator has its baleful counterpart in human solidarity under Sin's mastery: "all sinned" in Adam (Rom. 5:12; 1 Cor. 15:21–22). Consequently, what infects one human being infects all; and the effects upon personal relationships are disastrous.

Because the self that is enslaved to Sin insists on the enthronement of ego; because every other self behaves this way (since slavery to Sin is universal); and because pride is by nature competitive, Sin's slaves set about "biting and devouring one another" (Gal. 5:15). Paul reminds readers of the time when "we too were foolish, disobedient, deceived and enslaved by all kinds of passions and pleasures, [when] we lived in malice and envy, being hated and hating one another" (Titus 3:3 NIV). Conditions "in the last days," as described in 2 Timothy 3:1–4, merely intensify those which are to be seen in every generation. When human beings become "lovers of themselves" and "lovers of pleasure rather than lovers of God," it is certain that in relating to other people they shall become "boastful, proud, abusive, disobedient . . . , ungrateful, unholy, without love, unforgiving, slanderous, without self-control, brutal, not lovers of the good, treacherous, rash, conceited" (NIV).[83] All such mutual destructiveness perfectly serves Sin's pur-

---

80. Sin "signifies the unnature of man, the abnormal which has now become natural," writes Donald G. Bloesch, *Essentials of Evangelical Theology*, vol. 1 (San Francisco: Harper and Row, 1978), 95.

81. "Therefore, even though we grant that God's image was not totally annihilated and destroyed in [Adam], yet it was so corrupted that whatever remains is frightful deformity" (Calvin, *Institutes*, 189 [1.15.4]). In C. S. Lewis's *Prince Caspian* (New York: Macmillan, 1951), 182, Aslan says to Caspian: "You come of the Lord Adam and the Lady Eve. And that is both honour enough to erect the head of the poorest beggar, and shame enough to bow the shoulders of the greatest emperor on earth."

82. Writes Emil Brunner, *Man in Revolt*, trans. Olive Wyon (London: Lutterworth, 1939), 105, "Even as a sinner man can only be understood in light of the original Image of God, namely, as one who is living in opposition to it." It is just this note that is conspicuous by its absence from most contemporary talk about self-esteem, which therefore becomes childish, boring, and fruitless. Illuminating in this regard is "The Curse of Self-Esteem," *Newsweek*, 17 February 1992, 46–52.

83. Cf. Rom. 1:28–32; Gal. 5:19–21; Col. 3:5–9.

pose, which is ultimately the death of all its victims. Likewise, to see his schemes carried out with such efficiency fills Satan with glee.[84]

We have not yet come to the gospel according to Paul, but we have seen the urgent need for one. This is the approach that Paul himself uses: in Romans, having introduced the gospel of salvation (1:16–17), he demonstrates the universal need for salvation (1:18–3:20) before he expounds the gospel (3:21 *et seq.*; compare Gal. 4:1–3 to 4:4–7). Only when we have taken with all seriousness Paul's sober appraisal of the human condition can we rightly understand his gospel. Only when I perceive that *I* participate in human fallenness, only when I have been appalled by the reality of my own condition and recognize that *I* am bound to Sin and guilty before God, will I be ready to embrace Paul's message of grace and to experience the new life that it promises.[85]

> *O wretched man that I am! Who will rescue me from this body of death?* [Rom. 7:24]

---

84. In C. S. Lewis, *The Screwtape Letters* (New York: Macmillan, 1953), 29, Screwtape responds to Wormwood's joyous delirium over the outbreak of the Second World War: "For the first time in your career you have tasted the wine which is the reward of all our labours—the anguish and bewilderment of a human soul."

85. Paul Johnson, *Modern Times: The World from the Twenties to the Eighties* (New York: Harper and Row, 1983), shows how Freudian and Marxist analyses "combined to undermine, in their different ways, the highly developed sense of personal responsibility, and of duty towards a settled and objectively true moral code" (11). For Freud "feelings of guilt were . . . a sign not of vice, but of virtue" (11, cf. 6–8). "Within a few months of seizing power, Lenin had abandoned the notion of individual guilt, and with it the whole Judeo-Christian ethic of personal responsibility" (70; cf. 70–71). O. Hobart Mowrer, "'sin,' the Lesser of Two Evils," *American Psychologist* 15 (1960): 304, argues that by accepting one's "guilt and sinfulness," together with the "pain and effort" that entails, one may "pass from deep, pervasive self-rejection and self-torture to a new freedom, of self-respect and peace" (cited in Paul C. Vitz, *Psychology as Religion: the Cult of Self-Worship* [Grand Rapids: Eerdmans, 1977], 93).

3

The Saving Work of Christ

In the face of the manifold tyranny of Sin, Paul declares "the gospel"—the *euangelion*, his favorite term for his message of salvation and one that embraces all that he says about the person and work of Christ.[1] Christ, together with the powers at his command, comes to liberate persons from bondage to Sin and its agencies. This chapter focuses on salvation as an event of past history, the foundation for all that Paul says about the personal experience of salvation.

God's Saving Purpose

From first to last, salvation is God's achievement. In actively fulfilling that purpose, he foreknows, he predestines, he calls, he justifies, and he glorifies (Rom. 8:28–30). Having searched the limitless depths of God's intention for Jew and Gentile, Paul exclaims: "For from him and through him and unto him are all things. To him be glory forever. Amen" (Rom. 11:36). In Ephesians 1:3–14, a sustained celebration of God's plan to reclaim both humanity and the universe, *Theos* (God) is the subject of nearly every verb and participle. Where human beings are the subjects, they are

---

1. The noun *euangelion* occurs no fewer than sixty times in the thirteen letters. As I wrote in "Revelation and Tradition in the Pauline *Euangelion*," *WTJ* 48 (1986): 14, "Paul's gospel is about Christ *exclusively* (it is 'the gospel of *Christ*'—this gospel and no other) and about Christ *all-inclusively* (whatever can be affirmed about his person and work belongs to the gospel)."

described totally with reference to the work of the triune God: "in whom we have redemption" (1:7); "we were chosen" (1:11); "you were sealed" (1:13).

The Plan of God

Salvation begins in the unsearchable depths of the mind of God (1 Cor. 2:16a; Rom. 11:33–34). Of special note is Paul's usage of three terms, each of which contains the prefix *pro-* (before) as a witness to the priority of divine grace.

The first is the verb *protithemai*, together with the cognate noun *prothesis*. God "has saved us and called us to a holy life—not because of anything we have done but because of his own purpose (*prothesis*) and grace. This grace was given us in Christ Jesus before the beginning of time" (2 Tim. 1:9 NIV). God "purposed (*protithemai*) in Christ" to effect his will (Eph. 1:9). Believers are "called according to his purpose" (*prothesis*, Rom. 8:28), and chosen "according to the purpose (*prothesis*) of him who accomplishes all things according to the counsel of his will" (Eph. 1:11; cf. 3:11).

The second verb is *proginōskō*, "to know (*ginōskō*) beforehand (*pro*)."[2] In both instances, Romans 8:29 and 11:2, the knowing is deeply and thoroughly personal, not merely cognitive. Moreover, God's foreknowing is active in the very conceiving of his saving plan: "called according to his purpose. For those whom he foreknew (*proginōskō*) he also predestined" (Rom. 8:28–29). This introduces the third verb, *pro-orizō*, "to determine, appoint, fix (*orizō*) beforehand (*pro*)." This predetermination rests upon and perfectly accords with both God's plan and God's foreknowing: "predestined according to the purpose of him" (Eph. 1:11); "those whom he foreknew he also predestined" (Rom. 8:29). The language of election—the verb *eklegomai* and the noun *eklogē*—serves the same purpose. God establishes his purpose in accordance with election (Rom. 9:11, *kat' eklogēn prothesis*). Election and predestination are two names for one divine action: "he chose (*eklegomai*) us . . . before the foundation of the world . . . he predestined (*pro-orizō*) us" (Eph. 1:4–5).[3] The very ones who are called according to God's purpose, whom he foreknew and predestined (Rom. 8:28–29), are "God's elect" (*eklektōn*, Rom. 8:33).[4]

God's plan is effected in the actual experience of those he has chosen. His sovereign will does not obviate but incorporates human faith; this is

---

2. Paul does not use the matching noun *prognōsis*, "foreknowledge," which occurs only in Acts 2:23 and 1 Pet. 1:2.

3. Cf. 2 Thess. 2:13, "from the beginning God chose you. . . ." Here the verb comes from *haireō* (*heilato*) rather than *eklegomai*. For a defense of the reading *from the beginning* (*ap' archēs*) instead of "as firstfruits" (*aparchēn*, NIV mg.), see Ernest Best, *The First and Second Epistles to the Thessalonians* (New York: Harper and Row, 1972), 312–14.

4. See also the usage of *eklektos* in Rom. 16:13; Col. 3:12; 2 Tim. 2:10; Titus 1:1.

his appointed means for achieving his saving purpose, his ordained response to saving grace (Eph. 2:8). It is by God's design that human beings should "take hold of the eternal life to which [they] were called" (1 Tim. 6:12). Whereas this passage points especially to the heavenly prize (cf. Phil. 3:13–14), God's purpose embraces the entirety of Christian experience. "For he chose us . . . to be holy and blameless before him" (Eph. 1:4); "we are God's workmanship, created in Christ Jesus to do good works, which God prepared in advance for us to do" (2:10 NIV). In accordance with "his own purpose and grace," God "saved us and called us to a holy life" (2 Tim. 1:9 NIV; cf. 1 Thess. 4:7), which process reaches its predetermined goal when God glorifies his people and brings them into full conformity to the image of his Son (Rom. 8:29–30; cf. 1 Cor. 2:7; 2 Cor. 3:18).

God's redemption of fallen humanity stands at the heart of a plan to restore the whole universe—"to bring all things in heaven and on earth together under one head, even Christ" (Eph. 1:10 NIV; cf. Col. 1:20; Rom. 8:18–39). Once upon a time God the Father chose a bride for his Son (Eph. 1:3–6; 5:32), and thereafter created a home for them to live in (1:4, "the foundation of the world"). But the bride proved unfaithful, bringing disaster upon herself and her habitation (2:1–3). Yet through the sacrifice of the faithful Bridegroom (5:2, 25–27), and his triumph over all the powers of darkness (1:19–21), both the bride and her habitation will surely be restored (1:10–14, 22–23; 2:6–7). She will be more glorious as a rescued bride than as a created one.[5]

That imagery has already put the character of God's plan in a clearer light.

The Love of God

God's love accounts for his saving purpose. The love that first finds expression in God's foreknowledge of a people is consequently expressed in a predetermination on their behalf: "in love he predestined us" (Eph. 1:4–5).[6]

Correspondingly, election manifests God's love for his people: "knowing, beloved brethren, your election (*eklogē*) by God" (1 Thess. 1:4 NKJV; cf.

5. Ephesians presents the order in which events actually occur, not the order in which matters have been decreed in the mind of God. God has revealed the former in Scripture, but not the latter. Even to set forth a presumed "logical order" of thoughts within the mind of the incomprehensible God threatens to fashion God in man's image. See John M. Frame, *The Doctrine of the Knowledge of God* (Phillipsburg, N.J.: Presbyterian and Reformed, 1987), 264–65.

6. This rendering (NIV, RSV) is favored by John R. W. Stott, *God's New Society* (Downers Grove: InterVarsity, 1980), 37 n. 3, "because the context appears to be emphasizing love as the source rather than the result of our election." Yet the translation, "that we should be holy and without blame before Him in love, having predestined us" (NKJV, NRSV) is equally defensible; cf. the strong arguments in Andrew T. Lincoln, *Ephesians* (Dallas: Word, 1990), 15–18, 24–25.

2 Thess. 2:13).[7] Just how this comes about is stated most profoundly in Ephesians 1: God "has freely given us his grace in the Beloved" (*ēgapēmenō*, 1:6), namely, his beloved Son (Col. 1:13–14). God "chose us in him before the foundation of the world. . . . In love he predestined us" (1:4–5). In Paul's understanding, salvation is already *en Christō* at the very beginning, indeed before the beginning of time. There are no fewer than twelve instances of the phrase *in Christ* or its equivalent in Ephesians 1:3–14. From the very inception of the divine deliberations, God the Father sees the redeemed in his Son, and loves them for his sake. God "saved us . . . because of his own purpose and grace. This grace was given us in Christ Jesus before the beginning of time" (2 Tim. 1:9 NIV).

God's foreknowledge is deeply and thoroughly personal, not merely or even primarily cognitive, though the latter is of course not excluded.[8] In foreknowing a people (Rom. 8:29), God does not merely foresee that one day he shall love them; the foreknowing is itself an active expression of his love for them—the very love manifested in the cross (Rom. 5:6–8). God's foreknowledge may be likened, not to a woman's learning from the doctor that she is going to have a baby, but to the love that she sets upon the child as it grows and moves about in her womb.

God's mercy and grace arise from his love: "God, being rich in mercy, because of His great love with which He loved us . . . by grace you have been saved" (Eph. 2:4–5 NASB). At the beginning, no less than at the cross (Rom. 5:8), the divine *agapē* is not contingent upon the response or the condition of its objects: God "has saved us . . . not because of anything we have done but because of his own purpose and grace" (2 Tim. 1:9 NIV); "though [Jacob and Esau] were not yet born and had done nothing either good or bad, in order that God's purpose of election might continue, not because of works but because of his call" (Rom. 9:11 RSV). Therefore the loving and gracious God is alone worthy of honor and praise for the salvation of fallen humanity (1 Cor. 1:27–31; Eph. 1:3–14; 2:4–10).

The Power of God

God fulfills his purpose and exercises his love by "the immeasurable greatness of his power" (Eph. 1:19 NRSV). Just as God's actions before the creation of the world occurred "according to the good pleasure (*eudokia*) of his will (*thelēma*)" (Eph. 1:5), so too the sustained activity of his will brings his plan to full and perfect consummation: God "accomplishes all things according to the counsel (*boulē*) of his will (*thelēma*)" (1:11).

---

7. The verb *eklegomai*, in the middle voice, speaks of God's choosing a people to be his own: BAGD, "to choose, select (for oneself)" (*s.v.*). Cf. Titus 2:14, "to purify for himself a people that are his very own."

8. What was said in the preceding chapter about "the self's experience of knowledge" applies, *mutatis mutandis*, to God's knowledge of his people.

God carries forward that purpose, and exerts that power, by calling persons to himself.[9] Believers are "called according to his purpose ... those whom he predestined, he also called" (Rom. 8:28, 30). The very ones whom God chose in Christ before the creation (Eph. 1:4), he calls "into fellowship with his Son" (1 Cor. 1:9). Persons "who are called to belong to Jesus Christ ... are loved by God" for his sake (Rom. 1:6–7a NIV). "Those whom God has called," those whom "God chose," experience Christ's saving power (1 Cor. 1:18–31, especially vv. 24, 27–28). The scope of God's call accords with his purpose. Just as "he chose us ... to be holy and blameless before him" (Eph. 1:4), so too "God did not call us to impurity, but to holiness" (1 Thess. 4:7; cf. 2 Tim. 1:9). Beyond that, he calls his people into "eternal life" (1 Tim. 6:12), "into his own kingdom and glory" (1 Thess. 2:12; cf. 2 Thess. 2:13–14). "You were called to the one hope of your calling" (Eph. 4:4 NRSV; cf. 1:18). Paul presses on "toward the goal to win the prize for which God has called me heavenward in Christ Jesus" (Phil. 3:14 NIV).

The instrument of the call is the cooperative work of God's Word and God's Spirit. "The message of the cross ... is the power of God"; through this "demonstration of the Spirit's power" God calls his elect ones to salvation (1 Cor. 1:17–2:5). As a minister of the new covenant, anointed by the life-giving Spirit, Paul proclaims the gospel, God's appointed means for disclosing the glory of Christ (2 Cor. 2:14–4:6).[10] "Brothers beloved by God, we know that he has chosen you, because our gospel came to you not in word only but also with power and with the Holy Spirit and with full conviction" (1 Thess. 1:4–5).[11] "Brothers beloved by the Lord ... God chose you ... for salvation through sanctification by the Spirit and through belief in the truth" (2 Thess. 2:13). The Spirit, moreover, is "a seal" that both identifies and protects those whom God has called by "the word of truth" (Eph. 1:13), and "a deposit" who guarantees that God's saving purpose will reach its appointed goal (1:14).

No less indebted to God's power is the human response to the divine initiative. The very reason God employs the combined might of the Word and the Spirit in issuing his call is to evoke saving faith. "The gospel is the power of God for salvation to every one who believes" (Rom. 1:16). "My speech and my preaching were ... with a demonstration of the Spirit and of power, in order that your faith might not rest on the wisdom of men but on the power of God" (1 Cor. 2:4–5). God's call effects what it declares:

---

9. The terms are the verb *kaleō* (to call), the noun *klēsis* (calling), and the adjectives *klētos,-toi* (called ones).

10. Just as God brought light into being by his utterance (Gen. 1:3), so he creates "the light of the knowledge" of Christ by the utterance of the gospel (2 Cor. 4:4–6).

11. Cf. the sequence in 1 Thess. 2:12–13, "God, who calls you into his kingdom and glory ... when you received the word of God, which you heard from us ... the word of God, which is at work in you who believe." See also Acts 13:48.

here, as in the creation, God "calls into existence the things that do not exist" (Rom. 4:17 NRSV). Those who are "called [by God] to be saints" (Rom. 1:7; 1 Cor. 1:2) are holy by virtue of the call—persons whom God sets apart to serve him. Moreover, the call that sets them apart in the first place, remains at work throughout their struggle to grow in holiness. "May God himself . . . sanctify you wholly. May your whole spirit and soul and body be kept blameless. . . . Faithful is the one who calls you, and he will do this" (1 Thess. 5:23–24). Working in, by, with, and under all human exertions is the saving God, ineluctably carrying forward his purpose by his power. Philippians makes this especially clear. "He who began a good work in you will bring it to completion at the day of Christ Jesus" (1:6). "The fruit a righteous life comes through Jesus Christ" (1:11). "As you have always obeyed . . . work out your own salvation with fear and trembling, for God is the one working in you both to will and to work for his good purpose" (2:12–13). "I have strength for all things through the one who empowers me" (4:13).

What believers experience is not a new expression of God's power, but the progression or reverberation of a power released earlier in the events that are decisive for the achieving of God's saving purpose. To those events—the incarnation, the cross, and the resurrection of Christ—we now turn.

The Incarnation of the Son of God

"When the fullness of time had come, God sent forth his Son, born of a woman" (Gal. 4:4). Paul proclaims "the gospel of God . . . concerning his Son, who was born of the seed of David . . ." (Rom. 1:3; cf. 8:3, "God . . . by sending his own Son").[12] He does not hereby become God's Son; rather, he who is the eternal Son of the Father, is now sent forth. Why does he come, according to Paul?

The Revelation of God

Christ is "the image of the invisible God" (Col. 1:15), the One who makes God visible. "Christ, who is the image of God . . . God . . . made his light shine in our hearts to give us the light of the knowledge of the glory of God in the face of Christ" (2 Cor. 4:4, 6 NIV). Moreover, it is precisely as a man that Christ thus reveals God. "For in him all the fullness [of God] was pleased to dwell" (Col. 1:19). "For in him all the fullness of deity dwells bodily" (*sōmatikōs*, Col. 2:9).

---

12. In his resurrection, 1:4, he is "declared to be the Son of God," that is, manifested to be what he has always been.

Before becoming a man, Christ was "in the form of God" (Phil. 2:6a), that is, "equal with God" (2:6b)—terms that both distinguish him from God (*Theos*) and affirm his deity.[13] The expression of verse 6a "pictures the pre-existent Christ as clothed in the garments of divine majesty and splendour. He was in the form of God, sharing God's glory."[14] When Christ took "the form of a slave" (Phil. 2:7), he did not abandon "the form of God"; in becoming human he did not cease to be divine.[15] Philippians 2:7 speaks not of Christ's emptying himself of divine attributes (or indeed of anything), but rather of his giving utterly of himself by becoming a human being. By this action, far from abdicating or concealing his divinity, he discloses something of stupendous importance about the being and character of God. God is hereby shown to be a giving God, a humble God.[16]

Identification with Fallen Humanity

The One who by virtue of his deity is utterly different from ordinary human beings chooses to identify with them in the closest way. Christ "did not consider equality with God something to be grasped (*harpagmos*), but emptied himself (*heauton ekenōsen*)" (Phil. 2:6b–7a). Christ employed his equality with God, not for his own advantage but for the sake of his redemptive task.[17] Toward that end he expended himself to the full by becoming a human being.

13. "*Morphē* always signifies a form which truly and fully expresses the being which underlies it" (J. H. Moulton and George Milligan, *The Vocabulary of the Greek Testament* [Grand Rapids: Eerdmans, 1963], 417). The parallel phrase of Phil. 2:7, "the form (*morphē*) of a servant," points to the fact that Jesus actually became a slave. The words *to einai isa Theō* may be literally rendered "*the* being equal with God." "The function of the definite article [*to*] here is to point back to something previously mentioned"—namely, the equality with God of which Paul has just spoken in the equivalent phrase 'in the form of God'" (Gerald F. Hawthorne, *Philippians* [Waco: Word, 1983], 84). Paul's use of *Theos* for God the Father and *Kyrios* for Jesus Christ (2:11) is typical: see pp. 38–39.

14. Peter T. O'Brien, *Philippians* (Grand Rapids: Eerdmans, 1991), 211; he compares John 17:5 and Heb. 1:3. For strong arguments against recent attempts to exclude pre-existence from the passage, see ibid., 263–68.

15. See Col. 2:9; O'Brien, *Philippians*, 216–24. In John's language, "the Word was God" (John 1:1), and "the Word became flesh" (1:14) without ceasing to be God.

16. "Jesus displayed the self-giving humility which is the essence of divinity. . . . Service and self-giving are themselves the highest of divine attributes" (C. F. D. Moule, "Further Reflexions on Philippians 2:5–11," in *Apostolic History and the Gospel*, ed. W. Ward Gasque and Ralph P. Martin [Grand Rapids: Eerdmans, 1970], 265, 270). "He did not exchange the nature or form of God for that of a slave; instead, he displayed the nature or form of God in the nature or form of a slave, thereby showing clearly not only what his character was like, but also what it meant to be God" (O'Brien, *Philippians*, 223–24). The participial clause of 2:6a, "being (*hyparchōn*) in the form of God," is not concessive ("although he was in the form . . .") but causal ("because he was in the form . . ."); thus too O'Brien, ibid., 216.

17. O'Brien, *Philippians*, 215–16, following N. T. Wright, "[*Harpagmos*] and the Meaning of Philippians 2:5–11," *JTS* 37 (1986): 315–52. On one view *harpagmos* means "a thing to be snatched" (*res rapienda*), a prize not possessed but eagerly sought. Christ is not yet equal with God, and does not strive to become so; he is unlike Adam, who did so aspire. According to the other dominant view, the one adopted here, *harpagmos* means "something grasped" (*res rapta*), a prize already won. Jesus already possessed equality with God but did not selfishly employ it. This interpretation better accords with 2:6 as a whole; the other drives a wedge between v. 6a and v. 6b. For a discussion of these and other options, see Ralph P. Martin, *Carmen Christi* (Cambridge: Cambridge University Press, 1967), 134–64; O'Brien, ibid., 211–16.

The nature of his self-emptying is defined in the participial phrases *taking . . . being made . . .* and *being found*. "Taking the form of a slave" shows Jesus' willingness to relinquish the rights belonging to his heavenly status, and to experience to the extreme the distresses and deprivations of humanity.[18] "Being made in human likeness" does not deny the reality of Christ's humanity: he is made in the likeness of men, not of a man.[19] But Christ is not merely human; he is distinguished from other human beings. Unlike them, he is not sinful (Rom. 8:3). And unlike them, he belongs essentially to the heavenly world; even in his humanity he remains a divine being whose proper habitation is the heavenly glory. The third phrase, "being found in appearance as a man," does not mean that Christ merely appeared to be a man (as though his incarnation were an illusion) but that he manifested himself as a man, this being his chosen mode of self-revelation.

"God sent forth his Son, born of a woman" (Gal. 4:4)—not "of a virgin," for Paul here wants to emphasize Jesus' kinship with fallen humanity, rather than his distinction from them.[20] He expresses the kinship more starkly in Romans 8:3, "God . . . sending his own Son in the likeness of sinful flesh." Paul says neither "in the likeness of flesh" (for Christ's incarnation was genuine), nor "in sinful flesh," for Christ was without sin (2 Cor. 5:21).[21] God's Son "was born of the seed of David according to the flesh" (*kata sarka*, Rom. 1:3). The latter phrase stands parallel to the phrase "according to the Spirit" (*kata pneuma*, 1:4), the very terms by which Paul identifies the combatants in the Christian struggle (Rom. 8:1–17; Gal. 5:16–26). Romans 1:3 does not ascribe sinfulness to Jesus (again 8:3); but it does affirm, as did his reception of a "baptism of repentance for the forgiveness of sins" (Mark 1:4, 9), his willingness to identify fully with fallen humanity. The *sarx* of which this verse speaks is the very *sarx* that in the case of every other person has become the habitation and the tool of Sin.[22]

We now know more about Christ's disclosure of the character of God. For nowhere is the divine humility more evident than in Christ's willingness to identify utterly with human sinfulness.

---

18. "Slavery meant, in contemporary society, the extreme in respect of deprivation of rights" (Moule, "Reflexions," 268).

19. Paul uses the name *Jesus*, 2:10; and Christ had to be truly human in order to die, 2:8.

20. This is well observed by J. Gresham Machen, *The Virgin Birth of Christ* (New York: Harper, 1930), 259–60. Moreover he, like them, is "born under law" (4:4b).

21. See F. F. Bruce, *Romans* (Grand Rapids: Eerdmans, 1963), 161. Christ's identification with fallen humanity was closer still in the cross, where he became "sin" (2 Cor. 5:21).

22. Rom. 1:3–4 contains a pre-Pauline formulation (for evidence, see James D. G. Dunn, *Romans* [Dallas: Word, 1988], 5–6), which Paul incorporates into his own presentation of the gospel. "It must be judged highly probable that for Paul *kata sarka* in Rom. i.3 carries its normal note of depreciation" (James D. G. Dunn, "Jesus—Flesh and Spirit: An Exposition of Romans 1:3–4," *JTS* 24 [1973]: 49; for support, see 44–51).

The Conquest of Sin

Christ identifies with fallen humanity in his incarnation, in order to meet and to conquer the power that holds them all in terrible bondage. "By sending his own Son in the likeness of sinful flesh (*sarx*) and to deal with sin, [God] condemned sin in the flesh (*sarx*)" (Rom. 8:3 NRSV). As the flesh is the habitation and instrument of Sin (the phrase *sinful flesh* could also be translated "the flesh that Sin possesses"), it is in the arena of the flesh that Christ must encounter Sin. For the same reason, "God sent forth his Son [to be] born under law" (Gal. 4:4). For he came to "redeem those who were under law" (4:5), law being another means by which Sin enslaves people: as noted earlier, to be under Sin (*hypo hamartian*, Gal. 3:22) is to be under law (*hypo nomon*, Gal. 3:23). Christ willingly comes to the very places where Sin holds sway so that he may rescue its victims.

Yet the purpose and the extent of Christ's self-imposed slavery is not fully revealed until he encounters death, Sin's last and mightiest ally. He who "emptied himself" also "humbled himself and became obedient unto death—even death on a cross" (Phil. 2:7–8). God "condemned sin in the flesh" (Rom. 8:3 KJV), namely, "in the body of [Christ's] flesh through death" (Col. 1:22).[23] "God sent forth his Son . . . to redeem those under law" (Gal. 4:4–5), a deliverance accomplished in his death (3:13; Rom. 3:24–25). As these latter verses demonstrate, and as we shall see in the following section, the conquest of Sin entails atonement for the transgressions by which Sin's victims obey the master.

In face of this twofold need—victory over Sin and atonement for sins—the Savior had to be both divine and human. Only God possessed the power needed to end Sin's tyranny. But Sin had to be encountered in the realm of its tyranny, fallen humanity; Sin itself had to be conquered through the conquest of its agencies, the flesh, the law and death, together with the demonic powers. The same holds true in the case of the required atoning sacrifice, "which no one *can* make except God, and no one *ought* to make except man."[24] To achieve salvation in both respects, God became a man.

The Example of the Son

There is one further purpose of the incarnation to consider, one which will bring us closer to the cross. The Son of God became human in order to show how human beings were meant to live. Not only does Christ "the image of God" reveal the invisible God (Col. 1:15), he also restores the

---

23. The phrase *for sin* (*peri hamartias*) in Rom. 8:3 may also be rendered "to be a sin offering" (so NIV).
24. Anselm, *Cur Deus Homo?* ("Why God a Man?"), quoted by James D. G. Dunn, *Christology in the Making* (Philadelphia: Westminster, 1980), 1.

image that was marred by its first bearer, Adam. In Christ we see what Adam was meant to become (see chap. 4).

It is typical of Paul to leap from the incarnation to the cross, as many texts considered in the foregoing section illustrate (e.g., Rom. 8:3; Gal. 4:4–5). He tells us very little about Jesus' career, and he seldom draws upon the kind of material recorded in the Gospels about the life and teaching of Jesus.[25] When he does invoke Christ's example, it is typically something belonging to Passion Week or to the cross itself. Christ's "good confession" before Pilate provides a model for believers (1 Tim. 6:11–14). "For even Christ did not please himself," writes Paul, "but, as it is written: 'The insults of those who insult you have fallen on me'" (Rom. 15:3 NIV), the ultimate insult being to subject the sinless One to an accursed death (Gal. 3:13). Partly for that reason, Christ's "meekness and gentleness" (2 Cor. 10:1) are most poignantly evident during his passion. The supreme expression of Christ's selfless love (Phil. 2:1–4) was his obedience unto death (2:8).[26] It is possible that "the form [*typos*] of teaching" that Paul invokes in Romans 6:17, is Jesus himself—"Christ as the pattern of obedience, particularly in the epochal event of his death (5:19; cf. Phil 2:8), but probably also in the character of his whole life. . . ."[27]

The Cross of Christ

The cross stands at the very center of Paul's *euangelion*. His gospel is "the word of the cross" (1 Cor. 1:17–18); nowhere is there a comparable reference to the word of the resurrection. In 1 Corinthians 1:23–24 it is "Christ crucified" who is identified as "the power of God and the wisdom of God," not, as we might have expected (especially in the case of "power"), Christ resurrected.[28] Paul goes on to say, "For I determined to know nothing among you except Jesus Christ and him crucified" (2:2). Both the cross and the resurrection of Christ are "of first importance" in Paul's gospel (15:3–4). Unless Christ has risen from the dead the preaching of the cross (and of the resurrection) is a waste of time (15:14); but once the resurrection has occurred, the cross remains central. Whereas the received tradition of Romans 1:3–4 features incarnation and resurrection, in Romans 3:21–26, where Paul expounds the heart of the gospel introduced in 1:16–17, the entire focus is upon Jesus' death. The same is true in the corresponding

25. The absence of such references in Paul is "one of the strangest and most puzzling areas of early Christian history" (John Ziesler, *Pauline Christianity*, rev. ed. [New York: Oxford University Press, 1990], 20).

26. Christ is surely an example, but not merely an example, as Phil. 2 (and many another passage) shows. The fourfold rhetorical appeal of 2:1 provides the basis for the exhortations of 2:2–5. Persons must be in Christ (2:1) if they are to be like him (2:5).

27. Dunn, *Romans*, 353–54; see the arguments on 343–44.

28. For "the power of [Christ's] resurrection," see Rom. 1:4; 2 Cor. 13:4; Phil. 3:10.

passage of Galatians 2:15–21. The cross is literally the *crux* (Lat.: cross) of his preaching.

As we saw earlier, from the very conception of God's saving purpose he sees the redeemed in his beloved Son and loves them for his sake (Eph. 1:3–14). That love now comes to its supreme expression. "God demonstrates his own love for us in this: While we were still sinners, Christ died for us" (Rom. 5:8 NIV). God "did not spare his own Son, but gave him up for us all" (Rom. 8:32)—that is, for the very ones whom he "foreknew" and "predestined" (8:29–30). "In him we have redemption through his blood" (Eph. 1:7), "he" being God's beloved Son (1:6b), "we" being the ones whom God chose in him before the creation of the world (1:4).[29]

It has been well said that interpretations of Jesus' death are usually right in what they affirm, and wrong in what they deny. The cross is a multifaceted, diamond-shaped reality; nowhere is this so evident as in Paul's letters. To interpret the event he employs a variety of images, all of which are vital for understanding what happened in the cross. His language, drawn as it is from such quarters as the temple, the courtroom, the slave-market, and the battlefield, might elsewhere describe events that are rather impersonal. But Paul joins his terms together in the closest way, and uses each of them and all of them together to denote realities that are deeply personal. Moreover, each shows that the salvation accomplished here, occurs by the divine initiative through the divine power to fulfill the divine purpose.

Sacrifice

Crucifixion was literally excruciating; and it was the most shameful of deaths. But the closest Paul comes to reflecting on these two elements is Philippians 2:8, "becoming obedient to death—even death on a cross."

Paul also affirms that Christ died for other people. "Christ died for us" (Rom. 5:6): to be more exact, "while we were still sinners, Christ died for us" (Rom. 5:8). Even these verses do not quite explain the uniqueness of Christ's death: whenever one person dies for another, he dies for a sinner. The heart of the matter is stated in 1 Corinthians 15:3, "Christ died for our sins." Or in the language of Romans 4:25 (NRSV), Jesus "was handed over to death for our trespasses." The matter is stated most astonishingly in 2 Corinthians 5:21, "The one who knew no sin, [God] made to be sin for us, in order that we might become the righteousness of God in him." Christ thus represents his people, identifies in the closest way with their wrongdoing, and experiences the death that was their due. He represents them

---

29. Furthermore, those who have "redemption (*apolytrōsis*) through [Christ's] blood" (1:7) are the very ones whom the Spirit seals "until the redemption (*apolytrōsis*) of [God's] possession (*peripoiēsis*)" (1:14; cf. 4:30). Paul charges the Ephesian elders "to shepherd the church of God that he obtained (*peripoieō*) with the blood of his own Son" (Acts 20:28 NRSV).

by becoming their substitute; he acts on their behalf by standing in their place.[30]

In Romans 3:25 we meet the term *hilastērion*, which the Septuagint uses to translate the Hebrew *kaporet*, the "mercy seat," which covered the ark of the covenant in the Most Holy Place of the temple. But how is *hilastērion* to be translated? "God put forward [Christ Jesus, 3:24] as an expiation by his blood," says the Revised Standard Version; "to be a propitiation by His blood," says the New King James Version. Expiation is sinward, and denotes the eradicating or neutralizing of sin.[31] Propitiation is Godward, and speaks of appeasing or averting the divine wrath by sacrifice. Words akin to *hilastērion* are employed in nonbiblical Greek in this latter sense.[32] Yet the idea is thought by some (especially in light of pagan usage) to be sub-Christian. The critical difference is that according to Paul "God presented" Jesus as an *hilastērion* (3:25). The sacrifice is not offered to a capricious, irascible god, but by a loving God (Rom. 5:8).[33]

We must therefore not imagine that God's motives at the cross were different from Christ's, as though God were an implacable Judge who insists on punishing sin before he consents to impart his love, and Christ a passive victim who seeks to evoke that love for the sake of sinners by bearing the requisite punishment. On the contrary, the will of the Son perfectly accords with that of the Father and the motive for the Son's going to the cross is the same as the Father's. "God demonstrates his own love for us in this: . . . Christ died for us" (Rom. 5:8 NIV). For both it is a sacrificial love of incalculable cost. The Father "did not spare his own Son, but gave him up (*paradidōmi*) for us all" (Rom. 8:32).[34] "Christ loved us and gave himself up (*paradidōmi*) for us as a fragrant offering and sacrifice to God" (Eph. 5:2, cf. v. 25).

---

30. See Donald Guthrie, *New Testament Theology* (Downers Grove: InterVarsity, 1981), 467–71; Leon Morris, *The Cross in the New Testament* (Grand Rapids: Eerdmans, 1965), 216–24; John R. W. Stott, *The Cross of Christ* (Downers Grove: Inter-Varsity, 1986), 133–63 (on "the self-substitution of God"); James D. G. Dunn, "Paul's Understanding of the Death of Jesus," in *Reconciliation and Hope*, ed. Robert Banks (Grand Rapids: Eerdmans, 1974), 125–41; and my review in *WTJ* 38 (1976): 385–90. On Christ as representative man, see chap. 4.

31. In the Hebrew OT the verb *kaphar*, in the Qal stem, is used of the application of pitch to Noah's ark (Gen. 6:14): either "cover" with pitch or "wipe" (daub) with pitch. The same verb, in the Piel or intensive stem (*kipper*), means "cover over completely" or "wipe away completely." The latter term, used repeatedly in Lev. 16 (the ritual for the Day of Atonement), is translated *hilaskomai* in the LXX, and "to make atonement" in the NIV.

32. See Leon Morris, *The Apostolic Preaching of the Cross*, 3d ed. (Grand Rapids: Eerdmans, 1965), 145–47; David Hill, *Greek Words and Hebrew Meanings* (Cambridge: Cambridge University Press, 1967), 23–48.

33. "It cannot be emphasized too strongly that God's love is the source, not the consequence, of the atonement" (Stott, *Cross*, 174). So it was in the OT: "*I* have given [the blood] to you to make atonement [MT *kipper*; LXX *exilaskomai*] for yourselves on the altar" (Lev. 17:11). See Morris, *Apostolic Preaching*, 174–78.

34. The passive of the same verb in 4:25, "he was delivered over," likewise refers to the Father's action. Cf. 8:3, "God . . . sending his own Son . . . to be a sin offering" (NIV); for support of this rendering of *peri hamartias*, see Dunn, *Romans*, 422. It would have been easier (if we may put it so) for God the Father to have handed over himself than to have offered his only Son, just as Abraham would have readily offered himself in Isaac's place (an event, Gen. 22, to which Rom. 8:32 may allude).

"The Son of God . . . loved me and gave himself up (*paradidōmi*) for me" (Gal. 2:20). Here as elsewhere we find the Father and the Son to be distinct persons who are utterly united in being and character and purpose. In the cross "it is the Judge himself who in holy love assumed the role of the innocent victim, for in and through the person of his Son he himself bore the penalty which he himself inflicted."[35]

Earlier in Romans Paul declared that "the wrath of God is being revealed from heaven against all ungodliness and unrighteousness of men" (1:18). It is precisely in the face of his own wrath that God takes saving action. "For in [the gospel] the righteousness of God is being revealed (*apokalyptetai*). . . . For (*gar*) the wrath of God is being revealed" (*apokalyptetai*, 1:17–18). That dual revelation is still in view in 3:21–26. "But now . . . the righteousness of God has been disclosed" for the purpose of dealing justly with the sin that called forth the divine wrath (1:18). Integral to this purpose is the offering of Christ as "a sacrifice of atonement (*hilastērion*) by his blood" (3:25 NRSV).

Expiation and propitiation are in fact inseparable, and Romans 3:25 embraces both. The blood of Jesus expiates, or covers, the sins of God's people (cf. Rom. 4:7). Consequently God's wrath is averted, and his people are rescued from the terrors of the coming day of wrath (Rom. 2:5; 5:9; 1 Thess. 1:10; 5:9). In the death of Christ, as in the antecedent Levitical sacrifices, both human sin and divine wrath are taken with utmost seriousness; the expiating of sin is the essential means for propitiating the wrath; and the gracious God himself provides the atoning sacrifice which appeases and averts his own wrath.[36]

Justification

By manifesting his "righteousness" (*dikaiosynē*), God is shown to be "righteous" (*dikaios*). By virtue of this disclosure, he "justifies" (*dikaioō*) human beings, he grants them "justification" (*dikaiōsis*).[37] The crucial locus of that manifestation is the cross. "The righteousness of God is revealed (*apokalyptetai*)" in the gospel, says Romans 1:17. "But now the righteousness of God has been manifested (*pephanerōtai*)," says Romans

---

35. Stott, *Cross*, 159; see further 156–60.

36. This case is powerfully argued by Morris, *Apostolic Preaching*, 144–213. "The *hilastērion* which God has provided in Christ not only removes the ungodliness and unrighteousness of men but at the same time averts the wrath or retribution which is the inevitable sequel to such attitudes and actions in a moral universe" (Bruce, *Romans*, 106). BDB translates the Piel *kipper*, "cover over, pacify, make propitiation" (*s.v.*, 497a). See also Stott, *Cross*, 168–75; Guthrie, *Theology*, 468–71; Douglas Moo, *Romans 1–8* (Chicago: Moody, 1991), 231–38.

37. *Dikaiōma* is used once for the "righteous act" of Christ's death (Rom. 5:18), and once (as an equivalent to *dikaiōsis*) to mean "justification" (Rom. 5:16). Of all these terms, by far the most common are *dikaiosynē* (fifty-seven times in Paul, thirty-three in Rom. alone) and *dikaioō* (twenty-seven in Paul, fifteen in Rom. and eight in Gal.).

3:21. Paul here uses the Greek perfect tense to embrace the past event of Jesus' death together with its ongoing effects through the gospel. The saving verdict is here joined in the closest way to the cross. Persons are "justified (*dikaioō*) freely by [God's] grace through the redemption that is in Christ Jesus, whom God set forth to be a propitiation by His blood . . . to demonstrate His righteousness (*dikaiosynē*)" (3:24–25 NKJV; cf. 5:9, "justified by his blood").

Paul's teaching is deeply rooted in the Old Testament. The counterparts to *dikaiosynē* in Hebrew, *tsedek* and *tsedakah*, speak of a reality that is both active and relational. The *tsedek* of Yahweh is not a static attribute but a dynamic activity—not something Yahweh is but something he does: his vigorous and sustained faithfulness to the covenant that he has established with his people.[38] Thus Paul's language about the "revealing" or the "manifesting" of God's righteousness, whether in the cross or in the gospel (Rom. 1:17; 3:21), speaks not (except derivatively) of the imparting of information or the expounding of a concept, but of a divine exertion, a divine invasion into the territory over which Sin reigns.[39] As in the Old Testament, God activates his righteousness for a saving purpose (see Ps. 98:1–2; Isa. 46:13; 51:5–8; 56:1; 62:1, where in each case "righteousness" stands parallel to "salvation"). God manifests his righteousness in the cross in order to justify the ungodly (Rom. 3:21–26; 4:5). The gospel "is the power of God for salvation. . . . For (*gar*) in it the righteousness of God is being revealed. . . . For (*gar*) the wrath of God is being revealed . . ." (Rom. 1:16–18). The righteousness accounts for the power; the gospel of God is the channel along which the righteousness of God goes forth to save human beings from the wrath of God.

Furthermore, the revelation of Romans 3:21–26 (and 1:17) is eschatological in character—a gift of the last days. "But now, apart from law, the righteousness of God has been made manifest, as attested by the Law and the Prophets" (Rom. 3:21). The "now" (*nun*) is temporal, it pertains to "the present (*nun*) time" (3:26), the time inaugurated with Christ's coming, for which the time of "the Law and the Prophets" prepared (cf. Gal. 4:4–5).[40] Paul recognizes a prior revelation of God's righteousness in the Law: "The law is holy, and the commandment is holy and righteous (*dikaia*) and good" (Rom. 7:12). Moreover, to understand the present revelation of righteousness, it is essential to heed the witness both of the Law, notably Genesis 15:6 (Rom. 4:3), and of the Prophets, notably Habakkuk 2:4 (Rom. 1:17)

---

38. See Dunn, *Romans*, 40–43.

39. By the same token God's wrath is "revealed" (Rom. 1:18), that is, it goes out against, or falls upon, its objects, here expressed as God's "giving them over" to certain practices (1:24, 26, 28); cf. 1 Thess. 2:16, "the wrath [of God] has come upon them."

40. See Herman Ridderbos, *Paul: An Outline of His Theology*, trans. John R. DeWitt (Grand Rapids: Eerdmans, 1975), 161–66.

and Isaiah 40–66 (which anticipates every ingredient of Paul's own teaching). Nonetheless the revelation itself is unprecedented: it is the decisive irruption of God's righteousness into history, at his appointed time, to save his people through Christ's atoning death.

The foregoing discussion must not obscure the forensic nature of justification. Indeed it is within the courtroom that the active and relational character of God's righteousness is most poignantly revealed. Those who violate the terms of his holy covenant and the righteous commands of his law stand guilty before him, the Judge of all the earth; for him to view them otherwise would be to deny his very being and their very condition. If such persons are to be rescued from condemnation, the Judge himself must "justify" them, pronounce them "not guilty," declare them to be "in the right" and acquitted of all charges against them.[41]

The cross demonstrates as does no other event that God takes sin with utter seriousness and answers guilt with the full weight of his justice; and that he does so in order to exonerate the guilty and draw them into the closest fellowship with himself. "God presented [Christ] as a sacrifice of atonement (*hilastērion*). . . . He did this to demonstrate his justice (*dikaiosynē*), because in his forbearance he had left the sins committed beforehand unpunished—he did it to demonstrate his justice (*dikaiosynē*) at the present time, so as to be just (*dikaios*) and the one who justifies (*dikaioō*) those who have faith in Jesus" (Rom. 3:25–26 NIV).[42] In the cross "God made him who knew no sin to be sin for us, so that we might become the righteousness (*dikaiosynē*) of God in him" (2 Cor. 5:21). The wrath of God, which stood over the guilty (Rom. 1:18), is now poured out upon the sin with which Jesus has identified in the closest way; the result is that those whose sin has been placed upon him are acquitted of their guilt.[43] In manifesting his *dikaiosynē* in the cross, God shows that he is "both just and justifier" (Rom. 3:26). Both the combination and the order are significant; the second action is founded upon the first.[44] God justifies the ungodly (Rom. 4:5), because Christ has borne their ungodliness (Rom. 4:25; 2 Cor. 5:21).

---

41. In both OT and NT, the terminology belongs to the legal sphere. See especially Morris, *Apostolic Preaching*, 251–98.

42. We again see how inextricably joined are the language of the courtroom and the language of the temple. That sinners should be "justified freely by [God's] grace" (Rom. 3:24) is inconceivable apart from God's presenting Christ as the *hilastērion* (3:25).

43. See Isa. 53:4–6; Lev. 1:4. "In Jesus on the cross was focused not only man's sin, but the wrath which follows upon that sin. The destructive consequences of sin are such that if they were allowed to work themselves out fully in man himself they would destroy him as a spiritual being. This process of destruction is speeded up in the case of Jesus, the representative man, the *hilastērion*, and destroys him. The wrath of God destroys the sin by letting the full destructive consequences of sin work themselves out and exhaust themselves in Jesus" (Dunn, "Paul's Understanding of the Death of Jesus," 139).

44. "If there had been no death of Christ, God would have been unable to justify the sinner. Apart from the death of Christ, the only manifestation of righteousness is the sinner's condemnation in death" (George E. Ladd, *A Theology of the New Testament* [Grand Rapids: Eerdmans, 1974], 432).

Christ thus dies "for (*hyper*) sinners" (Rom. 5:6–8) and "for (*peri*) sin" (Rom. 8:3); he represents sinners, he identifies in the closest way with them and their sin, and in his death he stands in their place. Correspondingly, sinners must be united to Christ in the closest way. It is those who are "in Christ" (*en Christō*) whom God justifies (2 Cor. 5:21; Phil. 3:9). This is Paul's richest expression of the personal and relational character of the divine righteousness, a subject to which we shall return.

Redemption

Both before and during Paul's time, both within and beyond the Bible, to redeem typically meant to secure a release from some bondage or penalty by the payment of a ransom-price.[45] In accord with what was just said about righteousness, Paul declares that redemption occurs in Christ (Col. 1:14) and that Christ is the very embodiment of redemption (1 Cor. 1:30).

As with other aspects of salvation considered thus far, it is preeminently in the cross that Christ does his redeeming work.[46] His death is the ransom-price that secures the liberation of others. Here "the man Christ Jesus . . . gave himself as a ransom for all" (1 Tim. 2:6; cf. Titus 2:14).[47] Christians "were bought at a price" (1 Cor. 6:20; 7:23)—Christ's sacrificial death (1:18–31; 5:7; 11:23–26; 15:3). Sinners are "justified freely by [God's] grace through the redemption that came by Christ Jesus. God presented him as a sacrifice of atonement . . . in his blood" (Rom. 3:24–25 NIV). The shedding of blood signals not just the gift of life but the loss of life.[48] By the language of redemption, Paul does not imply that the ransom-price was paid to someone, whether to God or to the devil; his focus is on redemption's costliness, both to God and to Christ. A principal reason for its costliness to Christ is that he "became sin" so that sinners might be justified (Rom. 3:24–26; 2 Cor. 5:21). "In [Christ] we have redemption through his blood, the forgiveness of sins . . ." (Eph. 1:7; cf. Col. 1:14).[49] As in any

45. E.g., slaves, prisoners of war, and condemned criminals might be so released. For the evidence, see Morris, *Apostolic Preaching*, 11–64; Stott, *Cross*, 175–82. Speaking of the cross, Paul employs the nouns redemption (*apolytrōsis*), ransom (*antilytron*), and price (*timē*); and the verbs ransom/redeem (*lytroomai*) and buy (*agorazō* and *exagorazō*).

46. The final "day of redemption" (Eph. 4:30; cf. 1:14), including "the redemption of our bodies" (Rom. 8:23), depends upon the release accomplished in the cross (Eph. 1:7).

47. The verb used in these two verses is *didōmi*, "give," whose compound *paradidōmi* appears in other statements about Christ's voluntary sacrifice (Gal. 2:20; Eph. 5:2, 25).

48. Morris, *Apostolic Preaching*, 112–28; Stott, *Cross*, 179–81.

49. In both verses, "forgiveness" stands in apposition to and is virtually equated with "redemption," "for the deliverance in question is a rescue from the just judgment of God upon our sins, and the price paid was the shedding of Christ's blood when he died for our sins on the cross" (Stott, *God's New Society*, 40).

instance of genuine forgiveness, the offended party absorbs the wrong and thus prevents it from spreading and multiplying.[50]

In his death Christ the Redeemer liberates his people from bondage to Sin and its agencies, together with all the consequences of such bondage. God, "by sending his own Son in the likeness of sinful flesh, and as a sin offering, condemned Sin in the flesh" (Rom. 8:3)—in the very "body of [Jesus'] flesh through death" (Col. 1:22). "God did not redeem flesh by an act of incarnation; he destroyed flesh by an act of condemnation."[51] Moreover, by nailing sinners' certificate of indebtedness to the cross, Jesus "disarmed the rulers and authorities [and] made a public spectacle" of them (Col. 2:13–15).[52]

Of special interest to Paul is how Christ crucified delivers people from the law as Sin's instrument. God's Son came "to redeem those under law" (Gal. 4:5). Moreover, "Christ redeemed us from the curse of the law by becoming a curse (*katara*) for us, for it is written: 'Cursed (*epikataratos*) is everyone who is hung on a tree'" (Gal. 3:13, including a quotation from Deut. 21:23). Christ died for the accursed (Gal. 3:10, where *epikataratos* recurs in a quotation from Deut. 27:26). They are unmistakably "accursed by God," as the person to whom Deuteronomy 21:23 originally referred is expressly said to be (MT, LXX). They "rely on observing the law"; yet they do "not continue to do everything written in the book of the law," as shown by the fact that they are "under a curse" (*katara*, 3:10). They stand guilty, rather than justified, before God (3:11). The curse of the law is the penalty of death for failure to honor the demands of God's holy law and covenant—a penalty ultimately decreed, of course, not by the law but by the Lawgiver. Those whom Christ redeems are "under a curse," that is, destined for death. In buying their freedom, Christ himself experiences the very curse that was due them. That this experience personally affected Christ, we may be sure; how "becoming sin" and "becoming a curse" affected him, we cannot begin to imagine.[53] It remains significant that Christ is expressly said to have become "a curse" (*katara*), not "accursed" (*epikataratos*), nor "accursed by God" (*hypo Theou*), despite the language of the Old Testament texts that Paul invokes (Deut. 27:26; 21:23). For in both the plan and the work of salvation, the Father and the Son are utterly at

---

50. In the cross, "the holy God met the sin, accepted its entail, entered into its costliness, suffered redemptively in his own Son. . . . Here was no overlooking of guilt or trifling with forgiveness; no external treatment of sin, but a radical, a drastic, a passionate and absolutely final acceptance of the terrible situation, and an absorption by the very God himself of the fatal disease so as to neutralize it effectively" (C. F. D. Moule, *The Sacrifice of Christ* [Greenwich, Conn.: Seabury, 1957], 28).

51. Dunn, *Romans*, 440. Jesus' own death was the scene of the flesh's execution; the NIV of Rom. 8:3 ("he condemned sin in sinful man") is very misleading.

52. I follow the NIV of 2:15b, "triumphing over them by the cross." See the comments on "bondage to the spirits" on p. 54.

53. There are glimmers in the agony in Gethsemane (Matt. 26:36–46) and the cry of dereliction (27:46).

one; and Paul does not wish to place the one over against the other. Just as Christ "became sin" for sinners without himself being a sinner (2 Cor. 5:21), so he "became a curse" for the accursed without himself becoming accursed (Gal. 3:13).[54]

While affirming that Christ redeems persons who were "under law" (Gal. 4:5) by experiencing in their stead "the curse of the law" (3:13), Paul never says that believers are saved from the law itself. Instead, the law is wrested from Sin's grip and placed into the hands of a new Master (see chap. 6).

Reconciliation

Reconciliation establishes peace in the place of war, and attains unity and accord in place of alienation. In Paul, as in his antecedents, mutual alienation is presupposed. Human beings were willfully rebellious against God, suppressing his truth and resisting his will (Col. 1:21; Rom. 1:18–3:20). God consequently manifested his wrath "against all ungodliness and unrighteousness of men" (1:18). So when Paul says "we were God's enemies" (Rom. 5:10), both sides of the alienation are in view; observe the immediately preceding reference to God's "wrath" (5:9).[55]

Paul lays great emphasis upon the divine initiative in reconciliation: he who is both the offended party and the mightier party is the reconciler. "All this is from God, who reconciled us to himself through Christ" (2 Cor. 5:18). "Once you were estranged [from God] and hostile. . . . But now he has reconciled you" (Col. 1:21–22; cf. Eph. 2:16). "We were reconciled to [God] . . . we have now received reconciliation" (Rom. 5:10–11). We were responsible for the enmity; yet we contributed nothing whatsoever to the provision of the peace.

Moreover, God achieves reconciliation through the cross and does so by means of the saving actions already considered—sacrifice, justification, and redemption. Through Christ "God was pleased to reconcile to himself all things . . . by making peace through the blood of his cross. . . . He has now reconciled [you] in the body of his flesh through death" (Col. 1:19–22). Ephesians 2:11–18 declares that "through the blood of Christ" hostility is ended and peace established between Jew and Gentile; and more impor-

---

54. On this distinction, and the absence of the words *by God* from Paul's quotation of Deut. 21:23, see James Denney, *The Death of Christ* (London: Tyndale, 1951), 91–94; Morris, *Apostolic Preaching*, 56–58; Guthrie, *Theology*, 466 ("God could never curse his Son, but since he has already pronounced a curse on sin, his Son could not avoid the implications of this if he identified himself with man's sin"); and F. F. Bruce, *Galatians* (Grand Rapids: Eerdmans, 1982), 165–66, who observes (1) that Paul would hardly speak of Christ's being accursed by God for his supreme act of obedience; and (2) that Paul is not concerned with the question: By whom was Christ cursed? but with making plain "that the curse which Christ 'became' was his people's curse." Max Wilcox, "'Upon the Tree'—Deut 21:22–23 in the New Testament," *JBL* 96 (1977): 85–99, suggests that the words *by God* were lacking in the form of Deut. 21:23, which Paul quoted.

55. See Morris, *Apostolic Preaching*, 214–50; Stott, *Cross*, 192–203; Moo, *Romans*, 319–20.

tantly that by union with Christ "our peace," both parties are reconciled to God. "In Christ God was reconciling the world to himself, not counting their transgressions against them. . . . God made him who knew no sin to be sin for us, so that we might become the righteousness of God in him" (2 Cor. 5:19–21). "Therefore, since we have been justified through faith, we have peace with God. . . . Since we have now been justified by his blood, how much more shall we be saved from God's wrath through him! For if, when we were God's enemies, we were reconciled to him through the death of his Son, how much more, having been reconciled, shall we be saved through his life!" (Rom. 5:1, 9–10 NIV). Justification and reconciliation together save us from wrath and bring peace and the prospect of final salvation, confirming us in the belief that the alienation that reconciliation overcomes is dual in character.[56]

We now turn to the other great event of the past upon which our salvation depends.

The Resurrection of Christ

Christ's death and resurrection are inseparable, historically and theologically; in both respects, they stand together at the heart of Paul's gospel.[57] The significance of the one event is intelligible only in relation to the other. Both are essential for achieving God's saving purpose.

The Reality of the Event

Paul declares "that Christ died for our sins according to the Scriptures, that he was buried, and that he was raised on the third day according to the Scriptures" (1 Cor. 15:3–4). Jesus was raised in a body, a body moreover that was fully substantial and material. That which was put to death was buried, and that which was buried was raised to life.[58] As Jesus is "the first-

56. Note the parallels between Rom. 5:9 and 10, highlighted by Moo, *Romans*, 318. Cf. Dunn, *Romans*, 259 (on 5:10). He adds: "The same recognition of a harmony between the concepts of reconciliation and sacrifice, and that either can be used to speak of the turning away or ending of divine wrath (3:25 as the answer to 1:18–3:20; 5:9–10), should also discourage a revival of the view that it is only man who needs to be reconciled and not God; because God is the reconciler he does not cease to be judge" (260).

57. See 1 Cor. 15:3–4 (both are matters of "first importance"); Rom. 4:25; 6:4–5; 8:34; 2 Cor. 5:15; Gal. 1:1–4; Phil. 2:6–11; 3:10; 1 Thess. 4:14; Ridderbos, *Paul*, 54–57; J. Knox Chamblin, *Gospel according to Paul* (Ann Arbor: University Microfilms, 1979), 285–89. For emphasis on the centrality of resurrection, see Richard B. Gaffin, Jr., *Resurrection and Redemption: A Study in Paul's Soteriology*, 2d ed. (Phillipsburg, N.J.: Presbyterian and Reformed, 1987): "the resurrection of Christ is *the* pivotal factor in the whole of the apostle's soteriological teaching" (135).

58. The raising of Christ's body (*sōma*) is stated or implied in Rom. 8:11; 1 Cor. 6:13–14; 15:44. The words *on the third day* (1 Cor. 15:4) witness to the bodily character of the event (they may point as well to the fulfillment of Scripture, cf. Hos. 6:2). Also planting Christ's resurrection firmly in the past is Paul's habitual use of the aorist indicative, either "he was raised" or "God raised him" (e.g., Rom. 4:24–25; 8:11; 10:9; 1 Cor. 6:14; 2 Cor. 4:14; Gal. 1:1; 1 Thess. 1:10). Only in 1 Cor. 15:3 does the perfect tense appear (*egēgertai*, he has been raised), one indication that Paul here employs a received tradition (15:3a).

fruits of those who have fallen asleep" (15:20), his resurrected body is a "spiritual body" (*sōma pneumatikon*, 15:44)—not an immaterial body (which for Paul would be an oxymoron) but one animated and dominated by the Spirit (*Pneuma*) of God (Rom. 1:4; 8:11). It is moreover a transformed body, no longer subject to death: "we know that Christ, having been raised from the dead, will never die again" (Rom. 6:9; cf. 8:11). As Jesus is (again) "the firstfruits" of the resurrection, his mortal body is clothed with immortality (15:52–54) and thereby becomes a "glorious body" (Phil. 3:21). At the same time, it is Jesus who is raised, the very one who was crucified; he has not become a different person. He appears to, and is recognized by, those whom he knew before his death (1 Cor. 15:5–7). As the imagery of 1 Corinthians 15:52–54 indicates, his crucified body is not destroyed but is granted new qualities.[59]

All it takes is one resurrection from the dead for the reality of resurrection to be established. "If there is no resurrection of the dead, then Christ has not been raised" (1 Cor. 15:13). But in actual fact, Christ has been raised (15:20; cf. the evidence of 15:4–8), so that the statement of 15:13 may be reversed: "Now that Christ has been raised, there *is* resurrection of the dead." "If Christ has not been raised, our preaching is in vain and your faith is in vain" (1 Cor. 15:14). Unless he actually rose from the dead, it is futile to claim that he has. But, says Paul, he has actually been raised; the preaching has a sound historical basis.[60]

Assurance of Atonement

Paul declares that "Christ died for our sins" (1 Cor. 15:3). Yet a little later he says: "If Christ has not been raised, our preaching is in vain . . . you are still in your sins" (15:14, 17). Unless Christ was raised from the dead, the declaration of 1 Corinthians 15:3 is an untruth. Why is this so?

59. For an interesting explanation of the accounts in which disciples at first lack, and are then granted, recognition of the risen Christ (Luke 24:13–35; John 20:11–18; 21:1–14), see Peter J. Kreeft, *Everything You Ever Wanted to Know About Heaven . . . But Never Dreamed of Asking* (San Francisco: Ignatius, 1990), 98–102: "we now recognize character through body [but] Jesus' disciples recognized His body through His acts-in-character" (99). I suspect (though I certainly cannot prove) that Jesus' resurrected body was more substantial, more solid, denser, than his crucified body. In this case, if he did indeed pass through the grave clothes and through the wall of the cave, the explanation would be not that he had become a ghost (which would contradict Luke 24:39) but that he was now heavier than before (water is heavier than air, yet passes through air; a steel pipe is heavier than water, yet passes through it).

60. "Can Christ effect in me life through death, victory and deliverance from transitoriness, if he was not himself first raised from the dead, literally and in the completeness of his manhood, by the glory of the Father? . . . This is the burning question which will not stay for an answer" (Stephen Neill, *The Interpretation of the New Testament, 1861-1961* [London: Oxford University Press, 1964], 234). On the historical reality of Christ's resurrection, see Merrill C. Tenney, *The Reality of the Resurrection* (New York: Harper and Row, 1963), 105–44; Murray J. Harris, *Raised Immortal: Resurrection and Immortality in the New Testament* (Grand Rapids: Eerdmans, 1985), 57–71.

In his death, Jesus identified in the closest way with the sins of his people and in that capacity suffered in their place the consequences of their sins (2 Cor. 5:21; Gal. 3:13). Had he not risen from the dead, one could only conclude that he remained under sentence of condemnation, and that the wrath of God and the destructive consequences of sin had not exhausted themselves but were still at work upon him. There would therefore be no reason for those whom he represented to expect a different destiny and every reason for them to conclude that they remained in their sins: "And if Christ has not been raised, your faith is useless; you are still in your sins. Then those also who have fallen asleep in Christ have perished" (1 Cor. 15:17–18).

Christ "gave himself for our sins" (Gal. 1:4a); but the rescue from "the present evil age" was not complete until the Father "raised him from the dead" (1:1). Christ, says Paul, "was handed over to death for our transgressions and was raised for our justification" (Rom. 4:25). God justifies the ungodly on the basis of Jesus' atoning death (3:24–26; 4:5; 5:6–9). Yet it is by virtue of Jesus' resurrection that the verdict is upheld and its permanent validity guaranteed. The resurrection ratifies the achievement of the cross. The Father's raising of the Son is his mighty yes or amen to what the Son accomplished in his death: Christ "became obedient to death, even death on a cross. Therefore God exalted him to the loftiest height" (Phil. 2:8–9).[61] The death of Jesus remains the crucial locus of salvation; but it is so only because Jesus was raised from the dead. Because Jesus' death was followed by his resurrection from the dead, believers' faith is not futile, and those who have died have *not* perished (1 Thess. 4:14). In order to be saved and justified, one must believe "that God raised [Christ] from the dead" (Rom. 10:9), but the life here promised was pre-eminently secured in the cross (3:21–26).

Assurance of Victory

The Lord Jesus Christ "gave himself for our sins to rescue us from the present evil age" (Gal. 1:4). As atonement is secured in the cross and assured in the resurrection, so the conquest of Sin that commenced in the cross progressed in the resurrection.

In response to the Son's obedience unto death, God the Father "exalted him to the loftiest height" (Phil. 2:9, with its opening "therefore").[62] Thus

---

61. Only once does Paul say that Jesus "rose again" (*anistēmi*, 1 Thess. 4:14, probably a pre-Pauline formula). Otherwise he invariably says, whether directly or indirectly (by the passive voice), that "God raised (*egeirō*) him" from the dead (e.g., Rom. 4:24–25; 8:11; 10:9; 1 Cor. 6:14; 2 Cor. 4:14; Gal. 1:1; Eph. 1:20; Col. 2:12; 1 Thess. 1:10).

62. In the verb *hyperypsoō* the *hyper* (above) is "simply elative, indicating not an additional exaltation to a status higher than before, but simply the highest possible exaltation" (Moule, "Reflexions," 269)—that is, to the glorious estate which Christ had willingly relinquished (2:6–7).

enthroned, Christ is worthy of universal acclaim, worthy of the worship due Yahweh alone (2:10–11). He who governed all beings as "the firstborn over all creation" now rules over them as "the firstborn from among the dead" (Col. 1:15–20).[63]

Central to the purpose of Christ's reign thus begun is the conquest of all his and his people's enemies (1 Cor. 15:20–28). Sin exerted its rule by the agency of death; from Adam onward, death reigned as Sin's vicegerent (Rom. 5:12–21). Indeed, death subjugated Christ himself.[64] Sin hounded Jesus throughout his life, never succeeding, whether through the law or the flesh or the demonic powers, in mastering him. But at the end, Sin seems to have found a way to do so; by human agencies, Sin brings Jesus to his death. The crucified Jesus actually dies, and thereby becomes death's subject or prisoner. Had he remained under death's rule, one could only conclude that Sin remained in power.

However, Jesus' death marks the beginning of Sin's downfall. With his death, Jesus is placed beyond the reach of Sin. "For the one who has died has been freed from Sin" (Rom. 6:7): a dead person can no longer be tempted and assailed. But there would be scant comfort in that, had Jesus remained bound to death, the ally of Sin. Yet, declares Paul, Christ has conquered death by rising from among the dead: "death no longer reigns over him" (Rom. 6:9). Death's rule, inaugurated with the transgression of the first Adam, is now broken by the last Adam, and the reign of grace is established in its stead (Rom. 5:17–21).[65] Moreover, Christ is the first person to achieve total victory over death—"the firstfruits of those who have fallen asleep" (1 Cor. 15:20). His rising from the dead is categorically different from the experience of Lazarus, who would die again. "For we know that Christ, having been raised from the dead, will never die again; death no longer reigns over him" (Rom. 6:9). We can therefore understand the taunts of 1 Corinthians 15:55, "Where, O death, is your victory? Where, O death, is your sting?" The questions are not answered, for death has no answer to give; it is reduced to stunned and humiliated silence.

63. "Among all things (*en pasin*)" Christ is supreme (Col. 1:18), to my mind a better rendering than NIV's "in everything"; for every other instance of the plural of *pas* and *pan* in verses 15–20 speaks of creatures (cf. 2:10). Thus, too, C. F. D. Moule, *The Epistles to the Colossians and to Philemon* (Cambridge: Cambridge University Press, 1958), 69–70.

64. The God "who raised Christ from the dead will also (*kai*) give life to your mortal bodies" (Rom. 8:11)—i.e., to your mortal bodies as to Christ's mortal body.

65. In the words of J. A. T. Robinson, *The Body: A Study in Pauline Theology* (London: SCM, 1952), 40, "Paul sees Christ dealing with the forces of evil [by] going on and on and on, triumphantly absorbing their attack by untiring obedience, till eventually there is nothing more they can do. Or, rather, there is one thing more—and that is to kill Him. This they do. But in the very act they confess their own defeat. For all they achieve thereby is to deprive Him, still inviolate, of the flesh, through which alone they have any power of temptation over Him. He thus slips their grasp and renders them impotent. The Resurrection is the inevitable consequence of this defeat; death could have no grip on Him, since sin obtained no foothold in Him."

Jesus' personal triumph over the demonic powers, begun at the cross (Col. 2:14–15), now reaches its second stage. Had the powers known what was in store for them, "they would not have crucified the Lord of glory" (1 Cor. 2:6–8). Through human beings, they had Jesus put to death, not because they were ignorant of his identity, but because they knew he was "the Lord of glory" (cf. Mark 1:24, "I know who you are—the Holy One of God"). But being ignorant of "God's secret wisdom" (1 Cor. 2:7), they did not know that Jesus' death was the first step toward their own destruction (2:6, "who are doomed to perish").[66] By having Jesus crucified, they enable him to meet and thereby to conquer death.

God the Father, having raised Christ from the dead, "seated him at his right hand in the heavenly realms, far above all rule and authority, power and dominion, and every title that can be given, not only in the present age but also in the one to come" (Eph. 1:20–21 NIV)—that is, over all powers both human and angelic, over both the powers and the places of their rule, and over powers both good and evil.[67] All those beings that owe their very existence to him—creatures "in heaven and on earth, visible and invisible, whether thrones or dominions or rulers or authorities"—are now subject to his rule (Col. 1:15–20). Knowing his people's dread of spirits both real and imagined, and their vulnerability to their assaults, Paul especially emphasizes Christ's lordship over the malevolent spirits. Certain angels, rulers and powers want to separate people from God's love, but cannot (Rom. 8:38–39). Christ the King will surely destroy "every rule and every authority and power" (1 Cor. 15:24), thus completing the conquest begun at the cross (Col. 2:15).[68]

> *Thine is the glory, Risen, conquering Son;*
> *Endless is the victory Thou o'er death hast won.*[69]

66. I believe that "the rulers of this age" (*hoi archontes tou aiōnes toutou*, 1 Cor. 2:6–8) are demonic powers. See 2 Cor. 4:4, Satan "the god of this age" (*tou aiōnos toutou*); and Eph. 2:2, "when you followed the ways of this world (*ton aiōna tou kosmou toutou*) and of the ruler (*archonta*) of the kingdom of the air"; G. B. Caird, *Principalities and Powers: A Study in Pauline Theology* (Oxford: Clarendon, 1956), 1–30; C. K. Barrett, *First Corinthians* (New York: Harper and Row, 1968), 69–72; Clinton E. Arnold, *Powers of Darkness: Principalities and Powers in Paul's Letters* (Downers Grove: InterVarsity, 1992), 101–4. For the view that the rulers are human, see Ladd, *Theology*, 436 ("political rulers such as Pilate and Herod"); Gordon D. Fee, *The First Epistle to the Corinthians* (Grand Rapids: Eerdmans, 1987), 103–4. Guthrie, *Theology*, 143, thinks *archontes* embraces both ideas: "Although the political officials (Pilate, Herod, Caiaphas) are primarily in mind, Paul's statement here [2:8] must be interpreted via 1 Corinthians 15:24, where clearly the underlying spiritual powers are in mind."

67. See Stott, *God's New Society*, 59–60.

68. In view of such assertions, it is most likely that the hostile powers are especially in view in the more comprehensive statements noted. Eph. 1:20–21 should be read in light of 6:12, where the terms *archē* (rule) and *exousia* (authority) recur; and Col. 1:16 in light of 2:10, 15 (where the same terms recur). These two terms, together with *dynamis* (power), also occur in 1 Cor. 15:24. See the fine discussion of Christ's subjugation of the powers, with particular reference to Phil. 2:10–11, in Martin, *Carmen Christi*, 249–70.

69. Edmond Budry, "Thine Is the Glory" (1884) trans. R. Birch Hoyle (1923).

4

Life in the Son

Having considered the saving events of the past, we turn to the application of salvation to human beings, to their actual experience of salvation.

The New Humanity

Jesus Christ is no less than the inaugurator of a new humanity, a figure moreover who incorporates into himself all of those whom he represents and whose salvation he achieves. The closest Old Testament counterpart is Adam, and Paul explores the relationship between these two epochal figures in a variety of ways.

Creation and Fall

Paul calls Jesus Christ "the image (*eikōn*) of God" (2 Cor. 4:4), "the image (*eikōn*) of the invisible God" (Col. 1:15). This language is rooted in Genesis 1:26–27, "Then God said, 'Let us make man [MT, '*Adam*] in our image [LXX, *eikōn*]. . . .' So God created man ['*Adam*] in his own image (*eikōn*). . . ."[1]

Adam is a noble figure, the Creator's crowning achievement; yet it is strictly as a man that he discloses the invisible God. Christ however is "the

---

1. That 2 Cor. 4:4–6 and Col. 1:15–20 and Paul's Adam-Christology generally are rooted in Gen. 1 is recognized by Herman Ridderbos, *Paul: An Outline of His Theology*, trans. John R. DeWitt (Grand Rapids: Eerdmans, 1975), 68–86; and by Seyoon Kim, *The Origin of Paul's Gospel* (Grand Rapids: Eerdmans, 1982), 137–268.

firstborn over all creation" (Col. 1:15). "He is before all things" (1:17), he is already there when God's creative activity commences. More than that, he is the mediator through whom God the Father brings the whole creation, Adam included, into being: "it was through Him that the universe was created. Yes, all things in heaven and on earth . . .—they have all been created through Him and for Him" (Col. 1:16, FFB). Already in his preincarnate work as the mediator of creation, Christ is "the image of the invisible God."[2] As this title indicates, Christ's activity reveals a kinship with both God and Adam. As the One in whom all things cohere and endure (Col. 1:16–17), he rules on the Father's behalf. In doing so, he provides a model for the man and the woman, whom God commands to exercise responsible dominion over the earth (Gen. 1:26–28).

But Adam and Eve sought to become God's rivals rather than his subjects (Gen. 3:1–7), with catastrophic results: "Sin came into the world through one man, and death through Sin" (Rom. 5:12); "the many died by the transgression of the one man" (5:15). Christ comes into the world to deal with that disaster. At the critical hour Adam willfully disobeyed. In his own hour of crisis Christ steadfastly obeyed; he went down into death to bear the consequences of human sin and to conquer the powers of Sin and death that Adam's transgression had loosed upon the world. "Through the obedience of the one man," through his "one act of righteousness" (Rom. 5:18–19), namely, his saving death (3:21–26; 4:25–5:11), eternal life is provided for "the many" (5:18–21).

Christ the Last Adam

Adam and Christ represent two orders of existence, the first marked by *psychē*, the second by *pneuma*. "If there is a natural body (*sōma psychikon*), there is also a spiritual body (*pneumatikon*). So it is written: 'The first man Adam became a living being' (*psychēn zōsan*); the last Adam, a life-giving spirit (*pneuma zōopoioun*)" (1 Cor. 15:44b–45 NIV). Bodies marked by *psychē* perish, whereas those marked by *pneuma* are imperishable (15:42–44, 50–54).

Paul's language in this passage is consistent with his distinction between Adam as a created being and Christ as the pre-existent mediator of creation: "The first man was of the dust of the earth [Gen. 2:7], the second man from heaven" (15:47). Yet Paul here emphasizes the priority of Adam: "The spiritual (*pneumatikon*) did not come first, but (*alla*) the natural (*psychikon*), then the spiritual (*pneumatikon*)" (15:46). The reason for Paul's

---

2. Cf. p. 41. Kim, *Paul's Gospel*, having shown the kinship between *eikōn* (image) and *morphē* (form), 195–205, concludes (265) that "it is highly probable that the Adam-Christ antithesis . . . lies behind" Phil. 2:6–11, but rightly affirms that it is the pre-existent Christ who possesses "the form [*morphē*] of God," 2:6; so too Ridderbos, *Paul*, 73–78. As we saw in chap. 3, pp. 66–70, Christ revealed something of great importance about God's character when he decided to become a man: here, as in the creation, the preincarnate One proves to be "the image of the invisible God."

emphasis is both historical (the historical Adam antedates the historical Jesus) and theological (the new humanity rescues the old). The incarnation is presupposed: Christ is "the second man, the last Adam." But Paul's focus is upon the resurrection of Christ from the dead; it is by virtue of this event that Christ becomes "the last Adam."[3]

Colossians 1:15a, "He is the image of the invisible God," stands as a rubric over the whole of verses 15–20.[4] The Mediator of creation (1:15-17) is also the One through whose death and resurrection the fallen creation is reconciled (1:18–20). He, "the firstborn (*prōtotokos*) over all creation" (1:15b), is also "the firstborn (*prōtotokos*) from among (*ek*) the dead" (1:18). The preposition *ek* would be inappropriate at verse 15, for Christ is not one creature among many; but it is most appropriate in verse 18, for he fully identified with the dead by actually dying, and he rose as the "firstfruits" (*aparchē*) from among the dead (1 Cor. 15:20, 23). He is moreover "the beginning" (*archē*, 1:18a), also inappropriate in verses 15–17. Adam is "the beginning" of the first humanity. Christ is "the beginning" precisely as "the firstborn from among the dead" (1:18a, b): with his triumph over death, new creation begins; the new order of existence breaks in upon the old.

The New Creation

At the heart of this creation, as of the first, stands humanity, the handiwork of God—humanity now reclaimed and restored through identification with the last Adam. "As was the earthly man, so are those who are of the earth; and as is the man from heaven, so also are those who are of heaven" (1 Cor. 15:48 NIV). "The first man Adam became a living being (*psychēn zōsan*); the last Adam, a life-giving spirit (*pneuma zōopoioun*)" (1 Cor. 15:45)—not *pneuma zōn*, "living spirit." "The contrast is between man the recipient of the breath of life which constitutes him a living being, and Christ the giver of the life of the age to come, the life of the Spirit."[5] Moreover, like the first Adam, the last Adam is an inclusive figure, the very place of new life. "For since through a man came death, so also through a man comes the resurrection of the dead. For as in Adam all die, so also in

---

3. The original of Gen. 2:7b, quoted in 15:45a, reads (in both MT and LXX) "and man became a living being." In the interests of the contrast he is drawing, Paul enlarges upon the text: "The first man Adam became a living being," an instance of *midrash pesher*, "a quotation that is at once citation and interpretation" (Gordon D. Fee, *The First Epistle to the Corinthians* [Grand Rapids: Eerdmans, 1987], 788). The language of 15:45b is integral to the contrast between the two orders of existence: Adam belongs to *psyche*, Christ to *pneuma*; Adam receives life, Christ gives life; Adam's body was *psychikon*, Christ's *pneumatikon*. "This is by no means tantamount to equating Christ with the Holy Spirit" (C. F. D. Moule, "The New Testament and the Doctrine of the Trinity," *ExpT* 88 [1976–77]: 18; so also Fee, *First Corinthians*, 790 n. 15).

4. On the hymnic character and Pauline authorship of Col. 1:15–20, see Peter T. O'Brien, *Colossians, Philemon* (Waco: Word, 1982), 32–42.

5. James D. G. Dunn, *Christology in the Making* (Philadelphia: Westminster, 1980), 108; the emphasis is his.

Christ will all be made alive" (15:21–22). The "old man" (*palaios anthrōpos*, Rom. 6:6)—man in Adam (5:12–21)—is crucified, so that persons may be joined to the risen Christ (6:4–11). To "put on" the new man is to "clothe oneself" with Christ himself.[6] The "one new man" (*kainon anthrōpon*, Eph. 2:15) is the corporate Christ—Christ himself together with all those united to him in his death and resurrection. The proclamation of the peace that Christ secured in his reconciling death awaits his inauguration of the new humanity in his resurrection (2:14–17). On that reality rests the ethical imperative: "that you put off . . . the old man (*palaion anthrōpon*) which grows corrupt according to the deceitful lusts . . . and that you put on the new man (*kainon anthrōpon*) which was created according to God in righteousness and true holiness" (4:22–24, NKJV; cf. 1:4; 2:10; Col. 3:9–10).[7]

To be understood along the same lines, in my judgment, is "the inner man." This phrase identifies the person in Christ, in contrast to "the outer man," the person in Adam and destined to perish. "Although our outer man (*exō anthrōpos*) is wasting away, yet our inner (*esō*) man is being renewed day by day" (2 Cor. 4:16), anticipating the full realization of the new humanity in the heavenly glory (4:17–18). By the same token, "the inner man" of Romans 7:22 is equivalent to the "new man" implied in Romans 6:6. Ephesians 3:16, "that [God the Father] would grant you . . . to be strengthened . . . in the inner man (*esō anthrōpon*)" anticipates the commands of 4:22–24.[8]

Paul carefully distinguishes believers' present newness of life (Rom. 6:4, 11) from their awaited share with Christ in the resurrection of the body (6:5, 8). Only then shall they be fully conformed to his image (*eikōn*), that is, "glorified" (Rom. 8:29–30; Phil. 3:20–21).[9] Yet the process has already begun: "And all of us . . . are being transformed into [the Lord's] image (*eikōn*) from one degree of glory to another; for this comes from the Lord, the Spirit" (2 Cor. 3:18 NRSV). In prospect of the resurrection of the body and the fullness of glory (the main subject of 1 Cor. 15:42–58), Paul sum-

6. Observe the use of the middle voice of *enduō* ("clothe oneself") in Rom. 13:14; Gal. 3:27; Eph. 4:24.

7. On the "new man," see, e.g., Ridderbos, *Paul*, 223–31; C. K. Barrett, *From First Adam to Last* (London: A. & C. Black, 1962), 92–119; Russell Philip Sheed, *Man in Community: A Study of Saint Paul's Application of Old Testament and Early Jewish Conceptions of Human Solidarity* (Grand Rapids: Eerdmans, 1964), 126–99.

8. For this understanding of "the inner man," see C. K. Barrett, *The Second Epistle to the Corinthians* (New York: Harper and Row, 1973), 145–47; James D. G. Dunn, *Romans* (Dallas: Word, 1988), 394; Kim, *Paul's Gospel*, 321–26. Others take "inner and outer man" (as distinct from "old and new man") to denote the incorporeal and the corporeal aspects respectively: cf. Robert H. Gundry, *Sōma in Biblical Theology, with Emphasis on Pauline Anthropology* (Cambridge: Cambridge University Press, 1976), 135–40; and, with special reference to Eph., Andrew T. Lincoln, *Ephesians* (Dallas: Word, 1990), 204–6 (linking "inner man," 3:16, to "heart," 3:17, and "mind," 4:23).

9. On the relation between present resurrection life and the future resurrection of the body, and the basis for both in Christ's resurrection and the work of the Trinity, see Richard B. Gaffin, Jr., *Resurrection and Redemption: A Study in Paul's Soteriology*, 2d ed. (Phillipsburg, N.J.: Presbyterian and Reformed, 1987), 33–74.

mons readers to holiness of life: "Just as we have borne the image (*eikōn*) of the man of dust, let us also bear the image (*eikōn*) of the man of heaven" (15:49 NRSV mg.).[10] Transformation into Christ's image occurs in the very place where believers give themselves unstintingly to "the work of the Lord" (15:58).

Christ's mighty re-creative work is deeply personal; but it is not concluded until the whole universe has been renewed. God's purpose is nothing less than "to bring all things in heaven and on earth together under one head, even Christ" (Eph. 1:10 NIV). We saw in chapter 1 that the Christian *agōn* is part of an *agōn* which spans the whole of history and affects the entire creation; likewise, Christ comes to make his blessings flow as far as the curse is found (Rom. 8:18–39). Just as humanity was the crown of God's creative activity at the beginning, and just as God granted Adam dominion over the rest of creation, so too the persons whom Christ transforms will stand as glorified beings at the heart of a restored universe.

Both the personal and the cosmic dimensions are represented in 2 Corinthians 5:17, which may be literally rendered: "Therefore if anyone [is] in Christ—new creation (*kainē ktisis*); the old things have passed away, behold, new things (*kaina*) have come to be." The words *new creation* are more directly joined to the words *in Christ* than to the word *anyone*; and they embrace more than individual conversion and the replacement of old habits by new ones. The radical change in the person extends to the whole creation. The old corrupted order is being regenerated, paradise is being regained and superseded. "The accent falls on a person (*tis*) entering the new order in Christ, thus making the *kainē ktisis* an eschatological term for God's age of salvation."[11] The mediator of the creation is the very one through whom God reconciles and restores the fallen creation: "Through [Christ] God was pleased to reconcile to himself all things, whether on earth or in heaven" (Col. 1:19–20, the language of v. 16). This purpose is at least partly being achieved already through persons in whom God is cultivating the new image and whom he appoints as agents of reconciliation (2 Cor. 5:18–20).[12]

10. There are good textual reasons for choosing the hortatory subjunctive *phoresōmen* (let us bear) rather than the declaratory indicative *phoresomen* (we shall bear): see Fee, *1 Corinthians*, 787, n. 5; Metzger, *TC*, 569, opts for the indicative but acknowledges that it has "slender external support."

11. Ralph P. Martin, *2 Corinthians* (Waco: Word, 1986), 152. "When [Paul] speaks here of 'new creation,' this is not meant merely in an individual sense ('a new creature'), but one is to think of the new world of the re-creation that God has made to dawn in Christ, and in which everyone who is in Christ is included" (Ridderbos, *Paul*, 45). The cosmic dimension is captured in the NEB of 5:17b, "there is a new world" (text), "a new act of creation" (mg.).

12. On creation as the presupposition for redemption, on the inclusion of creation in redemption, and on Jesus as mediator of both creation and redemption, see John G. Gibbs, *Creation and Redemption: A Study in Pauline Theology* (Leiden: Brill, 1971), 139–54.

Union with Christ

Christ dies and rises from the dead for his people. They must die and rise with him. Just as Christ gained victory over death through his personal encounter with death, so too his people must be united with him in his death as the gateway to participating in his conquest of death. In both his death and his resurrection, Christ is a corporate figure.[13]

"In Christ"

Paul identifies believers as persons who are "in Christ" (*en Christō*) or "in Christ Jesus" (*en Christō Iēsou*).[14] "The formula 'in Christ' contains two fundamental ideas: believers are in Christ; salvation is in Christ. In both the *en* is taken at its full value. Sometimes one idea predominates and sometimes the other; they are held together by the conception of Christ as a corporate personality, who in his own person gained the salvation of believers, and of whose personality they are members."[15]

Paul's conviction that salvation is in Christ and no other is clear from the whole of chapter 3 and from everything considered thus far in this chapter.[16] Our main concern for now is the other idea: "believers are in Christ." Paul's usage is controlled by several factors.

The historical factor. The One to whom believers are united is not a purely spiritual being, but, astonishingly, a figure of recent history; and it is by virtue of specific events in his life that believers participate in salvation.[17]

The christological factor. In Paul's eyes, Christ is indeed a "corporate personality"; yet he remains, in keeping with his historical particularity, a distinct person. The relationship between Christ and believers is very intimate indeed. Not only are believers in Christ, Christ is in them (Rom. 8:10; Gal. 2:20). Yet the two are not absorbed into one another; the individuality of each is safeguarded. Christ remains the Lord, the object (not just the

---

13. Christ's death and resurrection for his people was the subject of chap. 3. For believers' union with Christ in his death and resurrection, see Rom. 6:1–11; Gal. 2:20; Eph. 2:4–18; Col. 2:9–12; 2 Tim. 2:11, together with other passages considered subsequently.

14. For the references in Paul, see Albrecht Oepke, *TDNT* 2:541–42.

15. Ernest Best, *One Body in Christ* (London: SPCK, 1955), 29, following a survey of the texts and the various views (1–29).

16. The point is stressed by Barrett, *First Adam to Last*, 77–78 (with special reference to Christ as "the seed" of Abraham, Gal. 3), 96 ("men are related to God, and participate in the last things [such as judgment, righteousness, and life] only in virtue of their relation with Christ"). Cf., e.g., Rom. 6:23; 8:2, 39; 1 Cor. 1:2, 4–5; 15:22; 2 Cor. 5:19–21; Gal. 2:4, 17; 3:14; Phil. 3:14.

17. Cf. C. F. D. Moule, *The Phenomenon of the New Testament* (London: SCM, 1967), 41: the early Christians "began to regard the Rabbi, whom some of them had known personally, whom all of them knew of as a recently executed victim of injustice, as the body in which they were limbs. Can you conceive of Paul speaking of himself as 'in Gamaliel'?" It is noteworthy that Paul employs the phrase *in Christ Jesus* more often than "in Christ."

sphere) of faith, and believers his subjects. It is a oneness of *communio* rather than *unio*. Thus to move from the words *Christ in me* to the words *Christ as me* (as some people are wont to say) is to cross a great divide and to enter exceedingly dangerous territory.[18]

The ecclesiological factor. "It is the corporate whole of believers who dwell in Christ"; therefore, "it is most emphatically . . . not the mere interpenetration of two individuals."[19] Life in Christ is inseparable from life in the church. In Paul's mind the individual's fellowship with Christ is inextricably joined to his or her participation in the Christian community. Allegiance to Christ finds expression in love for other believers (1 Cor. 13). At the same time, the experience of life *en Christō* is not exhausted in fellowship among Christians. To suggest so would be to ignore Christ's individuality and transcendent glory (he is "seated at the right hand of God," Col. 3:1), and also the personal and individual appropriation of Christ's life and power (Gal. 2:20; Phil. 4:13).[20] Paul does not allow the horizontal to eclipse the vertical: *en Christō* witnesses to believers' common life in the risen Christ, their common devotion to him in worship and obedience, and their common dependence upon his power.

The linguistic factor. While *en* is to be understood in a local or spatial sense, it is not to be taken literally. To think of believers' relationship to Christ in quasi-material terms, would be to ignore its deeply personal character.[21] But neither is the language purely figurative. Paul seeks to give expression to a transcendent reality (so that the language is better described as metaphysical or mythical than as figurative or metaphorical), one which the local *en* serves to express better than other language does. Furthermore, Paul indicates in what particular way he understands the local *en*: persons in Christ are joined together as members of a single body or organism (1 Cor. 12:12–27; Eph. 4:12–16). Paul's language is genuinely incorporative.[22]

18. "That it is not a *union of identity* is . . . clear, because of the strong sense of individual choice and responsibility, of dialogue with Christ, and of personal friendship, that pervades Paul's thought" (Moule, *Phenomenon*, 27). Cf. W. D. Davies, *Paul and Rabbinic Judaism*, 2d ed. (London: SPCK, 1955), 91 ("there is no loss of personal identity in mystical absorption"). Paul speaks much more often of believers "in Christ" than of Christ "in believers," almost the reverse of Paul's language about the Spirit (C. F. D. Moule, *The Origin of Christology* [Cambridge: Cambridge University Press, 1977], 56–58).

19. The respective quotations are from Best, *Body*, 9, and Moule, *Phenomenon*, 26.

20. "The aliveness of Christ, existing transcendentally beyond death, is recognized as the prior necessity for the community's corporate existence, and as its source and origin. Even if he is himself not called 'the body,' Christ, as a living, transcendent, inclusive, more-than-individual Person, is antecedent to the Church. . . . Paul conceived of Christ himself as a corporate entity, independently of his Church" (Moule, *Christology*, 70, 71). Cf. Richard N. Longenecker, *Paul, Apostle of Liberty* (New York: Harper and Row, 1964), 166–69.

21. See Longenecker, *Paul*, 169–70; Best, *Body*, 8–10; Moule, *Phenomenon*, 27.

22. Moule, *Phenomenon*, 27–28.

"The Body of Christ"

Paul identifies the Church as "the body (*sōma*) of Christ." The language is inspired by the individual body of Christ, both crucified and risen, and witnesses to believers' participation in both those events. Moreover, Paul consistently likens the church to the human organism. Yet his use of this image is by no means uniform; he exploits it for various pastoral purposes.

In 1 Corinthians and in Romans Paul accentuates believers' unity with one another proceeding from their common life in Christ. "For just as the body is one and has many members, and all the members of the body, though many, form one body, so it is with Christ" (1 Cor. 12:12). The church is emphatically not the "body of Christians" but the very "body of Christ."[23] Like the human organism, the church is a unity in diversity where independence and divisiveness would imperil the proper functioning of the whole (12:14–27).[24] The divisions in Corinth are therefore both inexcusable and extremely dangerous, especially when they appear at the very place where believers commemorate their participation in Christ's death (10:16–17; 11:17–34). Romans 12:4–5 presents a digest of 1 Corinthians 12:14–27, again amid a discussion of spiritual gifts (12:6–8) and the threat of conflict among believers (12:3, 9–21).

In the other two places Paul employs this language, the later epistles Colossians and Ephesians, we again hear calls for unity. "Let the peace of Christ rule in your hearts, for as members of one body (*sōma*) you were called to peace" (Col. 3:15). This note is especially strong in Ephesians. The rationale for the call is the incorporation of all believers into Christ: "His purpose was to create in himself one new man out of the two, thus making peace, and in this one body to reconcile both of them [Jew and Gentile] to God through the cross" (2:15b–16a NIV). "This one body" (*sōma*) is Christ's crucified body: reconciliation is achieved "in the body (*sōma*) of his flesh through death" (Col. 1:22; cf. Eph. 2:15). What happened there provides the basis for the subsequent declaration about the church: "There is one body (*sōma*) and one Spirit," and the attendant appeal, "Make every effort to keep the unity of the Spirit by the bond of peace" (Eph. 4:3–4; cf. vv. 12–16).

A distinctive feature of Ephesians and Colossians is that the appeals for unity are combined with the theme of the body's growth through corporate dependence upon Christ the church's Lord. In the picture of 1 Corinthians 12 the head is itself one of the members of the body: "the

---

23. The phrase *to sōma tōn Christianōn*, "the body of Christians," is first found in the fourth-century church historian Eusebius (Moule, *Christology*, 86).

24. The enclosing verses are very similar, referring to the human body and the church respectively: "Now the body (*sōma*) is not made up of one member but of many" (12:14); "Now you are the body (*sōma*) of Christ, and each one of you is a member of it" (12:27).

head (*kephalē*) cannot say to the feet, 'I have no need of you'" (12:21). In both Colossians and Ephesians Christ himself is the head of the church— its ruler and defender, its source of wisdom and knowledge—in the face of various perils both demonic and human, both spiritual and intellectual.[25] "He is the head (*kephalē*) of the body (*sōma*), the church" (Col. 1:18). He is indeed Lord of the whole universe (1:15–17). Yet his relationship to the church is by far the more intimate of the two: the creation is emphatically not his body, the church emphatically is.[26] Moreover, so closely is the church joined to Christ, that she shares in his universal reign: "And God placed all things under his feet and appointed him to be head (*kephalē*) over everything for the church, which is his body (*sōma*), the fullness of him who fills everything in every way" (Eph. 1:22–23 NIV).[27] All service in the church is similarly motivated: as a participant in Christ's own afflictions, Paul the apostle suffers "for the sake of his body (*sōma*), which is the church" (Col. 1:24); and the husband, identified as "the head (*kephalē*) of the wife as Christ is the head (*kephalē*) of the church, his body (*sōma*)," is called upon to love his wife "as Christ loved the church and gave himself up for her" (Eph. 5:23, 25).[28] If each believer is to be thus obedient, and if the church as a whole is to function properly, the power and wisdom must flow from the head into the body, as in a healthy human organism: "speaking the truth in love, we will in all things grow up into him who is the Head, that is, Christ. From him the whole body, joined and held together by every supporting ligament, grows and builds itself up in love, as each part does its work" (Eph. 4:15–16 NIV; similarly Col. 2:19).[29]

25. For a summary of the evidence, see F. F. Bruce, *Paul: Apostle of the Heart Set Free* (Grand Rapids: Eerdmans, 1977), 407–23 (on Colossians), 424–40 (on Ephesians). The principal meaning of *kephalē* in these and kindred texts, despite recent arguments to the contrary, is "rule" or "authority." Thus Wayne A. Grudem, "The Meaning of *Kephalē* ('Head'): A Response to Recent Studies," in *Recovering Biblical Manhood and Womanhood*, ed. John Piper and Wayne A. Grudem (Wheaton: Crossway, 1991), 425–68.

26. Thomas Boogaart, "Galileo, Fox, and the Reformed Tradition," *Perspectives* 6 (January 1991), 20, writes that Matthew Fox (in *The Coming of the Cosmic Christ*), "takes texts like Colossians 1:16–17 seriously . . . and helps us to image all over again how the cosmos is living, a part of the body of the living and reigning Christ." But this is just what Paul does not affirm in this passage. It may be said that Christ is to the creation what Rembrandt is to his paintings, and to the church what Rembrandt is to his son Titus. But the illustration is imperfect: see later comments on adoption.

27. The church is here called the *plērōma*, "that which is filled." The ascended Christ who "fills (*plēroō*) the whole universe" (4:10), "fills [the church] for himself [*tou* . . . *plēroumenou*, present middle participle]" (1:23c), with all the needed powers and gifts for sharing in his universal mission and his conquest of the demonic host.

28. We are again reminded of the inextricable connection between Christ crucified and the church: for the sake of his body the church, he handed over his own body to death.

29. Paul speaks fundamentally of the qualitative growth of the church, only derivatively of its quantitative growth. Such growth occurs amidst the lure of "power" and "wisdom" from spurious sources (Eph. 4:14; Col. 2:6–23). Christ the Head both supplies the true wisdom (Col. 2:3) and protects his people from the false wisdom (2:8–10).

The Family of God

The birth of a new humanity proclaims God's gracious and mighty rescue of mankind fallen in Adam and his renewal of the image defaced through Adam's disobedience. Paul's artistry exploits the imagery in another way. Besides being a new race, God's people are a newly created family, language more reminiscent of Abraham than of Adam. Christ himself, Christ individually, is "the seed (*sperma*) of Abraham" (Gal. 3:16), personal heir of God's covenantal promises to the patriarch. Now, declares Paul, persons in Christ become his fellow-heirs: "If you belong to Christ, then you are Abraham's seed (*sperma*), heirs according to the promise" (3:29; each "you" is plural, but "seed" significantly remains singular). Those whom Christ delivers from Sin are received into God's family: "God sent forth his Son . . . to redeem those who were under the law, that we might receive adoption as sons. . . . Therefore you are no longer a slave but a son, and if a son, then also an heir through God" (Gal. 4:4–7). The Spirit of God's Son enables adopted sons to cry out, "*Abba*, Father" (Rom. 8:15; Gal. 4:6). "I will be a Father to you, and you will be my sons and daughters, says the Lord Almighty" (2 Cor. 6:18, quoting the covenantal promise of 2 Sam. 7:14, 8).[30]

God's eternal purpose here finds fulfillment: "[God] predestined us for adoption as his children through Jesus Christ" (Eph. 1:5). "For those whom God foreknew he also predestined to be conformed to the image (*eikōn*) of his Son, that he might be the firstborn among many brothers" (Rom. 8:29). The language of adoption serves a dual purpose. On the one hand, it affirms the solidarity of Christ's people with him and with one another. Christ is not ashamed to call believers his brothers and sisters (Rom. 8:29), so let believers acknowledge one another to be members of the same family, and respect one another accordingly (Gal. 3:28, with 4:4–7). On the other hand, Paul's language safeguards the distinction between Christ and his people. Christ is the eternal Son of God who became a human being (Rom. 8:3; Gal. 4:4). Believers become God's sons and daughters by adoption (Gal. 4:5).[31] They are not, nor will they ever be, deified; the distinction between Redeemer and redeemed remains.[32] Nonetheless human beings are truly children of God by virtue of their identification with Jesus Christ, God's risen Son.

30. In the spirit of 2 Cor. 6:18 and of Gal. 3:28, the NRSV alters "sons" and "son" in Gal. 4:5, 7, to "children" and "child."

31. See C. S. Lewis, *Mere Christianity* (New York: Macmillan, 1954), 122, on the distinction between begetting (God's own Son) and making (God's sons and daughters by adoption). For Paul's language of adoption in its legal and social setting, see Frances Lyall, *Slaves, Citizens, Sons: Legal Metaphors in the Epistles* (Grand Rapids: Zondervan, 1984), 67–99.

32. Cf. preceding comments on "in Christ." Paul indeed speaks in Galatians 4 of passage from slavery to sonship. Yet in calling believers slaves of Christ, and the church the bride of Christ (Ephesians 5), he cautions against an absolute and exclusive use of the language of Rom. 8:29 (Christ as brother to believers).

Justification by Faith in Christ

Paul's favorite terms for a person's response to God's saving work in Christ are the noun faith (*pistis*) and the verb believe (*pisteuō*). The gospel "is the power of God for the salvation of everyone who believes. . . . For in it the righteousness of God is revealed through faith for faith" (Rom. 1:16–17a, NRSV).[33]

The Character of Faith

"The Law and the Prophets" (Rom. 3:21) bear joint witness to the cruciality of faith. "What does the Scripture say? 'Abraham believed God, and it was credited to him for righteousness'" (Rom. 4:3, quoting Gen. 15:6; so also Gal. 3:6); "as it is written, 'The righteous will live by faith'" (Rom. 1:17b, quoting Hab. 2:4). As both quotations show, "faith on man's side is the only possible and sufficient basis to sustain a relation to God."[34] With Paul as with Abraham and Habakkuk, and in accord with the active and relational character of the divine righteousness, faith rests fundamentally in God himself. Now that God's saving purpose has been achieved through his Son, faith in God must express itself also as faith in Christ.[35] Moreover, the Christ who is faith's object is also the very place where faith resides. Believers are incorporated into Christ: "a person is justified not by the works of the law but through faith in Jesus Christ. And we have come to believe in [or into] Christ Jesus (*eis Christon Iēsoun*), so that we might be justified by faith in Christ . . ." (Gal. 2:16 NRSV).[36]

Faith rests entirely on the divine achievement. Abraham was sure that "God was able to do what he had promised" (Rom. 4:21). Habakkuk waited for Yahweh to act (Hab. 2:3). In Paul, faith is always a response to God's saving work in Christ, never a basis of salvation; it is essential but

---

33. The words *through faith for faith* (*ek pisteōs eis pistin*) speak respectively of God's appointed way (faith alone) and of the requisite human response. Cf. Rom. 3:22, "the righteousness of God through faith in Jesus Christ for all who believe" (NRSV).

34. Dunn, *Romans*, 43. Rom. 4:3 is anticipated in 3:31, "Do we, then, nullify the law by this faith? Not at all! On the contrary, we uphold the law"—for the Torah itself, in Gen. 15:6 (the earliest use of faith terminology in the Bible), witnesses to the cruciality of such a response. In Rom. 1:17, as in Hab. 2:4, the accent is on faith rather than life; thus NRSV ("The one who is righteous will live by faith") improves upon RSV ("He who through faith is righteous shall live").

35. Paul speaks of faith in God (Rom. 4:3, 5, 24; 1 Thess. 1:8), more often of faith in Christ (Gal. 3:26; Eph. 1:15; Col. 1:4; 1 Tim. 3:13; 2 Tim. 1:13; 3:15).

36. References to believing "in Christ" (*en Christō*, cited in the preceding note) overlap considerably with references to believing "in [or into] Christ" (*eis Christon*; besides Gal. 2:16, see Phil. 1:29; Col. 2:5). Yet the two phrases are not exact equivalents; the latter expresses believers' incorporation into Christ more vividly: compare references to being baptized "into (*eis*) Christ" (Rom. 6:3; Gal. 3:27; cf. 1 Cor. 1:12–15; 12:13). In light of Gal. 2:16b, "we believed in [or into] Christ Jesus," I conclude that the flanking phrases of 2:16a (literally "faith of Jesus Christ") and 2:16c (literally "faith of Christ") likewise speak of Christ not as one who trusts but as the one who is trusted (so in most translations). The same can be said for the phrases of Rom. 3:22, 26; Gal. 2:20; 3:22; Eph. 3:12; Phil. 3:9.

not meritorious. One is saved "through faith" (*dia* or *ek pisteōs*), never "on account of faith" (*dia pistin*).[37] Faith is not a giant work, the finest accomplishment that one can offer to God. It is not self-assertion but self-abandonment, an utter trust in and reliance upon God.

The Believing Person

The whole person participates in that response. In the first place, faith is cognitive. The mind of God far transcends the human reason, as no one knew better than Paul; the very revelation of "the deep things of God" sharpened his awareness of the impenetrable mystery of Christ.[38] Yet for this very reason, the disclosure demands the most strenuous exertions of the mind. Genesis 15:6 records Abraham's response to God's promise, to which he, his reason included, continued to cling in the presence of overwhelming evidence to the contrary (Rom. 4:18–21). Habakkuk's response to Yahweh's challenge in the face of rampant wickedness (Hab. 2:4) is fully rational (3:1–19). Paul frequently speaks of believing something God has said, supremely the gospel. The obedient response to "the gospel of God . . . concerning his Son" is to believe it (Rom. 1:1–5).[39] God saves persons "through belief in the truth," that is, "through our gospel" (2 Thess. 2:13–14). Paul implores readers to be reconciled to God by embracing a message far more scandalous than that which Abraham or Habakkuk was asked to believe (1 Cor. 1:18–31; 2 Cor. 5:18–21)![40] Faith cannot "be defined as an act of surrender . . . without a clear awareness as to that to which it surrenders itself or for which it decides, but faith presupposes a knowing, on which it rests and from which it ever and anew derives its strength."[41]

Moreover, faith is an act of the will, both when the gospel is initially embraced and in the life that ensues. "The obedience of faith" (Rom. 1:5) is volitional as well as intellectual. Having understood the gospel, the Thessalonians "turned to God from idols" (1 Thess. 1:9). Paul commends readers for their "work produced by faith" (1 Thess. 1:3), exhorts them to "faith

37. One is "justified through (*ek*) faith" (Rom. 5:1), not "because of faith." "By grace you have been saved, through (*dia*) faith" (Eph. 2:8), "because of [God's] great love for us" (2:4).

38. Rom. 11:33–36; 1 Cor. 2:16; Col. 1:24–2:5 (the manifold mystery is now disclosed, but it remains a mystery and can now be more clearly recognized as a mystery). Because Paul possessed an extraordinarily deep understanding of God's saving purpose, he was exceptionally aware of the unfathomable depths of the mind of God.

39. "The obedience of faith" (Rom. 1:5) is not "the obedience that comes from faith" (NIV), but "the obedience that is faith." Cf. 10:16, "they have not all obeyed the gospel."

40. For Paul's insistence that faith embrace the message of Christ crucified, see also Rom. 3:21–26; 1 Cor. 2:1–5; Gal. 2:15–21. As in the original Passover (Exod. 12), the sacrifice of "Christ, our Passover lamb" (1 Cor. 5:7) must be personally appropriated.

41. Ridderbos, *Paul*, 242; see 242–45, on *gnōsis* (knowledge) as a dimension of faith in Paul. Cf. Günther Bornkamm, "Faith and Reason in Paul, " in *Early Christian Experience*, trans. Paul L. Hammer (New York: Harper and Row, 1969), 29–46; and (with special reference to 1 and 2 Thessalonians) Dieter W. Kemmler, *Faith and Human Reason* (Leiden: Brill, 1975), 147–211.

expressing itself through love" (Gal. 5:6), and challenges them to "fight the good fight of the faith" (1 Tim. 6:12).

The emotions are active as well. The Thessalonians welcomed Paul's message with joy (1 Thess. 1:6); believers may experience "progress and joy in faith" (Phil. 1:25). "May the God of hope fill you with all joy and peace in believing," Paul prays (Rom. 15:13). "For we by the Spirit through faith eagerly await the hope of righteousness" (Gal. 5:5).[42] In the meantime, "through faith in [Christ] we approach God with boldness and confidence" (Eph. 3:12).

To put the matter conversely: Christ, who by his Spirit dwells "in the heart through faith," empowers his people through the rational, emotional, and volitional faculties of the heart (Eph. 3:16–20).

God's Saving Verdict

Abraham's utter trust in God "was credited to him for righteousness" (Rom. 4:3)—that is, declared by God[43] to be the right response for being "right with God," for being rightly related to him. Correspondingly, while the basis of justification is Christ's death (Rom. 5:9, "justified by his blood"), the actual verdict awaits the answer of faith (Phil. 3:9; NEB, "righteousness . . . given by God in response to faith"). God declares righteous—pronounces "not guilty"—the person who is united to Christ by faith. It is not that I in myself am righteous, whereupon God pronounces me righteous; for God justifies the ungodly (Rom. 4:5). Nor is it true to Paul to say that I in myself am unrighteous but that God treats me as though I were righteous; God never deals with his people hypothetically. He declares a person righteous because he or she really is—in Christ. To conceive of righteousness merely as a commodity that God hands across a counter, or as a sum of money that he places in one's account, or as a garment in which he clothes his people is to fall far short of the reality. Here as everywhere God's righteousness is deeply personal and thoroughly relational. Christ himself is believers' righteousness, the very embodiment of God's *dikaiosynē* (1 Cor. 1:30; Rom. 5:21, grace reigns "through righteousness . . . through Jesus Christ our Lord"). In him the gift of righteousness is received (Rom. 5:17). Sinners are "justified . . . by faith in [or into] Christ" (Gal. 2:16). "There is therefore now no condemnation for those who are in Christ Jesus" (Rom. 8:1).[44]

---

42. Both within and among the three virtues of faith, hope, and love (1 Cor. 13:13; 1 Thess. 1:3; 5:8), the intellectual, volitional, and emotional aspects of believers' experience are tightly woven together. Observe the interlacing of faith, hope, and love in Rom. 5:1–11, together with the peace, joy, and endurance they together effect.

43. The verb *elogisthē*, "was credited," is an instance of the "divine passive."

44. See Ridderbos, *Paul*, 166–69 ("The Righteousness of God in Christ").

As we observed in chapter 3, Paul closely joins justification to reconciliation. It is God alone who takes the initiative to make peace, and he alone who provides the sacrifice necessary to end the hostility between himself and humanity. Yet as 2 Corinthians 5:14–6:2 makes clear, reconciliation is incomplete and the saving verdict withheld, until the offending party has heeded the summons to be reconciled to God and has been united to Christ: "God made him who knew no sin to be sin for us, so that we might become the righteousness of God in him" (5:21). It is persons who are "justified through faith" who have "peace with God" (Rom. 5:1). The same holds true for redemption. Christ alone redeems, but liberation from Sin is completed only when the rescued slaves begin to obey the new Master—as we shall see in the following chapters.

It is time to focus on the contribution of the third member of the Godhead to believers' experience of salvation.

The Gift of the Spirit

Christ the Lord imparts manifold grace to his people through the Holy Spirit. In some contemporary versions of psychotherapy, the existence of the Spirit is not even acknowledged. In others, while assent is given to orthodox doctrine ("I believe in the Holy Ghost"), the actual practice of counseling depends more on applying the right techniques than on invoking the Spirit's power and light. For Paul, on the contrary, the Spirit's work is vital; persons cannot be made whole without it.[45]

The Spirit of Life and Liberty

Believers experience life "in Christ Jesus" by action of "the Spirit of life" (Rom. 8:1–2). Through him they are incorporated into Christ: "For we were all baptized with [or in] one Spirit into one body . . . and we were all given the one Spirit to drink" (1 Cor. 12:13 NIV mg.).[46] The church that is the body of Christ is also a temple "in which God lives by his Spirit" (Eph. 2:21–22), animating both the whole edifice and its individual members.[47] Within the church the Spirit cultivates unity among persons formerly estranged from

---

45. "Where the NT differs from behaviourist psychology is over the actual reality of the work of the Spirit. . . . A psychologist takes a Christian conversion, and accounts for it . . . in terms of natural responses arising from such states as fear and inner stress. The NT would not deny such stresses, including guilt, but gives primacy to the Holy Spirit breaking in and supplying the dynamics of new life" (J. Stafford Wright, *NIDNTT* 2:568).

46. To say "we were all baptized *by* the Spirit" (NIV text) is misleading, for *Jesus* is the Baptizer (cf. Luke 3:16; Acts 2:33).

47. In 1 Corinthians Paul applies the language both corporately (3:16, "Don't you know that you yourselves are God's temple and that God's Spirit dwells in you?") and individually ("Do you not know that your body is a temple of the Holy Spirit, who is in you . . .?").

one another (Eph. 4:3–6; cf. 2:11–18). Within individuals once fragmented by slavery to Sin, the Spirit restores wholeness.[48]

God "saved us through the washing of rebirth and renewal by the Holy Spirit" (Titus 3:5), a statement that refers primarily to the Spirit's cleansing work and derivatively to baptism with water. As the Spirit of adoption he "cries out, '*Abba*, Father'" on behalf of believers (Gal. 4:6), enables them to do the same, and assures them that they are indeed God's children (Rom. 8:15–16).

Adoption occurs through redemption. The bestowal of life is simultaneously an act of liberation: "you are no longer a slave, but a son" (Gal. 4:7). The Spirit assaults all of Sin's agencies: the flesh, the demonic powers, the law, and death. Persons who "live by the Spirit" overcome the works of the flesh (Gal. 5:16–26). To walk according to the flesh is to die; to walk according to the Spirit is to live (Rom. 8:1–17). By the Holy Spirit believers withstand the demonic powers. "We have received not the spirit of the world but the Spirit who is from God" (1 Cor. 2:12); not "a spirit of slavery, [but] the Spirit of adoption" (Rom. 8:15).[49] By "the sword of the Spirit" and the prayer "in the Spirit," Christ's people combat "the spiritual forces of evil in the heavenly realms" (Eph. 6:10–18). "The law of the Spirit of life in Christ Jesus set me free from the law of Sin and death" (Rom. 8:2): the Law is wrested from the grip of Sin and death, now to be employed benevolently by Christ the Lord through his Spirit (8:4–8). At the end, by the same Spirit, God the Father will liberate his people from Sin's mightiest ally, death itself (Rom. 8:10–11).[50] For now, the Spirit is the seal who identifies and safeguards believers as "God's possession"; the deposit (*arrabōn*) that guarantees the day of final redemption when God's adopted children will receive their full inheritance; the firstfruits (*aparchē*) of the final harvest—our "adoption, the redemption of our bodies" from the chains of death; the One therefore by whose power believers "abound in hope."[51]

The Spirit of Truth and Light

The Spirit works in the closest conjunction with the Word of God. The gospel is declared "with a demonstration of the Spirit's power" (1 Cor. 2:4); the words by which Paul imparts spiritual realities are "taught by the

48. "For Paul the Spirit is the power of God which integrates emotion, thought and conduct in a life-giving way" (Dunn, *Romans*, 462).

49. In my judgment the phrases *spirit of the world* and *spirit of slavery* are neither metaphors nor linguistic foils to the matching references to the Holy Spirit, but names for personal spirits hostile to God (cf. Rom. 8:38; 1 Cor. 2:6–8; 2 Cor. 4:4).

50. In view of Rom. 8:2, 11, Rom. 8:10 should be rendered, not as in NIV ("your body is dead because of sin, yet your spirit is alive because of righteousness"), but as in NRSV ("the body is dead because of sin, the Spirit is life because of righteousness").

51. Rom. 8:23; 15:13; 2 Cor. 1:22; 5:5; Eph. 1:13–14; 4:30.

Spirit" (2:13). "Our gospel did not come to you in word only, but also with power and with the Holy Spirit" (1 Thess. 1:5): the proclamation is no bare word but one laden with the Spirit's power for driving home the truth about God (1:6, "you welcomed the word with joy inspired by the Holy Spirit"). The Spirit is likewise active in the mighty works that bear visible witness to the veracity of the apostolic message (Rom. 15:18–20).[52]

For understanding "the deep things of God," human beings are utterly dependent on enlightenment and instruction from the Spirit of God, he who alone "knows the thoughts of God" (1 Cor. 2:6–16). "The natural man does not receive the things of the Spirit of God, for they are foolishness to him. . . . But he who is spiritual judges all things" (2:14a, 15a NKJV). When Paul uses the word *spiritual* (*pneumatikos*) in a favorable sense, as here, he means not a person separated from the material and the physical, but one dominated by the Spirit (*Pneuma*) of God. By the same token the "natural (*psychikos*) man," far from being removed from what is spiritual or intellectual, is captive to "the wisdom of this age" and to "the rulers of this age" who propagate it (2:6–8). This is man in Adam; the other is man in Christ (15:42–49). The "spiritual man" of 2:15 has been given insight into spiritual realities by the tutelage of God's Spirit; has by this means become identified with Christ the last Adam; has been rescued from "human wisdom" and granted in its place the very "mind of Christ" (2:16); therefore has a capacity to know the natural man better than he knows himself;[53] and at the same time recognizes that he lacks exhaustive understanding of "the mind of the Lord" (2:16a).

The particular focus of the Spirit's tutelage is Christ crucified. The "wisdom [for] the mature" is imparted by the Spirit (1 Cor. 2:6–10); but it is in Christ crucified that "the wisdom of God" finds supreme expression (1:18–2:8). The Spirit never takes his pupils beyond the cross (the error of certain antagonists of Paul), but ever more deeply into the cross. One reason is theological: the cross is an unfathomable truth (cf. 2:16a). Another is practical: the person who becomes a Christian by believing "the message of the cross" (1:18; 2:5) is ushered into a life calling for unwavering fidelity to Christ crucified.[54]

---

52. Rom. 15:18–20 makes it plain that Christ has worked by his Spirit in what Paul has both "said and done," both in his preaching of the gospel and in the "signs and miracles." See also 2 Cor. 12:12.

53. While "the spiritual man makes judgments about all things" (2:15a), including the thought of "the natural man" (2:14), the former "is not subject to any man's judgment" (2:15b), the "man" in question being not a fellow Christian (cf. 14:29), but the "natural man"; so too Leon Morris, *The First Epistle of Paul to the Corinthians* (Grand Rapids: Eerdmans, 1958), 61.

54. See chaps. 7, 8. 1 Cor. 1:18–31 and 2:6–16 are joined together by 2:1–5, which speaks both of Paul's allegiance to "Jesus Christ and him crucified" and of his dependence on "the Spirit's power."

The Spirit of Power and Love

That "fellowship of [Christ's] sufferings" requires "the power of his resurrection" (Phil. 3:10), namely, the power of the Spirit (Rom. 1:4; 8:10–11). Ongoing faith and hope depend likewise on the Spirit's power (Rom. 15:13). Moreover, as Sin bred ever-increasing wickedness in its victims, so now the Spirit enables believers to grow in holiness. Through his Spirit, God the Father strengthens his people "in the inner man" (Eph. 3:16), that is, as members of the corporate Christ, for overcoming "the outer man," existence in Adam under the rule of Sin. Whereas adherents of the law as the tool of Sin "bore fruit for death," those who have been released from such use of the law and who experience the new life of the Spirit "bear fruit to God" (Rom. 7:1–6). The Spirit, far from discarding the law, internalizes it (2 Cor. 3:1–3; Jer. 31:31–34). The qualities that he cultivates in believers, supremely love (Gal. 5:22–23; Rom. 5:5; 15:30), are the very ones to which the Mosaic law summoned Israel (Lev. 11:44–45; Deut. *passim*).[55] Persons who live "according to the Spirit" are both able and willing to fulfill "the righteous requirement of the law" (Rom. 8:4–8), by which cooperative effort the "misdeeds of the body" are put to death (8:13). Having summoned the Thessalonians to sexual fidelity in marriage—that is, to obedience to the seventh commandment—Paul utters both a warning and a promise: "he who rejects this teaching rejects not man but God, who gives you his Holy Spirit" of power (1 Thess. 4:3–8). Moreover the Spirit, in concert with the other members of the Godhead, grants *charismata* so that the church may properly function (1 Cor. 12:4–31).

Paul exhorts, "Do not get drunk with wine, which leads to debauchery, but instead be filled with the Spirit" (Eph. 5:18). Both statements describe a person's being mastered and controlled by an outside power. The effects, however, are vastly different. Drunkenness is a means by which Sin seeks to destroy the human body and is in fact one of the ills from which the Spirit saves people (1 Cor. 6:9–11). But the fullness of the Spirit produces joy in worship and provides the power essential for combating the forces of evil in life's crucial relationships (5:19–21, with 5:22–6:9 and 6:10–18).[56]

---

55. Cf. Bruce, *Paul*, 188–202, especially 198–202; and J. Knox Chamblin, "The Law of Moses and the Law of Christ," in *Continuity and Discontinuity*, ed. John S. Feinberg (Westchester, Ill.: Crossway, 1988), 192–93.

56. Appended to the imperative of 5:18 ("be filled") are five participles—speaking (19a), singing and making melody (19b), giving thanks (20), and submitting (21)—all of which, like the imperative, are in the present tense. This structure is more evident in the Greek text than in the English translations, which often render the participles inconsistently. In NIV, e.g., the first three and the last are rendered as imperatives (and the fourth as a participle), suggesting that these terms are parallel to, rather than explanatory of, the imperative of 5:18. NIV further misleads by making the clause in which the fifth participle occurs a separate one-sentence paragraph, setting it apart both from what precedes and from what follows. The participles express the ways in which the fullness of the Spirit comes to expression; conversely, effectively worshiping and submitting requires the fullness of the Spirit.

The Renewal of the Person

Christ and the Spirit act to undo and to reverse the ruin and destruction that Sin and death visited upon their victims. The person united to Christ is transformed as a total being, and the self's unity in diversity is exploited for the new Master's benevolent purpose.[57]

Death to Sin (Rom. 6:1–14) entails death to the flesh (8:1–17). Paul never speaks of the resurrection of the *sarx*, only of its destruction. First Corinthians 5:5 speaks not (or not necessarily) of the physical death of the incestuous man but of the end of his rebellion against God—as when in Galatians 5:24, Paul calls for "the crucifixion of the flesh with its passions and desires."[58] "Human commands and teachings" do not restrain but only encourage the *sarx* (Col. 2:22–23). The power of the Holy Spirit is essential for conquering the flesh (Gal. 5:22–26; Rom. 8:1–17). Paul longs for the "fleshly" (*sarkinoi, sarkikoi*), persons still vulnerable to the *sarx* as the agent of Sin, to become "spiritual" (*pneumatikoi*), persons dominated by the Spirit, the agent of Christ (1 Cor. 2:14–3:3).

As the *kardia* is the integrating center of the person, renewal occurs from the heart outward. God causes the light of the gospel of the glory of Christ to "shine in our hearts" (2 Cor. 4:4–6). It is here that Christ dwells (Eph. 3:17), here that his peace reigns (Col. 3:15), and here that Christians are enlightened about God's saving purpose (Eph. 1:18). It is the heart that receives the Holy Spirit (2 Cor. 1:22), into the heart that God pours his love by the Spirit (Rom. 5:5), and "from a pure heart" that acts of love arise (1 Tim. 1:5). Similarly, it is Christ who explains Paul's "affection" (*splagchna*) for his people (Phil. 1:8). Corresponding to the depth of their former commitment to Sin, Christians believe the gospel "in the heart" (Rom. 10:9–10) and obey apostolic teaching "from the heart" (Rom. 6:17).

As part of the same process, believers are "transformed by the renewing of [their] mind" for discovering God's "good, acceptable and perfect will," and for employing his gifts in the church (Rom. 12:2–8; cf. Col. 1:9–10). Persons once duped by "the wisdom of this age" are given "the wisdom of God" for understanding (if only in part) the person and work of Christ, and God's saving purpose for both humanity and creation (1 Cor. 1:18–2:16; Eph. 1:8–10, 17–19; Col. 1:15–2:5). In place of the futile mentality and darkened understanding that marked existence in Adam, persons incorporated into Christ are "renewed in the spirit of [their] minds" for growth "in true righteousness and holiness" (Eph. 4:17–24). "The law of my mind" (Rom. 7:23) is God's law, to which the mind, now liberated by Christ, gives its hearty approval;

---

57. On the self's unity in diversity, see pp. 44–46. The renewal of the self may also be described as liberation from Sin through bondage to Christ, the subject of chap. 6.

58. Cf. Fee, *First Corinthians*, 212.

the new attitude of mind imparted by the Spirit is both able and willing to obey God's law, and to resist the assaults of Sin through the flesh (8:1–17).[59]

The believer's present *sōma* (body) is mortal. "God will destroy" the food that the stomach receives, and the stomach itself (1 Cor. 6:13), for this body belongs to a perishable order (1 Cor. 7:29–31; 15:42–44). Yet the *sōma* itself is destined for resurrection (6:13–14; 15:20–23). At the end the perishable will be clothed with the imperishable, and the believer's lowly body transformed into a glorious body like that of Jesus himself (1 Cor. 15:42–57; Phil. 3:20–21). Acutely aware of our mortality, "we eagerly await . . . the redemption of our bodies" (Rom. 8:23; cf. 7:24). Yet it is this perishable body that Jesus has purchased and now calls into his service, as we shall see in chapter 7. Moreover, even amid the present experience of the body's corruptibility, a renewal occurs as a foretaste of the transformation at the end. By his astonishing humility, the Spirit condescends to indwell this lowly body (1 Cor. 6:19) and to impart the very quality of life that will be fully realized at the resurrection; in helping believers put to death "the misdeeds of the body," he exercises the very power that will one day give life to their mortal bodies.[60]

Given the self's unity in diversity, the experiences of the *psychē* and the *pneuma* are bound up with those of the *sōma*. *Psychē* still designates "natural life" within the present order of existence. The believer is no longer a "natural man" (*psychikos anthrōpos*) but a "spiritual" (*pneumatikos*) one (1 Cor. 2:14–15); yet he retains a "natural body" (*sōma psychikon*), another name for the "mortal" and "corruptible" body (1 Cor. 15:42–44). The *psychē* will share in the transformation at the end (1 Thess. 5:23). Till then, the *psychē* is no less vulnerable than the *soma* to all the hazards of a deteriorating order and to the lures of "the present evil age." Yet as with the body, it is this very "life" that Christ calls into his service: "Whatever your task, put yourselves (*psychē*) into it, as done for the Lord and not for your masters" (Col. 3:23 NRSV); "as slaves of Christ, doing the will of God with your whole being (*psychē*, Eph. 6:6); "we were willing to share with you . . . our own lives (*psychai*) . . . because you had become dear to us" (1 Thess. 2:8). By the same token, the human spirit (*pneuma*) is destined for final salvation (1 Cor. 5:5; 1 Thess. 5:23); can still experience the defilements of sin (2 Cor. 7:1); can already experience deep communion with God through the Spirit (Rom. 8:16; 1 Cor. 14:2, 14–15); and is, together with the body, to be devoted to the Lord's service (1 Cor. 7:34).

The renewal of the person becomes evident in relationships.

---

59. For this understanding of Rom. 7:23, see Dunn, *Romans*, 394–96.

60. Rom. 8:2–13. As the "firstfruits" (8:23), the Spirit now mediates the realities to be fully experienced at the final harvest of the resurrection; cf. 1 Cor. 15:20, 23, where the same term is used of Jesus as the One whose resurrection guarantees that of his people. Accordingly, believers "abound in hope by the power of the Holy Spirit" (Rom. 15:13).

Relationships in the New Creation

Since the beginning of chapter 3, we have been considering the saving work of Christ and its manifold effects upon human beings. All along the way, consequences for the three relationships have come to light. We now seek to draw some of these together, especially to show how the catastrophic effects of Sin on all relationships (as described at the close of chapter 2), are reversed and overturned through bondage to Christ.

Relating to God

The knowledge of God, in the senses both of *savoir* and of *connaître*, is granted to the believer. By the cooperative work of the Word of God and the Spirit of God, the heart is enlightened and the mind is renewed concerning the Father's saving purpose and the Son's saving work (*savoir*). Through incorporation into Christ, one enters into deeply personal communion with all members of the Godhead (*connaître*). By both means the conviction begins to grow that "God, and God alone, is man's highest good,"[61] dispelling sin's propaganda that the self is the self's highest good, notions about God being barriers to self-fulfillment. Nor is there room for the idea that "man's chief end" is psychic wholeness and social well-being, and God the essential means. To encounter "the light of the knowledge of the glory of God in the face of Christ" (2 Cor. 4:6), is to realize (if only by degrees) that God is himself the end, himself the goal.[62] Paul affirms, not that "Christ exists to give me life," but that "for me to live is Christ" (Phil. 1:21).[63] To believe God is utterly to trust him (Rom. 4) and thereby to know him—that is, to love him (1 Cor. 8:1–3).

That dual knowledge occurs because the believer has learned about, and has experienced, liberation from the power of Sin and the consequences of sins. Persons who are "justified by [Christ's] blood" (Rom. 5:9) are freed from the guilt, both real and individual, that distanced them from God and evoked his wrath (Rom. 1:18). By manifesting his righteousness in the cross and in the gospel, God saves his people from his wrath (Rom. 1:16–17; 3:21–26; 5:9; 1 Thess. 5:9). The objects of his wrath

---

61. Herman Bavinck, *Our Reasonable Faith*, trans. Henry Zylstra (Grand Rapids: Baker, 1977), 17.

62. In the words of the Westminster *Larger Catechism*, "Man's chief and highest end is to glorify God, and fully to enjoy him forever." At the close of C. S. Lewis's *Till We Have Faces: A Myth Retold* (London: Bles, 1956), 319–20, Orual addresses the God: "I ended my first book with the words *No answer*. I know now, Lord, why you utter no answer. You are yourself the answer. Before your face questions die away. What other answer would suffice? Only words, words; to be led out to battle against other words."

63. "In consequence [of muting the cost of discipleship], our evangelism reaps large crops of still unconverted folk who think they can cast Jesus for the role of P. G. Wodehouse's Jeeves, calling him in and making use of him as Saviour and Helper, while declining to have him as Lord" (J. I. Packer, *Keep in Step with the Spirit* [Old Tappan, N.J.: Revell, 1984], 69).

are the very objects of his love (Eph. 2:1–10). Those "who once were far away [from God] have been brought near through the blood of Christ" (2:13). Through Christ's redemptive death, their sins have been forgiven (1:7). Now reconciled to God through the cross and delivered from the powers that used their guilt against them (Gal. 1:4; Col. 2:13–15), they may come freely into the divine presence (Rom. 5:1–11; Eph. 3:10–12). It is no accident that the most intimate communion with Christ is experienced at the very place where the cross is remembered (1 Cor. 11:23–26; 10:16–17).

Knowledge and liberation culminate in the adoration of God. Both the grand disclosures and the impenetrable mysteries of God's saving purpose, Romans 1–11, move Paul to worship, 11:33–36, concluding, "To him be glory forever! Amen."[64] The writing of theology in Ephesians 1:3–14 is simultaneously an act of worship, in which Paul takes delight in God the Father, Jesus Christ, and the Holy Spirit. The passage is but one sentence in the Greek text, a sustained offering of adoration from beginning ("Praise be to the God and Father") to end ("to the praise of his glory"). The prayers and exposition to follow (1:15–3:21) are likewise designed to evoke the worship of the church: "to him [God the Father] be glory in the church and in Christ Jesus throughout all generations, for ever and ever! Amen" (3:21 NIV). Whereas rebellious human beings "neither glorified him as God nor gave him thanks" (Rom. 1:21), God now receives praise both for the initiatives of his grace and for the astonishing transformations that he is effecting in the apparently hopeless objects of his love.[65]

Relating to Oneself

Freedom from God meant death for the self, but slavery to Christ frees the self to live (Rom. 6:15–23). Whereas nothing so demeans a person as self-worship, nothing is so healthy for the self as the praise of God. Life *en Christō*, far from dissolving or diminishing one's individuality, enhances it. "The more we get what we now call 'ourselves' out of the way and let Him

---

64. John Calvin, *Institutes of the Christian Religion*, ed. John T. McNeill, trans. Ford Lewis Battles (Philadelphia: Westminster, 1960), 2:952 (3.23.5), wrote that "God's hidden decree is not to be searched out but obediently marveled at," and in support quoted Augustine: "You, a man, expect an answer from me; I too am a man. Therefore, let both of us hear one who says, 'O man, who are you?' [Rom. 9:20]. Ignorance that believes is better than rash knowledge. . . . 'O depth!' [Rom. 11:33]. . . . Thou seekest reason? I tremble at the depth. Reason, thou; I will marvel. Dispute, thou; I will believe. I see the depth; I do not reach the bottom. Paul rested, for he found wonder."

65. 1 Cor. 1:26–31; 10:31; Eph. 1:4–12; 2:1–10. Peter T. O'Brien, "Thanksgiving Within the Structure of Pauline Theology," *Pauline Studies*, ed. Donald A. Hagner and Murray J. Harris (Grand Rapids: Eerdmans, 1980), 62, finds that "thanksgiving in Paul is . . . always a *response* to God's saving activity in creation and redemption . . . the great emphasis falls upon the mighty work of God in Christ bringing salvation through the gospel."

take us over, the more truly ourselves we become."[66] The only path to liberation for the pure and unvarnished "person," now inescapably bound to the "personage" ("a fragmentary and deformed image, an appearance" of the true person), is through union with Christ, who "alone is a person without a personage."[67]

With restored knowledge of God, and of God's knowledge of oneself, comes a new self-understanding.[68] In the first place, there is now a legitimate basis for self-respect. For the self has been embraced by God's love and redeemed from manifold bondage; has been adopted into God's own family; has been vindicated before the divine tribunal; is being transformed into the very likeness of Christ; and is a person whom God delights to honor ("them he also glorified," Rom. 8:30). An absence of joy over the personal effects of salvation, would raise doubts whether one has had the experience. Paul never commands a believer to love or to glorify himself, but integral to being a believer is an assurance that God loves his people and purposes to glorify them. A failure to take delight in that which delights God, would be an act of unbelief (cf. Ps. 149:4–5). "For it is not the one who commends himself who is approved, but the one whom the Lord commends," writes Paul in 2 Corinthians 10:18. At the moment he warns against self-commendation, he declares that it is possible to be commended by God and to receive his approval; and it would be a sin to think less of oneself than God does.[69]

Joined to that sense of personal worth is an ongoing and indeed a growing awareness of one's fallenness and proclivity to sin. The gospel reveals with shocking clarity the depth and breadth of human iniquity. In the cross the forgiving God faced the iniquity squarely and took it upon himself in the person of his Son. In a real sense the person who embraces the forgiveness must likewise be crushed under the weight of the sin and appalled by its enormity, thereby to recognize (if only to a small degree) what Christ

66. C. S. Lewis, *Mere Christianity* (New York: Macmillan, 1954), 174. "It is when I turn to Christ, when I give myself up to His Personality, that I first begin to have a real personality of my own. . . . Until you have given up your self to Him you will not have a real self" (174, 175). Contrast Terry Cole-Whittaker, quoted in *Christianity Today*, 21 September 1984, 73: "You can discover the God within yourself and be the creator of your own universe."

67. Paul Tournier, *The Meaning of Persons*, trans. Edwin Hudson (New York: Harper and Row, 1957), 15, 171.

68. "Again, it is certain that man never achieves a clear knowledge of himself unless he has first looked upon God's face, and then descends from contemplating him to scrutinize himself" (Calvin, *Institutes*, 1:37 [1.1.2]). On the gospel as the means of dispelling self-deception and recovering wholeness, see Dan O. Via, Jr., *Self-Deception and Wholeness in Paul and Matthew* (Minneapolis: Fortress, 1990), 46–53. Paul C. Vitz, *Psychology as Religion: the Cult of Self-Worship* (Grand Rapids: Eerdmans, 1977), 126–27, defines three stages in the "escape from the self": (1) The Naive Self or the Self As Object; (2) The Selfist Self or the Self As Subject; (3) The Transcendent Self or the Self as God's Object.

69. The four degrees of growth in love, according to Bernard of Clairvaux, are love of self for self's sake; love of God for what he gives; love of God for what he is; and love of oneself for God's sake (cited in Vitz, *Psychology*, 98–99).

bore on his or her behalf. As the Holy Spirit carries forward his work in the believer, and as one's life becomes the arena for increasingly fierce spiritual battles, the sense of personal sin becomes not less but more acute—the purpose of which is not to diminish one's sense of personal worth but to increase one's dependence on divine grace.[70]

In short, knowing God encourages a realistic dual view of oneself. To modify an image from Jonathan Edwards, the sense of personal worth is like a fire, which the sense of personal sin keeps within the fireplace so that it will not destroy the house. With that realism comes a sense of equilibrium as Christ the Lord exercises his gracious rule from the center of one's being.[71]

Relating to Other Selves

How well I know God and myself will come to light in my relationships with other people. "As long as man mistrusts his Creator he will in his anxiety for himself and his goods be unable to do anything in all his service of others but serve himself."[72] But the person who has newly trusted his Creator by embracing the gospel of Christ the Redeemer and who has thereby been incorporated into the new humanity may at least begin to behave differently.

As we saw earlier in the chapter, life in Christ radically challenges our natural inclination toward individualism and self-determination, and by its very nature compels us to take account of other selves. What was said about individuals in Christ applies again: individualism is de-personalizing, but individuality is heightened by the giving of the self to others. There is a sense in which this is true of relationships with all other human beings; for each of them is made in God's image and is therefore worthy of respect (1 Cor. 10:32; Rom. 13:1–7). Especially is it true of fellowship with other Christians, those in whom God's marred image is being restored (Gal. 6:1–10).[73] "Do not lie to one another, seeing that you have taken off the old man with its practices and have put on the new man, which is being renewed in knowledge according to the image of its Creator" (Col. 3:9–10). All of Paul's

70. Cf. pp. 23–26, on struggle and sin in Paul's life; and the discussion of the Christian struggle in chap. 7. The words of confession in *The Book of Common Prayer*: "There is no health in us . . . have mercy upon us, miserable offenders," "do *not* imply that cultivated misery is a required state, nor should they be read as . . . an expression of neurotic self-hatred and denial of personal worth. . . . Behind *miserable* lies the Latin *miserandi*, expressing the thought that as sinners we always stand in need of God's mercy and pity, and this is not the sick unrealism of neurosis, but healthy Christian matter-of-factness" (Packer, *Spirit*, 123–24).

71. See Anthony A. Hoekema, *Created in God's Image* (Grand Rapids: Eerdmans, 1986), 102–11, for an intelligent and balanced statement of what a Christian's "self-image" should be. In light of all that the Bible teaches about God's work of grace, the believer should have "a self-image that is primarily positive" (110). Cf. Joanna and Alister McGrath, *The Dilemma of Self-Esteem: The Cross and Christian Confidence* (Wheaton, Ill.: Crossway, 1992), especially chap. 5 (pp. 85–101) on the cross as the objective basis for self-esteem.

72. H. Richard Niebuhr, *Christ and Culture* (New York: Harper and Brothers, 1951), 173, speaking of Martin Luther.

73. On the corporate dimension of "the image of God," see Hoekema, *Created in God's Image*, 89, 99–100.

other instructions about relationships among believers are to be viewed in the same light. Moreover, whereas the male and the female are both distinct from the rest of the animate creation, they represent a unity in diversity, which to disregard is to rob both male and female of liberty and joy.[74]

It is most significant, I think, that Paul never encourages believers to forgive themselves but does urge them to forgive others; and he never commands Christians to love themselves but repeatedly exhorts them to love one another. How readers respond to the injunctions reveals how well they have understood the divine love and forgiveness; the sure sign that one knows the truth of the gospel is love for God and neighbor.[75] The two converge in the vertical and the horizontal offerings of praise in the worshiping community (Eph. 5:19–20; Col. 3:15–17).

The regained respect for other persons refashioned in God's image combines with a renewed sense of responsibility to fulfill the mandate of Genesis 1:28. Consider 1 Corinthians 9:9–10. Having quoted Deuteronomy 25:4 ("Do not muzzle an ox while it is treading out the grain"), Paul asks, "God is not concerned about oxen, is he?" (9:9b NASB).[76] Paul is not looking for a spiritual lesson beneath the plain meaning of Deuteronomy 25:4, but he is viewing the passage in the light of Genesis 1. First Corinthians 9:9–10 affirms, in accord with the latter, that human beings, the creatures made in the divine image, are of greater value to God than are animals; but the passage also affirms that the main responsibility for obeying Genesis 1:28 lies not with animals but with humans. "Oxen cannot read," as Martin Luther aptly noted.[77] The command *do not muzzle* is addressed not to cattle but to their owners. And if God is concerned that his people properly care for his animal creatures (Deuteronomy), then how much more should the people of God be attentive to the needs of God's human servants (1 Cor.; cf. 1 Tim. 5:17–18)?

As life progresses, our frustration and pain over present imperfections in all three relationships becomes more acute, and with that develops an ever deeper longing for the fullness of life in the heavenly glory (Rom. 5:1–4; 1 Cor. 13:9–13).

Almighty God, Father of all mercies, we thine unworthy servants, do give thee most humble and hearty thanks for all thy goodness and loving-kindness to us, and to all men. We bless thee for our creation, preservation, and

---

74. See Larry Crabb, *Men and Women: Enjoying the Difference* (Grand Rapids: Zondervan, 1991). For the outworkings of this, see in this book chaps. 8 (on husband and wife) and 9 (on male and female in public worship).

75. See Rom. 13:8–9; 1 Cor. 8:1–3; 13:1–13; 2 Cor. 2:10; Gal. 5:14; Eph. 4:32–5:2; Col. 3:13–14; 1 Thess. 3:12; 4:9–10; and p. 34.

76. Whether 9:10a is translated as in NRSV ("does he not speak entirely for our sake?") or as in NIV ("Surely he says this for us, doesn't he?"), the accent is clearly on men, not oxen.

77. Quoted in R. C. H. Lenski, *I and II Corinthians* (Minneapolis: Augsburg, 1937), 361.

all the blessings of this life; but above all, for thine inestimable love in the redemption of the world by our Lord Jesus Christ; for the means of grace, and for the hope of glory. And, we beseech thee, give us that due sense of all thy mercies, that our hearts may be unfeignedly thankful; and that we show forth thy praise, not only with our lips, but in our lives, by giving up our selves to thy service, and by walking before thee in holiness and righteousness all our days; through Jesus Christ our Lord, to whom, with thee and the Holy Ghost, be all honour and glory, world without end. Amen.[78]

---

78. *Book of Common Prayer*, "A General Thanksgiving," in The Order for Daily Morning Prayer.

5

The Conquest of Pride

"There is one vice of which no man in the world is free; which every one in the world loathes when he sees it in someone else; and of which hardly any people, except Christians, ever imagine that they are guilty themselves. . . . The vice I am talking about is Pride." So wrote C. S. Lewis.[1] Yet, says Paul, God offers victory over pride. The subject is crucial for our study.

The Character of Pride

Pride is essentially competitive. It "gets no pleasure out of having something, only out of having more of it than the next man. We say that people are proud of being rich, or clever, or good-looking, but they are not. [That is *vanity*.] They are proud of being richer, or cleverer, or better looking than others. . . . It is the comparison that makes you proud: the pleasure of being above the rest. . . . If I am a proud man, then, as long as there is one man in the whole world more powerful, or richer, or cleverer than I, he is my rival and my enemy."[2] The proud person loathes those who are above him and despises those who are beneath him. As the proud are always surrounded by the proud, personal conflicts of the gravest sort arise. Out of pride flow

---

1. "The Great Sin," in *Mere Christianity* (New York: Macmillan, 1954), 94. On pride in world history and literature, see Robert Payne, *Hubris: a study of Pride* (New York: Harper and Row, 1960).
2. Lewis, *Mere Christianity*, 95, 96.

"hatred, discord, jealousy, fits of rage, selfish ambition, dissensions, factions and envy" (Gal. 5:20–21 NIV).

"Pride always means enmity . . . , not only enmity between man and man, but enmity to God."[3] Indeed, God is the supreme rival to the proud. For pride's competitive ardor is not satisfied until it is crowned king of its universe. Pride is "the sin of trying to be as God."[4] So truth about the real God has to be suppressed (Rom. 1:18). To embrace that truth would be to acknowledge One who is infinitely greater than I, who brings my true condition to light, and with whom it is futile to compete. The hearts of the proud *must* become "darkened" with respect to the true knowledge of God (1:21); otherwise he poses too great a threat to them.[5]

In thus competing with God and with other human beings, the self opposes the self. For in striving to outdo other people and to convince ourselves that we are better than they, we inevitably exaggerate our own importance. But nowhere do we betray ourselves so absurdly and so tragically as when we seek to deify ourselves.[6] Pride, then, is the cardinal human sin, whose effect upon the self's three relationships is catastrophic.

The Humbling of Paul

What happens when a person does acknowledge God and seek to obey him? Pride, far from being vanquished on this account, finds new avenues of expression.

Paul the Pharisee was as zealous for God as anyone (Acts 22:3). Yet his religious pedigree and achievements were the very things that nourished his pride. As he recalls in Philippians 3:4–6, his belonging to God's chosen people, to a family in which the ancient language was spoken ("a Hebrew of Hebrews"), and to the party of the Pharisees, all gave him cause for "confidence." By the standard of the Mosaic law his conduct was "faultless"; his "righteousness according to the law" was genuine, not spurious or imagined (3:6). But this made the temptation to pride all the stronger. It is

3. Ibid., 96.

4. Dorothy L. Sayers, "The Other Six Deadly Sins," in *Creed or Chaos?* (New York: Harcourt, Brace, 1949), 82. So it was in the garden. The serpent promises Eve, "You will be like God"(Gen. 3:5b). To heighten the appeal, the tempter cunningly depicts God as an insecure monarch proudly—therefore jealously—protecting his turf (3:5a).

5. As noted in chap. 2, an idolater determines what his religion shall require of him and thus in a sense becomes his own god.

6. Robert Farrar Capon, *Health, Money, and Love* (Grand Rapids: Eerdmans, 1990), 103, speaks of "the great baboon of . . . 'the endless struggle to think well of yourself'"(the quoted phrase is from T. S. Eliot). For a human being's successful "struggle against joy" in order to preserve his self-importance (comical to everyone but himself), see the picture of the dwarf and the tragedian ("that great, ugly doll") in C. S. Lewis, *The Great Divorce* (London: Bles, 1946), 99–109.

authentically good works of which one is most tempted to boast (Eph. 2:9); the sin lies not in the working, but in the boasting.[7]

Philippians 3 witnesses, moreover, to pride's competitiveness. "If anyone else thinks he has reason for confidence in the flesh, I have more" (3:4). Paul belonged to Israel, not to a lesser nation. Unlike some Jewish families, his spoke Hebrew. Unlike the vast majority, he lived "according to the strictest sect of our religion" (Acts 26:5; cf. Phil. 3:6b). And even among Pharisees, Paul excelled. "I advanced in Judaism beyond many of my contemporaries, for I was far more zealous for my ancestral traditions"—as his persecuting activity demonstrated (Gal. 1:13–14; Phil. 3:6). What other Pharisee so passionately and effectively opposed the church?[8]

Paul's pride is shattered through his encounter with Jesus on the Damascus road. The impact of Christ's glory literally brings him low.[9] Whatever confidence he may have felt on account of his past is demolished in an awful moment of disillusionment. His opposition to Jesus and the church, formerly a chief source of pride, is now seen to be an attack on the very God whose honor he sought to defend. So what really jolts Paul, once he knows who the figure is, is that Christ has come not to destroy but to save him. At the moment he unveils his glory, Christ condescends to bestow his grace (1 Cor. 15:8–10; Gal. 1:13–16; 1 Tim. 1:13–17).

Recognition leads to renunciation. "But whatever was to my profit I now consider loss for the sake of Christ. What is more, I consider everything a loss compared to the surpassing greatness of knowing Christ Jesus my Lord, for whose sake I have lost all things" (Phil. 3:7–8a NIV). Paul is not thinking primarily of his sins but of the things that were to his "profit," not of transgressions of the law but of his scrupulous obedience to its commands (v. 6b). With the single exception of his persecuting activity, Paul's heritage is honorable indeed. But as he now sees, the danger lies just here: the nobler one's lineage and the more virtuous one's attainments, the greater the temptation to pride. Paul does not disown his pedigree (as though he is now embarrassed to have been born a Jew) or disparage his achievements (as though what once appeared to be genuine rectitude is now seen to be spurious). But if he does not denounce these things, he does

7. The only work in the testimonial of Phil. 3:4–6 which is inherently sinful is Paul's persecuting activity. "Flesh" embraces all that is natural and human in Paul's case, perhaps circumcision especially. The sin that is latent in the flesh (since both humanity and nature are fallen) becomes patent in the confidence. Rudolf Bultmann says of Phil. 3:3–7 and kindred passages that zealous adherence to the law, fostering as it does self-reliance and ill-founded confidence before God, is the most virulent form of existence "according to the flesh" (*Theology of the New Testament*, trans. Kendrick Grobel [New York: Scribners, 1951], 1:239–46).

8. "He must have a *kauchēma*, a ground of pride. . . . Paul must at all costs excel. He creates for himself an ideal of scrupulous perfection which to many of his fellow-Pharisees must have seemed fantastic"(C. H. Dodd, "The Mind of Paul, I.," in *New Testament Studies* [Manchester: Manchester University Press, 1953], 73, 75).

9. Paul is felled by the brilliant light from heaven and left speechless and blinded (Acts 9:3–8; 22:6–11; 26:13–14).

renounce them all for Christ's sake. What he once considered "gain," he now calls *skubala*—"rubbish," even dung (3:8)—to express his revulsion over the effect those things had on him, and the radical character of his conversion. *Skubala* describes not the nature of the things Paul abandoned, but his view of them in that twofold light.

"Boasting" remains, but its object has changed. We "boast in Christ Jesus, and put no confidence in the flesh" (Phil. 3:3). Paul abandons both his confidence and the sources of his confidence. Pride in his attainments "has been displaced . . . by pride in that which empties him of pride"[10]— "the surpassing greatness of knowing Christ Jesus my Lord" (3:8). "I want to know Christ," he says (3:10); "to me, to live is Christ" (1:21). Pride seeks to establish its own righteousness as a basis for reward (Rom. 4:4; 10:3). The humility that abandons (without denying) its own righteousness, is ready to receive "the righteousness that comes from God" (Phil. 3:9). The pride that boasts of human righteousness is the cardinal sin; the humility that rejects all reliance on human righteousness, and trusts instead in the righteousness of God, is the supremely righteous act.[11]

Paul's recognition of his guilt as a persecutor does not leave him engulfed in self-pity, nor does his renunciation of the past leave him frozen in inactivity. On the contrary, the grace that crushes his pride renews and redirects his zeal (1 Cor. 15:9–10). The "thorn in the flesh" that keeps Paul "from exalting himself" over his ecstatic experiences (2 Cor. 12:7) is the very means by which Christ's empowering grace is released in his life (12:9–10).

Out of his experience, Paul addresses the churches. His letters make it painfully clear that the pride subdued at conversion, far from being vanquished, gains a new lease on life among Christians. How does pride manifest itself, and how does Paul combat it? Four of the Epistles are especially instructive.

Confronting Pride in Galatians

"There is neither Jew nor Greek, there is neither slave nor free, there is neither male nor female; for you are all one in Christ Jesus" (Gal. 3:28 NKJV). Apart from Christ, each of these factors provides pride with limitless opportunity. In Galatians it is especially the Jews' sense of national superiority over the Gentiles that Paul assails. He does so principally by accentua-

---

10. Dodd, "The Mind of Paul," 78.

11. Among ancient Greeks, both *hybris* (pride) and *tapeinōsis* (humility) were viewed unfavorably (Georg Bertram, *TDNT* 8:295–99; Walter Grundmann, ibid., 1–5). On the favorable sense of the latter in the OT and in Judaism, as preparation for NT teaching, see ibid., 6–15. Humility expresses itself "through faith in Christ" (Phil. 3:9). As God declared to Abraham, Gen. 15:6 (quoted in Rom. 4:3 and Gal. 3:6), faith was the right response for being right with God.

ting the achievement of Christ, especially in his death: "May I boast of nothing but the cross of our Lord Jesus Christ . . ." (6:14). Through that event God has justified the Gentiles, in fulfillment of his ancient promise to Abraham (3:6–14). By incorporation into Christ, the Gentiles have become Abraham's children: "If you belong to Christ, then you are the seed of Abraham, heirs according to the promise" (3:29). So much for the Jews' vaunted superiority![12] The sole way of acceptance, for Jews no less than for Gentiles, is trust in Christ crucified (2:15–21). Every personal pedigree and achievement on which one might otherwise rely is as nothing (6:15).

That faith expresses itself in love (5:6). "For the whole law [so highly respected by the Jews] is summed up in a single commandment: 'You shall love your neighbor as yourself'" (5:14), which now embraces Gentile neighbors. Love, together with the other qualities that the Spirit cultivates in believers (5:22–23), combats "the works of the flesh" (5:19–21), notably the "hatred, discord, jealousy . . . selfish ambition, dissensions, factions and envy" which betray the foundational sin of pride.

Of special note is 6:1–5. A fellow believer has been "caught in a sin" or "overtaken by a trespass" (6:1). Such news offers a fresh opportunity to place myself above the other person, the more so if the sin is especially scandalous and one which I've never committed. In face of such an event, Paul commands: "Bear one another's burdens, and thus you will fulfill the law of Christ" (6:2), the law of love (5:14).

How are 6:3–5 to be related to 6:1–2? In particular, how does 6:2 ("Bear one another's burdens") relate to 6:5 ("For each one shall bear his own load")? I believe that verse 2 states the burden of the passage, and verses 3–5 the supportive argument. "For if anyone thinks he is something, when he is nothing, he deceives himself," says Paul in 6:3 (RSV), with the "for" connecting this statement to 6:2. Paul here denounces the conceit or vainglory of which he has spoken in 5:26. Such a posture precludes burden bearing, because the vainglorious individual puts himself above the other and insists on being served. But if I regard myself as nothing, then I can more readily serve the other; for as a "nobody," I am beneath him, from which position I can more easily bear his burden.

Paul continues: "But let each one test his own work, and then his reason to boast will be in himself alone and not in his neighbor" (6:4 RSV). This is the attitude of a person who is no longer self-deceived. The "boasting" is now based on what he really is and has truly done. It has not arisen from a comparison with "his neighbor"—that being, in this case, the erring brother.[13] And what, in this context, is "his own work"? Nothing other

---

12. See T. David Gordon, "The Problem in Galatia," *Interpretation* 41 (1987): 32–43.

13. Behind RSV's "his neighbor" is *ton heteron*, "the other." I believe that "the other" in question is the person of 6:1.

than the task of bearing the fellow believer's burden. The very act of doing so is the remedy for my putting myself above him. Or, in the language of 6:5, "Each one shall bear his own load": one's "load" is the personal responsibility to bear the burdens of other Christians.[14]

Let us note in closing that the other party may also fall prey to pride. Does this not explain why many an "erring brother" refuses the proffered help? Is this not especially likely to happen in the case of a person who is accustomed to offering help?

Confronting Pride in 1 Corinthians

The factionalism addressed in the opening chapters reveals pride at its most competitive. The partisans of 1:12 are all "boasting about men" (3:21). Each party says in effect to the others, "We are better than you." The pride contributed by each member is combined with that of all the others, resulting in a corporate pride whose potency exceeds the sum of its parts.[15] The relational problems are exacerbated by individuals who call themselves the *teleioi*, the "mature" or the "perfect" (2:6).[16] They consider themselves to be the favored recipients of deep spiritual mysteries and special privileges, and therefore to be standing on a loftier plane than others: they are "spiritual," whereas ordinary believers are only "fleshly."[17]

Pride's effects are calamitous. As we saw in the preceding chapter, the church is not "the body of Christians," but "the body of Christ" (12:27). So when members of the body break away from one another into competing factions, it is as though Christ himself has been torn limb from limb (1:10–13a, concluding with the question, "Has Christ been divided?"). The church is also "God's temple," which Corinthian factionalism threatens to destroy (3:16–17). When the "living stones" of the temple break loose from each other, the stability of the whole edifice is threatened. Moreover, in destroying relationships, pride robs its slaves of great riches. "Therefore, let no one boast about men. For all things are yours, whether Paul or Apollos or Cephas . . .—all are yours" (3:21–22). Those who boasted, "I follow Paul" (1:12) were depriving themselves of what God had to teach them through Apollos and Peter.

14. *Baros* (burden, 6:2) is Paul's own term. The synonymous *phortion* (load, 6:5) belongs to the maxim that he quotes. Cf. Richard N. Longenecker, *Galatians* (Dallas: Word, 1990), 278.

15. On the power of the group to intensify individual good and evil, see C. S. Lewis, "Friendship," *The Four Loves* (New York: Harcourt Brace Jovanovich, 1960), 87–127.

16. Elsewhere in Paul, *teleios* bears a favorable sense (e.g., 1 Cor. 14:20; Col. 1:28). In 1 Cor. 2:6 the term is probably borrowed from Corinthian usage, and is at least partially ironical to denote persons who think they are *teleioi* but in fact are not. Those who embrace Paul's teaching show that they are truly *teleioi*. See Gordon D. Fee, *The First Epistle to the Corinthians* (Grand Rapids: Eerdmans, 1987), 102–3.

17. Note the terms *pneumatikoi* (spiritual ones) and *sarkinoi* and *sarkikoi* (fleshly ones) in 1 Cor. 2:13–3:3.

At the heart of Paul's response to the Corinthian problem stands "the cross of Christ" (1:17). Through the preaching of "Christ crucified" (1:18–25), God brings down "the wisdom of this age," which by assorted means propagates the notion that man attains fulfillment by his own achievement for his own glory. On the contrary, says Paul, human wholeness—or salvation—is God's accomplishment for God's glory (1:29–31).

In his wisdom, God appoints a means of salvation that is sure to expose human pride, whether its Jewish or its Grecian variety (1:22). To those who boast of their power ("Jews ask for signs") and of their understanding ("Greeks seek wisdom"), the cross appears to be utterly weak and foolish (1:23). But this view simply brings to light the blindness of the interpreters. For Christ crucified is in fact "the power of God and the wisdom of God" (1:24). One's failure to perceive this demonstrates that God conceals the truth from those who insist on employing "the standards of this age" (3:18 NIV). The first step in the conquest of pride, and the initial evidence of true wisdom, is to recognize not merely that one is proud, but that the whole system of thought ("the wisdom of this age" in one of its manifestations), which has nurtured pride and provided the basis for its competitiveness, is itself spurious, ridiculous, and doomed to destruction (1:19–20).

In other words, to perceive what happened in the cross leaves no room for boasting—except boasting "in the Lord" (1:29–31). Paul's "weakness and fear, and much trembling" among the Corinthians reflect not a dread of personal rejection but a humility born of preoccupation with "Jesus Christ and him crucified" (2:1–3). It was the sheer weight of "the message of the cross" that made him feel weak, first as a proud exemplar of "the wisdom of this age,"[18] and then as a redeemed sinner and commissioned apostle (1:17–21).

Understanding "the power and the wisdom of God" in the cross (1 Cor. 1:18–31) requires enlightenment by God's Spirit (2:6–16).[19] The Spirit does not take his pupils beyond the cross, but ever more deeply into it. The meaning of the event that eluded even "the scholar [and] the philosopher of this age" (1:20 NIV) and "the rulers of this age" (2:6–8), God discloses by his Spirit (2:6–11). The purpose of the instruction is that "we may understand what God has freely given us" (2:12), namely, the "wisdom . . . righteousness, holiness and redemption" (1:30) that reside in "Christ crucified."

18. Like other nonbelieving Jews, Paul the Pharisee found the message of Christ crucified to be a "stumbling block"(1:23) and therefore persecuted its advocates.

19. 1 Cor. 2:1–5 forges the link between 1:18–31 and 2:6–16. "The message of the cross" (1:18)—of "Jesus Christ and him crucified" (2:2; cf. 1:23)—is communicated "in words taught by the Spirit" (2:13) and "in demonstration of the Spirit's power" (2:4).

Moreover, the Spirit (*Pneuma*) is given not just to a favored few (the self-styled *pneumatikoi*), but to all Christians (12:4–13). The true *teleioi* (2:6) are those who embrace the Spirit's teaching about Christ crucified and become united to him who is the "wisdom of God" (1:24, 30). As persons instructed by the Spirit, they "have the mind of Christ" (2:16). The Corinthians who pride themselves on being *teleioi* and *pneumatikoi*, yet at the same time scorn Paul's preaching of the cross, thereby reveal that they are neither *pneumatikoi* (for they ignore the Spirit's teaching) nor *teleioi* (those whose lives are not patterned after "Christ crucified" are at best *sarkinoi*, "mere infants in Christ," 3:1; cf. 4:8–13).

How may one respond to Paul's teaching about the cross and the Spirit, so that pride is effectively opposed and its disastrous consequences averted?

In the first place, it is essential to receive God's teaching. The initial step toward doing so is to abandon the teaching—some version of "the wisdom of this age" (2:6)—upon which one has previously relied. One has to revert to being an intellectual "fool," a scholarly "nobody." For it is just such persons—"the foolish, the weak, the lowly, the despised," the very "things that are not"—whom God calls through the Spirit's instruction (1:26–28). The relatively few among the called who were "wise by human standards . . . powerful . . . of noble birth" (1:26), must abandon all reliance on those things and join the ranks of "those that are not" (cf. 3:18), that their boast may be in the Lord alone. The very fact that a person understands "the message of the cross" shows that he or she is a "thing that is not" who therefore has nothing at all to boast about (1:29). Only a nonperson who knows oneself to be a nonperson, can embrace the message that salvation is entirely Christ's achievement for Christ's glory alone (1:30–31). Moreover, one evidence of discernment from the Spirit (2:14–15) is a growing recognition that one is far from fathoming "the mind of the Lord" (2:16a). Becoming *teleios*, or "putting away childish things," means acknowledging that one "knows in part" (13:11–12). Those who claim to "know in whole" merely show how puerile is their understanding.[20] By the same token, to boast over having "the mind of Christ" (2:16b) would show that one has not really grasped the Spirit's exposition of the cross—in other words, that one lacks "the mind of

---

20. "Socrates was declared by the Delphic oracle of Apollo to be the wisest man in the world. He interpreted this to mean that even though he had no wisdom at all, he had the wisdom to know that he had no wisdom, while everyone else, who also had none, thought they did. . . . In other words, there are only two kinds of people: the wise, who know they are foolish, and the foolish, who think they are wise" (Peter J. Kreeft, *Everything You Ever Wanted to Know about Heaven . . . But Never Dreamed of Asking* [San Francisco: Ignatius, 1990], 260). On the self-deceptive character of "the wisdom of the world," see Dan O. Via, Jr., *Self-Deception and Wholeness in Paul and Matthew* (Minneapolis: Fortress, 1990), 19–21.

Christ." Such pride would resurrect the very spirit that Paul seeks to slay.[21]

In the second place, Paul urges readers to receive God's gifts. The first gift is the apostolic teaching itself. To those who have willingly become "fools," God imparts the true knowledge (*gnōsis*) and the highest wisdom (*sophia*), the very "mind of Christ," by the agency of the Spirit (3:18; 2:16; cf. 1:5; 12:8). Believers can now understand what God in his grace (*charis*) "has freely given (*charisthenta*) us" (2:12)—both in Christ (1:18–31) and in the Spirit (2:6–16), both for entry into life and for the sustaining of life.[22] Once the Spirit's pupils grasp the reality and the magnitude of the gifts, and recognize that they are just that—gifts of grace, not awards or accolades for human accomplishments—they can logically draw only one conclusion: "And so there is no place for human pride (*kauchēsetai*) in the presence of God" (1:29 NEB). "For who makes you different from anyone else? What do you have that you did not receive [from God]? And if you did receive it, why do you boast (*kauchasai*) as though you did not?" (4:7 NIV).

While thus interpreting the totality of Christian experience as a gift of grace (*charis*), Paul also speaks of "spiritual gifts" (*pneumatika*) and "gracious gifts" (*charismata*) in a more restricted sense (1 Cor. 12–14).[23] These gifts are by nature corporate exercises designed to challenge pride's self-centeredness: "to each person the manifestation of the Spirit is given for the common good" (12:7). As the parts of the human organism are interdependent, so it is with the body of Christ (12:12–27). A *charisma* comes into being in an act of service to another person (12:8–11, 28–31).[24] The recipient of the gift receives its blessing not before, but precisely in, the service. What if all believers behave this way? Since it is the nature of servanthood to place oneself beneath the other, the only competition that remains is to outdo one another in showing care and bestowing honor (12:25–26). But Paul goes a step further. As with the human organism, so in the church the less honor-

---

21. Gordon D. Fee observes (*1 Corinthians*, 120) that in the church's application of 1 Cor. 2:6–16, "Paul's own point has been almost totally lost in favor of an interpretation nearly 180 degrees the opposite of his intent. Almost every form of spiritual elitism, 'deeper life' movement, and 'second blessing' doctrine has appealed to this text. . . . One special brand of this elitism surfaces among some who have pushed the possibilities of 'faith' to the extreme, and regularly make a 'special revelation' from the Spirit their final court of appeal. Other 'lesser' brothers and sisters are simply living below their full privileges in Christ. Indeed, some advocates of this form of spirituality bid fair to repeat the Corinthian error in its totality. What is painful about so much of this is not simply the improper use of this passage, but that so often it is accompanied by a toning down of the message of the cross. . . . Being spiritual does not lead to elitism; it leads to a deeper understanding of God's profound mystery—redemption through a crucified Messiah."

22. Christ's "wisdom, righteousness, holiness and redemption" (1:30) are essential not just for conversion but for the whole of the Christian life. Conversely, the Spirit, through whose gifts believers grow, was also active in their conversion (6:11; 12:13).

23. I take the verb *charizomai*, 2:12, in the widest sense, as distinct from the more restricted usage of the noun *charisma* in 1 Cor. 12.

24. "Speaking in tongues," the one gift that can be exercised individually, is placed at the bottom of the lists. Prophecy is superior to tongues because it helps other people (14:1–5).

able and the less presentable members are to be accorded special honor and respect (12:22–24). Only by such drastic action can pride, with its congenital insistence on being the most honorable and the most presentable, be effectively assaulted; and only the conquest of pride will forestall divisions (*schismata*) in the body (12:25).[25]

Finally, Paul exhorts the Corinthians to love one another. "Let all that you do be done in love" (16:14). Whereas pride is the cardinal sin from which all others spring, love is the greatest of the Christian virtues (13:13), the exercise of which is essential for the conquest of pride. "Knowledge puffs up, but love builds up" (8:1). It is possible for a Christian's newfound knowledge, and the liberty that springs from it, to become a vehicle for pride, particularly when one is surrounded by persons who have obviously not been enlightened or liberated (8:1–7, "We know. . . . But not everyone knows this"). But if the exercise of liberty is motivated by love, then one is willing to relinquish his or her rights for the sake of the weaker brother or sister (8:7–9:23); love "does not insist on its own way" (13:5 NRSV).[26] The same holds true for the exercise of the spiritual gifts. These endowments are indeed bestowed for the sake of combating pride; but pride being what it is, these very gifts afford many avenues for its expression, as is eminently clear from 1 Corinthians 12–14. For some gifts are "higher" than others; some provide opportunities to dominate other people; and some promise more exciting experiences than others. It is therefore urgent that the gifts of the Spirit be joined in the closest way to love, the foremost fruit of the Spirit. Exercised independently, the gifts are almost certain to foster pride (13:1–3). The most effective antidote is love, which by its very nature "does not envy . . . does not boast . . . is not proud . . . is not self-seeking" (13:4–5 NIV).

Love in turn proves to be the strongest motivation for employing one's spiritual gifts in service to other people. It is Paul's love for Christ and for the believers under his care that accounts for the rigorous discipline to which he subjects himself, and to which he calls his readers (9:24–27). The "competition" he urges upon them ("only one receives the prize . . . so run that you may win it") is to outdo one another in acts of mutual love and service (cf. Rom. 12:10; Phil. 2:3–4).[27]

When one discovers that the basis for human pride has been destroyed, and that all things needed for life (now and hereafter) are God's achievement and gift; when one begins to experience the charismatic joy reserved for those who are liberated from pride's competitiveness into the service of

---

25. For more on the corporate dimension of Christian experience, and on the spiritual gifts, see chap. 9.

26. For a development of this theme, see the following chapter.

27. To press the point that "only one gets the prize" would exceed the purpose of the analogy and fly in the face of everything Paul says in 1 Cor. about competitive pride.

the body's "common good"; and when one witnesses (however fleetingly) the conquest of pride by the power of love, the result is worship: "Let him who boasts boast in the Lord" (1:31). Being captivated by God is the ultimate remedy for pride's self-intoxication.

Confronting Pride in Philippians

In Philippi pride is at work among both preachers and recipients of the gospel. Both groups described in 1:15–18 "preach Christ."[28] Yet the one does so "out of selfish ambition"; so their "envy and rivalry" is inevitably aroused by the greater effectiveness of the group more closely associated with Paul. Consequently they seek to "stir up trouble" for Paul, in order to bring him down (along with those sympathetic to him)—which in turn serves their "selfish ambition" to be above all competitors.[29] Most tragically, they preach Christ "from false motives" (1:18); rather than serving and exalting him, they seek to use him to elevate themselves.

The same "selfish ambition" is at work in the Philippian church (2:3, *eritheia*, as in 1:17): favoring one's own interests above those of others, considering oneself better than others (2:3–4), and therefore promoting conflicts rather than harmony in personal relationships (1:27; 2:2, 14).

To address the pride that lies at the root of the Philippians' disunity (1:27–2:4), Paul invokes the supreme example of humility: "Let this attitude be in you which was also in Christ Jesus" (2:5), as celebrated in the following hymn (2:6–11).[30]

In his preincarnate state (2:6), Christ Jesus occupied "the highest place" (cf. 2:9). He did not aspire to be above all others, he already was. He did not suffer from a "divinity complex," he was actually divine. According to this passage, what does Christ make of his identity and position? He does not employ his power to safeguard his supremacy, nor does he tyrannize those under his rule: he is too secure and too serene in his majesty to have to resort to that. He does not behave as a proud sovereign would. Instead, he "empties himself" (2:7) and gives utterly of himself to his subjects. Far from cloaking or abdicating his deity, he hereby discloses the divine being and character. He is the humble God who looks "to the interests of others" (2:4). He relinquishes his rights and places himself beneath his subjects by becoming their slave (*doulos*, 2:7). Normally a person is coerced into slavery. Christ on the contrary "emptied himself" and "humbled himself" (2:7, 8). In doing so he does not abdicate power but expresses it. By an exer-

---

28. The concern here is rival messengers of the true gospel; the subject of Phil. 3 is rival messages.

29. The first group was "jealous of Paul"; so Gerald F. Hawthorne, *Word Biblical Themes: Philippians* (Waco: Word, 1987), 15, 37. Members of the other group (1:16, also 1:14), on the contrary, love Paul (and so are not jealous of him) and are encouraged (not scandalized) by his chains.

30. The comments on this passage on pp. 67–68 are presupposed.

cise of his authority as the heavenly King, he abandons his heavenly status—which accords perfectly with his character as the humble God.[31]

The humility of the incarnation and the ministry came to supreme
expression in the cross (2:8). "*Therefore* God exalted him" to the lofty place
he had previously occupied (2:6, 9). It is as the humble One that Christ is
extolled; his humility is his glory (cf. Matt. 23:12). "The name that is above
every name" (2:9) is *Kyrios*, "Lord," which represents the Hebrew *Yahweh*,
the personal name of Israel's covenant God.[32] Christ is now acclaimed to
be what he has always been, very God of very God. Just as there is a distinction of person between God the Father and God the Son, there is also
an identity of being and character. In confessing that "Jesus Christ is Lord,"
the creatures acknowledge both the fact and the character of his deity. They
bow their knees in worship (2:10), they humble themselves, before the
humble God.

Certain individuals have in fact adopted the attitude of Christ Jesus
(2:5). Like Jesus himself, they demonstrate that genuine humility, unlike
disabling self-denigration, finds expression in purposeful activity for the
sake of others. Timothy is Christ's slave (*doulos*, 1:1), so his whole being
is devoted to obeying the Master. This he does by enslaving himself to
other people (*edouleusen*, 2:22). "I have no one else like him, who takes a
genuine interest in your welfare. For everyone looks out for his own
interests (*ta heautōn*), not those of Jesus Christ" (2:20–21 NIV). Timothy's
life is thus a model of the humility to which Paul calls his readers (2:3–4,
where "own interests," *ta heautōn*, recurs), and an image of Christ's own
humility (2:5–11).

Epaphroditus too is worthy of honor (2:29). Like Timothy, he fulfills his
duty to Christ (2:25a) by enlisting in service to other believers—both the
Philippians, whom he represents (2:25b), and Paul, for whose sake he risks
his life (2:26–27, 30). Such is his mentality that he is less concerned about
his sickness than about the effect of this news on the Philippians (2:26).

Paul's own life is exemplary. His love for the Philippians pervades the
whole letter (1:3–8; 2:12; 4:1). He sacrifices self-interest for their sake (1:24–
26). In an astonishing echo of the command to emulate Christ (2:5–11), Paul
exhorts readers to follow his own example: "Put into practice the things
which you learned and received from me, which you heard and saw in me"
(4:9).[33] Here is confirmation that humility is vastly different from self-pity

31. Christ both exercises his own will and submits to his Father's will (he "became obedient to death").
Cf. Rom. 8:32 (the Father "gave [the Son] up for us all") and Gal. 2:20 (the Son of God "gave himself for
me"). Gerald F. Hawthorne, *Philippians* (Waco: Word, 1983), 78–79, suggests that Phil. 2:6–11 reflects the
influence of the event recorded in John 13:3–17.

32. For God's disclosure of the meaning of *Yahweh*, see Exod. 3. In the LXX, *Yahweh* is represented by
Kyrios.

33. Moisés Silva, *Philippians* (Chicago: Moody, 1988), 178, suggests that Phil. 3:7–11, with its "sequence
of privilege-death-exaltation," echoes 2:5–11, a suggestion "confirmed by explicit verbal parallels."

and self-denigration, both of which are egotistical. So far removed is Paul from self-centeredness, and so occupied with other people and with Christ, that he may invoke his own example as freely as those of Timothy and Epaphroditus and speak as disinterestedly in the one case as in the others.[34]

In the light of such models of humility, Paul makes his appeal to the Philippians. "Do nothing from selfish ambition or vain conceit, but in humility consider others better than yourselves" (2:3): that is, do what is appropriate for a *doulos* and place yourself beneath them, from which position you can more readily serve them (cf. above on Gal. 6:1–5).

Paul first buttresses this appeal by invoking "love" (*agapē*). As Christ's self-emptying proceeded from his love (2:1), so believers must have "the same love" (2:2) if they are to relate to one another in humility. For *agapē* by its very nature "is not proud [or] self-seeking" (1 Cor. 13:4–5). Accordingly, Paul prays that his readers' "love may abound more and more" (1:9). Secondly, following the Christ-hymn Paul challenges readers to "work out [their] salvation with fear and trembling" (2:12). Such emotions are stirred, not by questions about "eternal security," but by the presence of God in one's life (2:13, with its opening "for"). What better spur to a humility trembling with fear than the knowledge that the high and lofty One has condescended to dwell in one's heart (Isa. 57:15)?

Confronting Pride in Romans

Romans 12:1–15:13 embraces, although it is not confined to, conditions in Rome. In particular, 14:1–15:6 reflects Paul's awareness of "a crisis . . . of some magnitude" in the Roman church.[35] Here he addresses a conflict between the "weak" and the "strong" (15:1), which is "also, to a large extent at any rate, a division between Jewish and Gentile Christians" respectively.[36] The parties are at loggerheads over Old Testament laws about foods and special days (14:2–6). Pride now has its opportunity. Each group puts itself above the other: he who eats everything "looks down on" him who does not; he who does not, "condemns" him who does (14:3, 10). The very act of passing judgment on another (14:13) presumes that the judge occupies loftier ground.

To combat this and attendant problems, Paul first challenges his readers to think. "For by the grace given to me I say to every one of you: Do not think of yourself more highly than you ought to think, but rather think

34. Cf. 1 Cor. 15:9–10, and the discussion of chap. 1 on Paul's self-understanding.

35. James D. G. Dunn, *Romans* (Dallas: Word, 1988), 812. He calls attention to "the climactic and inordinately lengthy treatment" of the problem at hand.

36. C. E. B. Cranfield, *The Epistle to the Romans*, vol. 2 (Edinburgh: T. & T. Clark, 1979), 695. See Rom. 15:7–13. As Dunn reminds us (*Romans*, 802), the "weak" doubtless included Gentiles previously attracted to Judaism; and the "strong," Jews like Paul himself (15:1, "we who are strong").

with sober judgment, in accord with the measure of faith that God has granted to each of you" (12:3). This admonition rests on verse 2: "thinking with sober judgment" entails a refusal to be "conformed to this world" (and to "the wisdom of the world," 1 Cor. 1–2) and a willingness to "be transformed by the renewing of your mind." And this happens through grasping "God's mercy" (12:1), a succinct expression for the gospel expounded in Romans 1–11 (note the opening "therefore" of 12:1). Here, as in Galatians, 1 Corinthians, and Philippians, one of the most potent weapons against pride is rigorous thinking about the person and work of Christ. The revelation of the righteousness of God in face of human unrighteousness *and righteousness,* is the mightiest assault ever on human pride (3:21–4:2).

Right thinking also means recognizing pride as the sin from which all others spring (1:18–23). The injunction of 12:3 stands as a rubric over the whole section. All that Paul proceeds to say about life in the church will go for nought unless the foundational sin of pride is addressed. Furthermore, to "think with sober judgment" is to perceive that pride poses a threat to all members of the church: "I say to every one of you" (12:3). Paul enjoins all his readers, "Do not be proud" (12:16).

Those more general exhortations pave the way for Paul's response to the dispute over food laws and special days. His appeal that the strong and the weak "accept one another" (14:1; 15:7) is based on God's acceptance of both in the gospel (1:16; 14:3b; 15:1–13). In "judging one another," they usurp the prerogative of God, the one righteous Judge; revert to the presumption and arrogance described in 1:18–3:20; and show that they are not sufficiently mindful of the radical sin from which they themselves have been delivered, or of their own destined appearance before God's judgment seat (14:10–12).

Founded upon the challenge to think is a challenge to act. The person who understands God's mercy, submits to God; and the one whose mind God has transformed, understands God's will (12:1–2). Avenues for obeying his will are provided in the "different gifts" (12:4–8). Here too the starting point is right thinking, namely, perceiving that in Christ "each member belongs to all the others" (12:4–5), and that Christ's own ministry surmounted racial and cultural barriers (15:7–12). The exercise of the gift is by nature a service, which places the giver beneath the recipient. Pride is overcome through "associating with the lowly" (12:16). Identifying with a lowly person, by an act of mercy, for example (12:8), puts oneself in a lower position still and thus honors another above oneself (12:10). One rebuttal to the temptation to compare one's own gifts to those of others is faithful stewardship of what God has given: "If it is serving, let him serve; if it is teaching, let him teach" (12:7 NIV; cf. 1 Thess. 4:11).

In Romans, as in the three other letters considered, the principal action for combating pride is love for one another. Sincere love (12:9) is not one of the "disputable matters" (14:1). The freedom of the "strong" from certain particulars of the Mosaic law does not exempt them from its fundamental command, "Love your neighbor as yourself" (Rom. 13:9; Lev. 19:18). "Love does no wrong to the neighbor" (Rom. 13:10); therefore, "if your brother is distressed because of what you eat, you are no longer conducting yourself in love" (14:15). Let the "strong" remember that "even Christ [the strongest of all] did not please himself," but instead, by the supreme expression of both his power and his love, died for "the powerless" (15:3; 5:6–8).[37] And let the "weak" who seek to honor Mosaic rules about foods and special days remember that "love is the fulfillment of the law" (13:10); and that Jesus the Messiah became a servant of the Jews in order to confirm God's promises to the Gentiles (15:7–12) through their faith alone (3:27–4:25). Love does not abolish or ignore differences between strong and weak, but on the contrary comes to its most powerful expression precisely in face of such differences.[38]

God's Grace to the Proud

Let us now highlight what God has done to save the proud. "Christ died for our sins" (1 Cor. 15:3), including the cardinal sin of pride. "God made [Christ] to be sin for us, in order that we might become the righteousness of God in him" (2 Cor. 5:21): he who was the very incarnation of humility became pride, in order that we might be changed from proud to humble people. Yet he who became pride "had no sin" of his own (2 Cor. 5:21a). Indeed, the greatest witness to the Savior's sinlessness and to the depth of his humility is that he willingly "became pride" for his people.

This conversion occurs "in Christ" (2 Cor. 5:21b). He dies and rises for us; we are crucified and raised with him (Rom. 6:4–6; Gal. 2:20; Eph. 2:4–7). Congenitally proud persons need more than Christ's example. The basis for Paul's appeal, "Let this attitude be in you which was also in Christ Jesus" (Phil. 2:5), is his readers' common life in Christ (2:1). Simply to be exhorted to be humble like Christ leaves all but the most naive with a deepened sense of their own pride and their inability to be otherwise. But union

---

37. Rom. 15:3 refers principally to Christ's passion, as is evident from the quotation of Ps. 69:9 (cf. Dunn, *Romans*, 838–39). The "weak" of Rom. 5:6 and 14:1–2 are denoted, respectively, by the adjective *asthenēs* and the participle *asthenōn*.

38. The contemporary writer Iris Murdoch says that genuine love is "the nonviolent apprehension of differences"(quoted in *Reformed Journal*, August 1989, 13). It was said of Father Brown, Roman Catholic priest and amateur detective: "He did not encourage her psychic views; quite the contrary; but he discouraged them as if they mattered and not as if they did not matter. It was not so much that he did not sympathize with her opinions, as that he did sympathize but did not agree"(G. K. Chesterton, *The Penguin Complete Father Brown* [New York: Penguin, 1981], 488).

with the very One whom we are asked to emulate gives us hope: "I can do all things through him who empowers me" (Phil. 4:13). By "knowing Christ and the power of his resurrection" (Phil. 3:10a), I can at least begin to become like him. By "sharing in his sufferings [and] becoming like him in his death" (3:10b), I participate in the event in which Christ's own self-emptying came to supreme expression.

Furthermore, God "saved us through the bath of rebirth and renewal by the Holy Spirit" (Titus 3:5). No less humble than other members of the Godhead, the Spirit condescends to indwell those whom he has renewed (1 Cor. 6:19; Rom. 8:9). Here he assaults pride and its offspring (Rom. 8:13 NIV, "if by the Spirit you put to death the misdeeds of the body, you will live"), principally by granting to his people the love that is essential for pride's conquest (Rom. 5:5, "the love of God has been poured out in our hearts by the Holy Spirit"). As the sins of Galatians 5:19–21 arise from pride, so the virtues of 5:22–23 witness to the Spirit's cultivation of humility in believers' lives.[39] Only "walking by the Spirit" (5:25) can combat pride's "vain glory" (5:26).[40]

The Three Avenues of Humility

We conclude by inquiring how Paul's teachings apply to our three relationships.

True humility begins with magnifying God. "Pride does not only go before a fall but is a fall—a fall of the creature's attention from what is better, God, to what is worse, itself."[41] Paul invites us to reverse that process by contemplating the manifold splendor and the amazing humility of God—a singular evidence of the latter being that he glorifies persons who once refused to glorify him and sought to deify themselves.[42] In both 1 Corinthians and Philippians, Paul calls upon the proud and self-confident to "boast" or "glory" in the Lord (1 Cor. 1:29–31; Phil. 3:3). He expects Roman believers to achieve unity among themselves, not by eradicating their differences of opinion but by worshiping God together (Rom.

39. Only the humble person, one whose mind is off himself and on others (Phil. 2:3–4), is free to show "love, joy, peace, patience, kindness, goodness, faithfulness, gentleness and self-control"(Gal. 5:22–23 NIV). Of these qualities, "gentleness"(*prautēs*) comes closest to being a synonym for "humility"(*tapeinophrosynē*, used in Phil. 2:3). These two terms occur together in Col. 3:12 and Eph. 4:2. The *tapeinophrosynē* of Col. 2:18, 23, is a "false humility"(NIV) that simultaneously masks and displays pride (cf. 2:18b).

40. The adjective *kenodoxos* (Gal. 5:26) means "conceited, boastful" (BAGD), or literally, "vainglorious." Correspondingly, the noun *kenodoxia* means "conceit, excessive ambition"; and the verb *kenodoxeō* "hold a false opinion, vainly imagine" (BAGD). Proud persons have distorted and inflated ideas of their importance.

41. C. S. Lewis, "Christianity and Literature," *Christian Reflections*, ed. Walter Hooper (Grand Rapids: Eerdmans, 1967), 7, following Augustine.

42. The only instance of *doxazō* (glorify) in Rom. prior to 8:30 is 1:21. "It is a finely conceived reversal that the [glory] which man failed to give to his Creator in the beginning is finally resolved in God's [glorifying] of man" (Dunn, *Romans*, 485).

15:5–6).[43] Those whom God glorifies are the very ones who ascribe glory to him.[44]

Paul's capacity to cope with rival preachers was directly related to his resolve that Christ should be exalted in his body, whether by life or by death (Phil. 1:15–21). His determination to live for Christ rather than for himself was founded upon his understanding of the cross (2 Cor. 5:14–21). The singular object of his boasting was "Christ crucified" (1 Cor. 1:18–2:5). It was especially this event that assaulted Paul's own pride: "May I never boast except in the cross of our Lord Jesus Christ, through which the world has been crucified to me, and I to the world" (Gal. 6:14 NIV). Likewise we shall learn to "hate what is evil" (Rom. 12:9), in this case pride, by meditating upon the divine condescension—especially as manifested in the death of Christ. In struggling with this besetting sin, I find it helpful to reflect on the fact that Christ emptied himself, and went to the cross, for the express purpose of conquering my pride.

> When I survey the wondrous cross
> On which the Prince of Glory died,
> My richest gain I count but loss,
> And pour contempt on all my pride.[45]

Seeing God as he truly is means seeing ourselves as we truly are. The conquest of pride begins with the recognition that one is indeed proud (1 Cor. 1–3), and that pride's effects on oneself are uniformly destructive.[46] We may identify with a prayer offered by Michel Quoist: "Lord, deliver me from myself. . . . I'm suffering dreadfully. Locked in myself, prisoner of myself, I

43. In the kind of worship Paul envisages in Rom. 15:6, the meat eater and the vegetarian can unitedly and openly "give thanks to God" (14:6) for their divergent practices!

44. In view of Rom. 8:30, note the usage of "glory" and "glorify" in 4:20; 11:36; 15:6–9. Richard F. Lovelace, *Dynamics of Spiritual Life* (Downers Grove: InterVarsity, 1979), 42, echoes Jonathan Edwards's warning that "fallen human nature is fertile ground for a fleshly religiosity which is impressively 'spiritual' but ultimately rooted in self-love. High emotional experiences, effusive religious talk, and even praising God . . . can be self-centered and self-motivated. In contrast to this, experiences of renewal which are genuinely from the Holy Spirit are God-centered in character, based on worship, an appreciation of God's worth and grandeur divorced from self-interest. Such experiences . . . leave the believer hungering and thirsting after righteousness instead of satiated with self-congratulation."

45. Isaac Watts, "When I Survey the Wondrous Cross" (1707). At the close of Flannery O'Connor's story "The Artificial Nigger," *The Complete Stories* (New York: Farrar, Straus and Giroux, 1979), 269–70, the main character, Mr. Head, "stood appalled, judging himself with the thoroughness of God, while the action of mercy covered his pride like a flame and consumed it. He had never thought himself a great sinner before but he saw now that his true depravity had been hidden from him lest it cause him despair. He realized that he was forgiven for sins from the beginning of time, when he had conceived in his own heart the sin of Adam."

46. "Sigmund Freud wrote in his notebook of aphorisms that the worst egoist is the person to whom the thought has never occurred that he might be proud" (Alice Miller, *Prisoners of Childhood* [New York: Basic, 1987], xiv). Charles Colson describes how C. S. Lewis's teaching on pride affected him: "Suddenly I felt naked and unclean, my bravado . . . gone. I was exposed, unprotected, for Lewis's words were describing me. . . . In those brief moments . . . I saw myself as I never had before. And the picture was ugly" (*Born Again* [Old Tappan, N.J.: Chosen, 1976], 113, 114).

hear nothing but my voice, I see nothing but myself. . . . Lord . . . take me by the hand. . . . Show me the way, The path leading to joy, to light."[47]

If nothing is so enervating as trying to maintain one's status atop a pinnacle of pride, nothing is so invigorating as to be freed at long last from the joylessness of a self-centered faith. As liberation from pride released new energy in Paul (1 Cor. 15:9–10), so it can be for us. Salvation by grace through faith, by relieving us from trying to establish a basis for "boasting" (Eph. 2:8–9), paves the way for genuine self-fulfillment: "For we are God's workmanship, created in Christ Jesus to do good works, which God prepared in advance for us to do" (2:10 NIV). Release from self-absorption frees us to understand what "good works" really are.

We all know from painful experience what pride does to personal relationships: it breeds misery, resentment, jealousy, and alienation. What is the effect of humility?

The humble person does not constantly demean himself, nor does he dwell upon his humility; both are subtle forms of egocentricity. Like Timothy and Epaphroditus (Phil. 2), "he will not be thinking about himself at all."[48] As with Paul, the object of boasting will shift away from oneself to other people.[49] "*Humble* comes from *humus*, earth. Sages are earthy. They feel at home with you, and they make you feel at home with them. . . . They are not thinking about themselves, but about you, caring about you. [Like Christ, Phil. 2], they are selfless not by being small but by being empty, open, commodious; they always have plenty of room in themselves for you and your needs. . . . The person suffering from a divinity complex cannot empty himself because there is not much of a self there to empty. He is incapable of caring about you for the same reason he is incapable of insight into you: he is only into himself."[50]

My chosen profession of teaching provides innumerable opportunities to pour one's life into other people. Yet the intellectual community testifies as eloquently as any other to pride's self-deification and ruthless competitiveness. Paul "calls people who are trained to speak as intellectual authorities to admit their ignorance and foolishness,"[51] and to rely on Christ cru-

---

47. *Prayers of Life* (Dublin: Gill and Son, 1963), 87, 89.

48. Lewis, *Mere Christianity*, 99.

49. 2 Cor. 1:14; 7:4, 14; 8:24; 9:3; 1 Thess. 2:19–20; 2 Thess. 1:4. Such boasting finds its explanation and matrix in Paul's boasting about Christ (1 Cor. 15:31, "I exult over you in Christ Jesus our Lord").

50. Peter J. Kreeft, *Between Heaven and Hell* (Downers Grove: InterVarsity, 1982), 58–59, 63.

51. Nathan O. Hatch, "Evangelical Colleges and the Challenge of Christian Thinking," *Reformed Journal*, September 1985, 16. "The Christian scholar walks a precarious path because the deadliest vices of all, autonomy and pride, are so pervasive and so beguiling within academe" (ibid.). "Karl Barth describes the ethics of the New Testament as a downward pull, the pull from the heights to the depths, from riches to poverty, from victory to defeat, from triumph to suffering, from life to death. . . . Doesn't Yale instill in its students the desire to move upward from weakness to power, from poverty to wealth, from ignorance to knowledge, from servant to master?" (Henri Nouwen, in Colin Williams, "Purpose in a University Divinity School," *Theological Education* 14 [1978]: 67).

cified, "the wisdom of God" (1 Cor. 1:24). In proclaiming a Savior who "did not please himself" (Rom. 15:3) but instead "emptied himself" (Phil. 2:7), Paul summons professors away from their arrant egotism back to renewed attentiveness and service to their students: "if it is teaching, let him teach" (Rom. 12:7).

Casper Rene Gregory once paid tribute to Fenton John Anthony Hort, a New Testament scholar of another generation: "He was a great man, and at every moment a complete man, whether he was caring for the children suffering from scarlet fever in his rural parish, or occupying himself with the translation of Plato, or discovering and describing some new plant, or recovering some forgotten utterance of a Father of the Church, or sitting in his study wrestling with some problem of the transmission of a text, or standing on the summit of the Matterhorn [trying] to identify the surrounding mountains. . . . He was a student of the things and the people whom God had created; and in this study he forgot one thing only—himself."[52]

Let us be realistic. God is gently but firmly bringing his people into conformity to the image of Jesus Christ, the humble King and Savior. But the good work that God has begun, he has not yet completed (Phil. 1:6; 3:12). Humility may have been born in us, but it is by no means full grown; it is probably at best in its adolescence. Pride grows like a weed, humility like a delicate oriental flower. For us to imagine that humility has reached maturity in us, only reveals that we are still very immature.

Humble me to the dust before thee [O Lord]. . . . Break the Dagon of pride in pieces before the ark of thy presence. Demolish the Babel of self-opinion, and scatter it to the wind. Level to the ground my Jericho walls of a rebel heart. Then grace, grace, will be my experience and cry.[53]

52. In Stephen Neill, *The Interpretation of the New Testament 1861–1961* (London: Oxford University Press, 1964), 74.

53. Arthur Bennett, ed., *The Valley of Vision: A collection of Puritan prayers and devotions* (Edinburgh: Banner of Truth, 1975), 188.

6

Freedom in Slavery

"Freedom *in* slavery"? But surely Paul teaches freedom *from* slavery: "For freedom Christ has set us free. Stand firm, therefore, and do not submit again to a yoke of slavery" (Gal. 5:1 NRSV). Yet Paul speaks also of a slavery that grants liberty and life to its captives. "When you were slaves to sin, you were free from the control of righteousness. What benefit did you reap at that time from the things you are now ashamed of? Those things result in death! But now that you have been set free from sin and have become slaves to God, the benefit you reap leads to holiness, and the result is eternal life" (Rom. 6:20–22 NIV).

The importance of this subject for our purpose cannot be exaggerated. I must say that this strand of Paul's teaching has had a profoundly liberating effect in my own life.

We begin by observing the distinction between slavery (*douleia*) and service (*diakonia*). In our day a servant can work for more than one person: he may pump gas during the day and wait tables at night. Not so a slave in Paul's time; he was owned and controlled by one master only.[1] "No one can be slave (*douleuein*) to two masters [said Jesus]. . . . You cannot be slave (*douleuein*) to both God and Money" (Matt. 6:24). The significance of this distinction will become apparent as we proceed.

1. On this distinction, see C. H. Dodd, *Romans* (London: Hodder and Stoughton, 1932), 97, on Rom. 6:15–23. For the background of Paul's usage of this terminology, see Dale B. Martin, *Slavery as Salvation: The Metaphor of Slavery in Pauline Christianity* (New Haven: Yale University Press, 1990).

From One Bondage to Another

As we saw at the close of chapter 2, Paul speaks of sin much more often as a power than as an action: a person outside of Christ is enslaved to Sin, under whose mastery he or she commits sins. We saw also that Sin captures and controls its victims through several agencies—the flesh, the law of God, the demonic powers, and death—and that the effect upon each of the three relationships is catastrophic.[2]

Jesus Christ, himself victor over Sin, proceeds to liberate persons from Sin and all the powers at its command. Yet such persons, far from becoming autonomous, are ushered immediately into a new bondage: they become Christ's slaves (*douloi*), he becomes their Lord (*Kyrios*).[3] We now consider several aspects of this passage from the old slavery to the new.

Paul employs the term flesh (*sarx*) to denote the whole person in rebellion against God and in thrall to Sin. By Christ's incarnation and death, Sin is "condemned . . . in the flesh," and its victims freed from existence "according to the flesh" (Rom. 8:3–4). They are no longer "in the flesh," but "in Christ" (8:1) and "in the Spirit" (8:9). Those who belong to Christ have crucified the flesh with its passions and desires, and are impelled by the Spirit to love and good works (Gal. 5:22–26). The Lord is for the body (*sōma*), but against the flesh (*sarx*); the body will be raised, but the flesh is doomed for destruction (1 Cor. 6:13–14; 5:5).[4]

To be freed from the flesh as thus understood is to be freed from bondage to oneself—the fallen self, the self within the old humanity. "Our old man was crucified with [Christ] so that the body under Sin's control might be rendered powerless, that we should no longer be slaves (*douleuein*) to Sin" (Rom. 6:6), but slaves to Christ instead. As Christ's slave, I can be slave to no one else, myself included. "You are not your own; you were bought with a price" (1 Cor. 6:19–20). "[Christ] died for all, that those who live should no longer live for themselves but for him who died for them and was raised again" (2 Cor. 5:15).[5]

2. See pp. 49–59.

3. Believers (including Paul) are called *douloi* of Christ (or of God) in Rom. 1:1 (cf. 6:15–23); 1 Cor. 7:22; 2 Cor. 4:5; Gal. 1:10; Eph. 6:6; Phil. 1:1; Col. 4:12; 2 Tim. 2:24; Titus 1:1. The verb *douleuō* is so used in Rom. 12:11; 14:18 (cf. 16:18); Eph. 6:7; Phil. 2:22; Col. 3:24; 1 Thess. 1:9; *douloō*, in Rom. 6:22. *Kyrios* occurs 275 times in Paul, almost always with reference to Christ. Paul applies *despotēs* to earthly masters of slaves (1 Tim. 6:1–2; Titus 2:9), but never directly to Christ (but see 2 Tim. 2:21).

4. Jerome Murphy-O'Connor, *1 Corinthians* (Wilmington, Del.: Michael Glazier, 1979), 42, rightly says of 5:5 that neither *sarx* (flesh) nor *pneuma* (spirit) "is to be understood as designating part of the person. Each designates the whole person as viewed from different angles. 'Spirit' means the whole person as oriented towards God. 'Flesh' means the whole person as oriented away from God." For supportive arguments, see Gordon D. Fee, *The First Epistle to the Corinthians* (Grand Rapids: Eerdmans, 1987), 210–13; and my discussion of Pauline anthropology in chap 2.

5. Cf. Gal. 2:20, "I have been crucified with Christ and I no longer live . . ."; Phil. 1:21, "For to me to live is Christ. . . ."

In the process Christ frees me from bondage to other people. Bound to Christ alone, Paul is "free from all men" (1 Cor. 9:19a). He and his colleagues "are not trying to please men" and are "not seeking praise from men," for they have been commissioned by God and Christ and are accountable to them alone (1 Thess. 2:4–7). "Am I now seeking the favor of men, or of God? Or am I trying to please men? If I were still trying to please men, I would not be a slave (*doulos*) of Christ," reasons Paul in Galatians 1:10.[6]

As an integral part of that same work, Christ redeems his people from bondage to the law and joins them to himself instead (Gal. 4:5–7; 5:1; Rom. 7:1–6). In the hands of Sin, the law of God is enslaving; persons who are "under Sin" are "under law" as well (Gal. 3:22–23). But those whom Christ has freed from Sin "are not under law but under grace" (Rom. 6:14). The age of law has been superseded by the age of Messiah (2 Cor. 3:4–18). Paul and others are "servants of a new covenant, not of the letter (*gramma*) but of the Spirit (*Pneuma*); for the letter kills, but the Spirit gives life" (3:6). The Spirit of the Lord indeed grants freedom (3:17), but not from the "law" (*nomos*) or from the "writing" (*graphe*), only from the "letter" (*gramma*, Rom. 7:6; 2 Cor. 3:6). "What Paul denotes by *gramma* (when contrasted with *pneuma*) is . . . that mere letter, which is what one is left with in the [Old Testament] as a whole or in any part of it, when one insists on interpreting it independently of the illumination of the Holy Spirit and so without out reference to Him to whom the [Old Testament] bears witness, Jesus Christ."[7] Now that Christ has come, the law is not jettisoned but is put at the disposal of a new Master. In the hands of Sin the law is deadly; wielded by Christ the Lord through the empowering Spirit, it becomes a means of grace (Rom. 7:7–13; 8:4–8). When believers "carry one another's burdens," they fulfill "the law of Christ" now implanted in their hearts by the Spirit (Gal. 5:22–6:2); and they bear visible witness to the heart of the Old Testament law (5:13–14).[8]

Believers likewise share in Christ's victory over the hostile spirits. In his death he "disarmed the rulers and authorities" by snatching from them the record of his people's guilt and "nailing it to the cross" (Col. 2:13–15). More radically still, Christ saves his people from the demons' destructive use of the law through human instruments, and summons them to purposeful

---

6. On this translation (RSV mg.), the questions are parallel. The Greek might also be rendered, "Is it human beings or God that I am trying to persuade now? Or am I seeking to please human beings?" In this case Paul may mean that he persuades men (not God) and pleases Christ (not men). See F. F. Bruce, *Galatians* (Grand Rapids: Eerdmans, 1982), 84–85.

7. C. E. B. Cranfield, *The Epistle to the Romans* (Edinburgh: T. & T. Clark, 1979), 870. Owing to the veil that covers their minds, the opponents whom Paul addresses in 2 Cor. 3 fail to see that the very raison d'être of the Mosaic order was to prepare the way for a new, more glorious order. To be true to Moses is to turn, as he did, "to the Lord"—which now means turning to Christ (3:14, 16).

8. See p. 101 on "the Spirit of Power and Love."

law-keeping under his own headship (Col. 2:16–23). Now exalted to the
Father's right hand, he reigns over all the powers that terrorize humanity;
and he does so for the sake of his people: "God placed all things under his
feet and appointed him to be head over all things for the church" (Eph.
1:22).[9] Persons who are "raised with Christ" are thereby rescued from "the
ruler of the kingdom of the air" and the "spiritual forces of evil" at his command (Eph. 2:1–10; 6:10–18). "When [Christ] ascended on high, he led prisoners captive, he gave gifts to men" (Eph. 4:8): the "captives" are the hostile
powers, the "men" their former victims, now released to serve Christ the
King (Eph. 4:7–13).[10] Persons once devoted to "the wisdom of this age"
through indoctrination by "the rulers of this age," or to "hollow and deceptive philosophy" at the instigation of "the elemental spirits," are now
taught by the Holy Spirit and granted "the mind of Christ" (1 Cor. 1:18–
2:16; Col. 2:1–23). The final conquest of the powers awaits the future (1 Cor.
15:24; Phil. 2:9–11). Yet as long as the warfare continues, God supplies his
people with the needed weaponry (Eph. 6:10–18) and prevents the
demonic powers from separating his people "from the love of God that is
in Christ Jesus our Lord" (Rom. 8:38–39).

Finally, Jesus conquers Sin's mightiest ally on his people's behalf. In
confronting death, he redeems them from death, "the curse of the law"
(Gal. 3:13). Whereas Sin reigned through death, grace established its rule
by the bestowal of eternal life (Rom. 5:21; 6:23). Christ's personal triumph
over death has yet to be fully experienced by his people; for them "the last
enemy" remains to be destroyed (1 Cor. 15:20–26, 42–58). Nonetheless,
they have already "been brought from death to life"; even now they "may
live a new life" and experience "life and peace" through the indwelling
Spirit (Rom. 6:4, 13; 8:1–17).

The Implications of Bondage to Christ

Like any slave, a Christian belongs to one master only; he or she is duty-
bound to obey Christ alone. The purchased possession of Christ the Lord
cannot logically remain the slave of Sin or of any of those powers by which
Sin maintained its mastery.[11]

9. See Herman Ridderbos, *Paul: An Outline of His Theology*, trans. John R. DeWitt (Grand Rapids: Eerdmans, 1975), 387–92. The portrait of Christ as Lord of all is "to keep the church from being overawed by
any other power" (391).

10. On this view the "captives" of 4:8 are or represent the hostile rulers or authorities mentioned (or
included) in 1:21; 3:10; and 6:12. Cf. Gerhard Kittel, *TDNT* 1:196 (Eph. 4:8 speaks of "the subjection of spirits
to Christ"); Andrew T. Lincoln, *Ephesians* (Dallas: Word, 1990), 242 (citing 1:21–22; Col. 2:15); and (more
tentatively) F. F. Bruce, *Paul, Apostle of the Heart Set Free* (Grand Rapids: Eerdmans, 1977), 436–38.

11. Especially Rom. 6–8. On Paul's asseverations both of achieved victory and of ongoing struggle in
this passage, see chap. 7.

What does Christ require of his newly acquired slaves? The question is crucial: if I am to be utterly dominated by another, it matters terribly what sort of master he is and what he plans to do with me. We have learned more than enough of Sin's character and designs, and of the disastrous consequences of slavery to ourselves and to other slaves of Sin. What of the new Master?

Christ exercises his lordship not to please himself (Rom. 15:3), but to help his slaves. It is a tyranny of love that moves him to action—supremely the action required for delivering them from Sin. "Christ loved us and gave himself up for us as a fragrant offering and sacrifice to God" (Eph. 5:2; cf. 5:25; Gal. 2:20). By the same power he moves his redeemed people to act on his behalf. As Paul puts it in 2 Corinthians 5:14a, "Christ's love [as demonstrated in his death, v. 14b] compels us [to fulfill the ministry of reconciliation, vv. 11–21]."[12] Nowhere else is such despotism to be found. Jesus Christ is "the only one in the universe who can control us without destroying us."[13] Only under the mastery of Christ's love does the slave attain true liberty.[14]

Not surprisingly, then, the Lord's supreme command is that his slaves should impart his love to others. References to loving God and Christ are not lacking in Paul. But his emphasis lies on God's love for his children and their answering love for other people, both within and beyond the church. A Christian shows that he loves God by loving other human beings.[15]

Slavery to Christ, like slavery to Sin, entails slavery to other people. But now the experience is radically different, owing to motivation from the new Master. "You were called to freedom, brothers. But do not use your freedom as an opportunity for the flesh; rather, be slaves (*douleuete*) to one another in love. The entire law is summed up in a single command: 'Love your neighbor as yourself'" (Gal. 5:13–14). Persons who once "lived in malice and envy, hateful themselves and hating one another," may now, because they are justified by grace and renewed by the Spirit, "devote themselves to good works" to the profit of everyone (Titus 3:3–8).

12. Grammatically, "the love of Christ" (v. 14a) may denote Christ's love for us or our answering love for him. 5:14b–15a suggest that Paul is speaking primarily if not exclusively of the former. But this in turn evokes Paul's love for Christ (v. 15b) and for the recipients of the gospel (vv. 16–20).

13. Rebecca Pippert, *Out of the Salt-Shaker and into the World* (Downers Grove: InterVarsity, 1979), 64. See the whole chapter "Jesus the Lord," 45–64, especially "A Question of Control," 52–58. Speaking from the other side of the relationship, Richard J. Foster, *Money, Sex and Power* (San Francisco: Harper and Row, 1985), 126, says that "God is our only legitimate obsession."

14. Jesus declares in John 15:15, "I no longer call you slaves (*douloi*), because a slave does not know what his master is doing. Instead, I have called you friends [cf. v. 12b, "as I have loved you"]. . . ." Paul's language is more striking; for, he says, it is within a relationship of slavery that such friendship exists.

15. Some of the evidence: believers' love for God or Christ, Rom. 8:28; 1 Cor. 16:22; God's or Christ's love for believers, Rom. 5:5, 8; Gal. 2:20; believers' answering love for others, Rom. 13:8–10; 1 Cor. 8:1; 13:1–13; Gal. 5:14; Eph. 5:1–2; 1 Thess. 4:9. See Victor Paul Furnish, *The Love Command in the New Testament* (Nashville: Abingdon, 1972), 91–131.

We can now appreciate more fully the comprehensiveness of Christ's liberating work. Just as Sin affected all three of the self's relationships, exploiting their inseparability to the full, so does Christ. The self, having been justified by Christ's blood, is now at peace with God. The self, having surrendered its insistence on self-determination, experiences self-fulfillment for the first time. And the self, now freed from people, is for the first time free for them (1 Cor. 9:19).

The rest of the chapter will explore some of the implications for believers. How does adherence to Paul's gospel of salvation, together with his concept of bondage to Christ, affect one's understanding and practice of Christian liberty? What are the practical consequences for one's attitude toward other people? toward the law of God? toward religious traditions and social customs? (Liberation from the demonic powers and from death is largely reserved for later chapters.) We seek answers first in the practice of Paul himself.

The Liberated Apostle

With his conversion Paul becomes a *doulos* of Christ; Christ becomes his *Kyrios*.[16] Henceforth "the mind of Christ" governs his thinking (1 Cor. 2:16), and the command of Christ his behavior (Acts 22:10). Consequently he is freed from bondage both to himself and to others.

The effect of bondage to Christ may be illustrated from the account of the crisis at Antioch (Gal. 2:11–14). Paul's adherence to the conviction of Galatians 1:10 ("If I were still trying to please men, I would not be a slave [*doulos*] of Christ"), and Peter's violation of it, are equally in evidence during the crisis. Peter withdrew from table-fellowship with the Gentiles, says Paul, because he feared the members of the circumcision party (2:12). As fellow Jewish Christians who belonged (as he did) to the Jerusalem church, they wielded an influence upon Peter which the Gentiles of Antioch (in Jewish eyes, lesser Christians from a lesser church) could hardly be expected to equal. He feared them because their favor (together with that of James's group) was vital, or so he thought, for his sense of theological and social security; and thus he allowed them to dictate his actions and, in the process, to override his personal convictions.

Paul in response "opposed [Peter] to his face" (Gal. 2:11), and thus demonstrated in the most dramatic way his freedom from the sort of fear that still bound Peter. For Paul challenged not merely the most eminent of apostles but the stupendous authority of the Jerusalem church as well. His

16. Paul calls himself Christ's "slave" in Rom. 1:1; Phil. 1:1. He repeatedly speaks of "our Lord"(e.g., Rom. 1:4) but only once of "my Lord" (Phil. 3:8)—a witness to the centrality of Christian community in his thought.

action is all the more astonishing when we remember his concern for the unity of the church.[17] Yet he takes his stand, despite all the risks, because "the truth of the gospel" demands it,[18] and because slavery to Christ leaves no room for the fear of men (Gal. 1:10).

We might, of course, interpret Paul's boldness at Antioch very differently: he asserts his colossal ego in the face of threats to his turf, his message, and his apostolic claims.[19] Paul, unlike Peter, finds (or at least seeks) relief from bondage to other people in willful enslavement to himself. This view, however, fails to take account of the decisive effect of Paul's theology on his conduct. Paul is in fact, not just in theory, a slave of Christ. For Sin's slaves, of course, self-enslavement is the quite predictable reaction. Perceiving that others think ill of me, or little of me, I can compensate for this by feeding my ego or improving my "self-concept," the effect of which process is certain to be a distorted view of myself.[20] But for Paul the *doulos*, what Jesus the *Kyrios* says about him is vastly more important than what he might say about himself. By the same token, the judgment of Christ matters far more than that of other people: even if every last person in Galatia and Jerusalem denies the genuineness of his apostleship, Paul remains an *apostolos* because Christ has declared him to be so (Gal. 1:1–17).

Paul also appropriates his teaching about liberation from the law. "I myself am not under the law," he declares (1 Cor. 9:20a); the *doulos* of Christ cannot be under a second master, even the law of God. Yet to forestall misunderstanding, Paul quickly adds, "I am not free from God's law but am bound by Christ's law" (*ennomos Christou*, 9:21b).[21] *En Christō* provides the inspiration, so to speak, for *ennomos Christou*; life "in Christ" provides the essential context for law-keeping. Paul is subject to Christ's law because he is subject to Christ himself—the One who has wrested the law from the grip of Sin, and now employs it for his own gracious purpose.

"The law of Christ," implanted on the heart by the Spirit, shows believers how to bring love for other people (one of the law's fundamental com-

17. Gal. 2:2b, "for fear I was running or had run in vain." "A cleavage between his Gentile mission and the mother-church would be disastrous" (Bruce, *Galatians*, 111). Cf. 2:10, and Paul's later collection for the Judean Christians.

18. "The truth of the gospel" (Gal. 2:5, 14) is that one is "justified by faith in Christ and not by works of law" (2:16). Peter's action insinuates to the Gentiles of Antioch that they cannot be saved unless they keep the law of Moses. Peter's personal slavery (to the champions of the law) contributes to the enslavement of the Gentiles (to the law itself): "How is it, then, that you compel Gentiles to follow Jewish customs?" (2:14b).

19. Paul considered himself to be, by Christ's commission, the apostle to the Gentiles (Gal. 1:16; 2:8–9). Antioch had become the headquarters for this mission (Acts 11:20, 25–26; 13:1–3).

20. I say "certain to be distorted," because one's thinking is controlled by Sin, through the flesh (or the fallen self). Evidence that the thinking is distorted is the belief that one escapes bondage to others by slavery to oneself—when in fact slavery to oneself always means slavery to others.

21. NIV's rendering of *ennomos Christou* as "under Christ's law" is misleading. The preposition is not *hypo* (under), but *en* (in), here attached to the noun *nomos* (law); so better to translate "bound by the law of Christ" (FFB).

mands, Gal. 5:14) to concrete expression. In one of his foundational statements about the Christian life, Paul declares: "Although I am free from all
men, I have enslaved (*edoulosa*) myself to all, that I might win the more"
(1 Cor. 9:19). Normally a person becomes a slave against his will; here the
act of enslavement is voluntary and deliberate, an exercise of Christian liberty: "I have enslaved myself." As Christ's slave, Paul was free to "become
all things to all men" (9:22). It is possible, of course, to be "all things to all
men" in a bad sense—to be a Christian chameleon that changes color
depending on the circumstances and the audience.[22] If we consider Paul to
have been such a person, we had better reread Galatians. First Corinthians
9:22 is the testimony of a man who has found security in bondage to Christ,
and who is consequently free to relate to all kinds of people and to tolerate
all sorts of differences within the context of a common commitment to the
gospel.[23] It was precisely Paul's slavery to Christ that equipped him to love
other people; only by being freed from them could he be free for them. "For
we do not preach ourselves [we are delivered from bondage to ego], but
Jesus Christ as Lord [we are now his slaves], and ourselves as your slaves
(*douloi*) for Jesus' sake [we submit to him by submitting to you]" (2 Cor. 4:5;
cf. 5:14–20).

We shall now look at the two principal passages where Paul applies this
idea of freedom in slavery to personal relationships within the Christian
community.

Liberty and Love in 1 Corinthians 8–10

Paul here replies to the Corinthians' inquiry (7:1) about "food sacrificed
to idols" (8:1). His response may be considered in three stages.

Gifts from God

In the first place Paul acknowledges that God has granted certain gifts
to his people. The first is knowledge: "We all possess knowledge" (8:1).
Christians know truth about God and Christ (8:4–6). This insight in turn
yields the right understanding of food. Christians know that food is a good
gift from God (10:25–26); that neither eating nor abstaining is the basis for
God's acceptance (8:8); and that the idol to which food is offered is "nothing in the world" (8:4).

---

22. Denis Mack Smith wrote in his biography of Mussolini, that he was "an actor, an exhibitionist who
changed his role from hour to hour to suit the occasion. . . . It was an awkward fact that there is not a single
belief or idea in all his voluminous writings that he did not directly contradict somewhere else" (quoted in
Newsweek [14 June 1982]: 89).

23. See Henry Chadwick's superb essay, "'All Things to All Men' (I Cor. ix. 22)," *NTS* 1 (1955): 261–75.
Paul states his inflexibility respecting the truth of the gospel in Gal. 1:6–9.

The knowledge brings to light certain privileges—the right to food and drink, to marriage, and to payment for one's services as a herald of the gospel (9:4–18).[24]

Moreover, God gives his people the liberty to act upon that knowledge and to exercise those rights. "Everything is permissible" (10:23, *bis*).[25] "Am I not free?" asks Paul (9:1). He is indeed: he may marry if he so chooses, and he is at liberty to receive payment for his services. Not only so: "If some unbeliever invites you to a meal and you want to go, eat whatever is put before you without raising questions of conscience. . . . For why should my freedom be judged by another's conscience? If I take part in the meal with thankfulness, why am I denounced because of something I thank God for?" (10:27, 29b–30 NIV; for the moment we omit vv. 28–29a).

The Perils of Freedom

At the very moment he proclaims Christian liberty, Paul sounds a warning, precisely in the face of those gifts. "'Everything is permissible'—but not everything is beneficial. 'Everything is permissible'—but not everything is constructive" (10:23 NIV).[26] The first danger is that believers' freedom will "become a stumbling block to the weak" (8:9). For "not everyone knows" the truth about God and Christ and idols and food (8:4–8). The unenlightened one, the "weak brother," is thus offended when he sees fellow Christians eating food which has been (or which recalls food that has been) sacrificed to idols. (We may compare the reaction of a former alcoholic to a Christian's having a glass of wine over a meal, or of a strict Sabbatarian to a professing Christian's mowing his lawn on Sunday afternoon.) What makes the situation especially serious is that the genuinely mature Christian—and thus the one whose conduct the weaker brother is most likely to respect and long to emulate—is the very one who feels secure and liberated enough to eat such meat without pangs of guilt.

But the weaker Christian's being offended is his defense against a graver danger, namely, the defiling of his conscience (8:7b). His conscience, informed by Christian truth, tells him that idol worship is a grievous sin. Yet, having witnessed the practice of believers whom he respects and the boldness with which they have partaken of idolatrous sacrifices, he fails to make the proper distinction between paganism and Christianity and may himself "be encouraged to eat what has been sacrificed to idols" (8:10–11)—which may in turn tempt him to revert to paganism. The peril is that

---

24. The term *exousia* (right, authority) occurs six times in 1 Cor. 9:4–18.

25. Here, as in all probability in 8:1, Paul quotes a Corinthian slogan with approval; note the NIV's use of quotation marks in both passages (in the text at 10:23, in the margin at 8:1).

26. "Nothing hurts us, nothing destroys us, but the ill use of that liberty with which God has entrusted us," writes William Law, *A Serious Call to a Devout and Holy Life* (Grand Rapids: Eerdmans, 1966), 282. The book was first published in 1728.

the weak believer will act out of accord with—that is, "violate"—his conscience, and be "destroyed" as a result (8:7, 11).

But there are perils too for Christians whose knowledge gives them freedom to partake of pagan foods. The warning of 10:23 applies to these "stronger brothers" as surely as to the "weaker." Indeed, lacking as they do the danger signal of a wounded conscience (8:12), the former may be at greater risk. One's very strength, or to be more exact, confidence in it, makes him exceptionally vulnerable: "So, if you suppose you are standing firm, beware lest you fall" (10:12). Says Paul to the "strong": Beware lest a practice that is not sinful draw you into one that is. It is quite true that idols themselves, and the sacrifices offered to them, amount to nothing; but the demons behind them are very real indeed (10:18–22). They represent the host of so-called gods and lords (8:5). They are not really divine, but they behave as though they were: they bring human beings under their dominion, and draw them into an intimacy akin to that of the Lord's Supper (10:20–21). To be oblivious to the existence or the presence of such powers, or to be confident of one's capacity as a liberated or mature Christian to withstand them, makes a person more susceptible than ever to their baleful influence (10:12).

Therefore Paul urges his readers, weak and strong alike: "Flee from idolatry" (10:14). Learn a lesson, he says, from Israel's experience in the wilderness. They all received God's manifold provision and protection (10:1–4); nevertheless the majority fell under God's judgment on account of their sins, starting with idolatry (10:5–10). We too have received God's grace—grace in the fullness of its eschatological manifestation (10:11); so let us beware of misplaced confidence (10:12).[27] To be sure, God provides a way of escape amidst the temptation (10:13); but one cannot rightly claim that word of promise while disobeying the attendant word of command (10:14).

That brings us to the third and crucial stage of Paul's response to the problem of food offered to idols.

Bondage to Love

In the conduct of the genuinely mature (*teleios*) believer, liberty acts in concert with love. "'A Christian man is a most free lord of all, subject to none. A Christian man is a most dutiful servant of all, subject to all.' 'Subject to none' in respect of his liberty; 'subject to all' in respect of his charity."[28] More than that, it is in love for other people that one's freedom finds its fullest expression.[29]

27. The Corinthians were apparently tempted to view the sacraments of baptism and the Lord's Supper (cf. 10:2–4) as talismans against evil.

28. Bruce, *Paul*, 202, quoting Martin Luther.

29. "How does this freedom [that we have in Christ through the Spirit] come to realization in us? The decisive answer is in love. It is not in isolation but in life with others that the Christian attains to freedom" (Heinrich Schlier, *TDNT* 2:500).

To be sure, "we all possess knowledge" (8:1b); but even the right kind of knowledge may be wrongly employed. "Knowledge puffs up, but love builds up" (8:1c). The gift of the Spirit (in this case "knowledge," *gnōsis*) must not be divorced from the fruit of the Spirit, the foremost quality of which is love, *agapē* (13:2; Gal. 5:22). Indeed, the absence of love betrays a lack of knowledge. "The one who loves God is known by him" (8:3). We might have expected, "The one who *knows* God is known by God" (cf. Gal. 4:9). For Paul the essence of knowing God is loving God; he who does not love God, shows that he does not really know him.[30]

One test of how well I love God is whether I love his people—those "for whom Christ died" (8:11). With respect to the issue at hand, Paul concludes: "Therefore, if food causes my brother to fall, I will never eat meat again, lest I cause my brother to fall" (8:13). Based on his knowledge (which far exceeded that of any of his readers), Paul has the right to eat food sacrificed to idols. But as he has freedom to partake, he also has freedom to abstain; he has the freedom not to exercise his freedom. "A truly emancipated spirit such as Paul's is not in bondage to its own emancipation."[31] Proud persons must be so bound, because for them (as 1 Corinthians shows) liberty is a means of establishing superiority over other people. But the person whose security is in Christ alone (not in Christ together with the liberty he gives); who is being liberated from pride (which is by nature competitive); and in whose heart the Spirit is cultivating the love that is neither proud nor self-seeking (13:5) has freedom and power to relinquish freedom for the sake of another.[32]

In bondage to love for the weaker brother whose conscience is threatened with defilement, Paul will, if necessary, become a vegetarian. He is not required to eat flesh (he is a slave to Christ, not to food); his survival does not depend upon his doing so.[33] Paul was willing to assent to the apostolic decree, one stipulation of which pertained to "food polluted by idols" (Acts 15:20, 29). But he responded as a liberated Christian to the law of love implanted on the heart by the Spirit (2 Cor. 3:2–3).

By the same token, Paul is free to relinquish, as he was free to receive, payment for his services (1 Cor. 9:14–23). That such payment is a right makes the decision the more noteworthy. But Paul is not bound to his rights, only to the Lord who granted them. Moreover, it is the apostle's love both for Christ and for the people under his care that explains his rigorous discipline (9:24–27). By enslaving himself to himself ("I beat my body and

---

30. "God is known in proportion to the extent that He is loved" (Herman Bavinck, *Our Reasonable Faith*, trans. Henry Zylstra [Grand Rapids: Baker, 1977], 30). As we saw in chap. 2, this is knowledge in the sense of deeply personal communion, as distinct from the idea of knowledge as chiefly or purely cognitive.

31. F. F. Bruce, *The Book of the Acts* (Grand Rapids: Eerdmans, 1956), 432 n. 39.

32. For Paul's assault on pride in 1 Cor., see pp. 116–21; on the nature of humility, pp. 126–29.

33. The term chosen in 1 Cor. 8:13, *kreas*, means strictly "meat," not "food" in general.

enslave it [*doulagōgō*]," v. 27), he both resists the attacks of Sin through the flesh and shows himself loyal to Christ the Lord (cf. 6:19–20). The Corinthians too can only run freely in a context of enslavement to training; the greater the discipline, the greater the liberty (9:24–25). Or, in terms of the subject of 1 Corinthians 8–10, only in bondage to love for God and neighbor does a Christian discover what freedom really is.

First Corinthians 10 likewise makes it clear that Christian liberty is governed by love: "No one should seek his own good, but that of the other person" (v. 24). Thus the statements of 10:27, 29b–30, are qualified by the parenthesis concerning the weaker brother, 10:28–29a.[34] Let it be observed, however, that while Paul refrains from food out of respect for the brother's conscience, he does not violate his own conscience in the process (10:29b–30). Such an effect must be avoided at all costs in the life of any Christian, whether oneself or another.[35] Paul still adheres to the conviction of 10:26 (he has not capitulated to the notion that food belongs to idols or to demons), and he still recognizes his right to the food. His right is relinquished, not invalidated. It is precisely as the one who holds these convictions that Paul acts on behalf of the weaker brother. His decision to refrain is not a loss of freedom but an expression of freedom.[36]

Liberty and Love in Romans 14–15

The dispute addressed here is reminiscent of 1 Corinthians 8–10, but rather more complex and critical. Moreover, the theological underpinnings of Paul's argument are closer to the surface in the present passage; given his definitive exposition of the gospel in Romans 1–11, together with his insistence on a mode of conduct consistent with the gospel, the stakes are higher in Romans 14–15.[37] At the same time, Paul's counsel to believers in the Roman church and beyond is principially very much in keeping with that of 1 Corinthians; and it gives us opportunity, as it did Paul, to underscore and to amplify points from the earlier discussion.[38]

34. In my judgment the reference to "the other man" also embraces the nonbeliever (cf. 10:27, 32).

35. Corresponding to the corruption of both mind (*nous*) and conscience (*syneidēsis*) in the nonbeliever (Titus 1:15), the conscience participates with the mind in God's renewing work and is therefore to be respected, even as its fallibility is clearly recognized (1 Cor. 4:4–5; cf. Rom. 2:15–16).

36. On 10:27–30, see C. K. Barrett, *The First Epistle to the Corinthians* (New York: Harper and Row, 1968), 243–44; and Peter Richardson, *Paul's Ethic of Freedom* (Philadelphia: Westminster, 1979), 129, who thinks Paul raises the question of 10:29b in response to "weak Christians [who] were using their weakness aggressively, to keep others from doing things that offended them."

37. At issue in Rom. 14–15 is "the definition of Christianity itself" (James D. G. Dunn, *Romans* [Dallas: Word, 1988], 811). As part of the same question, Jewish Christians, and Gentiles associated with Judaism before receiving the gospel, face "nothing less than a crisis of identity"(ibid.).

38. See T. W. Manson, "St. Paul's Letter to the Romans—and Others," *Studies in the Gospels and Epistles*, ed. Matthew Black (Manchester: Manchester University Press, 1962), 225–41. For linguistic and conceptual parallels between 1 Cor. 8–10 and Rom. 14–15, see C. E. B. Cranfield, *The Epistle to the Romans*, vol. 2 (Edinburgh: T. & T. Clark, 1979), 691–92. Did the Roman Christians possess a copy of 1 Corinthians at this time?

The Existing Situation

The division is principally between Jewish and Gentile Christians, here called the "weak" and the "strong" respectively (15:1).[39] At issue are certain Old Testament and Jewish laws about food and special days (14:1–6). In the terms of 1 Corinthians 8–10, Christians whose consciences are weak (and thus easily violated) are at loggerheads with those whose consciences are strong (and thus easily desensitized to the vulnerabilities of the weak). Jewish Christians, together with Gentile Christians of their persuasion, "could not with a clear conscience give up the observance of such requirements of the law as the distinction between clean and unclean foods, the avoidance of blood, the keeping of the Sabbath and other special days."[40] In face of the difference, each side cultivated a censorious spirit toward the other (14:1, 10, 13).

"Strong" and "weak" are meaningful terms: the strong possess deeper understanding of the ethical implications of Christ's work than do the weak. The former correspond to those in Corinth who possess "knowledge" (rightly conceived), the latter to those who lack it. In Paul's mind, the person who "eats everything" and who "considers every day alike" (14:3, 5) is the more liberated of the two. Significantly, Paul places himself among the strong (15:1); from this position he offers a twofold response to the crisis.

The Example of Christ

Foundational to Paul's argument is a fact which no reader would dispute: that Jesus Christ is Lord over both parties in the dispute, and that the conduct of each person involved is ultimately directed "to the Lord" (14:3–8). It is therefore most appropriate that Paul should invoke the conduct of Christ himself as a guide for persons under his lordship. How has Christ dealt with the problem addressed in these chapters?

In the first place, Christ offered himself in service, both in life and in death, for both kinds of people: he became a servant to the Jews for the express purpose of bringing to fulfillment God's covenantal promises to the Gentiles (15:3–12).

Secondly, in keeping with that saving action, Christ continues to receive the diverse expressions of worship and obedience offered to him by the Jewish and the Gentile members of his household (14:3–8). He does not insist that the practices of the one (of whichever party) conform to those of the other to be worthy of acceptance. For God's reception of Jew and Gen-

---

39. See the introduction to the discussion of this passage in the preceding chapter, p. 123.

40. Cranfield, *Romans*, 695; cf. Acts 15:20, 29. Paul is hardly referring to the Sabbath exclusively. But it would be a mistake, in my judgment, to take 14:5 to refer to all special days except the Sabbath, for Jews the most special day of all (Gen. 2:3; Exod. 20:8–11). Cf. Paul's use of *Sabbatōn* in Col. 2:16 (NIV, "a Sabbath day"). We shall return to this subject in a later section.

tile alike is founded solely upon his grace: "For the kingdom of God is not
a matter of eating and drinking [whether one partakes or abstains], but of
righteousness, peace and joy in the Holy Spirit [all three of which qualities
have their origin in the saving God, as the preceding chapters of Romans
eloquently testify], because anyone [whether Jew or Gentile, whether weak
or strong] who serves (*douleuōn*) Christ in this way [that is, in dependence
on God's sovereign grace and in servitude to Christ alone] is pleasing to
God and approved by men [including both the weak and the strong within
the church]" (14:17–18 NIV).

The Obedience of the Slaves

The ultimate allegiance of each disputant belongs to Christ alone. "The
one who eats, eats to the Lord, for he gives thanks to God; and the one who
abstains, does so to the Lord and gives thanks to God" (14:6). Christ's claims
are exclusive, readers of both persuasions are his slaves: "Who are you to
judge the servant of another? To his own master he stands or falls" (14:4; cf.
14:18, *douleuōn*). Therefore the weak cannot logically be enslaved to both
Christ and the law, nor the strong to both Christ and their liberty; either dual
commitment would compromise and dilute the utter dependence upon God
and Christ that stands at the heart of Paul's understanding of faith (Rom. 4).

Paul exhorts Christ's slaves on both sides of the conflict to follow their
Lord's example. His unconditional acceptance of both Jew and Gentile is
to be mirrored in the conduct of strong and weak toward each other. "Let
not him who eats despise him who abstains, and let not him who abstains
pass judgment on him who eats; for God has welcomed him" (14:3 RSV; cf.
v. 10, where the same verbs, "despise" and "pass judgment on," recur).
"Therefore let us stop judging one another" (14:13). "Therefore welcome
one another, just as Christ welcomed you" (15:7; cf. vv. 5–6). Let the
strong stop despising the weak; let them instead, after Christ's example,
bear their weaknesses even at risk of insult (15:1–3). And let the weak
stop judging the strong for their perceived lawlessness; let them instead
show them the very mercy which the covenant God extended to lawless
Gentiles (15:8–12).

Such acceptance entails respect for diverse expressions of liberty. The
weak are free to refrain from certain foods, and to regard some days above
others; the strong are likewise free to eat meat along with vegetables, and
to regard all days alike. To have "the mind of Christ" is to tolerate in one's
own attitude the breadth of practice that the Lord himself permits. In the
terms of 1 Corinthians 8–10, each side must beware lest conscience be violated, whether one's own or that of the other (14:13–23).[41] The weak and

---

41. The term conscience, frequent in 1 Corinthians 8–10, is absent from Rom. 14–15; but the teaching
of Rom. 14:13–23 is very close to that of 1 Cor. 8:7–13.

the strong must accept one another as they are, rather than as potential converts to one's own position. "Disputable matters" (14:1) are almost certain to remain so. The weak and the strong are each relieved of the arduous and inevitably frustrating task of shaping the other into one's own image. Conversely, each is free to assist the other in becoming conformed to the image of him who alone is Master of both. What a relief to realize that the other, whether weak or strong, belongs to Christ and not to me.[42]

Paul thus calls both sets of disputants to a change in attitude. Yet as noted, he believes that the strong have a firmer grasp of the implications of Christ's saving work than do the weak; and the strong are therefore the ones to whom he makes his stronger appeal. "Welcome the one whose faith is weak," he counsels them at the very outset (14:1). As in 1 Corinthians, it is especially the conscience of the weaker believer that is to be safeguarded (14:13–23). It is most significant that Paul, himself one of the strong (15:1), does not employ his apostolic authority to impose his personal convictions upon the weak. Nor does he counsel the strong to try by whatever means to convert the weak into the strong. On the contrary: "We then that are strong ought to bear the infirmities of the weak, and not to please ourselves" (15:1 KJV). Not for a moment does he ask the strong to renounce their liberty (which would be to repudiate their very being as Christians), but he does challenge them to practice it in a certain way. They are free both to exercise and to restrict their freedom, for they are enslaved to Christ, not to the liberty he has granted them. Paul urges them to "let their strength be made perfect amid weakness" (cf. 2 Cor. 12:9). The strong are free to defend expressions of the very weakness from which they themselves have been liberated. More than that, they have strength and freedom actually to *"bear (bastazō)* the infirmities of the weak" (15:1).[43]

In short, diversity in the Christian community provides love (*agapē*, 14:15) its greatest opportunity. Love in turn honors both the liberty that is the concern of the strong (as noted earlier, freedom comes to fullest expression in acts of love), and the law that is the concern of the weak ("for love is the fulfillment of the law," 13:8–10). The effect is the praise of God (15:6–7).

---

42. Ernst Käsemann, *Commentary on Romans*, trans. and ed. Geoffrey W. Bromiley (Grand Rapids: Eerdmans, 1980), 379, comments on 14:23, "Christ remains the only measure for all. No one must make his faith a norm for others as they seek to serve Christ. The weak want uniformity by making their law binding for brothers, and the strong seek it too by forcing their insight on the weak. We thus try to make others in our own image and in so doing sin, since faith has to do always and exclusively with the image of Christ."

43. NIV's "to bear with the failings" is inadequate. *Bastazō* is similarly used in Gal. 6:2, "carry each other's burdens." It is the weak believer's acute sensitivity and deep conviction, not his practice as such, that determines the conduct of the strong (Dunn, *Romans*, 820, 830, on Rom. 14:14).

From Paul's Day to Ours

How may we apply Paul's teaching about Christian liberty to believers living in today's world? The questions posed earlier are still before us. What are the practical consequences for one's attitude toward other people? toward the law of God? toward religious traditions and social customs? In each case there is potential for both slavery to Sin and liberty in Christ.

People: Bondage and Freedom

For us, as for Paul's original readers, victory over Sin and its agencies is real but incomplete. Thus Christians too know what it is to be bound to self and to other selves in a destructive way.

As we saw at the close of chapter 2, the slaves of Sin produce "works of the flesh," among which are "hatred, discord, jealousy, fits of rage, selfish ambition, dissensions, factions and envy" (Gal. 5:20–21 NIV). In other words, slavery to Sin and to oneself always results in slavery to other people.

Consider jealousy and anger, although any selection from Galatians 5:20–21 could illustrate the point. Jealousy's essential competitiveness witnesses to its origin in pride. Jealousy is a monster that saps creative energy.[44] It can cause such absorption with another person's gifts and attainments that one becomes riveted in inactivity. Jealousy longs for the other's failure. Paul exhorts: "Rejoice with those who rejoice, weep with those who weep" (Rom. 12:15). But jealousy makes me rejoice when they weep, and weep when they rejoice. It may also find expression as a murderous ardor[45] intent upon destroying its object. However manifested, jealousy enslaves me to the other person; it has become he, not I, who determines the way I function.

It is possible to be angry without sinning (Eph. 4:26), to display anger that is compatible with and indeed expressive of "self control" (Gal. 5:22). But we are speaking of anger as a "work of the flesh." In this case I lose my temper and am brought under the control of another. Amid a fit of rage, my mind may become incapable of curbing my words and actions. Says an old Amish saying, "Anger is the wind that blows out the lamp of the mind." If my anger causes me to assault or even kill someone, I thereby demonstrate just how fully he has mastered me.

We have been describing what happens when a person, by the exertions of his own ego, enslaves himself to someone else. But enslavement to oth-

---

44. Does this help to explain why the man who received one talent "went and buried it in the ground" (Matt. 25:25)?

45. It is noteworthy that one Greek word, *zēlos*, serves for both "zeal" and "jealousy."

ers can become crueler still. It may also happen (even within the same relationship) that the other person, no less a slave of Sin than I, aggressively and deliberately makes me his slave and crushes my ego under the weight of his own. This is just what happened to hundreds of people in Jonestown, Guyana, some years ago.

Let us see how this might occur within more conventional relationships. One of our greatest fears (certainly one of mine) is rejection by another person, a fear that makes us dependent upon others' opinions and desperately desirous of their approval.[46] According to James Dobson, loss of self esteem is the principal source of depression in women. If so, his attendant judgment is all the more sobering: "At least 90 percent of our self-concept is built from what we think others think about us."[47] What if my perception of their thinking is correct? What if they are really, not just supposedly, against me? And what if they are among those whose judgment matters the most to me, and whose affirmation I most crave? Then there exists a psychological slavery with potentially devastating results.

We have been showing how Sin ruins personal relationships through the flesh, that is, through the fallen self. Let us remind ourselves that Sin's other agencies are also at work in the processes we have been describing. Satan contributes to the deterioration of relationships (as noted earlier) by encouraging anger, infidelity, slander, and coldness of heart; significantly, Paul especially warns against such acts among the people of God.[48] Moreover, as we shall see presently, Sin finds both in God's law, and in human traditions masquerading as divine law, instruments for enslaving human beings to one another. In the end, by the agency of death, Sin fulfills its purpose by destroying relationships altogether.[49]

But what if I am the purchased possession of Jesus Christ, redeemed by his blood and enslaved to his lordship? How does this affect my view both of myself and of other people? Henceforth my self-understanding must be reshaped by the mighty utterances of the divine Lord. No longer am I shackled to the deceptions of a psyche ruled by self and Sin. By virtue of

46. C. S. Lewis writes about Mark Studdock in *That Hideous Strength* (New York: Macmillan, 1968), 218: "Mark had always felt that Dimble disliked him. This had not made him dislike Dimble. It had only made him uneasily talkative in Dimble's presence and anxious to please. . . . For Mark liked to be liked. A snub sent him away dreaming not of revenge but of brilliant jokes or achievements which would one day conquer the good will of the man who had snubbed him. If he were ever cruel it would be downwards, to inferiors and outsiders who solicited his regard, not upwards to those who rejected it."

47. *What Wives Wish Their Husbands Knew about Women* (Wheaton: Tyndale House, 1975), 24. He continues: "I can hardly respect myself, obviously, if the rest of the world seems to believe that I am dumb or ugly or lazy or boring or uncreative or undesirable" (ibid.). See further 22–41.

48. See p. 54, where reference was made to 1 Cor. 7:5; 2 Cor. 2:11; Eph. 4:27; and 1 Tim. 5:14–15.

49. A person currently experiencing an especially hard relationship might think that death would bring welcome relief. But that can hardly be the case if, as Paul teaches (2 Cor. 5:1–10), death also causes the disintegration of the self; and if, as he also teaches (Rom. 14:7), selfhood is achieved in relation to other selves.

"the truth that is in Jesus," I can heed Paul's admonition to "be transformed by the renewing of [my] mind" (Rom. 12:2; Eph. 4:20–24).

Let us imagine ourselves at a dinner party. We hardly need to be reminded of the various threats and pressures in such a situation; most of us know them from painful experience. If we are slaves of Sin, we cannot really enjoy the party. We lack the freedom to do so; joy is a fruit of the Spirit, not a work of the flesh. We shall be too self-centered, and consequently too preoccupied with the impressions that we are making on the other guests, and too concerned with the approval or the disapproval that we are gaining, by our appearance or conversation or accomplishments. The ego's strategy in the social battle will vary, depending on one's particular temperament. One of two things is likely to happen, and both are equally egotistical. Either we will assert ourselves, seeking by such a means as gossip or wit or verbosity to establish our centrality or supremacy. Or else we will withdraw ourselves, perhaps by leaving the room or by hiding behind a facial or verbal or sartorial façade. Either response bespeaks an insecurity born of slavery to Sin, and a fear in the face of persons who are viewed as threats to the health or the stability of one's ego.[50]

But if we have become slaves of Christ the Lord, and if on this occasion the reality of this relationship is shaping our thinking (and consequently our feelings and our conduct), the effect can be very different. Being transformed by the renewing of our minds means discovering, amid the practical exigencies of a dinner party, that our security comes from Christ, not from ourselves or from the other guests. We no longer require their acceptance and approval. We are free to risk rejection. For we know that God, the one whose approval matters most, "chose us in [Christ] before the creation of the world [and] predestined us to be adopted as his sons through Jesus Christ" (Eph. 1:4–5 NIV), a bond from which nothing, least of all the indifference or contempt of others, can separate us (Rom. 8:31–39). Our sense of well-being no longer depends upon the praise of other people. For we know that God, the only one whose judgment ultimately matters, has purposed to glorify his people—to honor them, to declare their worth, by virtue of their union with his beloved Son.

The point is that until we have been freed from other people, we cannot be free for them (1 Cor. 9:19). Those who have been liberated from the other guests at the dinner party are the persons best equipped to establish and to maintain genuine relationships. They are free to be real, to be instead of merely to seem. There is no further need to pretend. Those whose hearts

---

50. On our social life as an ongoing game whereby we conceal the "person" behind the "personage," see Paul Tournier, *The Meaning of Persons*, trans. Edwin Hudson (New York: Harper and Row, 1957), 28–39. Cf. Eric Berne, *Games People Play: The Psychology of Human Relationships* (New York: Grove, 1964).

are given unreservedly to Christ are the very ones capable of loving other human beings most freely and most deeply.[51]

The Law of God: Bondage and Freedom

The law of God, like its Giver, is holy, righteous, and good; yet in the hands of Sin even God's holy law becomes an instrument of destruction (Rom. 7:7–13). How often has the fifth commandment, "Honor your father and your mother" (Exod. 20:12), been invoked as an excuse for enslaving a child to a parent? Paul's application of that command is taken up in chapter 8. For now we focus on the fourth commandment, "Remember the Sabbath day, to keep it holy" (Exod. 20:8–11); which seems an apt choice, given Paul's own references to the Sabbath in Romans 14 and Colossians 2. Four questions are pertinent.

1. Whose law am I obeying? Does it come from God? or is it human in origin? The "elemental spirits" (stoicheia, Col. 2:8, 20) seek through human agencies to subjugate persons to purely human teaching in the guise of divine law. Such rules—"Do not handle! Do not taste! Do not touch!"—are "all destined to perish with use, because they are based on human commands and teachings" (Col. 2:20–22 NIV). How many Christians have become shackled to purely human traditions about Sabbath observance in the firm conviction that they possess divine authority, thus falling prey to a "hollow and deceptive philosophy" propagated by the spirits (Col. 2:8)?

2. Who is my master? Is it Christ, or the demonic powers? Under the latter, allegiance to the fourth commandment is certain to generate misery rather than the intended joy (Isa. 58:13–14). How often have human beings, assured that they are championing God's cause, actually used this command to bring people under their own power, thereby revealing that they have been influenced (however unwittingly) by the spirits? But Paul is addressing persons who with Christ "died to the elemental spirits of the universe" (Col. 2:20 NRSV), and who are now bound instead to Christ who is head (kephalē) both over the church and "over every ruler and authority," including the elemental spirits (1:18; 2:8–15, 19). As an instrument of his

---

51. "The person who is still bound to sin and enslaved to others is not free to truly love his neighbor. . . . When we are free from the control of our neighbor, we are able to obey God. And as we obey God with a single heart, we are given a new power and desire to serve our neighbor, from whom we are now free" (Richard J. Foster, *Freedom of Simplicity* [San Francisco: Harper and Row, 1981], 62, 63). C. S. Lewis, *Mere Christianity* (New York: Macmillan, 1954), 173, says that Christians "love you more than other men do, but they need you less." For practical help in being freed from slavery to other persons (notably parents and spouses), and being controlled by God instead, see Robert Hemfelt, Frank Minirth, and Paul Meier, *Love Is a Choice: Recovery for Codependent Relationships* (Nashville: Nelson, 1989). Their closing counsel (270–75) is to be utterly dependent on God and fully surrendered to Christ. "With His love encompassing you, you need no longer tie yourself in the codependent knots of an unhealthy relationship, grasping, enmeshing, suffocating and being suffocated"; instead, you may now at long last freely choose to love other persons (275).

gracious rule, the Sabbath becomes a channel for the life-giving Spirit, and one means by which Christ's people may show their gratitude for salvation (Rom. 8:1–4). Moreover, under the dominion of the One "in whom are hidden all the treasures of wisdom and knowledge" (Col. 2:3), his people can more readily distinguish the purity of the divine commandment from the accretions of human tradition. Colossians 2:16–23 does not recommend that the fourth commandment be abandoned; but it does insist that the salutary use of the command depends upon the most intimate union with Christ the head, and alertness to the ongoing threat of the deceptive powers.

3. How do I obey? If Paul is not advocating that the Sabbath command be jettisoned, how does he counsel readers to obey it? We have just seen that the command must be viewed christologically. It must also be viewed eschatologically—that is, in the full awareness that the last days have been inaugurated with Christ's coming. Paul respects Jewish Christians whose way of honoring Christ is to regard "one day [in this case, the Sabbath] more important than another" (Rom. 14:5–6). But he also considers such a person's faith, albeit genuine and sincere, to be "weak" (14:1). The strong (in Paul's mind, truly so) understand more fully than the weak that Old Testament Sabbath regulations are a shadow pointing to the reality that is Christ (Col. 2:16–17); and that Jesus' coming marks the dawn of the great Sabbath Age to which all prior history pointed. Those who are inattentive to that great epochal shift are bound to interpret the fourth commandment as "letter" rather than as sacred "writing."[52] The new insight afforded by the Spirit (Rom. 7:1–6) makes it possible to "consider every day alike" (14:5). The "hallowed" character once reserved for the Sabbath is now extended to all other days of the week. Yet the Sabbath Age is only inaugurated. While the present order of creation continues, and until the eschatological tension is finally resolved, the creation ordinance of the Sabbath rest remains in effect. One can esteem all days alike (as just indicated) and at the same time recognize that human beings *as creatures* urgently need the Sabbath rest.[53] At the same time, the Sabbath rest must not be riveted to a particular day, as though the efficacy of the rest depended on its being

52. See the discussion on p. 133. John Calvin, *Institutes of the Christian Religion*, ed. John T. McNeill, trans. Ford Lewis Battles (Philadelphia: Westminster, 1960), 395–401, distinguishes three conditions in which the keeping of the fourth commandment consists. The first was the foreshadowing of the spiritual rest that would be fully realized in Christ. "It would seem . . . that the Lord through the seventh day has sketched for his people the coming perfection of his Sabbath in the Last Day"(396). Now that the reality has come, the shadow is no longer needed (397).

53. Neither in Rom. 14 nor anywhere else does Paul call into question the ongoing validity of this principle. Indeed his acute awareness of the mortality of the body (*sōma*) represents tacit approval of God's provision of rest. Calvin's second condition, one which remains "equally applicable to every age," is that the sabbath offers "surcease from labor" (*Institutes*, 398). Cf. John Murray, *Principles of Conduct* (Grand Rapids: Eerdmans, 1957), 30–35.

observed on this day instead of that.[54] But what of persons who stand, as I do, within a tradition that identifies the first day of the week as the Christian Sabbath, the day now appointed for rest as surely as the seventh used to be? Such persons may freely relinquish the freedom, or the right, to choose another day. Their conscience has not been violated; their understanding of Paul remains unchanged. Yet it is to Christ alone that they are bound, not to a view of the fourth commandment; and they make their choice, both because it is convenient and also in genuine support of believers who are otherwise persuaded.[55]

4. What is my motive? If I am under the mastery of other people (perhaps having been duped into thinking that slavery to them is tantamount to slavery to Christ), whose approval is therefore vital for my self-esteem, there is a danger that my conduct on Sundays will owe more to the judgments of my fellow Christians than to those of Christ. "Therefore do not let anyone judge you by what you eat or drink, or with regard to a religious festival, a New Moon celebration or a Sabbath day" (Col. 2:16 NIV): Christ alone is your Head and Judge (Col. 2:19; Rom. 14:1–12). Furthermore, if I dissociate the fourth commandment from Paul's gospel and Paul's eschatology, there is a danger that I shall view Sabbath-keeping as a way to curry the divine favor or atone for my guilty past (Col. 2:13–15), forgetting that my adherence to the law rests upon God's gracious initiative (Rom. 8:1–8). But once the gospel has me in its mighty grip (1:16–17), the way is open for a new motivation: to seize upon the Sabbath rest as opportunity to celebrate the wonders of grace with weak and strong alike.

Ethical Choices: Bondage and Freedom

Let us apply Paul's counsel about eating "food sacrificed to idols" to the contemporary question, often hotly debated among Christians, about alcoholic beverages. In light of the "knowledge" that we have gained from

54. Calvin's third condition is that God appointed the Sabbath for his people to gather for worship and teaching (*Institutes*, 395). This principle remains in effect for God's people, together with the principle of rest. However, with Christ's coming the choice of day becomes a matter not of law but of convenience. To insist on a particular day is to perpetuate "crass and carnal Sabbatarian superstition" (ibid., 400) not unlike that which Paul combats in Gal. 4:10 and Col. 2:16. The weak of Rom. 14 seem to have considered the strong to be insufficiently "sabbatarian." Some of the material in this paragraph is drawn from J. Knox Chamblin, "The Law of Moses and the Law of Christ," *Continuity and Discontinuity*, ed. John S. Feinberg (Westchester, Ill.: Crossway, 1988), 196, 370.

55. The Westminster *Confession of Faith*, prior to calling the first day of the week "the Christian Sabbath" (chap. 23), declares that "God alone is Lord of the conscience" (chap. 23, including Rom. 14:4 as a prooftext). From earliest times Christians assembled for worship on "the first day of the week" (1 Cor. 16:2; Acts 20:7), that is, "the Lord's Day" (Rev. 1:10), in honor of Christ's resurrection. Yet nowhere does the NT call the first day of the week the Christian Sabbath, or prescribe it as the day of rest. (This is good news for a pastor accustomed to preaching three times on Sunday morning.) See the discussions in D. R. deLacey, "The Sabbath/Sunday Question and the Law in the Pauline Corpus," in *From Sabbath to Lord's Day: A Biblical, Historical, and Theological Investigation*, ed. D. A. Carson (Grand Rapids: Zondervan, 1982), 159–95; and A. T. Lincoln, "From Sabbath to Lord's Day: A Biblical and Theological Perspective," ibid., 342–412.

1 Corinthians, we may say that wine is a good gift from God, brought forth from the earth for his people's enjoyment (1 Cor. 10:26; cf. 1 Tim. 4:3–5).

But there are Christians who "have not that knowledge"; whose sole acquaintance with alcohol has been within a context of paganism; for some of whom heavy drinking was an integral part of an indulgent or a wanton past; and who therefore cannot dissociate such a practice from a pagan worldview. Moreover, there are Christians for whom alcohol continues to threaten manifold destruction, and for whom even a minimal use of such drink would pose the risk of a return to alcoholism. But even those with the knowledge must be on guard. For we have also learned from Paul not to dishonor our bodies (1 Cor. 6:9–20); to beware lest too confident an exercise of liberty enslave us to a power other than Christ (10:12); and to avoid drunkenness (Eph. 5:18).

Thus we conclude that abstinence is the virtue of the weak and temperance the virtue of the strong. But situations may arise in which the strong are called upon to relinquish their right to a moderate use of alcohol, for the sake of weak fellow believers. The strong do not hereby violate their consciences. Their knowledge remains the same (they do not trade the teaching of 1 Corinthians 10:26 for the view that wine comes from the devil); and they do not conclude that what was once considered a right is really a wrong. But they freely relinquish the right (without invalidating it) out of deference to the sensibilities and vulnerabilities of weaker believers (10:25–30).

Let us imagine that my wife and I have just begun to serve (as my wife's sister and her husband have in fact served for many years) as missionaries to native North Americans in British Columbia. Among them alcoholism is rampant: it enslaves people; it swallows up money; it destroys families; it begets violence; it is associated in the closest way with philosophical and practical paganism. My wife and I used to enjoy an occasional glass of wine with a meal. But as we embark upon this particular ministry, we decide to become teetotalers. We still believe that a moderate use of wine is our right—also that it is a right which we have the right freely to surrender out of respect for the weak believers (actual and potential) among whom we serve. We do not have to drink wine (just as Paul did not have to eat flesh); slavery to Christ is commanded, slavery to wine forbidden.

The Ongoing Struggle

It has been said that insecure people make poor servants. Paul speaks of finding security in slavery to Christ, who grants the liberty needed to serve other people effectively—just as a person once bound to thievery but now freed for purposeful activity has "something to share with those in need" (Eph. 4:28). Yet grasping the practical implications of the principle for a host of ethical decisions, and then seeking to apply them, is likely to be a painfully slow process. For me at least, it has been one thing to grasp the idea, and quite another to live accordingly. The spiritually mature may have difficulty identifying with the struggles of us who are less advanced. "It is hard for a free fish to understand what is happening to a hooked one."[56]

Yet in the human arena, unlike the aquatic, the struggle is not the end of freedom but the way to freedom. As we strive to grow, let us purpose to do three things.

1. Be answerable to Christ the Lord. Christians pledge their supreme allegiance to him alone. His redeemed slaves are duty-bound to obey his commands; when they do, they discover their true liberty.[57] "Fear him, ye saints, and you will then have nothing else to fear; make his service your delight, your want shall be his care."[58] As the divine Arbitrator exercises his gracious rule and bestows his liberating power, the effect is a sense of equilibrium and stability at the center of one's being, especially in face of the clamorous demands of the self upon the self.[59]

2. Be appropriating the Spirit's power. The antidote to "the works of the flesh" is "the fruit of the Spirit." It is not enough to recognize and to explain the presence of jealousy and anger and the like in our lives. What we need is their destruction by the Spirit of God (Rom. 8:13), and his cultivating in their place such qualities as "patience, kindness, goodness, faithfulness, gentleness and self-control" (Gal. 5:22–23 NIV). For Paul there is no contradiction between reliance upon the Holy Spirit and the exertions of obedience. On the contrary, it is vital that the two be joined together.[60]

3. Be available to other people. "The man who is liberated from himself ... perceives his neighbor. His life becomes, like the life of his Lord, vicarious service for all fallen, perverted and subjugated creatures."[61] He or she is free, as Paul was, to run risks, to move out into relationships with all kinds of people, both within and beyond the church, including relation-

56. Karl Menninger, quoted in Chaim Potok, *The Chosen* (New York: Simon and Schuster, 1967), 7.

57. "If we want to be disciples, we place ourselves, like the football player and the instrumentalist, under someone's direction. He tells us what to do, and we find our happiness in doing it. . . . Freedom lies in keeping the rules" (Elisabeth Elliot, *Discipline, the Glad Surrender* (Old Tappan, N.J.: Revell, [1982]), 37.

58. Nahum Tate and Nicholas Brady, "Through all the Changing Scenes of Life" (1696).

59. "Within all of us is a whole conglomerate of selves. There is the timid self, the courageous self, the business self, the parental self, the religious self, the literary self, the energetic self. And all of these selves are rugged individualists. [But when Christ lives as the Center], our many selves come under the unifying control of the divine Arbitrator. . . . Everything becomes oriented to this new Center of reference. . . . [O]ur many selves have been stilled by the Holy Within" (Foster, *Simplicity*, 80–81).

60. Rom. 8:13 ("if by the Spirit you put to death the misdeeds of the body . . ."); Phil. 2:12–13. Jerry Bridges, *The Pursuit of Holiness* (Colorado Springs: NavPress, 1978), well brings out the Bible's insistence that one grows in holiness by both trusting and obeying God. Cf. 1 Cor. 10:13–14.

61. Ernst Käsemann, "On Paul's Anthropology," *Perspectives on Paul*, trans. Margaret Kohl (Philadelphia: Fortress, 1971), 30.

ships that appear at the outset to be the most threatening and the most hopeless.[62] Even there—or especially there—we shall discover that the power of the Master is made perfect in the weakness of the slave (2 Cor. 12:9–10).

> *Make me a captive, Lord, and then I shall be free;*
> *Force me to render up my sword, and I shall conqueror be.*
> *I sink in life's alarms, when by myself I stand;*
> *Imprison me within Thine arms, and strong shall be my hand.*
>
> *My heart is weak and poor, until it master find;*
> *It has no spring of action sure—it varies with the wind.*
> *It cannot freely move, till Thou hast wrought its chain;*
> *Enslave it with Thy matchless love, and deathless it shall reign.*[63]

---

62. Lawrence J. Crabb, Jr., *Understanding People* (Grand Rapids: Zondervan, 1987), 196, judges that "a mature pattern of relating involves whatever actions represent the abandonment of self-protection." Sheldon Vanauken recalls how, in the days of his newfound faith at Oxford University, he was surrounded by "Catholics and Evangelicals and Atheists and all shades of Betwixts and Betweens, all talking happily and spiritedly on equal terms" (*A Severe Mercy* [San Francisco: Harper and Row, 1977], 113).

63. George Matheson, "Make Me a Captive, Lord" (1890).

7

The Christian Struggle

Christ's conquest of Sin, and believers' consequent liberation from its power, is an accomplished fact: "we died to Sin" (Rom. 6:2); God "rescued us from the tyranny of darkness and brought us into the kingdom of his beloved Son" (Col. 1:13). Yet the fight against Sin, like every other aspect of the Christian life, testifies to the "already" and the "not yet" of eschatology. The decisive battle was fought and won in Christ's death and resurrection, but the war will last until his triumphant return.

From the standpoint of believers' actual experience, the real war commences with incorporation into Christ. Their lives now become daily battlegrounds for the ongoing war between Christ and Sin. Moreover, as they seek to grow in holiness and to resist the unrelenting assaults of Sin through the flesh, the law and the demonic host, the struggle not merely persists but intensifies—offering hope in the process of outbreaks of the Spirit's power more than enough to quell that of the opposition.

We have already considered Paul's own *agōn*.[1] We shall now look at his portrayal of the *agōn* in store for all Christians.

The Call to Faithfulness

God's promises are harmonious with his commands. The indicatives of the gospel are inextricably joined to, and foundational for, the imperatives

---

1. For Paul's apostolic *agōn* within the context of his eschatology, see chap. 1.

of Christian living. "In Christ" (*en Christō*) chiefly denotes the indicative, believers' incorporation into Christ; "in the Lord" (*en Kyriō*), denotes the imperative, the outworkings of that union in Christian behavior.[2]

As Paul implores his hearers to trust in God and to believe the gospel, so he summons them to lives of unswerving allegiance to Christ's lordship and unquestioning obedience to his commands. Those upon whom Christ has shined are duty bound to "live as children of light [and to] discover what is pleasing to the Lord" (Eph. 5:8–14). One cannot rely on the word of promise and simultaneously reject the word of command (1 Cor. 10:13–14). The *pistis* of faith is inseparable from, and manifests itself in, the *pistis* of faithfulness.[3] "You were bought with a price [the good news of redemption]. Therefore honor God with your body [the consequent ethical demand]" (1 Cor. 6:20). "Therefore, I urge you . . . in view of God's mercy, to offer your bodies as living sacrifices, holy and pleasing to God. . . . Never be lacking in zeal, but keep your spiritual fervor, serving (*douleuontes*) the Lord" (Rom. 12:1, 11 NIV). God's mercy kindles the zeal; the servitude gives it expression. Titus is to insist "that those who have trusted in God may be careful to devote themselves to good works" (Titus 3:8).

Dependence on God is fully compatible with human exertions.[4] The Christian is not passive but fully cooperates with God for achieving the divine purpose. "Offer yourselves to God. . . . You have become enslaved to God" (Rom. 6:13, 22). "As you have always obeyed . . . work out your own salvation with fear and trembling, for God is the one working in you both to will and to work for his good purpose" (Phil. 2:12–13; cf. 4:13). "For we are God's workmanship, created in Christ Jesus to do good works, which God prepared in advance for us to do" (Eph. 2:10 NIV)—but which do not become a reality until we take action. Paul both urges Timothy to "be strong in the grace that is in Christ Jesus," and summons him to the devotion of the soldier, the discipline of the athlete, and the toil of the farmer (2 Tim. 2:1–6). "If by the Spirit you put to death the misdeeds of the body, you will live" (Rom. 8:13). "If we live by the Spirit [declarative], let us also walk by the Spirit [hortatory]" (Gal. 5:25). Ephesians 5:18 joins passive voice to imperative mood: "be filled with the Spirit."[5]

---

2. For this distinction, see C. F. D. Moule, *The Origin of Christology* (Cambridge: Cambridge University Press, 1977), 58–60.

3. *Pistis* is used in the first sense in Gal. 2:16 (NIV, "faith"), in the second in Gal. 5:22 (NIV, "faithfulness"); cf. 5:6, "faith expressing itself through love." The Hebrew *'emunah* likewise embraces both trust and fidelity.

4. "*Moral effort is in no way antithetical to faith*; it is rather the outworking and expression of faith" (James D. G. Dunn, *Romans* [Dallas: Word, 1988], 350; the emphasis is his).

5. Moreover, the tense is present. "The fullness of the Spirit is not a once-for-all experience which we can never lose, but a privilege to be renewed . . . by continuous believing and obedient appropriation" (John R. W. Stott, *God's New Society* [Downers Grove: InterVarsity, 1979], 209).

The incarnation of truth in the life of obedience witnesses to the transforming power of the gospel. How firmly the gospel has been grasped will be evident from the way one lives. Paul speaks of "the knowledge of the truth that leads to godliness" (Titus 1:1 NIV), and warns of those who "profess to know God but by their actions deny him" (1:16). He exhorts Timothy to "set an example for believers . . . in conduct, in love, in faith" (1 Tim. 4:12), and to "watch [his] life and teaching closely" (4:16).

In other words, there is no division in Paul's thinking between Christ as Savior and Christ as Lord. How could there be? It is by exercising his lordship that Christ saves his people from Sin and death (Rom. 5:12–21). "If you confess with your mouth that Jesus is Lord, and believe in your heart that God raised him from the dead, you will be saved" (10:9).[6] It is the very "grace of God that brings salvation" which teaches believers "to say 'No' to ungodliness and worldly passions, and to live self-controlled, upright and godly lives in the present age" (Titus 2:11–12 NIV); that same grace energizes them to do so (1 Cor. 15:9–10). To say yes to ungodliness is a serious affront to saving grace, and puts one in grave danger. Christ saved his people from wickedness, for the express purpose that they might be "eager to do what is good" (Titus 2:14); Christ's commands provide avenues along which the eagerness may find practical expression. Allegiance to the Master is the believer's means of offering thanks for salvation by grace.

Slavery to Sin, far from affording escape from personal responsibility, comes about through the self's willful surrender to Sin's demands. The same holds true (*mutatis mutandis*) for the slaves of Christ. Ethical decisions matter; we shall be answerable for them on the day of judgment (1 Cor. 3:12–15; 2 Cor. 5:10). Moreover, just as Sin exploited the self's unity in diversity, so Christ calls for the dedication of the whole person—corporeal and incorporeal; internal and external; heart and body; mind, emotions and will—in the life of obedience as in the initial response of faith. Paul prays that his readers may have "knowledge and all insight," so that, having discerned "what is best," their conduct may be blameless and righteous (Phil. 1:9–11). The prayer of Colossians 1:9–11 calls for the activating of the mind (v. 9), the will (v. 10), and the emotions (v. 11, "with joy"). Christ does not merely tug on our emotions, asking only that we be moved by the story of his sacrifice or excited by his triumph over death. Nor does he merely inform us of his way. Here, as with bondage to Sin, the critical factor is the mobilizing of the will: "offer your bodies" (Rom. 12:1); "flee from idolatry" (1 Cor. 10:14); "flee the evil desires of youth, and pursue righteousness, faith, love, and peace" (2 Tim. 2:22; cf. 1 Tim. 6:11). Enduring hardship like a soldier or athlete or farmer (2 Tim. 2:3–6) calls for the cooperation of all

---

6. To confess "Jesus is Lord" is to affirm his deity (cf. chap. 2, p. 39), and therefore his sovereignty over one's life.

the self's faculties, and especially for the exertions of the will.[7] Standing on the promises is one thing, sitting on the premises quite another.

The Call to Holiness

Faithfulness to Christ manifests itself in a life of holiness. The call to be saintly or holy pertains not just to a select company of Christians (the error of certain of Paul's opponents), but to every one of Christ's purchased possessions.

Heeding the Call

Like every other aspect of Paul's theology, holiness is to be understood within the context of eschatology. "Holiness" describes what happens both at the threshold of Christian experience and throughout the life there begun. Those who are "called [by God] to be saints" (*klētois hagiois*, Rom. 1:7; 1 Cor. 1:2), are "holy" by virtue of the call—persons whom God sets apart to serve him: "you were sanctified" (*hēgiasthēte*) by God (1 Cor. 6:11, a reference to Christian initiation, like the flanking clauses *you were washed* and *you were justified*). Yet integral to that same call is the command that converts honor Christ throughout the life on which they now embark. By obeying God amid a multitude of ethical decisions, they become holy in their conduct.[8]

Paul sounds this call throughout his letters. "This is the will of God, that you should be holy (*hagiasmos*). . . . For God called us to holiness, not to impurity" (1 Thess. 4:3, 7 NEB). "Just as you used to offer the parts of your body in slavery to impurity and to ever-increasing wickedness, so now offer them in slavery to righteousness leading to holiness. . . . But now that you have been set free from sin and have become slaves to God, the benefit you reap leads to holiness, and the result is eternal life" (Rom. 6:19, 22 NIV). Just as "the truth that is in Jesus," namely, "the word of truth, the gospel," opposes every contrary belief system, so Christians' pattern of conduct is to be radically different from the old way of life (Eph. 1:13; 4:17–32).

---

7. In C. S. Lewis, *The Screwtape Letters* (New York: Macmillan, 1953), 37, Screwtape counsels Wormwood: "Think of your man as a series of concentric circles, his will being the innermost, his intellect coming next, and finally his fantasy. . . . You must keep on shoving all the virtues outward till they are finally located in the circle of fantasy, and all the desirable qualities inward into the Will. It is only in so far as they reach the will and are there embodied in habits that the virtues are really fatal to us." The devil does not care if our fantasy is full of "the fruit of the Spirit," so long as our wills are motivated to do "the works of the flesh."

8. By the same token, Paul is "called to be an apostle" (*klētos apostolos*, Rom. 1:1; 1 Cor. 1:1): he is an apostle by virtue of the divine commission (Gal. 1:15), and he becomes one by actually going forth as missionary to the Gentiles. On the dual sense of "holiness" as standing and behavior, see Horst Seebass and Colin Brown, "Holy [etc.]," *NIDNTT* 2:223–32.

The call that "sets them apart" in the first place, remains effectually at work throughout believers' lives, spurring them to steadfastness. "May God himself . . . sanctify (*hagiasai*) you wholly. May your whole spirit, soul and body be kept blameless. . . . The one who calls you is faithful and he will do this" (1 Thess. 5:23–24). Working in, by, with, and under all human exertions is the saving God, ineluctably carrying forward his purpose by his power (Phil. 1:6; 2:12–13).[9]

Restoring the Image

God calls persons away from conformity to this age into conformity to the image of his Son, by the transforming power of his Spirit (Rom. 12:2; 8:29; 2 Cor. 3:18). God's purpose is that they shall thereby be equipped to do the "good works" which he has appointed for his human creation from the beginning (Eph. 2:10); and that they shall manifest the qualities of "true righteousness and holiness" to which Adam and Eve had been called (Eph. 4:24). In other words, God's design is not so much the cultivation of personality as the growth of character.[10] The latter occurs, not by preoccupation with "the image of man," or with one's "self-image," but by attentiveness to "the image of God" and to Christ, its perfect bearer. The apostle calls his readers to holiness of life for the singular purpose that they may become increasingly conformed to the likeness of Christ, the eventual effect of which will be not the abolition of the self but its full realization.[11]

Persons "called to be holy," set apart to God through union with Christ, are thereby granted restored knowledge of the triune God, both as *savoir* and as *connaître* (as we saw at the close of chap. 4). Upon this, every other experience of knowledge depends—just as when the sun rises on a clear day, we behold both the light of the sun and, in its light, everything else. The person whose highest aspiration is to know and love God ("first things") is prepared to understand and to delight in the creation ("second things"). But to ignore or suppress first things, and to treat second things as though they were first things, threatens one with the loss of both first and second things.[12] "The body is not meant for sexual immorality, but for the Lord" (1 Cor. 6:13): under his ownership and direction, the body is

---

9. On holiness as a gift of God's grace, see Jerry Bridges, *Transforming Grace: Living Confidently in God's Unfailing Love* (Colorado Springs: NavPress, 1991), 101–17.

10. "Alas, the modern age is concerned with 'personality' rather than character [the latter being the object of the much-derided 'Victorian morality']" (George F. Will, *Newsweek*, 17 June 1991, 70). Stephen R. Covey, *The Seven Habits of Highly Effective People* (New York: Simon and Schuster, 1989), traces a shift from a "character ethic" (the first 150 years of our nation's history) to a "personality ethic" (the past 50 years), and urges a return to the former.

11. See Dick Keyes, *Beyond Identity: Finding Your Self in the Image and Character of God* (Ann Arbor: Servant, 1984).

12. See Rom. 1:18–32; and C. S. Lewis, "First and Second Things," in *God in the Dock*, ed. Walter Hooper (Grand Rapids: Eerdmans, 1970), 278–81.

meant for sex itself (6:19–20; 7:2–5). "Demas, in love with this present world, has deserted me and gone to Thessalonica," reports Paul (2 Tim. 4:10 NRSV). Demas risks losing not only God and his servant Paul, but also the world to which he has unreservedly given himself (behind "love" is *agapaō*). It is not in fact the world as God's creation that he loves, but "the present age" (*ton nun aiōna*), life in the world (*kosmos*) as affected by the rule of Sin (Gal. 1:4; Eph. 2:2). Nothing less than love for God (Rom. 8:28, *agapaō*) frees fallen human beings from a distorted view of the world and an illicit use of creation. The Christian must therefore, at whatever cost and by however strenuous an effort, maintain communion with God and loyalty to Christ. Growth in holiness in this respect is critical for all others.[13]

On that basis, the restoring of God's image entails respect for all human beings and especially for fellow believers, those in whom the image is being restored. "You were taught . . . to put on the new man, created to be like God in true righteousness and holiness. Therefore let each of you speak truth to his neighbor, for we are members of one another" (Eph. 4:22–25). "As we have opportunity, let us do good to all persons, especially to those who belong to the household of faith" (Gal. 6:10). Reading this verse in the light of the rest of Galatians makes it plain that Paul is not speaking in mere generalities. "As many of you as were baptized into Christ have clothed yourself with Christ," he declares in 3:27. That statement of fact is followed immediately by another: "There is neither Jew nor Greek, there is neither slave nor free, there is neither male nor female; for you are all one in Christ Jesus" (3:28 NKJV). Efforts to realize those indicatives in personal relationships, whether in Paul's day or in ours, puts Christians' commitment to one of its sternest tests but at the same time offers hope of incontrovertible evidence that the image of God is being restored.[14]

With the restored knowledge of God comes a new capacity to see his handiwork and benevolence in the natural world. "For everything God created is good, and nothing is to be rejected if it is received with thanksgiving, because it is consecrated by the word of God and prayer" (1 Tim. 4:4–5 NIV). There is also a deepened awareness of human responsibility to exercise dominion over the rest of creation (Gen. 1:28); for the enjoyment of foods, which God created (1 Tim. 4:3), entails human toil (1 Cor. 9:10; cf. 3:7).[15] Believers grow in holiness, not in some spiritual stratosphere, but

---

13. Exod. 20:3. For what happens when the first commandment is disobeyed, see Rom. 1:18–32. Jerry Bridges, *The Practice of Godliness* (Colorado Springs: NavPress, 1983), 66, says of Phil. 3:10, that Paul "wants both Christ-centeredness and Christlikeness. This is godliness: God-centeredness, or devotion to God; and Godlikeness, or Christian character."

14. Richard N. Longenecker's *New Testament Social Ethics for Today* (Grand Rapids: Eerdmans, 1984), is largely built on the triad of Gal. 3:28.

15. On the basis of Gen. 1:26–28, Anthony A. Hoekema, *Created in God's Image* (Grand Rapids: Eerdmans, 1986), 75–82, speaks of man the image of God in a threefold relationship—to God, to his fellow men, and to nature.

amid the concrete demands of daily obligations in the world. "Our people must learn to devote themselves to doing what is good, in order that they may provide for daily necessities and not live unproductive lives" (Titus 3:14 NIV). Invoking his own example, Paul admonishes the idle "to work quietly and earn the bread they eat" (2 Thess. 3:6–13), lest undue strain be put on others.

Responsibilities to people and to nature are joined in Paul's teachings about exercising and submitting to authority.

The church. Elders are exhorted to be wise and temperate in their leadership (1 Tim. 3:1–7), to be "self-controlled, upright, holy and self-disciplined" (Titus 1:8). Members are urged to respect their leaders, to "hold them in the highest esteem in love because of their work" (1 Thess. 5:12–13), and to honor their right to payment for their services (1 Cor. 9:9–14).[16]

The home. To qualify for service in the church, the elder "must manage his own household well" (1 Tim. 3:4–5), as must the deacon (3:12). The father is to respect his children and to "bring them up in the training and instruction of the Lord" (Eph. 6:4; cf. Col. 3:21), and to see that they in turn "obey him with all respect" (1 Tim. 3:4). Failure to provide for one's family is a denial of the faith (1 Tim. 5:8). Women are counseled to "have children, to manage their homes" (1 Tim. 5:14), a twin fulfillment of Genesis 1:28. Wives and mothers are challenged to "continue in faith, love and holiness with decency" (1 Tim. 2:15), "to love their husbands and children . . . [and] to be working at home" (Titus 2:4–5). In response children must obey and honor their parents (Eph. 6:1–3; Col. 3:20),[17] and in time provide needed care for them (1 Tim. 5:3–8, 16).

The workplace. As persons who are both accountable to Christ the Lord, master and slave are to treat one another with respect—the latter by industry and honesty, the former by justice and fairness (Eph. 6:5–9; Col. 3:22–4:1; Titus 2:9–10).[18]

The state. "The governing authorities" are in a special sense responsible for exercising dominion on God's behalf, and for doing so in accord with his moral law (Rom. 13:1–4). Accordingly, citizens owe them due honor and submission (13:5–7); and the authorities are among the neighbors whom believers are commanded to love (13:8–10).[19]

Paul's admonitions entail both personal and corporate responsibilities, for both the individual believer and the church as a whole partake of the

---

16. See the comments on 1 Cor. 9:9–10 at the close of chap. 4.

17. Cf. Titus 1:6 ("whose children . . . are not open to the charge of being wild and rebellious"); and 2 Tim. 3:2 ("disobedient to their parents, ungrateful, unholy").

18. The evidence of Philem. is taken up in chap. 8. For Paul's response to slavery in relation to today's world, see Peter Richardson, *Paul's Ethic of Freedom* (Philadelphia: Westminster, 1979), 40–56.

19. So too John Murray, *The Epistle to the Romans*, vol. 2 (Grand Rapids: Eerdmans, 1965), 159–61. Cf. Titus 3:1–2 ("Remind the people to be subject to rulers and authorities, to be obedient . . . to show true humility toward all men"). One mark of respect for rulers is to offer prayer on their behalf (1 Tim. 2:1–2).

restored image. Our main focus for now is the former; the latter is taken up in chapter 9.

Putting Off the Old, and Putting On the New

With a variety of images, Paul urges believers under his care to say a resolute no to certain practices, and to give themselves assiduously to holy living. Persons who have "died to Sin" and are now "alive to God" through union with Christ must stop offering the parts of their bodies to Sin "as instruments of wickedness," and offer them to God instead "as instruments of righteousness." Habits associated with life in Adam are to be "put off" or "put to death," and those compatible with life in Christ cultivated instead.[20] "Everyone who confesses the name of the Lord must turn away from wickedness," in order to become "an instrument for noble purposes, made holy, useful to the Master and prepared to do any good work" (2 Tim. 2:19–21 NIV). Grace instructs God's people to "say 'No' to ungodliness and worldly passions," and instead to "live self-controlled, upright and godly lives in the present age" (Titus 2:12 NIV). "Do not take part in the unfruitful works of darkness" in which you once walked, but instead "live as children of light" by showing forth "the fruit of the light in all goodness, righteousness, and truth" (Eph. 5:8–11).

Such commands sound a discordant note in many quarters today, even within a church that too readily allows the mentality of a "crooked and depraved generation" (Phil. 2:15) to determine moral standards. Particularly unpopular are the apostolic injunctions that persons who confess Christ as Lord should categorically reject certain practices.[21] The words "Put to death your members which are on the earth" (Col. 3:5 NKJV), demand action no less painful than literal amputation—the termination of conduct characteristic of "the present evil age." In today's climate, churchgoers understandably welcome a message that relieves pain; they do not so readily embrace one which inflicts it. Says Paul: "Don't let the world around you squeeze you into its own mold, but let God remold your minds from within" (Rom. 12:2 *Phillips*). One effect of the transformation is to realize that the crucifixion of the old man, and the excruciating pain inevitably associated with it, is essential if the person is to become whole (as the pain inflicted by surgery is designed to relieve a greater pain). In keeping with his own violent assault on the powers of darkness (Rom. 8:3; Col. 1:13; 2:14–15), Christ the King orders his subjects not to negotiate with

20. Cf., e.g., Rom. 6:1–14; Gal. 5:16–26; Eph. 4:22–24; Col. 3:1–14.

21. James D. Hunter, "Evangelicals: Strangers in a Strange Land," *RTS Ministry* (Winter 1989): 10, cites as an example of Christians' accommodation to contemporary society "attitudes toward the self. The traditional Protestant view of the self held it to be something to be denied and kept under control. . . . Today, any form of self-denial has been largely abandoned in favor of self-help books and therapeutic introspection. How can you deny the self when the self is constantly being examined, probed, and 'understood'?"

sins, or to declare a truce, but to fight them to the death—*their* death (Rom. 8:13; Col. 3:5).

Heeding "the whole counsel of God" as mediated by Paul safeguards us on the one hand from a moral reductionism in which ethical imperatives are loosed from their essential moorings in the great declarations of the gospel; and on the other hand from "cheap grace" (Dietrich Bonhoeffer's phrase), the effect when the gospel of salvation is severed from the attendant call to godly living. With the general admonitions ringing in our ears, we consider some particular areas in which Paul calls his readers to holy conduct.

Respecting the Body

Paul calls for a realistic view of the human body. It is not to be worshiped (its Creator is alone worthy of adoration), but neither is it to be despised (it is God's good creation).[22] It both belongs to a perishing order and is destined for resurrection. Recognizing its mortality, Paul can say that "physical training is of some value, but godliness has value for all things, holding promise for both the present life and the life to come" (1 Tim. 4:8 NIV). At the same time, it is this perishable body which Jesus has liberated from Sin's dominion, and which is therefore to be given unreservedly to his service (Rom. 6:11–23; 12:1; 1 Cor. 6:19–20); and it is for deeds done in this very body that the believer shall one day be judged (2 Cor. 5:10).

The body's mortality offers Christians not the slightest excuse for indulging its cravings or yielding it to Sin's directives. Paul censures persons whose master or god is "the stomach," that is, gluttony and the like.[23] "Do not get drunk with wine," he warns (Eph. 5:18). Drunkards will not inherit the kingdom (1 Cor. 6:10). Qualified elders and deacons must not be "given to much wine" (1 Tim. 3:2–3, 8; Titus 1:7), nor must the older women be so addicted (Titus 2:3). At the same time, slavery to Christ frees one to enjoy both food and drink as gifts of a gracious Creator.[24]

22. C. S. Lewis, *The Four Loves* (New York: Harcourt Brace Jovanovich, 1960), 142–43, rejecting the views both of the "ascetic Pagans," who think the body shameful, and of the "Neo-Pagans" who think it glorious, follows St. Francis in calling the body "Brother Ass": one can neither revere nor hate a donkey, "a useful, sturdy, lazy, obstinate, patient, lovable and infuriating beast . . . both pathetically and absurdly beautiful."

23. "For such people are enslaved (*douleuousin*), not to our Lord Christ, but to their own stomach" (Rom. 16:18); "their god is their stomach" (Phil. 3:19). F. W. Beare, *The Epistle to the Philippians* (New York: Harper and Row, 1959), 136, comments that "there is no need to go beyond the obvious meaning; these are people who are interested chiefly in the pleasures of the table—if not gluttons or drunkards, they are gourmets, with no thought of anything else in life." Paul never employs the word *phagos* (glutton).

24. The key terms are "enslavement," "much wine," and "addiction." Cf. 1 Tim. 5:23, "Stop drinking only water, and use a little wine for the sake of your stomach . . ."; the above comments on "first and second things"; and the comments in chap. 6, pp. 151–52. Paul never prescribes or prohibits fasting. It is uncertain whether the deprivations (*nēsteiai*) of 2 Cor. 11:27 are voluntary ("in fastings often," KJV) or involuntary ("often without food," RSV); cf. Ralph P. Martin, *2 Corinthians* (Waco: Word, 1986), 380.

With respect to the use of the body, sexuality is by far Paul's major concern. In his day, as in ours, sexual practices appear to have posed the most formidable threat to the holiness of the body. Paul repeatedly alerts readers to the dangers posed by a society in which sexual immorality is not only condoned but encouraged, celebrated, and blessed with religious sanctions.[25] He repeatedly warns Timothy against the lure of sexual sins.[26] In his catalogs of vices, forms of sexual immorality are typically placed first: Colossians 3:5–9 begins with "sexual immorality, impurity [and] lust"; Ephesians 5:3–5, with "sexual immorality [and] impurity"; Galatians 5:19–21, with "sexual immorality, impurity and debauchery"; and 1 Corinthians 6:9–10, with "fornicators, idolaters, adulterers, male prostitutes [and] sodomites" (NRSV).[27] So grave is the peril that believers must refrain from fellowship with professing Christians involved in such practices (1 Cor. 5:6–13). In 1 Thessalonians, the first matter taken up for instructing readers "how to live in order to please God" (4:1–12) is sexual fidelity in marriage (4:3b–6), the seriousness of which is accentuated by the enclosing words of verses 3b ("This is the will of God, your holiness") and 7 ("For God did not call us to impurity, but to holiness").[28] In 1 Corinthians Paul successively commands that an incestuous man be excommunicated (5:1–13); warns that union with a prostitute draws a member of the holy Christ into a most unholy and intimate alliance (6:15–18);[29] and teaches married believers that habitual attentiveness to the partner's sexual needs provides one safeguard against marital infidelity (7:1–9).[30]

25. Rom. 1:32 ("they not only do these things but also approve of those who practice them," with 1:24–27); Phil. 3:19 ("their glory is in their shame," probably an allusion to sexual misconduct); in which respects the church can outdo the world (1 Cor. 5:1–6). See Friedrich Hauck and Siegfried Schulz, *TDNT* 6:579–95.

26. "Set an example for believers . . . in purity" (1 Tim. 4:12); "Treat . . . younger women as sisters, with absolute purity" (5:1–2); "Flee the evil desires of youth" (2 Tim. 2:22).

27. The term *porneia*, translated "sexual immorality" in the preceding examples, can denote adultery, fornication, homosexuality, incest, and bestiality (Hauck and Schulz, *TDNT* 6:579–95). In a catalog that includes various sexual offenses, *porneia* (or its nominal counterpart *pornoi*) can denote "fornication" specifically, as in 1 Cor. 6:9–10. In this passage there are two terms for homosexual behavior, denoting the passive and active partners respectively (C. K. Barrett, *The First Epistle to the Corinthians* [New York: Harper and Row, 1968], 140). 1 Cor. 5 addresses a case of incest in the church (*porneia* occurs twice in 5:1). For the association of idolatry with both heterosexual and homosexual offenses, see (besides 1 Cor. 6) Rom. 1:18–32.

28. The word *hagiasmos* (holiness) occurs also in 4:4, linking the instances of vv. 3 and 7. Some think that Paul turns to matters of commerce in 4:6 (as it were from the seventh to the eighth commandment). I believe that the singular concern of 4:3–6 is sexual conduct. For the same view see, e.g., F. F. Bruce, *1 and 2 Thessalonians* (Waco: Word, 1982), 84–85.

29. The law of Gen. 2:24 holds true even in such an alliance as this (1 Cor. 6:16). Whereas drunkenness and gluttony (6:10) differ only in degree from legitimate satisfactions of thirst and hunger, it is the very fact of *porneia* which is sinful, not its frequency; the uniqueness and intimacy of the union makes it a "sin against the body" that is categorically different from the others (6:18).

30. Counsel about divorce follows (7:10–16). If the "concession" of 7:6 is the instruction of 7:5a, Paul is making it clear that couples need not deprive one another even "for a time"; and in no case is prayer to be an excuse for avoiding sexual responsibility in marriage.

Such passages make it plain that Paul encourages sexual passion within the marital bond. He declares that "the body is not meant for sexual immorality" (1 Cor. 6:13); but never does he say that the body as such is not meant for sex. The very reason for his urgent warnings against various kinds of *porneia* is that sex might be received on God's terms and therefore become a source of pleasure—both in itself and in its issue.[31] It is precisely because "restraining sensual indulgence" is vital that one must avoid "human commands and teachings" and cling instead to Christ, who stands ready to offer the gifts of marriage and children under his headship (Col. 2:16–3:21).[32] Contrary to the "doctrine of demons" that forbids people to marry, Paul views marriage, including its sexual dimension, as a bestowal of the Creator that is to be "received with thanksgiving" (1 Tim. 4:1–4). The joyous intimacy of the marital bond provides the closest earthly counterpart to the relationship of Christ to his church (Eph. 5:30–33).[33]

Controlling the Tongue

Given Paul's belief in the power of words divine, human, and demonic, it is not surprising that speech figures prominently in his calls to holiness. He urges believers to "put to death" language that gives vent to unrighteous anger; that voices irreverence to God and disrespect to persons made in his image, and disloyalty to both, by propagating falsehood; and that further expresses contempt or ridicule toward God's creation by speaking of sexuality and related matters in a vulgar or an obscene manner. Corresponding to what happens in actual speech, the various verbal offenses are often joined in Paul's admonitions. "But now you must rid yourselves of all such things as these: anger, rage, malice, slander, and filthy language from your lips. Do not lie to each other . . ." (Col. 3:8–9 NIV). "Nor should there be obscenity, foolish talk or coarse joking, which are out of place" (Eph. 5:4 NIV). The Pastoral Epistles warn against malicious and quick-tempered speech (1 Tim. 3:11; Titus 1:7), and against gossip and slander (1 Tim. 5:13; Titus 2:3; 3:2). Especially pernicious is the wedding of "godless chatter" to the propagation of false teaching (2 Tim. 2:16–18). To Paul's mind the most damnable of all utter-

---

31. See the preceding references to childbearing. The point of 1 Tim. 2:15 is not that a woman must become a mother in order to be saved, but that God offers his blessing at the very place of his judgment (Gen. 3:16).

32. In demanding "the harsh treatment of the body (*sōma*),"those pseudo-laws (propagated by the hostile spirits through human agencies) actually serve "the flesh" (*sarx*, 2:23). See Peter T. O'Brien, *Colossians, Philemon* (Waco: Word, 1982), 151–55.

33. Eph. 5:25–33, with its quotation of Gen. 2:24, is also Paul's strongest argument against homosexuality (see also Rom. 1:26–27; 1 Cor. 6:9–10; 1 Tim. 1:9–10). See John Stott, *Involvement II: Social and Sexual Relationships in the Modern World* (Old Tappan, N.J.: Revell, 1985), 215–44.

ances are those that oppose the Word of God, especially the *euangelion* but also the exhortations built upon it.[34]

As with Paul's ethical teachings generally, those commands have their positive counterpart. The vulgarities of the past are to be replaced by utterances of thanksgiving (Eph. 5:4). Now that they have "put off" rage, slander, and the like, let believers "put on" such qualities as "compassion, kindness, humility, gentleness and patience" (Col. 3:8, 12), each of which can find verbal expression. Whereas false teaching destroys, God's Word heals and restores. Especially is this so of the Word's great indicatives. The gospel is "the power of God for salvation" in the most comprehensive sense (Rom. 1:16). The church is nurtured when Christians speak to one another "the word of truth, the gospel of your salvation" (Eph. 1:13 with 4:15), together with the songs of praise that the gospel evokes (Eph. 5:18–19). "Therefore encourage each other with these words," says Paul (1 Thess. 4:18)—the words he has just written about Christ's return (4:13–17). Prophetic utterances imparted by the Spirit "speak to other people for their upbuilding and encouragement and consolation" (1 Cor. 14:3 NRSV). Paul calls on readers to honor the Word of God by actually declaring it, both to believers and to nonbelievers (Eph. 5:19; 6:15, 17); by presenting it courageously and persuasively (Phil. 1:14; Col. 4:3–6);[35] and by conducting themselves in a way that will not violate but visibly match what they say (Phil. 2:12–16).[36]

Employing Money and Material Things

Paul's teaching on this twofold subject is deeply rooted in both creation and redemption. On the one hand, faithfulness to the Creator prohibits worshiping and serving created things, and bondage to Christ leaves no room for slavery to money and to the things that money can buy. Veneration of self finds expression in devotion to money: in the last days people will be "lovers of themselves (*philautoi*), lovers of money (*philarguroi*), boastful, proud . . . " (2 Tim. 3:1–2); arrogance and reliance on wealth go hand in hand (1 Tim. 6:17). Greed is a form of idolatry (Col. 3:5), whose devotees easily fall into thievery. Therefore church leaders must neither love money (1 Tim. 3:3) nor pursue "dishonest gain" (1 Tim. 3:8; Titus 1:7);

---

34. See, e.g., Gal. 1:8–9; 1 Thess. 5:19–22 (where the command to "avoid every kind of evil" applies especially to utterances that claim divine authority); Rom. 16:17–20; 2 Cor. 11:1–15; Phil. 3:2–21; Col. 2:8–23; and the helpful survey by E. Earle Ellis, "Paul and his Opponents," *Prophecy and Hermeneutic in Early Christianity* (Grand Rapids: Eerdmans, 1978), 80–115.

35. In Col. 4:6 Paul is concerned with the manner in which Christians speak ("Let your speech always be gracious, seasoned with salt"), to the end that nonbelievers may be attracted to the content of the message (4:2–5). Thus too O'Brien, *Colossians, Philemon*, 242.

36. In my judgment, Phil. 2:16 exhorts Philippian believers to "hold on to the word of life" (NIV mg.) by striving for unity among themselves, the dominant practical concern of 1:27–2:18. By doing so, they shall behave in a way that is "worthy of the gospel" (1:27a) and shall more effectively "hold out the word of life" (2:16 NIV) to a world both watchful and hostile (1:27b–30; 2:15). Cf. 1 Tim. 4:12, 16.

Christian citizens are not to withhold revenue from the governing authorities (Rom. 13:6–9); and Christian slaves are not to steal from their masters (Titus 2:10). Paul recognizes the folly of seeking security in so unstable a god (1 Tim. 6:17), and warns of the catastrophic effects of disobedience in these respects: "For the love of money is a root of all kinds of evil. Some people, eager for money, have wandered from the faith and pierced themselves with many griefs" (1 Tim. 6:10 NIV).

But on the other hand, the renewal of the mind that comes with participation in the new creation (Eph. 4:23) puts money and material things in a wholly new light; and Christ the Lord, by freeing his people from bondage to wealth, frees them to take delight both in receiving it and in giving it away. The secret of Paul's contentment "whatever the circumstances . . ., whether full or hungry, whether in plenty or in want" was the Christ who mastered and empowered him (Phil. 4:11–13; 1:21). In contrast to the grief in store for lovers of money, godliness (*eusebeia*) joined to contentment with life's necessities ("food and clothing") is "great gain" (1 Tim. 6:6–10).[37] To put one's hope in God rather than in wealth is to discover that he "richly provides us with everything for our enjoyment" (1 Tim. 6:17), including the wealth that once held us in thrall. Persons "who believe and know the truth" are able to see that "everything God created is good," and can therefore receive it "with thanksgiving" and consecrate it "by the word of God and prayer" (1 Tim. 4:3–5). Attentiveness to the same word calls for relinquishing what has been received. "Command them to do good, to be rich in good deeds, and to be generous and willing to share" (1 Tim. 6:18 NIV). Let the former thief "work hard and do good with his own hands, that he may have something to share with the person in need" (Eph. 4:28). "Share with the saints who are in need. Practice hospitality" (Rom. 12:13). Here, as in other respects, "Happiness lies more in giving than in receiving" (Acts 20:35b NEB); see 20:33–35, where Paul, appealing to the Ephesian elders to work hard in order to help the weak and needy, invokes both his own example and the words of Jesus. Yet Paul's own instructions about the collection for the poor saints of Judea (2 Cor. 8–9) make it plain that admonitions about money, however appealing the principles they embody, are not readily heeded. God indeed "loves a cheerful giver"; but who of us has not given "reluctantly or under compulsion" to a Christian cause (2 Cor. 9:7)? And who of us has not been tempted, even as a Christian, to cheat on an income tax return or to steal from one's employer (Rom. 13:6–9; Titus 2:10)? The struggle continues.[38]

37. In the Pastoral Epistles, *eusebeia* (godliness or piety) denotes "conduct in relation to God," "a manner of life [which is] honouring to God the Creator and Redeemer of all men" (Werner Foerster, *TDNT* 7:183).

38. For an intelligent treatment of both the perils and the salutary uses of money, see Richard J. Foster, *Money, Sex and Power* (San Francisco: Harper and Row, 1985), 19–87.

Looking Beneath the Surface

Obeying Paul's commands to "put off" certain habits and "put on" others instead may not be a simple matter. It is possible that an alcoholic or a homosexual, or a person who habitually lies or loses his temper, or a shoplifter or an extortioner, may want to change but feels incapable of doing so. In many a case, probably in most, there is need to probe beneath the surface. An addiction to pornography or anger or drink may be like the red light on the dashboard of a car—a signal that someone needs to look under the hood, someone who knows how to interpret and to deal with what is there. The help of a professional counselor may be needed to bring the deepest problem to light. Such disclosures may be unsettling, even terrifying, but at the same time they hold out promise of deep healing, which will in turn have a salutary effect upon outward behavior. This is not to evade or to rationalize the apostolic directive to "put to death" certain habits; it is rather a way of radically obeying it.[39]

Through psychotherapy a person may be better able to make responsible ethical choices in accord with God's word.[40] Yet personal wholeness requires more than the enlightenment and cure of the psyche. Release from the radical effects of bondage to Sin demands just what Paul declares—a saving work of the mighty God himself, by which persons are reborn, reconciled to God, and transformed from the heart of their beings. By the concerted workings of his Word, his Spirit, and his people, God slowly but surely sanctifies his children, gently yet persistently bringing to light the breadth and depth of their need, all the while disclosing to them the wonders of his healing grace.[41]

39. With Lawrence J. Crabb, Jr., *Inside Out* (Colorado Springs: NavPress, 1988), 49, we may recognize Christians' responsibility both to obey God's commands about "actions, thoughts and feelings," and to seek "awareness and resolution of deep problems." In other words, there is need both for "change in our conscious direction" and "change in the direction of our being" (ibid., 201–18). For both reasons, a counselor who cannot or will not recognize the reality and radicality of sin is ill-equipped to help, just as I can know that something is wrong with my car but remain quite incapable of detecting or dealing with the real problem.

40. See C. S. Lewis, "Morality and Psychoanalysis," in *Mere Christianity* (New York: Macmillan, 1954), 69–73. He sounds a warning against psychotherapy founded on a philosophy that is antagonistic to the Christian faith.

41. Paul Tournier, *The Strong and the Weak*, trans. Edwin Hudson (London: SCM, 1963), 228, writes that "a thorough clearing of the ground on the psychological level often opens the spiritual channels through which God's grace may flow." On the Spirit, the Word, and the people of God as three means of bringing one's true condition to light, see Crabb, *Inside Out*, 153–70. In Paul, the three always work in concert. This holds true for public worship (1 Cor. 14:26–40; Eph. 5:18–20), and also for a counseling session in which the counselor is competent in his field, committed to the lordship of Christ, and granted the Spirit's wisdom and insight (1 Cor. 12:4–11). On the important place of pastoral counseling in church renewal, see Richard F. Lovelace, *Dynamics of Spiritual Life* (Downers Grove: InterVarsity, 1979), 216–23.

The Way of the Cross

Paul's resolve to "know nothing . . . except Jesus Christ and him crucified" (1 Cor. 2:2), pertains both to his proclamation and to his experience.
The cross stands at the very heart of his gospel (as we saw in chap. 3), and
identification with Christ crucified defines the whole character of his apostolic life and ministry (as we saw when discussing the Pauline *agōn*, chap. 1).

For other believers, no less than for Paul, suffering is central to the struggle. How could it be otherwise? To be incorporated into Christ is to be summoned into the "fellowship of his sufferings" (Phil. 3:10). For the people of
God, the whole span of history between the advents of Jesus is marked by
suffering—by trouble, hardship, persecution, famine, nakedness, peril,
sword, and death (Rom. 8:18, "the sufferings of this present time," *tou nun
kairou*, 35–36).[42] Not surprisingly, such a notion met with resistance. More
than once, Paul had to address a "Christian triumphalism," which proclaimed in one way or another that the "already" of eschatology had swallowed up the "not yet," and that resurrection-life had eclipsed crucifixion-
life, a message as appealing as it was erroneous.[43]

A principal reason for believers' afflictions is the opposition and oppression that their allegiance to Christ arouses. It is "for your [God's or Christ's]
sake," says Paul, that we face death and a host of other troubles at the
hands of enemies both human and demonic (Rom. 8:35–39).[44] Satan
obstructed Paul's ministry (1 Thess. 2:18); his "thorn in the flesh" was "a
messenger from Satan, to torment me" (2 Cor. 12:7). The Philippians
together with Paul are granted the privilege "not only to believe on
[Christ], but also to suffer for him" (1:28–30). The Thessalonians and other
Christians are destined for trials on account of their allegiance to Jesus
(1 Thess. 2:14–15; 3:2–4). Invoking his own experiences of peril and of
deliverance, Paul tells Timothy that "all who want to live a godly life in
Christ Jesus will be persecuted" (2 Tim. 3:10–12)—a way of life, significantly, set in contrast to one that goes "from bad to worse" (3:13).

Other causes of pain are life in a mortal body within a perishing order;
the crucifixion of the old self; recurrent failures and agonizingly slow
progress on the path to spiritual maturity, seen both in oneself and in others; and the chastening judgment of God in response to his children's sins.[45]

---

42. See chap. 1, pp. 34–35. "The Son of God suffered unto the death, not that men might not suffer, but
that their sufferings might be like His," wrote George Macdonald, *Unspoken Sermons*, quoted by C. S.
Lewis, *The Problem of Pain* (New York: Macmillan, 1955), vi. Thus, as Lewis himself writes, "the real problem is not why some humble, pious, believing people suffer, but why some do *not*" (ibid., 92).

43. For more on this view, see the treatment of 1 Corinthians in chap. 5, and of 2 Corinthians in chap. 8.

44. Human foes—those who incite persecution and wield swords (8:35)—are agents of demonic op-
pressors (8:38). Both sets of enemies are bent on separating believers from the love of God in Christ (8:35, 39).

45. A judgment that is restorative in purpose (e.g., 1 Cor. 5:5; 2 Cor. 2:5–11), but not less painful on that
account.

Whatever the cause or occasion of suffering, God means to address his children in that very place, and to use that very experience to make them more like Christ (Rom. 8:29, with 8:18–39).[46] It is instructive to notice how, in 2 Corinthians, Paul testifies to the salutary effect of his suffering upon each of his three relationships. The prospect of imminent death caused him to rely not on himself "but on God, who raises the dead" (1:8–10). Through the thorn in the flesh, he gained deeper understanding about false and true ways to self-fulfillment (12:7–10). His troubles drew him to other people, both to impart God's consolation to them (1:3–7) and to find solace in their company (2:12–13; 7:5–16).

Probably more than any other problem, suffering causes thinking and feeling people, Christians included, to raise doubts about God. God cannot be all-loving and all-powerful, it is said; either he is good and cannot stop suffering, or else he is mighty and will not stop it. The problem has been effectively addressed by contemporary Christian writers.[47] I want only to insist, in keeping with Paul's *euangelion*, that the cross must be central in any Christian statement on suffering. Let us liken our view of life to the examining of a fabric under a large magnifying glass: the fabric is most clear in the center, and quite blurred around the edges. If the cross, as interpreted by Paul, stands in the center of our glass, then in the face of much that is puzzling and incomprehensible, we cannot remain in doubt about the ultimate question. We shall know assuredly that God is both all-loving and all-powerful; for the cross was the supreme manifestation both of his love (Rom. 5:8; Eph. 5:2) and of his power (Rom. 8:1–3; 1 Cor. 1:24). This event assures us "that in all things God works for the good of those who love him, who are called according to his purpose"; for "he who did not spare his own Son but gave him up for us all, will he not also, with him, freely give us all things?" (Rom. 8:28, 32, with 8:29–39).[48]

The Divided Self

The structure of Paul's argument in Romans 6–8 is instructive. Through union with Christ, believers have "died to Sin" (6:2–11). They are thereby

---

46. "God whispers to us in our pleasures, speaks in our conscience, but shouts in our pains: it is His megaphone to rouse a deaf world" (Lewis, *Pain*, 81). David Watson, *Fear No Evil: One Man Deals with Terminal Illness* (Wheaton: Harold Shaw, 1984), 129, found it fruitless to ask God for the cause of his cancer ("Why?"), but fruitful to ask for the purpose ("What are you saying to me, God? . . . What response do you want me to make?").

47. I especially recommend Lewis, *Pain*; Peter Kreeft, *Making Sense Out of Suffering* (Ann Arbor: Servant, 1986); and the more personal perspective of Watson, *Fear No Evil*.

48. On present suffering as the gateway to future glory, see Rom. 5:2–4; 8:18–25; 2 Cor. 4:17; and chap. 11. On the importance of the cross for one's view of suffering, see John R. W. Stott, *The Cross of Christ* (Downers Grove: InterVarsity, 1986), 311–37.

liberated from Sin's agencies, especially the law (7:1–6; "you died to the law," v. 4), the flesh (8:1–17; "you are not in the flesh . . . not [debtors] to the flesh, to live according to the flesh," vv. 9, 12), and death (8:18–39).[49] Yet the victory is incomplete. These chapters bring sharply into focus the eschatological tension between the "already" and the "not yet" of salvation. Believers must still be urged to yield themselves to God, not to Sin (6:12–23). The struggle to obey the law as the will of God rather than the tool of Sin persists (7:14–25). The flesh remains a serious threat to the believer (8:12–13). Present sufferings are a constant reminder that death has not been swallowed up in victory (8:18–23, 35–36).[50]

Our chief concern for now is the struggle described in Romans 7:14–25, a passage as crucial as it is controversial.[51] The three major views: (1) this is an autobiographical account of Paul's own preconversion experience; (2) the account is not autobiographical, but depicts humanity in general, or Jews in particular, apart from Christ and under the law; and (3) Paul is describing his Christian experience.[52] I shall defend the view that Romans 7:14–25 describes a Christian struggle, one that is exclusively Christian, and one in which Paul represents Christians generally.

The Perspective of the Speaker

The "I" of this passage is Paul himself.[53] It is Paul who writes. Moreover, he is too deeply involved in what he is saying—the existential anguish of these verses is too real—for us to regard the "I" as merely a rhetorical device.[54] It is indeed doubtful that Paul speaks in purely autobiographical terms, and likely that he speaks as representative, or example, of a larger company. But let us not generalize the "I" so as to exclude Paul.

Paul is speaking, moreover, as a Christian. Even those who argue that he reflects here upon preconversion experience acknowledge that he does so with Christian insight. "The misery of the unredeemed man is described

49. Paul refers to demonic opposition in 8:15 ("spirit of slavery") and 8:38 ("rulers" [NIV "demons"] . . . powers").

50. A "structural feature of chaps. 6–8 [is] the way Paul makes an in-principle statement in clear-cut unequivocal terms at the start of each chapter, only to go on immediately to qualify it and to blur the clean-cut lines by showing that the reality of the believer's experience is more ambivalent" (Dunn, *Romans*, 302–3).

51. James D. G. Dunn, "Rom. 7,14–25 in the Theology of Paul," *Theologische Zeitschrift* (1975): 257, judges that Rom. 7 is "one of the few really pivotal passages in Paul's theology," and that our "understanding of it will in large measure determine our understanding of Paul's theology as a whole." C. E. B. Cranfield, *The Epistle to the Romans*, vol. 1 (Edinburgh: T. and T. Clark, 1975), 344, lists seven interpretations of the "I" of verses 14–25.

52. As summarized by Dunn, "Rom. 7,4–25," 257.

53. The subject *I* appears in every verse of the Greek text of 7:14–25, either in the verb or as a pronoun. The only verb in the first person plural is the "we know" of verse 14.

54. So rightly Dunn, "Rom. 7,14–25," 260.

from the standpoint of the redeemed man," writes Günther Bornkamm.[55] Thus if 7:14b ("sold as a slave to Sin") describes the nonbeliever, it is a condition which becomes plain only to the eyes of faith. For Sin deceives its slaves (7:11), blinding them to their actual state. Only the Christian can know that "nothing good dwells within me, that is, in my flesh" (7:18), and perceive that one is (or used to be) Sin's prisoner (7:23).

Let us examine further the verbs of the passage. Romans 7:7–13, clearly a recollection of Paul's pre-Christian experience, is dominated by past tenses (the aorist and the imperfect in Greek). In 7:14–25, however, with the exception of the "will rescue" of 7:24, every indicative verb is in the present tense. The change of tense is natural if Paul wishes, at 7:14, to turn to Christian experience.[56] Three ideas are expressed by the present indicative verbs used with the subject *I* in 7:14–25, namely, willing (*thelō, synēdomai, symphēmi*), doing (*poieō, prassō, katergazomai*), and seeing (*oida, heuriskō, blepō*). The last category represents reflections upon the discrepancy between the willing and the doing. We have already found reason to take the verbs of "seeing" as expressive of the viewpoint of Christian faith. The most natural reading of the passage is to place the verbs of "willing" and "doing" within the same period—both because these verbs too are in the present tense, and also because in some instances the "willing" appears to be inextricably joined to the "seeing": "I agree" (*symphēmi*, 7:16), and "I delight in" (*synēdomai*, 7:22).

A much more important point is that with the insight, or the "seeing," the struggle really begins—when the "I" finds that "when I want to do good, evil lies close at hand" (7:21), when the "I" sees "another law at work in the members of my body, waging war against the law of my mind and making me a prisoner of the law of sin at work within my members" (7:23 NIV). There are indeed passages where Paul the Christian expresses anguish and shame over his attitude as a Pharisee; but he does not portray a deeply troubled *Pharisee*.[57] Moreover, if our passage represented insight into Paul's struggle as a Pharisee, would he not more likely speak of doing good but willing evil, rather than the reverse (Rom. 7:18–19; compare Phil. 3:3–6 to Rom. 7:7–13)?

---

55. "Sin, Law and Death," in *Early Christian Experience*, trans. Paul L. Hammer (New York: Harper and Row, 1969), 89. Compare Rudolf Bultmann, *Theology of the New Testament*, trans. Kendrick Grobel, 2 vols. (New York: Scribner's, 1951), 1:266, "Rom. 7:14–25 is not a confession of Paul describing his erstwhile inner division under the Law, but is that picture of the objective situation of man-under-the-Law which became visible to him only after he had attained the viewpoint of faith."

56. Some who view 7:14–25 as an elaboration of 7:7–13, explain the shift in tense as a means of achieving greater vividness.

57. See chap. 1, pp. 24–24; and the quotation from Bultmann in note 55. The conflict of Acts 26:14 did not arise over the demands of the Mosaic law.

Two Views of the Self

Paul's anthropology is thoroughly Hebraic, as we saw in chapter 2. The terms *flesh* (7:18), *mind* (7:23), and *inner man* (7:22) do not denote parts or compartments of the self, but view the whole self in a variety of ways. From one standpoint the self is a fleshly being. Bornkamm rightly speaks of the words *that is, in my flesh* (7:18) as a definition rather than a limitation of the "I" as here conceived.[58] Likewise is 7:14 to be understood. From the standpoint of my participation in Adam (5:12–21), and my continued vulnerability to the agents of Sin, I as a Christian am still "fleshly" (*sarkinos*), still subject to Sin's power.[59] Behind the words "sold as a slave to sin," 7:14b, lies the perfect participle *pepramenos*, denoting a condition that began before conversion and carries over into Christian experience.

From another viewpoint the self is renewed. I have already argued that "the inner man" (7:22) is the self in Christ, what Paul elsewhere calls "the new man," in contrast to "the outer man," or "the old man," man in Adam; and that "the law of my mind" (7:23) is God's law, to which the mind, now renewed by Christ, gives its approval and allegiance.[60] Only as a renewed being can I delight in God's law for the right reasons. As a nonbeliever, my doing so was adversely affected by Sin's use of the law, or by my own perverse motive (cf. Rom. 10:3). But whereas the mind (*nous*) used to capitulate to Sin's seductive uses of the law (7:7–11; Gal. 3:22–23), it now resists (7:23). From the standpoint of the renewed self, I do not *recognize*, I do not *acknowledge*, the very things that I do (7:15).[61] Paul the Christian knows what he does, and he understands what he does (7:15b), and why (7:17–18). But he does not approve, or acknowledge the legitimacy of, what he does. Even when succumbing to the dictates of Sin, he repudiates and loathes what he does. Sin's claims on the Christian are always illegitimate (Rom. 6).

Two Kinds of Slavery

A servant (*diakonos*) can serve more than one master, but a slave (*doulos*) cannot, as we saw in chapter 6. Yet consider Romans 7:25b, "So then, I myself (*autos egō*) am enslaved to (*douleuō*) the law of God with the mind, but to the law of Sin with the flesh." "I myself" do both; the verb *douleuō* governs both parts of the sentence. Given our definition of a slave, the only

---

58. "Sin, Law and Death," 98.
59. It is noteworthy, however, that Paul never in 7:14–25 speaks of the "I" as being "in the flesh." For the Christian is by definition "in Christ," 8:1, and "in the Spirit," 8:9, cf. 7:5.
60. See chap 4, pp. 88, 102–3.
61. The italicized words represent an interpretation of the verb *ginōskō* (know) in 7:15, following (respectively) C. K. Barrett, *The Epistle to the Romans* (New York: Harper and Row, 1962), 147, and Cranfield, *Romans*, 358.

explanation is that "I myself" participate in two humanities (represented by Adam and Christ respectively) and in two realities (the present evil age and the age to come). I am capable of giving myself totally to each, not alternatively but simultaneously.

This reading of 7:25b is confirmed by the order of clauses in 7:24–25. First comes the cry "O wretched man that I am!" (7:24a), and finally the recognition of a deeply divided self (7:25b). In between come the question "Who will rescue me from this body of death?" (7:24b) and the exclamation "Thanks be to God through Jesus Christ our Lord!" (7:25a). Significantly, this unmistakable reference to Christian experience is integral to the present discussion, not appended to it.[62] The cry of 24a is echoed in the more sober statement of 25b. The verb of 25a (*herusetai*) is a true future: Jesus Christ indeed "will rescue me from this body of death." Yet it will happen, not within this life but only in the resurrection (already affirmed in 6:5, 8, and to be reaffirmed in 8:10–11)—when the body is liberated from bondage to death, and one's "perishable body," belonging as it does to a perishing order, is transformed into a glorious body like that of Jesus himself.[63] It is not merely the struggle against Sin (7:25b) that accounts for the anguish (7:24a). To have tasted the "already" of salvation creates a longing that is not fully satisfied until the "not yet" becomes "already" (8:18–25; 13:11–14). Assurance of eventual rescue prevents anguish from degenerating into despair; and the very division within the self shows that Sin is being effectively resisted in anticipation of final victory.[64]

The Passage in Context

Romans 7:14–25 relates to the earlier part of the chapter as Rom. 6:12–23 relates to 6:1–11, as noted in the opening paragraph of this section. In view of the forthright declarations of 7:1–6 that believers have "died to the law" and are now married to Christ instead, verses 14–25 are a needed qualification to make it clear that while one has died to the law conceived as mere "letter" (*grammatos*, 7:6), the righteous requirements of the law endure, calling the renewed mind and the whole of the "inner man" to obedience

---

62. James Moffatt, *The New Testament: A New Translation*, rev. ed. (London: Hodder and Stoughton, 1935), 228, rearranges 7:24–25 into the order 25b, 24, 25a, and explains: "Restoring the second part of ver. 25 to its original and logical position before the climax of ver. 24." But there is no textual support whatsoever for this order; to say "to its original position" is purely speculative; to say "logical position" begs the question. Moffatt is followed by C. H. Dodd, writing in the Moffatt Commentary: "We do seem to have here one of the cases . . . where a primitive corruption of the text has affected all our surviving MSS., and we cannot avoid trusting our own judgment against their evidence" (*The Epistle to the Romans* [London: Hodder and Stoughton, 1932], 115).

63. Cf. 1 Cor. 6:13–14; 15:42–57; Phil. 3:20–21. It is the body's rescue from death (*thanatos*) that is in view in Rom. 7:24–25; note that 7:25 echoes 1 Cor. 15:57. In the present struggle, it is the "mortal body" (*thnētō sōmati*, Rom. 6:12) that one is to withhold from Sin and yield to God.

64. See Dunn, "Rom. 7,14–25," 268, 272–73.

(7:22–23; 8:4); and that even for persons wed to Christ, the struggle to submit to the law as God's will rather than as Sin's tool is by no means over.

The voicing of the self's anguish and dividedness at the close of Romans 7 well prepares for Romans 8. Paul opens the new chapter with the assurance that amid the ongoing struggle and despite the repeated failures, there is no condemnation for those who are in Christ Jesus, who are justified by his blood, and upon whom God has bestowed the gift of righteousness (3:21–5:21).

Moreover, Romans 8 promises power to the vulnerable and impotent self. To be sure, as renewed beings Paul and those he represents can "delight in God's law" (7:22); but the self in Christ, as surely as the self under Sin, is incapable of obeying the law when left to itself (7:15–20). I cannot depend upon myself any more as a Christian than I could as a nonbeliever; Paul understands conversion to be passage from bondage to Sin into bondage to Christ, not into self-reliance. "The discord pictured in Romans 7 consists . . . in the absolute impotence of the I to break through the barrier of sin and the flesh in any degree at all."[65] It is only by the Spirit that the law can be wrested from Sin and death and become an instrument of life instead (8:2; cf. 7:10); only by the Spirit that one can meet the righteous requirements of the law (8:4–8); only by the Spirit that the deeds of the flesh can be put to death (8:13). By depicting the battle as he does in Romans 7 (where the lone reference to the Spirit comes in v. 6), Paul better prepares readers for the good news of the Spirit in Romans 8.

At the same time, Romans 8, far from marking an end to the struggle of 7:14–25, views it in a new light. It is when Christ the conqueror of Sin (8:3) sends forth his Spirit to assault Sin and the flesh that the battle commences. "The struggle so vividly depicted in Romans 7, 14–25 does not end when the Spirit comes; on the contrary, that is when it really begins."[66] For one thing, there is the continuing threat of the flesh, to which Paul has referred in 7:18, 25. It is illogical and senseless for Christians to live according to the flesh, for they are not "in the flesh" but "in the Spirit"; yet they may choose to behave illogically and irrationally (8:5–9, 12–13). They owe the flesh nothing but ingratitude, but they may choose

65. Herman Ridderbos, *Paul: An Outline of His Theology*, trans. John R. DeWitt (Grand Rapids: Eerdmans, 1975), 127. J. A. T. Robinson, *Wrestling with Romans* (Philadelphia: Westminster, 1979), 88, 89, believes that the contrast of 7:14–25 "is not between what I was and am, but between the law and myself (the *ego* in the Greek is emphatic). The law is all right, in fact it is divine; but human nature is incapable of fulfilling it. . . . When Paul uses the word *ego* here he has not in mind either Paul the Jew or Paul the Christian but Paul simply *qua* man, the self in its own unaided human nature, or in biblical terms, man as 'flesh' (*sarx*)." This point remains valid when we view the passage (as in my judgment we must) as a statement of Christian experience.

66. Dunn, "Rom. 7,14–25," 263. *The Scots Confession*, chap. 13, affirms that "as soon as the Spirit of the Lord Jesus . . . takes possession of the heart . . . that continual battle [begins] which is between the flesh and the Spirit in God's children. . . . Other men do not share this conflict since they do not have God's Spirit."

to live as though they have a debt to repay (8:12). The perils posed by the flesh's assaults call for counterassaults in kind, in the Spirit's power: "if you live according to the flesh, you will die; but if by the Spirit you put to death the deeds of the body, you will live" (8:13 NRSV; cf. 8:6; Gal. 5:16–26). For another thing, there is the abiding relevance of the law of God (8:4–8), the law to which Paul has pledged his allegiance in 7:22–23. The internalizing of the law by the lifegiving Spirit (8:2) implies that a new and radical obedience is called for (cf. Rom. 7:6; 13:8–10). This in turn provides new opportunities for Sin to employ the law as its own tool (7:7–13, 23, 25), and to encourage law keeping "according to the flesh." Not only does the manifold struggle carry over into Romans 8. When the evidence of Romans 8 is added to that of Romans 7, we see the intensity of the struggle with far greater clarity.

There is a healthy realism about Romans 7:14–25. The Christian is granted new understanding both of God's law (7:16, 22–23) and of Sin's designs. Moreover, with growth in holiness comes a deeper awareness of the powerlessness of the self. The ones most acutely aware of the struggle depicted here are not the spiritually infantile but the spiritually mature. The more one experiences the presence of Christ and the power of the Spirit, the more one recognizes the inadequacy of the autonomous self. "The man in whom the power of sin is really being seriously and resolutely challenged, in him the power of sin is clearly seen. The more he is renewed by God's Spirit, the more sensitive he becomes to the continuing power of sin over his life and the fact that even his very best activities are marred by the egotism still entrenched within him."[67] Thus with ever more fervent longing, he utters the cry of 7:24–25a.[68]

Christian Warfare

In closing, we amplify the note on which the chapter began. Persons whom Christ calls to faithfulness, to holiness, and to a share in his sufferings, are drawn into battle with Sin and all its agencies, as Romans 6–8 makes especially clear. Paul frequently speaks like a commanding officer preparing soldiers for battle: "Let us be alert and self-controlled" (1 Thess. 5:6). "Be on your guard; stand firm in the faith; be courageous; be strong" (1 Cor. 16:13). "Fight the good fight of the faith" (1 Tim. 6:12; cf. 2 Tim.

---

67. Cranfield, *Romans*, 341–42. In this regard, J. I. Packer, *Keep in Step With the Spirit* (Old Tappan, N.J.: Revell, 1984), 163, warns us against "making too much of our continuing sinfulness and too little by comparison of the scriptural expectation of ongoing moral change into Christ's image through the Holy Spirit."

68. For strong arguments favoring the foregoing interpretation of Rom. 7:14–25, see Cranfield, *Romans*, 355–70; and Dunn, "Rom. 7,14–25," 257–73; *Romans*, 387–99, 403–12. For a recent defense of the view that all of 7:7–25 depicts "the history and experience of Jews under the law," see Douglas Moo, *Romans 1–8* (Chicago: Moody, 1991), 448–98.

4:7). "Endure hardship with us like a good soldier of Christ Jesus" (2 Tim. 2:3). "Let us put off the deeds of darkness and put on the armor of light" (Rom. 13:12).

Our focus at present is believers' warfare against demonic powers. In some quarters of the church, such language is common, and the danger is a distorted view of the demonic, or such an obsession with it that the devils are blamed for everything and personal responsibility is abdicated. In other quarters, biblical teaching about the powers is "demythologized," or the process of sanctification is conceived in altogether different terms.[69] Paul is not obsessed with the demonic: God is his only obsession, and he speaks more often of Sin's power than of Satan's. Yet he knows the devil to be "the evil one," "the adversary" of Christ and his people; to have a host of demons at his command; to have an endless number of schemes for promoting his cause; and to be alert to every means of setting traps for believers and of gaining a foothold in their lives.[70] In that light Paul prepares the Christians under his care for battle.

The intellectual dimension of the battle is critical. Arrayed against "those who believe and who know the truth" are "deceiving spirits and teachings of demons" (1 Tim. 4:1–3). In the face of Satan's manifold appeal to accept as true that which is false, God summons his people to "belief in the truth" (2 Thess. 2:9–15). Knowing that "the god of this age has blinded the minds of unbelievers, so that they cannot see the light of the gospel of the glory of Christ," Paul proclaims this very gospel, by means of which God cures the blindness, pierces the veil of unbelief, and causes the heart to behold "the glory of God in the face of Christ" (2 Cor. 4:1–6). The perpetrators of the "different gospel" about "another Jesus," together with the "different spirit" (2 Cor. 11:4), serve Satan's purpose (11:13–15)—in opposition to which Paul preaches the true gospel of the real Jesus by means of the Holy Spirit, wielding weapons that "are mighty through God for demolishing strongholds," particularly the pretentious arguments advanced against the knowledge of God (10:3–5; 11:1–6; cf. 6:7). It is therefore not at all surprising that Satan seeks to impede the progress of the apostolic mission (1 Thess. 2:18).

---

69. Virginia Stem Owens, "Gone for a Soldier," *Perspectives* (March 1991): 8, observes that "our metaphors for sanctification come at present from codependency and support groups, not from spiritual warfare."

70. See Eph. 4:27; 6:11; 1 Tim. 3:7; 2 Tim. 2:26; and chap. 2, p. 54. Paul invariably speaks of *"the* devil" (*ho diabolos*), literally "the slanderer" ; and of *"the* Satan" (*ho Satanas*), "the adversary" (2 Cor. 12:7 is no exception). Paul calls the devil "the evil one" (*ho ponēros*) in Eph. 6:16 and 2 Thess. 3:3. The latter instance may be impersonal ("the evil"), but "the evil one" provides a better antithesis to "the Lord" of 3:3a (thus Bruce, *1 and 2 Thessalonians*, 200).

Ephesians is especially instructive.[71] In his resurrection from the dead and his exaltation to God's right hand, Christ won a decisive victory over "the ruler of the kingdom of the air" and all his host (1:20–21; 2:2; 4:8–10). Persons united to Christ participate in this conquest (2:6), and are endowed with the gifts necessary for building up the church in the world (4:7–16; cf. 2:19–22). Indeed, so stupendous have past victories been, and so mighty is the presence of Christ in his church by his Spirit, that believers might easily become blind or indifferent to present and future danger. Perhaps for this reason Paul devotes the last section of the letter before the postscript (6:21–24) to preparing both himself and his readers for battle (6:10–20). Our principal enemies, he warns, are not human but demonic: "For our struggle is not against flesh and blood, but against the rulers, against the authorities, against the powers of this dark world and against the spiritual forces of evil in the heavenly realms" (6:12 NIV).[72] Their assaults, furthermore, will be of every conceivable kind (6:16).[73] And not only does the war continue; it is sure to intensify before it is over: present "days are evil" (5:16) in anticipation of the climactic "day of evil" (6:13).

Confronted with "the devil's schemes," believers are granted "the full armor of God" (6:11). The principal source of the imagery of 6:14–17 is not equipment worn by the Roman legionary but Old Testament language about both Yahweh and his Messiah. Furthermore, Paul's chief interest is the six theological realities being enunciated, not the armament with which each is associated (Eph. 6:14 speaks of "the breastplate of righteousness," 1 Thess. 5:8 of "the breastplate of faith and love").[74] Each of the six is supplied by God, and each remains his to wield (as in the Old Testament) even as he imparts it to his people; only so can the warriors be expected to "stand their ground." Moreover, personal responsibility is in view throughout the passage: believers must obey the imperative to "be strong in the Lord," and must "put on" the armor that God provides (6:10–11). At the same time, we may recognize a distinction within the list. Believers' cooperation with God is especially evident in the first four (6:14–16; cf. 2:8–10): "fidelity" (for *alētheia*, usually rendered "truth"); "righteousness" (an ethical quality, as in 4:24; 5:9); "readiness" for battle owing to one's appropriation of "the

---

71. On spiritual warfare in Eph., see Clinton E. Arnold, *Ephesians: Power and Magic* (Cambridge: Cambridge University Press), 1989. For a more general treatment see idem, *Powers of Darkness: Principalities and Powers in Paul's Letters* (Downers Grove: InterVarsity, 1992).

72. The "rulers" (*archai*) and "authorities" (*exousiai*) are among the heavenly powers over which Christ now reigns (1:21; 3:10).

73. "All the flaming arrows of the evil one" (6:16) denotes "not just temptation to impure or unloving conduct but also false teaching, persecution, doubt, and despair" (Andrew T. Lincoln, *Ephesians* [Dallas: Word, 1990], 450).

74. On these two points, see Lincoln, *Ephesians*, 435–37. The principal OT passages are Isa. 11 (of Messiah), and 59 (of Yahweh). "The Lord" of Eph. 6:10 is probably Christ, as normally in Paul.

gospel of peace"; and "faith." The latter two are pure gifts from God: "salvation" and "the word of God."[75]

With the command to "pray in the Spirit" (6:18), Paul again calls on believers to cooperate with God. Prayer is not associated with a particular armament, but it is vital if "the full armor of God" is to be effectively appropriated, and if Christians are to "stand firm" against the powers of darkness.[76] Prayer is addressed to the God of heaven, and the believers who invoke Christ's authority over the demons are themselves seated with Christ in the heavenly realms. At the same time, Christians engage in cosmic warfare in very down-to-earth conditions, in those places of responsibility of which Paul speaks earlier in Ephesians, most immediately in 5:21–6:9. It is precisely by faith and fidelity in these places, in dependence all the while upon the divine power (5:18; 6:10–20), that Christians can "extinguish all the flaming arrows of the evil one" (6:16).

Even as "the day of evil" draws nearer (Eph. 6:13), Christian warriors may rest assured that "the God of peace will soon crush Satan under your feet" (Rom. 16:20).

> *O LORD GOD, thou art my protecting arm, fortress, refuge, shield, buckler. Fight for me and my foes must flee; uphold me and I cannot fall; strengthen me and I stand unmoved, unmoveable; equip me and I shall receive no wound; stand by me and Satan will depart; anoint my lips with a song of salvation, and I shall shout thy victory; give me abhorrence of all evil, as a vile monster that defies thy law, casts off thy yoke, defiles my nature, spreads misery. . . . And may holiness be the atmosphere in which I live.[77]*

---

75. For this distinction, and for the above understanding of "truth" and "righteousness," see Lincoln, *Ephesians*, 447–51. To be sure, "faith" responds to "salvation" ; but the salvation itself is God's work exclusively (1:1–14; 2:1–10). By the same token, Paul proclaims "the gospel of salvation" (or "the word of God"); but he is its ambassador, not its source, and he requires the Spirit's power if his preaching is to be effective (6:17–20).

76. See Lincoln, *Ephesians*, 451–53, who correctly notes that Paul lists six armaments, not seven (despite the attractiveness of this number). Still, the "prayer in the Spirit" (6:18) matches "the sword of the Spirit" (6:17); and Paul's stress on prayer in 6:18–20 testifies to its crucial function in spiritual warfare.

77. Arthur Bennett, ed., *The Valley of Vision: A collection of Puritan prayers and devotions* (Edinburgh: Banner of Truth, 1975), 100 (structure altered).

8

Power in Weakness

At this point in our study, you may be discouraged. The three preceding chapters may have confirmed you in the belief that you are a proud person, or slave to the opinions of others, or prey to a selfish heart or an uncontrollable temper. Despite the help that Paul has offered, you may still be convinced that the Christian struggle is more than you can bear, that for you there is no hope of peace and victory until you go to heaven or Christ returns.

But take heart. It is just such people that God helps. Paul often speaks of "power" (*dynamis*), usually as exercised by God or a particular member of the Godhead.[1] In many of these instances, the divine power is promised in the face of human weakness, inadequacy, and failure.[2] In other words, God's *dynamis* acts in concert with his *charis* (grace). By his power he manifests his grace (Rom. 1:16; Titus 2:11), and by his grace he energizes his people (1 Cor. 15:10; 2 Tim. 2:1).

Of special importance is 2 Corinthians 12:8–10, "Three times I pleaded with the Lord [i.e., Christ] to take it [the thorn in the flesh, v. 7] away from me. But he said to me, 'My grace (*charis*) is sufficient for you, for my power (*dynamis*) is made perfect in weakness.' Therefore I will boast all the more

---

1. Of the 48 instances of *dynamis* in Paul, only six bear an unfavorable sense (e.g., 1 Cor. 15:24). Most of the rest refer to exercises of divine power. Paul associates *dynamis* with God the Father (Rom. 1:16; 1 Cor. 2:5); with Christ (1 Cor. 1:24; 5:4; 2 Cor. 12:9); and with the Spirit (Rom. 15:13, 19; Eph. 3:16).

2. E.g., Rom. 1:16; 15:13; 1 Cor. 2:3–5; 2 Cor. 6:4–7; Eph. 3:16–20; 6:10; Phil. 4:13; Col. 1:11; 1 Tim. 1:12–14; 2 Tim. 1:7–8; 2:1; 4:17. Cf. David Alan Black, *Paul, Apostle of Weakness* (New York: Peter Lang, 1984), 228–40.

gladly about my weaknesses, so that Christ's power (*dynamis*) may rest on me. . . . For when I am weak, then I am strong" (NIV).[3] Thus does Paul reach one of his profoundest convictions about Christian living.[4] What does he mean? and what are the implications for our three relationships?

The Saving Work of Christ

In seeking to answer those questions, we begin with the person and work of Jesus Christ. For Paul's convictions about strength in weakness are deeply rooted in his Christology.[5] What Jesus the Lord teaches Paul (2 Cor. 12:9–10), he himself has experienced.

"For you know the grace (*charis*) of our Lord Jesus Christ, who, though he was rich, yet for your sakes became poor, in order that through his poverty you might become rich" (2 Cor. 8:9). God's saving plan was conceived before the world began (Eph. 1:4–5), when Christ was still "rich." But saving grace actually began to reveal itself (cf. Titus 2:11), when Christ "became poor"—when he relinquished his rights and "emptied himself" by becoming a man (Phil. 2:6–7). According to the saving plan, believers would "become rich," not through Christ's riches but "through his poverty." What Christ taught Paul about the *dynamis* of *charis* (2 Cor. 12:9–10), he himself honored in inaugurating his mission. He mediated the power of his salvation through the weakness of his incarnation. By an act of sovereign power, Christ surrendered the power of his pre-existent glory in order to activate the power of his grace.

That self-emptying culminated in the cross (Phil. 2:8; cf. Isa. 53:12). "Christ crucified . . . [is] the power of God," declares Paul (1 Cor. 1:23–24). To devotees of "the wisdom of this age" (2:6), the idea of salvation in (rather than from) destruction, or of a triumph in (rather than over) failure, is nonsense (1:23). Yet according to "God's secret wisdom" (2:7), God's saving power came to supreme expression in the very place where his weakness came to supreme expression. Christ was indeed "crucified in weakness" (2 Cor. 13:4); but it is this very One—"the Weakness of God"—who is "the Power of God." The Lord's teaching in 2 Corinthians 12 arose out of his own experience. "The key to [the] mystery of strength in weakness is the Cross of Christ."[6]

3. In 12:9, *charis* has the personal pronoun ("my grace"), *dynamis* does not; but as v. 10 refers to "the power of Christ," the NIV rendering of 12:9 is justified. Ralph P. Martin, *2 Corinthians* (Waco: Word, 1986), 419, rightly views *charis* and *dynamis* as "synonymous."
4. Philip Edgcumbe Hughes, *Paul's Second Epistle to the Corinthians* (Grand Rapids: Eerdmans, 1962), 451, calls 2 Cor. 12:9 "the summit of the epistle, the lofty peak from which the whole is viewed in true proportion."
5. This is well emphasized by Black, *Weakness*, 2, 234–40.
6. Peter J. Kreeft, "Unraveling the Mystery of Weakness and Strength," *Christianity Today*, 21 April 1989, 23. Dorothy L. Sayers says of Christ, "He will be victor and victim in all his wars, and will make his triumph in defeat" (*The Man Born to Be King* [London: Gollancz, 1943], 54).

Death generates power to rise from the dead: "Unless a grain of wheat falls into the ground and dies, it remains alone. But if it dies, it bears much fruit" (John 12:24). My zoology professor, Russell Mixter, used to say that there is a biological parallel for every spiritual truth. The natural world is real, but it is also metaphorical, pointing to realities beyond itself.[7] Paul writes: "What you sow does not come to life unless it dies. When you sow, you do not plant the body that will be, but just a seed, perhaps of wheat or of something else. . . . So will it be with the resurrection of the dead. The body that is sown is perishable, it is raised imperishable; . . . it is sown in weakness, it is raised in power" (1 Cor. 15:36–37, 42–43 NIV). The harvest of resurrection power depends upon the sowing of the body in the weakness of death.

The inspiration for Paul's teaching about the resurrection of believers (1 Cor. 15:35–58) is Christ's own resurrection (15:1–28). He "was crucified in weakness, yet he lives by the power of God" (2 Cor. 13:4). The Father hereby acclaims the Son's lowly obedience (Phil. 2:9, "Therefore God exalted him"). Yet Christ's character is unchanged: it is the very One who was "crucified in weakness," who "lives by God's power." "The power of his resurrection" (Phil. 3:10) is the very power at work in his death.[8]

The one whom Paul identifies as "the power of God," is "Christ having been crucified" (*estaurōmenon*). The cross is not relegated to the past; the exalted Savior remains "Christ crucified."[9] He exercises his sovereignty as "the serving and sacrificing one."[10] "Always his lordly power is conditioned by his continuing weakness, obedience and humility."[11] So it must be, therefore, for his subjects: "Likewise," says Paul in 2 Corinthians 13:4b (cf. 13:4a, quoted above), "we are weak in him, yet by God's power we will live with him to serve you" (NIV).[12]

In speaking thus, Paul is not merely reflecting upon his personal spiritual condition. He also writes as a pastor, in the face of a serious threat to the Corinthian believers.

7. "The physical world furnishes us with endless metaphors, not by our poking about and extracting occult significance from things but simply by our observing what is perfectly plainly going on"(Thomas Howard, *The Reformed Journal* [February 1979]: 13).

8. Interpreting Paul, Walter Grundmann speaks of the power of God "concealed . . . in weakness and mortality" in the cross, "hidden in the power of death," in order—by that very concealment—to overcome the power of death (*TDNT* 2:316–17).

9. Paul uses the participle in the perfect tense, *estaurōmenon* (1 Cor. 1:23; 2:2; Gal. 3:1), never in the aorist (past) tense, *staurōthenta*. See C. F. D. Moule, *An Idiom-Book of New Testament Greek*, 2d ed. (Cambridge: Cambridge University Press, 1959), 14, 202.

10. E. Earle Ellis, "Christ Crucified," in *Reconciliation and Hope*, ed. Robert Banks (Grand Rapids: Eerdmans, 1974), 75.

11. Martin, *2 Corinthians*, 475. Cf. Luke 12:37.

12. Paul's "we will live" refers not to the afterlife, but to his ongoing work among the Corinthians (cf. Martin, ibid., 477).

Paul's Opponents in 2 Corinthians

Since the writing of 1 Corinthians, certain individuals have arrived at Corinth. They are Jewish Christians, at least nominally so, who represent themselves as Christ's "servants" and "apostles" (2 Cor. 11:13, 22–23). They come from the Jerusalem church, in hopes of bringing the Corinthian Christians under the authority of that church and into conformity with its practices.[13] To advance their cause, they produce "letters of recommendation," recite their spiritual experiences and accomplishments, and actually exert their authority over the Corinthian congregation.[14]

To the same end, the Judeans seek to undermine Paul's credibility among the Corinthians. They assault his person. He is not a "trained speaker" (11:6). "His letters are weighty and forceful, but in person he is unimpressive and his speaking amounts to nothing" (10:10 NIV). When he does speak, and even when he writes, his teaching is obscure and hard to understand (1:13; 4:3). He also vacillates, saying one thing and doing another (1:15–23). Besides (they say) our spiritual experiences are more spectacular than his (if he has had them at all), and our achievements more impressive (see n. 14).

They also raise questions about Paul's ministry. What proof do we have (they say) that Christ really speaks through him (10:7; 13:3)? Where are his letters of recommendation (cf. 3:1)? Does not his refusal to accept payment for his services show that he knows himself to lack the required apostolic commissioning (11:7–9; 12:13)? And if his claim to apostolic status is questionable, so then are his motives. If he claims to be an apostle, knowing that he is not an apostle, then he is (to put it mildly) insincere (2:17). And why does he claim to be what he is not? Clearly in order to gain mastery over the Corinthians and to bring them under his power (cf. 1:24). Toward this end he must use "trickery," "craftiness," and "deception" (4:2; 12:16). He "distorts the Word of God" to make it more palatable to his hearers (cf. 4:2). And what is really afoot in this collection being made for the poor saints in Jerusalem? Is Paul, the very one who has refused payment for his services, exploiting the Corinthians by furtively taking their money for himself and Titus (see 8:20–21; 12:16–18)?

The teachings and tactics of the newly arrived, self-styled apostles have favorably impressed the Corinthians; and they now compare Paul

13. Circumcision is not an issue in 2 Cor.; the Jerusalem Council settled the matter (Acts 15) before Paul ever came to Corinth (Acts 18:1). The emissaries from Jerusalem may be attempting to impose the Jerusalem decree, especially the food regulations (15:20, 29), on the Corinthian church (thus F. F. Bruce, "Paul and Jerusalem," *Tyndale Bulletin* 19 [1968]: 16). Paul's opponents, the "false apostles" (2 Cor. 11:13), are to be distinguished from "those 'super-apostles'" (11:5). The latter are the Jerusalem apostles (the "pillars" of Gal. 2:9), the legitimacy of whose apostleship Paul never questions, and whose authority the emissaries from Jerusalem wrongly claim. See Martin, *2 Corinthians*, 342.

14. 2 Cor. 2:16b; 3:1–5; 4:5, 7; 5:12–13; 10:7, 12–13, 18; 11:7–9, 12, 16–23; 12:1, 13.

unfavorably with his detractors.[15] The basic issue thus raised is the "legitimacy of apostleship"—as claimed by both Paul and his opponents.[16] How then does a person prove that he is a genuine apostle? How does Paul seek to do so in 2 Corinthians?

Paul's Counterattack: The Message

Paul's ministry (*diakonia*), he declares, is fundamentally one of proclamation (2 Cor. 2:14–7:16; 10:1–13:10).[17]

Glory

Paul's proclamation discloses the glory (*doxa*) of God.[18] The supreme such disclosure is found "in the face of Christ" (2 Cor. 4:6). As "the image of God" (4:4), he reflects, he radiates forth, he embodies, the very glory of God (cf. Heb. 1:3). Yet Paul speaks also of "the light of the gospel of the glory of Christ" (4:4): the glory belongs to Christ; but it is here, in the gospel, that his glory is disclosed. The gospel is God's chosen means for imparting knowledge of the glory of God in Christ (4:4, 6).

Understanding that disclosure, says Paul, requires attentiveness to its Old Testament background, Exodus 34 in particular.[19] Here Yahweh reveals his glory to Moses by both his Presence and his Word. Exodus 34:29 accentuates the latter: "When Moses came down from Mount Sinai with the two tablets of the Testimony in his hands, he was not aware that his face was radiant because he had been speaking with Yahweh."[20] The glory of Yahweh and the word of Yahweh belong inextricably together. Accordingly, Moses must not wear a veil when he listens to Yahweh or when he addresses the people (Exod. 34:33–35), for the veil would eclipse the glorious Word. At other times Moses wears the veil; lest the people be overcome, Yahweh's glory is disclosed to them only when it is essential that it be disclosed, namely, when Yahweh's word is proclaimed to them.

15. See C. K. Barrett, "Paul's Opponents in II Corinthians," *NTS* 17 (1971): 233–54; and Donald A. Carson, *From Triumphalism to Maturity: An Exposition of 2 Corinthians 10–13* (Grand Rapids: Baker, 1984),156–59.

16. Ernst Käsemann, "Die Legitimität des Apostels. Eine Untersuchung zu II Korinther 10–13," *ZNW* 41 (1942): 33–71.

17. Paul's favorite term for his apostolic message, *euangelion*, occurs eight times in 2 Cor. I believe that Paul speaks of "our gospel" (4:3) in conscious allusion to the "different gospel" being propagated in Corinth (11:4). He does the same in Galatians 1–2.

18. The Greek noun *doxa* occurs fifteen times in 2 Corinthians 3–4.

19. Paul's opponents are champions of the law of Moses, and the "five books of Moses" (the Torah) are authoritative Scripture for both them and Paul. In 2 Corinthians 3, as elsewhere, Paul uses his adversaries' own weaponry to refute their arguments.

20. "As regards the OT promise, when man is set in a relation of *kavod* [glory], all the emphasis lies on *sight* [e.g., Lev. 9:6]. . . . The story that the face of Moses shone after his *speech* with Yahweh (Exod. 34:29f.) is an isolated one" (Gerhard Kittel, *TDNT* 2:249; the emphasis is added).

That veil remains, says Paul; only now it does not cover the face of the one who mediates Yahweh's word (Moses) but the hearts of those who receive it (the Israelites), blinding them to Yahweh's glory (2 Cor. 3:14–15). Nothing but "turning to the Lord" will take the veil away (3:16). Doing this means turning to Christ, in whose face God's glory is revealed (3:14; 4:5–6). And doing this requires attentiveness to the gospel Paul preaches, for it is here that Christ's glory is disclosed (4:4). The spurious gospel, far from providing the needed illumination, darkens the understanding of its recipients. By means of the "different gospel," "the god of this age" blinds unbelievers' minds (4:3–4; 11:3–4).

Power

Paul's gospel witnesses to God's power, especially as revealed in Christ's death and resurrection. But the gospel also manifests the divine power. By "speaking through" Paul, Christ shows himself to be "powerful" (*dynatei*) among the Corinthians (13:3). The "treasure" of "the gospel of the glory of Christ," displays the "all-surpassing power (*dynameōs*)" of God (4:4, 7). Paul commends himself "by the word of truth, by the power of God" (*en logō alētheias, en dynamei Theou*, 6:7); here, in the word, the power expresses itself.[21] Engaged as he is in spiritual warfare, Paul employs "weapons [that are] mighty (*dynata*) through God for demolishing strongholds" (10:4a).[22] Consequently, "We cannot do anything against the truth [efforts to impede or withstand or destroy it, are all in vain],[23] but only for the truth [by declaring it, we provide an avenue for its power]" (13:8).

Authenticity

What can Paul say to certify that he is a legitimate apostle of Christ? Nothing but the gospel. Second Corinthians 4:2–7 is especially noteworthy. The very way Paul and his colleagues "commend themselves to every man's conscience in the sight of God" is by refusing to "preach themselves." They resolve not "to tamper with God's word," but instead to "set forth the truth plainly"—that is, to "preach the gospel of Christ." What further proof is needed? For here, in the *euangelion*, the glory of God is revealed (4:4, 6) and the power of God expressed (4:7). The gospel needs no

21. I believe that Paul refers here, not merely to "truthful speech" (NIV), but to "the word of truth" (KJV)—the *euangelion*, "the word of God" (4:1–4)—and to the manifestation of "the power of God" precisely here, in the message (4:7; 1 Thess. 1:5; 2:13; Rom. 1:16; 1 Cor. 1:17–18; 2:4–5). Thus too Martin, *2 Corinthians*, 178. Corresponding to, and supportive of, the "power" (*dynamis*) in the proclamation are the "mighty works" (*dynameis*) that Paul accomplished among the Corinthians (2 Cor.12:12).

22. Paul's weapons are chiefly verbal (10:4b–5; and 2:14–7:16; 10:1–13:10, *passim*), corresponding to those wielded by "the god of this age" and his servants the "false apostles" (4:3–4; 11:3–15).

23. The Judaizers in Galatia "are trying to pervert the gospel of Christ" (Gal. 1:7); but all they can actually do is to replace it with another—spurious—"gospel" (1:6).

outside authentication; it authenticates itself.[24] By contrast, the very proclamation of the "different gospel" about "another Jesus" (11:4) will eventually demonstrate its falsity.

Paul's Counterattack: The Messenger

The message is crucial, but it does not stand alone. Such a proclamation affects its bearer, and the character of the messenger can "do things for the truth" of the message (2 Cor. 13:8).

Humility

The messenger's task is to unveil the glory of Christ, by "setting forth the truth plainly" (4:2). Unlike Moses, "the ministers of the new covenant" never wear a veil, so that Christ's glory may be perpetually revealed (3:6–18).[25] The effect of this disclosure is to humble the messenger under its impact: "For we do not preach ourselves, but Jesus Christ as Lord" (4:5). We are mere "earthen vessels" commissioned to bear "the treasure," namely, "the gospel of the glory of Christ" (4:4, 7). "The god of this age" is of course dedicated to concealing the divine glory (4:3–4). Toward this end he encourages human beings to magnify themselves, and in Paul's opponents he finds willing allies. Their "different gospel" does not disclose but rather conceals the glory of Christ (theirs is an inglorious "different Jesus," 11:4). Instead, they "commend themselves" (10:12a) by producing letters of recommendation and parading their spiritual experiences.[26]

Paul too engages in "boasting," but of a very different character: "'Let the one who boasts boast in the Lord.' For it is not the person who commends himself who is approved, but the one whom the Lord commends" (10:17–18). As the inclusion of the quotation (from Jer. 9:24) shows, it is not merely the person who refuses to commend himself whom the Lord commends, but the one who "commends" the Lord instead. Paul is therefore extremely reluctant to dwell on "visions and revelations from the Lord" (12:1); he knows that such experiences encourage self-exaltation (12:7).[27] Having spoken of them, he confesses: "I have been making a fool of myself;

---

24. C. H. Spurgeon once said, "Defend the Bible? I would as soon defend a lion" (quoted in J. I. Packer, *"Fundamentalism" and the Word of God* [Grand Rapids: Eerdmans, 1960], 6).

25. According to 2 Cor. 3:12, Moses wore the veil so that the Israelites "might not see the glory come to an end and thus be led to disparage Moses as being of no more than temporary importance" (C. K. Barrett, *2 Corinthians* [New York: Harper and Row, 1973], 119). But now that Christ has come to inaugurate "a new covenant" (3:6), one without end, no such concealment is needed.

26. Moreover, says Paul, the others "measure themselves by one another" (10:12b). Is he implying that to compare oneself with the glorious Christ would be too threatening to the proud ego?

27. The fact that Paul's own "visions and revelations from the Lord" (12:1) could compare with anyone's—and doubtless surpass what most others actually experienced—lends greater weight to his refusal to regard these matters as decisive.

it was you who drove me to it" (12:11).[28] Paul's own choice is to boast about his weaknesses, for they provide opportunity to boast about the Lord whose power is thereby manifested (11:23–30; 12:5, 9–10).

Weakness

Paul's *euangelion* is indeed "the power of God," but its chosen medium is human impotence. "Not that we are adequate in ourselves to claim anything as from ourselves. On the contrary, our adequacy comes from God; he has made us adequate to be ministers . . ." (3:5–6a). "We are weak in [Christ], yet by God's power we will . . . serve you" (13:4). "Jars of clay," not vessels of steel, are chosen to bear the treasure of the gospel, "to show that this all-surpassing power (*dynameōs*) is from God and not from us" (4:7). This helps to explain Paul's resolve not to preach himself (4:5); such an assertion of human power would rob him of the divine power.

The messenger is kept weak through suffering (12:7–10). Moreover, Paul interprets his suffering as identification with Christ crucified.[29] The apostle's life is one of perpetual crucifixion: "We always carry around in our body the killing of Jesus" (4:10); "we . . . are always being given over to death" (4:11). Although repeatedly "put to death" (*nekrōsis*, 4:10), Paul never finally dies. We are "dying, and yet we live on," he says (6:9; cf. 1 Cor. 15:31, "I die every day").

Paul writes those words, not as the victim of a martyr complex, but as one who has learned well the lesson of the thorn in the flesh. His suffering must be perpetual, for suffering is requisite for the divine power. Amidst his anxiety over Titus and the Corinthians (2:13), Paul experiences victory (2:14, "God, who always leads us in triumphal procession").[30] His undying death is not an end in itself: "We always carry around in our body the killing of Jesus, in order that the life of Jesus may also be manifested in our body. For we who are living are always being given over to death for Jesus' sake, in order that the life of Jesus may be manifested in our mortal flesh" (4:10–11). With Paul, as with Jesus, the power of life presupposes the weakness of death (13:4).[31] Consequently, he is reticent to rehearse his ecstatic experiences. Nothing—not even "surpassingly great revelations" from God (12:7)—must eclipse the life of crucifixion, the essential path to power.

Let us turn for a moment to Philemon for a fine example of apostolic power in weakness. Clearly Paul desires that Onesimus be free; but he also respects Philemon, who is both Onesimus's owner and a fellow believer.

---

28. Verse 11 appears to mean: "Those who capitalize—as do the false apostles—on such ecstatic experiences, are fools. You have insisted that I speak to you on their terms. To do so, I too must become a fool."

29. This is emphasized in Black, *Weakness*, 239. See also Martin, *2 Corinthians*, lix, 418–23.

30. The link between 2:12–13 and 7:5–7 must not obscure the link between 2:12–13 and 2:14–17.

31. For a different formulation, cf. Phil. 3:10, where Paul, reversing the order of the historical events, indicates that "the power of [Christ's] resurrection" is essential for "sharing in his sufferings."

Paul might have led from strength by refusing to allow Onesimus's return, or by issuing a decree to Philemon ("I could be bold and order you to do what you ought to do," v. 8 NIV). Instead, Paul leads from weakness. In the face of a strong urge to the contrary, he sends Onesimus back to his owner (vv. 12–13). And rather than throwing his apostolic weight around, he appeals to Philemon "on the basis of love" (vv. 8–9). "I did not want to do anything without your consent, so that any favor you do will be spontaneous and not forced" (v. 14 NIV). By taking this path, Paul risks Philemon's refusal and the loss of further service from Onesimus; that is, he risks a kind of crucifixion. But Paul's very vulnerability to this, together with his appeal from love, brings resurrection-power to bear on the situation. The very preservation of the letter signals that Philemon granted Paul's request—in other words, that Philemon himself experienced power in weakness by abandoning his rights and relinquishing his hold upon his slave.[32]

As Philemon shows, the power is not Paul's private possession; it comes to expression precisely in his ministry to other people. The "all-surpassing power" of the gospel is revealed only in its proclamation (2 Cor. 4:4–7). "So then, death is at work in us, but life is at work in you" (4:12); "by God's power we will live . . . to serve you" (13:4). By the same token, when the Macedonian Christians, themselves impoverished, determined nonetheless to contribute to the needs of the Judean Christians, they discovered God's ability to bring much out of little: "Out of the most severe trial, their overflowing joy and their extreme poverty welled up in rich generosity" (8:2 NIV; cf. 9:6–15).

God releases his *dynamis* in order to make persons slaves (*douloi*) of Christ. Should a bearer of the gospel seek to employ that power to make others slaves to himself, this very action would deprive him of the power. Human weakness is the agency of divine power, but divine power never condescends to be the instrument of human power. Paul's is a real weakness (as 2 Corinthians makes clear), not strength masquerading as weakness as a subtle way to gain mastery over people. He preaches the gospel to the Corinthians, not as a means of enslaving them to himself, but as a way of enslaving himself to them for Christ's sake (2 Cor. 4:5).

Paul's opponents have failed to learn these lessons. Whereas Paul leads from weakness, they lead from strength. Their self-commendation, their accent on spectacular experiences, and their "different gospel" (11:4), are simultaneously assertions of human power and rejections of divine power. That they claim to be (and doubtless believe themselves to be) exercising God's power makes it easier to bring the Corinthians under their control

---

32. F. F. Bruce, *Paul, Apostle of the Heart Set Free* (Grand Rapids: Eerdmans, 1977), 406, observes that "if Philemon had hardened his heart and refused to pardon and welcome Onesimus he would certainly have suppressed the letter."

(11:20). The threat is extremely serious, for their power is not apparent but real. Its ultimate source is "the god of this age" (4:4; 11:13–15) who, by the agency of the "false apostles," seeks to draw the Corinthians away from Christ into bondage to himself (11:3).

Authenticity

Branded an "impostor" or "deceiver" (*planos*) by his opponents, Paul declares himself to be "true" or "genuine" (*alēthēs*, 6:8). What makes him so?

Paul found security in who he was—Christ's apostle (1:1) and ambassador (5:20). Ultimately he is answerable to Christ alone. He is therefore free from the judgments of both the Judeans and the Corinthians. In one sense it does not matter what these people make of his apostolic claims. Jesus has commissioned him, so he is an apostle even if everyone else denies it. This frees him from having to pretend, and from throwing his apostolic weight around, and from striving to win people's approval. Paul does not have to prove his apostleship to them, or impose his apostleship on them, by insisting on payment for his services (12:13–18). He has stupendous authority, but he does not use it to subjugate people (1:24; 13:10). He has power not to throw his power around, and the right not to insist on his rights.[33] Paul views his relationship to the Jerusalem apostles in the same light. He is enslaved to Christ, not to Peter; having been commissioned directly by Christ, he stands beside, not under, the Jerusalem leaders ("I do not think I am in the least inferior to those 'super-apostles,'" 11:5 NIV). But knowing he is free from them, he is free for them (1 Cor. 9:19); far from severing his ties with Jerusalem, he oversees the collection (2 Cor. 8–9) in order to unite the Gentile Christian churches with the needy believers of Judea.

Paul also found security in what he said. The gospel he preaches generates its own power and discloses its own glory. As the bearer of a self-authenticating message, the apostle is relieved of enormous pressure. He does not have to resort to trickery. He is free to be genuine: "We do not use deception, nor do we distort the word of God. On the contrary, by setting forth the truth plainly we commend ourselves to every man's conscience in the sight of God" (4:2 NIV). The testimony in 1 Thessalonians 2:3–6 is very similar:[34] "For the appeal we make does not spring from error or impure

33. In 1 Cor. 9:7–18, Paul speaks of exercising his apostolic authority to relinquish his apostolic right to payment for his services. In 1 Thess. 2:7–9, he recalls that "as apostles of Christ, we could have been a burden to you [or thrown our apostolic weight around]" by charging for our services, but that instead "we worked night and day in order not to be a burden to anyone" (NIV).

34. The Thessalonians are threatened not by Judaizers, but by advocates of various pagan religions. Yet their tactics are reminiscent of Paul's opponents in 2 Cor. Günther Bornkamm, *Paul*, trans. D. M. G. Stalker (New York: Harper and Row, 1971), 64, says of them: "They were itinerant apostles and miracle-workers of the most varied persuasions, heralds of heathen gods, and dispensers of salvation, adroit and eloquent, ardent and evoking ardor, but also smart and conceited in extolling the mighty acts of their gods and fooling the masses. . . . General popular opinion expected the Christian missionaries to be able to vie with them."

motives, nor are we trying to trick you. On the contrary, we speak as men approved by God to be entrusted with the gospel [so pretense is unnecessary]. We are not trying to please men but God, who tests our hearts [so pretense is futile]. You know we never used flattery, nor did we put on a mask to cover up greed—God is our witness. We were not looking for praise from men, not from you or anyone else" (NIV). As a person who is neither slavishly dependent upon the Thessalonians' approval nor bent upon enslaving them to himself, Paul is free to care for them as a mother and to encourage them as a father (2:7–12).[35]

Paul also learned genuineness through suffering. Self-abandonment (2 Cor. 12:9–10) was his way to self-realization.[36] The experience of "always being given over to death for Jesus' sake" (4:11) freed him from having to insist on his rights: what rights does an executed victim have? He is also free to be real: what need is there for phoniness if one is about to die?

It is not Paul but his opponents who are the *planoi*, the "imposters." They are "false apostles, deceitful workers," servants of Satan masquerading as apostles of Christ (11:13–15). Their message is false—a "different gospel" about "another Jesus" (11:4). And their power is false—human, ultimately demonic, power disguised as divine power. As there is no genuineness in what they are, or say, or do, they have to lead from strength. They are not secure enough to lead from weakness.

Second Corinthians thus affirms the legitimacy of Paul's apostleship by its threefold witness to his humility, his weakness, and his authenticity— by this and nothing more. "The apostle's legitimacy appears not in the power of his personality, not in his spiritual experiences, not in his commissioning by the right ecclesiastical authorities, but only in the extent to which his life and preaching represent the crucified Jesus."[37]

Leading from Weakness

What are the implications of Paul's teaching about apostleship in 2 Corinthians and elsewhere for Christian ministry today?

The Pattern

Today's minister is no apostle; but he is a slave of Christ, just as surely as was Paul. Herein lies his security. As Christ's slave, he is free from his

---

35. Paul's willingness to liken himself to a nursing mother (2:7; cf. Matt. 23:37), is, if anything, a signal of his sense of security as a male in Christ.

36. C. H. Dodd, "The Mind of Paul: I.," *New Testament Studies* (Manchester: Manchester University Press, 1953), 80–81, observes that 2 Cor. 12:9–10 is "not mere 'paradox.' It has profound psychological truth. So long as [Paul] chafed against unavoidable disabilities and reverses which wounded his prestige, he was losing the spiritual liberty and power which come from the abandonment of personal claims. But when he accepted his limitations he was liberated afresh." Cf. Mark 8:35.

37. Barrett, *2 Corinthians*, 30.

people; and only on this basis can he be free for them (1 Cor. 9:19). Slavery to a people ceases to be destructive only when it happens "for Jesus' sake" (2 Cor. 4:5). The ministerial *doulos* shows his allegiance to Christ the *Kyrios*, by his verbal proclamation of the *euangelion* about Christ crucified and by a corresponding visible proclamation in a life of perpetual crucifixion. By this twin witness the divine power is released, the divine glory is revealed, and the messenger is shown to be a true heir of the apostles.[38]

That power is exerted in the face of human impotence, and that glory disclosed in the face of human obscurity. Nothing could be more liberating for a minister.[39] He is relieved of the enormous burden of maintaining control over his people, and of striving to remain glorious in their eyes. He is not hereby called upon to be as incompetent or as disgraceful as possible (as if to say, "Let us fail that grace may abound"); such behavior would only assure that he remains the center of attention. But he is to be attentive to those qualities of his that make him most confident and offer most hope of success. It is his native strengths, not his native weaknesses, of which the minister must be especially wary.[40]

Leading from strength is the safeguard of the insecure. If a person trades the true gospel for a spurious one, and trades the life of crucifixion for one of triumphalism, and thereby abandons the divine power and glory, counterfeit expressions of power and glory inevitably arise. Strong-armed tactics are now essential to assure that everyone knows who is in charge. Attention may be shifted from what is said to what is done. A powerless message encourages an achievement-centered ministry (5:12). Or attention may be diverted from the message to the messenger. As a "different gospel" (of whatever content) lacks glory, its advocate may more conveniently clothe himself with glory, thereby converting the "earthen vessel" into a "treasure." Or to compensate for the impotence of his message, he may arrogate apostolic authority to himself. Moreover, since the size or prestige of one's church, or the performance or ecclesiastical credentials of the preacher, are indeed counterfeits, great effort is

38. Conversely, "service severed from obedience [to Christ] degenerates into spiritual stardom," writes Richard J. Foster, *Money, Sex and Power* (San Francisco: Harper and Row, 1985), 231. His whole discussion of power (175–246) is valuable.

39. Henri J. M. Nouwen, *The Wounded Healer* (Garden City, N.Y.: Image, 1979), 81–96, speaks of the wounds of ministerial loneliness as a major source of healing power.

40. D. Martyn Lloyd-Jones counsels preachers: "Watch your natural gifts and tendencies and idiosyncrasies. . . . What I mean is that they will tend to run away with you. It can all be summed up in a phrase—watch your strength. Not so much your weaknesses: it is your strength you have to watch, the things at which you excel, your natural gifts and aptitudes. They are the ones that are most likely to trip you because they are the ones that will tempt you to make a display and pander to self" (*Preaching and Preachers* [Grand Rapids: Zondervan, 1971], 255).

required to maintain the illusion of glory and power, and to hold people under its spell.[41]

The Purpose

Second Corinthians says as much about "boasting" (*kauchēma* and *kauchēsis*) as about power (*dynamis*).[42] And no wonder, for the two are very closely related; what we think about power determines the focus of our boasting.

Since pride is by nature competitive (as we saw in chap. 5), it craves for power. "Power is what Pride really enjoys: there is nothing makes a man feel so superior to others as being able to move them about like toy soldiers. What makes a pretty girl spread misery wherever she goes by collecting admirers? Certainly not her sexual instinct. . . . It is Pride."[43] A minister who seeks to control people is acting both out of and into pride. Pride moves him to wield the power, and wielding the power bolsters his pride; pride is both the root and the fruit of power. The minister may more easily dominate others when he wields power under a pretext of humility—a deception assured of some success, given the perception of this profession as one of service to others.[44]

How then can a minister employ real power without its becoming the handmaiden of pride? Only by his following Paul's example. For Paul too, pride was both the root and the fruit of power. His "boast in the Lord" (2 Cor. 10:17) provided the impetus for his exercise of power. As that power came from the same Lord (12:9–10), and as its exercise caused "the glory of God in the face of Christ" to be revealed (4:4–7), the effect was to intensify Paul's boast: "For all things are for your sakes, that grace, having spread through the many, may cause thanksgiving to abound to the glory of God" (4:15 NKJV). It is right and it is healthy for the minister's heart to be swollen with pride to the point of bursting, so long as it is God and Christ of whom he boasts.[45]

41. According to Paul, "the one who claims to be strong is often in fact weak. . . . Is it possible that sometimes those who seem to know what everyone else should do are in fact weaker brothers? Is it possible that the one who seems extremely vulnerable is in fact more likely to know the supporting power of God?" (Peter Richardson, *Paul's Ethic of Freedom* [Philadelphia: Westminster, 1979], 140–41). Cf. our discussion of 1 Cor. and Rom. in chap. 6.

42. The noun *kauchēma* occurs three times in 2 Cor., the noun *kauchēsis* six times, and the verb *kauchaomai* twenty times.

43. C. S. Lewis, *Mere Christianity* (New York: Macmillan, 1954), 95. Scarlett O'Hara was such a woman, who nonetheless despised those who let her dominate them: "she could not love anyone who was weak" (Margaret Mitchell, *Gone with the Wind* [New York: Macmillan, 1936], 419).

44. The *tapeinophrosynē*, "false humility," of Col. 2:18, 23, becomes a tool of legalists bent upon enslaving others (2:16–23). Uriah Heep (in Charles Dickens's *David Copperfield*), by his incessant talk about how "'umble" he is, draws people under his power.

45. For the applicability of 2 Cor. to the life and leadership of the contemporary church, see Carson, *From Triumphalism to Maturity*.

The Power of Submission

Let us now apply the teaching of 2 Corinthians 12:9–10 to our three relationships. Our main text is Ephesians 5:21–6:9. The fullness of the Spirit (5:18)
finds expression in the actions denoted by the five participles of 5:19–21,
namely, in praising and submitting.[46] We are presently concerned with the
latter: "Submitting yourselves to one another out of reverence for Christ"
(5:21), a statement that governs the discussion of the three crucial relationships in 5:22–6:9. What Paul teaches here is closely akin to what he says about
ministry in 2 Corinthians. Here too he talks about using power in a context
of spiritual warfare (5:18 vis-a-vis 6:10–18). And here too he insists that submission—that is, weakness—is essential for the release of divine power.

Relating to God

"Submitting yourselves to one another out of reverence for Christ," says
Paul (5:21). Submission to Christ the Lord, not to the partner in the human
relationship, is the foundational reality. Only thus are we protected from
the temptation to devour, or to let ourselves be devoured by, other people.
Each person in each relationship stands under Christ's lordship and is ultimately subject to him alone.[47] Without this safeguard, one shudders to
think what some husbands might do with the command of 5:24, or some
fathers with the command of 6:1. As the purchased slaves of Christ the
Redeemer, all persons addressed stand on equal footing (Gal. 3:28). No
partner is superior or inferior to the other.

At the same time, to revere Christ is to recognize the pattern of authority
that God has established. "The husband," says Paul, "is the head (kephalē)
of the wife as Christ is the head (kephalē) of the church" (Eph. 5:23). In the
one case, as in the other, "headship" denotes rule.[48] Correspondingly, children are to "obey" and "honor" their parents (6:1–3); and slaves are to
"obey" their masters "with respect and fear" (6:5).

Furthermore, these relationships are scenes of titanic conflict between
the triune God and "the spiritual forces of evil in the heavenly realms"
under the devil's command (6:11–12; 2:2). Accordingly, in order to live by
the counsel of 5:22–6:9, one must recognize Christ's victory over the hostile
powers (1:20–22), and appropriate "the full armor of God" (6:10–18). One

46. Cf. chap. 4; p. 101, including note 56.
47. In each instance Paul addresses Christians: 5:22 ("as to the Lord"), 25 ("just as Christ loved"), 29
("just as Christ does"); and 6:1 ("in the Lord"), 4 ("in the Lord"), 5 ("just as you would obey Christ"), 6
("like slaves of Christ"), 7 ("serving the Lord"), 9 ("both their Master and yours").
48. See also 1 Cor. 11:3; Eph. 1:22; 4:15; Col. 1:18; 2:10. For an able defense of this reading of kephalē, see
James B. Hurley, Man and Woman in Biblical Perspective (Grand Rapids: Zondervan, 1981), 144–48, 163–68;
and Wayne Grudem, "The Meaning of Kephalē ('Head'): A Response to Recent Studies," in Recovering Biblical Manhood and Womanhood, ed. John Piper and Wayne Grudem (Wheaton: Crossway, 1991), 425–68.

must also obey the command and claim the promise of 5:18. For the fullness of the Spirit finds expression in the practice of submitting, and submitting to one another requires the fullness of the Spirit. Moreover, reliance on God calls for attentiveness to the totality of this passage—to everything that the ascended Christ authorizes his apostle to impart for the growth of his people (cf. 4:7–13).

Relating to Ourselves

It is a great relief to recognize that every person in the relationships of Ephesians 5:22–6:9, including oneself, is a slave of Christ. This frees me from bondage to other people. As Jesus' slave, I cannot also be a slave to my spouse, or to my children or parents, or to my employer or employees—a truth especially important for persons who stand under the authority of another. I am also spared the onerous task of mastering other people and holding them in bondage to myself—a truth especially important for a person who exercises authority over another. For both reasons, my submission is not coerced but voluntary: "submitting yourselves to one another."[49]

Self-awareness also means perceiving my spiritual impotence in face of the demands of the relationships themselves on the one hand, and the relentless assaults from the demonic powers on the other. Moreover, the submission to which Paul summons me is itself an act of weakness: it signals a willingness to yield to the other person and to expose myself to his or her exertions of power. Yet when, acutely aware of my impotence and vulnerability, I nonetheless obey, I learn the lesson of 2 Corinthians 12. As Christ crucified was "the power of God," and as Christ's power was perfected in the apostle's weakness, so the Spirit's power comes to expression in the very act of my submitting.

Relating to Other People

The fullness of the Spirit is not a private experience; it is by nature relational and communal. Moreover, the Spirit acts where there is reciprocity: "submitting yourselves to one another" (5:21; cf. 5:19, "speaking to one another"). Each partner in the relationship must submit to the other, and do so (as noted) voluntarily.[50] Only thus does the Spirit's power come to

---

49. The participle *hypotassomenoi* could by itself be rendered as a passive; but with the reciprocal pronoun *allēlois* following, it must be middle. Paul has already applied this principle to himself: "Although I am free from everyone [for I am Christ's slave], I have made myself a slave of everyone" (1 Cor. 9:19); it is a decision of Christian liberty.

50. The verb *hypotassō* often denotes submission to authority: that of Christ (1 Cor. 15:27–28; Eph. 1:22; 5:24; Phil. 3:21), or the state (Rom. 13:1; Titus 3:1), or one's husband (Eph. 5:24; Col. 3:18; Titus 2:5), or one's master (Titus 2:9), or church leaders (1 Cor. 16:16). Never does Paul use *hypotassō* to denote an authority's submission to his subjects. Cf. Hurley, *Man and Woman*, 139–44. But Paul does use the verb to denote mutual submission: 1 Cor. 14:32 (with vv. 29–31); and Eph. 5:21, the one place where Paul joins this verb to the

full expression. In calling for mutual submission, Paul does not threaten the structure of authority; rather, he is showing how the authority is to be employed. In the previous section, we applied Paul's model of leadership from weakness to the ecclesiastical sphere. The same holds true in the home and in the workplace. Here too, strength is made perfect in weakness—not only when a person is yielding to authority, but also (and more profoundly) when one is wielding it. To illustrate, we focus chiefly, as does Paul, on the husband-wife relationship.[51] We do so, moreover, in the awareness that Ephesians proclaims the creation of a new humanity at the center of a restored universe. The partners' mutual submissiveness recalls both the metaphysical equality of male and female in Genesis 1:27, and their services to one another according to Genesis 2:18 (the woman a "helper suitable" for the man) and 24 (the man leaves his parents and cleaves to his wife).

In view of what Ephesians 5:21 says about the partners' mutual submissiveness and their common allegiance to Christ, it will be helpful to begin by recalling Paul's counsel to married believers in an earlier letter. Closer in spirit to Ephesians 5 than is sometimes recognized is 1 Corinthians 7:1–5. Paul astonishingly declares that Christ's ownership of the body (6:19–20) entails ownership by the spouse: "For the wife does not have authority over her own body, but the husband does; likewise the husband does not have authority over his own body, but the wife does" (7:4 NRSV).[52] This is a particular instance of slavery to others as a mark of one's slavery to Christ. Significantly, "depriving each other" must be "by mutual consent" (7:5). Both in this opening section and beyond, 1 Corinthians 7 respects the metaphysical equality of husband and wife (cf. 7:10–16, 32–35). This prepares for the richer development of Ephesians.

The wife submits to her husband by respecting him, which includes acknowledging his headship (Eph. 5:22–24, 33). This is meaningful, because she has the power (though not the right) not to do so. A wife may subtly manipulate her husband into thinking he is in charge, in order to establish herself as the real ruler of the domestic realm. But such an asser-

---

reciprocal pronoun *allēlois*. Moreover, in this passage Paul commands each authority figure to serve, which is by nature a submissive act: as Christ "gave himself up" for the church, so the husband is to love his wife (5:25); the parent is to "bring [the children] up in the training and nurture of the Lord" (6:4); and masters are to "treat . . . slaves in the same way" (6:9), i.e., to serve them (6:7).

51. In Eph. 5:22–6:9, this is the first relationship to be considered (as also in Col. 3:18–4:1), and the one which Paul discusses at greatest length. As this relationship goes, so go the other two. The uses of power in marriage are therefore of critical importance. Helen Singer Kaplan, *The New Sex Therapy* (New York: Times Books, 1974), 160, speaks of "the violent power struggles which transpire between some couples . . . [when] each spouse is dominated by the need to control the other and conversely to avoid being subjected to domination." I am indebted to Mrs. Mignonne Tadlock for this reference.

52. NIV's additions "does not belong to her alone but also to her husband" and "does not belong to him alone but also to his wife" do not occur in the Greek text.

tion of human power, in violation of Christ's directive (5:21–22), would rob the relationship of the divine power.

The wife's model is the church (5:24); but the husband's is Christ himself—a testimony to the cruciality of the husband's function in the relationship. As Christ showed his love for the church by giving himself up for her, so the husband is to do for his wife (5:25). This means that he will serve his wife "in a way that is holy and honorable" (1 Thess. 4:4).[53] Such conduct is significant because the husband may choose not to do so; instead he may use his headship to tyrannize his wife, or throw his weight around by being unfaithful to her (1 Thess. 4:4–6). But the crown that Christ bestows upon the husband is made not of gold but of thorns.[54] As Christ crucified is the power of God (1 Cor. 1:23–24), so power is released into the marital relationship when the husband lays down his life for the sake of his wife, which may well include the crucifixion of the urge to commit adultery. Such a husband encourages his wife to become all that God created and redeemed her to be.[55]

The structure of 5:25–28 is instructive. The enveloping verses (25, 28) call upon husbands to "love their wives." The enclosed verses (26–27) describe how this happens. Christ loved the church, not just for what she was, but for what she by his oversight would one day become—"a radiant church, without stain or wrinkle or any other blemish, but holy and blameless" (v. 27 NIV). So too, says Paul, a husband should love his wife not just for what she is, but for what by God's grace she can become. How many a wife, viewed by her husband with contempt because in some way she falls short of his expectations, becomes in response yet more contemptible? But how many a wife, viewed by her husband with respect and love in face of a ruinous physical or psychological condition, has grown more lovable as a result? Amid marital weaknesses and hardships, as amid their apostolic counterparts, the power of Christ crucified is perfected.[56]

---

53. I believe that the *skeuos* (vessel) of 1 Thess. 4:4 is the man's "own wife" (NIV mg.) rather than his "own body" (NIV text). The first view is defended by Ernest Best, *The First and Second Epistles to the Thessalonians* (New York: Harper and Row, 1972), 161–65; the second by F. F. Bruce, *1 and 2 Thessalonians* (Waco: Word, 1982), 83–84.

54. "Christ loved the church and gave himself up for her" (5:25), the very language used of his atoning sacrifice in 5:2.

55. John Stott believes that the husband's task "is a headship more of care than of control, more of responsibility than of authority" (*Involvement II: Social and Sexual Relationships in the Modern World* [Old Tappan, N.J.: Revell, 1985], 145). But as *kephalē* denotes rule, it is preferable to say that the husband exercises authority by protecting, encouraging, and serving his wife—just as Christ did not abandon but exercised kingly rule when he went to the cross. As Stott goes on to say, "Masculine 'headship' is the God-given means by which their femininity is protected and enabled to blossom. . . . Masculine headship is intended not to smother but to serve them, and to ensure that they are—and may more fully become—themselves" (ibid., 147).

56. See the story of Mother Gerda in Walter Trobisch, *I Married You* (New York: Harper and Row, 1971), 128; and the comments on Eph. 5 in C. S. Lewis, *The Four Loves* (New York: Harcourt Brace Jovanovich, 1960), 148–49.

As noted, submission in these relationships must be both voluntary and mutual. Moreover, on the analogy of Christ's saving work, the initiative rests with the authority figure.[57] If he or she insists on leading from strength—remaining unbending and unbreakable before the partner—the healthy growth of the relationship is impeded.[58] But when, following Christ's example, the husband, or the parent, or the employer chooses to lead from weakness, divine power is released for evoking a kindred submissiveness from the partner.[59]

The power of submission, here applied to the home and the workplace, is also evident in Paul's teaching about relationships within the church, the subject of the next chapter.

O God, I know that I often do thy work without thy power, and sin by my dead, heartless, blind service. . . . But thou dost show thy power by my frailty, so that the more feeble I am, the more fit to be used, for thou dost pitch a tent of grace in my weakness. . . . Teach me that I must act by a power supernatural, whereby I can attempt things above my strength, and bear evils beyond my strength, acting for Christ in all, and having his superior power to help me. Let me learn of Paul whose presence was mean, his weakness great, his utterance contemptible, yet thou didst account him faithful and blessed. Lord, let me lean on thee as he did, and find my ministry thine.[60]

---

57. Salvation occurs by Christ's initiative, which is by nature self-emptying (Phil. 2:7) and self-sacrificing (Eph. 5:25).

58. John Steinbeck, in *East of Eden* (New York: Penguin, 1979), 13, says of Liza: "She frightened her grandchildren because she had no weakness."

59. Cf. Paul Tournier, *The Strong and the Weak*, trans. Edwin Hudson (London: SCM, 1963), 230–38. On the working out of the principle of "exchanged life"—"my life for yours"—in the family, see Thomas Howard, *Hallowed Be This House* (Wheaton: Harold Shaw, 1979), 22–28 *et passim*. For an illustration from labor-management relations (at Pittron Steel), see R. C. Sproul, *Stronger than Steel: the Wayne Alderson Story* (New York: Harper and Row, 1980).

60. Arthur Bennett, ed., *The Valley of Vision: A collection of Puritan prayers and devotions* (Edinburgh: Banner of Truth, 1975), 187.

9

Life in Community

"In and through community lies the salvation of the world." Paul would agree with these words of a contemporary author.[1] Understanding what Paul means requires attentiveness to his whole theology. The viability of community depends upon salvation from bondage to Sin (chap. 2) by the work of Christ (chap. 3). Life in Christ is by nature communal (chap. 4). One of the best remedies for pride's self-absorption (chap. 5) is the corporate life of the church—both its vertical dimension (the common worship of God) and its horizontal (the exercise of the gifts of the Spirit for the sake of others). Servitude to other people in obedience to Christ the Lord (chap. 6) requires community. Christians engaged in the manifold struggle (chap. 7) need both the encouragement and the accountability of the church. Christ reveals his strength amid our weakness (chap. 8) by the agency of his people.

1. M. Scott Peck, *The Different Drum: Community Making and Peace* (New York: Simon and Schuster, 1987), 17. On Americans' urgent need of "communities of memory" (including the church) in the face of rampant and destructive individualism, see Robert Bellah et al., *Habits of the Heart: Individualism and Commitment in American Life* (Berkeley: University of California Press, 1985). For a stirring call for the renewal of the church's witness in and for the world, see Charles Colson with Ellen Santilli Vaughn, *The Body* (Dallas: Word, 1992).

Paul's Accent on Community

The very act of being joined to Christ unites one to other human beings. This Paul affirms in various ways, all of which are woven together in his letters.[2]

The Church

Behind "church" in our English translations is *ekklēsia*. Paul employs the term sixty-two times (in eleven letters), invariably to denote a people, namely, those who belong to God and who have been incorporated into Christ.[3]

Moreover, in accord with ancient usage generally, *ekklēsia* in Paul denotes a gathered people.[4] In each case it is the people's common life in Christ that accounts for the gathering and determines what happens there; and the accent is always upon the assembling of persons or the persons assembled, not upon the places where they gather. This does not mean that such places are without importance, only that they are denoted by terms other than *ekklēsia*—unlike our practice of using "church" to denote a building or a denomination.

It was common for the Christians to whom Paul writes to congregate in private homes.[5] In some cities at certain times one such place would probably have sufficed: "the church that meets in [Philemon's] house" (Philem. 2) may have been the only gathering of believers in Colosse. In other cities the Christians assembled on occasion as one body and on occasion as smaller groups in various homes. At the close of Romans Paul's opening greeting to Priscilla and Aquila, and to "the church that meets at their house" (16:3–5a), is followed by many more (16:5b–15, including "the brothers" and "all the saints" with named individuals, vv. 14–15), evidence that the gathering of 16:5 did not encompass all the Roman believers.[6] Paul

2. The present discussion builds upon the remarks about "union with Christ" in chap. 4, pp. 90–94.

3. Such a church is "not simply a human association or a religious club, but a divinely created entity" (Peter T. O'Brien, *Colossians, Philemon* [Waco: Word, 1982], 59). For "the church [or the churches] of God," see 1 Cor. 1:2; 10:32; 11:16, 22; 15:9; 2 Cor. 1:1; Gal. 1:13; 2 Thess. 1:4; 1 Tim. 3:5, 15. For "the church [or the churches] in Christ [or of Christ]," see Rom. 16:16; Gal. 1:22. 1 Thess. 1:1 speaks of "the church . . . in God the Father and the Lord Jesus Christ" (2 Thess. 1:1 is almost identical); and 2:14 of "God's churches . . . which are in Christ Jesus."

4. For the antecedents in Greek and Jewish usage, see Karl Ludwig Schmidt, *TDNT* 3:513–17, 527–29; Lothar Coenen, *NIDNTT* 1:291–96.

5. For instances of *ekklēsia* in this sense, see Rom. 16:5, 23; 1 Cor. 16:19; Col. 4:15; Philem. 2. Cf. Robert Banks, *Paul's Idea of Community: The Early House Churches in Their Historical Setting* (Grand Rapids: Eerdmans, 1980), 33–42. "It was not until about the middle of the third century that early Christianity owned property for purposes of worship" (O'Brien, *Colossians*, 256).

6. The same distinction between a smaller and a larger number of believers in one locale is present in 1 Cor. 16:19–20 ("Aquila and Priscilla greet you warmly in the Lord, as does the church that meets in their house. All the brothers send you greetings") and Col. 4:15 ("Greet the brothers at Laodicea, also Nympha and the church in her house").

speaks of times when "the whole church [at Corinth] comes together in one place" (1 Cor. 14:23 NKJV), implying that there were smaller assemblies as well.[7] Romans (written from Corinth) points to a place that was adequate to house all the Corinthian believers: "Gaius, who is host to me and to the whole church" (16:23).

That Paul employs the term *ekklēsia* to denote a Christian gathering (of whatever size) in a private home is noteworthy indeed. But the foregoing passages witness to something that is yet more significant: where several congregations within a city come together, they do not become "the churches" (*ekklēsiai*) but remain *the church*. Paul does use the plural when speaking in broader geographical terms.[8] But he consistently uses the singular when identifying Christians by the city in which they live, he addresses his letters to the whole company of believers in the city, and he directs his instructions to their gatherings as a "whole church": "Paul . . . to the church of the Thessalonians" (1 Thess. 1:1), a letter to be read "to all the brothers" (5:27); "Paul . . . to the church of God in Corinth" (1 Cor. 1:2; chaps. 11–14); "And when this letter has been read among you [the church of Colosse], see that it is read also in the church of the Laodiceans . . ." (Col. 4:16).[9] It is "the whole church" of a given city that will most clearly demonstrate believers' unity (or lack of it); and "the whole church" that will bear the most telling witness, for good or ill, to the surrounding populace.

Despite Paul's accent on the local church, he offers not the slightest encouragement to an independent spirit. His letters repeatedly remind readers of their connection to believers elsewhere: "The churches of Asia send you greetings. Aquila and Priscilla, together with the church that meets in their house, greet you warmly in the Lord. All the brothers send you greetings" (1 Cor. 16:19–20).[10] Paul's letters to the Colossians and the

---

7. NKJV well represents both the verb *synerchomai* (come together, assemble) and the prepositional phrase *epi to auto* (to the same place); so too BAGD, *s.v. epi*. The full assembly is again in view in 1 Cor. 11:17–34, where *synerchomai* occurs five times and where we again meet the words *come together in one place* (11:20).

8. Paul consistently uses *ekklēsiai* when identifying believers by province: "the churches of Galatia" (Gal. 1:2; 1 Cor. 16:1); "God's churches in Judea" (Gal. 1:22; 1 Thess. 2:14); "the Macedonian churches" (2 Cor. 8:1); "the churches of Asia" (1 Cor. 16:19). The same holds true for the more comprehensive phrases of Rom. 16:4 ("all the churches of the Gentiles"), 16 ("all the churches of Christ").

9. See also Rom. 16:1; 2 Cor. 1:1; 2 Thess. 1:1. Paul sometimes speaks to a group or an individual within the larger community; but nowhere does he expressly address a house-church within the city-church, though of course some instructions to the general assembly (e.g., 1 Corinthians 11 and 14) would apply to the smaller ones too. Where he distinguishes one *ekklēsia* from another, congregations in different cities are always in view: Phil. 4:15 ("no church shared with me . . . but you alone"); 1 Cor. 4:17; 7:17; 2 Cor. 12:13. 1 Cor. 14:33b–34, "As in all the churches (*ekklēsiais*) of the saints, women should be silent in the churches (*ekklēsiais*)" (NRSV), teaches that Corinthian practices must accord with those elsewhere. The latter instance of "churches" may refer to a succession of joint assemblies or (more likely) to a plurality of assemblies, each of which may be termed an *ekklēsia* (as in 1 Cor. 16:19), and which together compose "the church (*ekklēsia*) at Corinth" (1 Cor. 1:2).

10. See also Rom. 16:3–16, 21–24; 2 Cor. 13:13; Phil. 4:21–22; Col. 4:10–15; 1 Thess. 5:26; 2 Tim. 4:19, 21; Titus 3:15; Philem. 23–24; and the salutation of every letter.

Laodiceans respectively are to be exchanged (Col. 4:16). Ephesians has the marks of a circular letter, addressed to several churches in the province of Asia and perhaps beyond.[11] Churches offer hospitality to traveling Christians, including Paul and his coworkers; Paul sends emissaries to, and receives helpers from, local churches.[12] A church, or group of churches, offers financial aid to believers elsewhere.[13] Paul and his colleagues pray for the churches under their care, and he asks readers to pray for his work and for other Christians beyond their own number.[14] By all these means, Paul "sought to build up enduring relationships of a personal, rather than institutional, character."[15]

We are now ready to consider a broader usage of *ekklēsia* in Paul's letters. When recalling that he "persecuted the church of God" (1 Cor. 15:9; Gal. 1:13; "the church," Phil. 3:6), he is probably still thinking of believers gathered in a particular locale, Jerusalem.[16] The same may be said of 1 Corinthians 10:32 ("Give no offense to Jews, or to Greeks, or to the church of God"), in view of the usage of *ekklēsia* in the letter generally. But by the time Paul writes Colossians and Ephesians, his understanding of the *ekklēsia* has deepened considerably. He now builds as never before upon his foundational conviction that the church is God's creation and Christ's purchased possession. God "raised [Christ] from the dead and seated him at his right hand in the heavenly realms" (Eph. 1:20). Not only so: "God raised us up with him and seated us with him in the heavenly realms in Christ Jesus" (Eph. 2:6); "Since therefore you have been raised with Christ, seek the things that are above . . . , your life is hidden with Christ in God" (Col. 3:1, 3). Those "blessed . . . in the heavenly realms" are "the saints . . ., the faithful in Christ Jesus" (Eph. 1:1–3), the members of the new humanity (Eph. 2:11–22)—in other words, the church. The church that Christ loved and for whose sake he died (Eph. 5:25) already participates in his heavenly glory (Eph. 3:21). There the church bears its witness: God's "intent was that now, through the church, the manifold wisdom of God should be made known to the rulers and authorities in the heavenly

11. On this matter, see Donald Guthrie, *New Testament Introduction*, 4th ed. (Downers Grove: Inter-Varsity, 1990), 530–31. On the collection of Paul's letters for the sake of the whole church, see ibid., 986–1000.

12. See Rom. 1:11–13; 15:23–33; 16:1–2; 1 Cor. 16:10–11; 2 Cor. 7:5–16; 8:16–24; Eph. 6:21–22; Phil. 1:19–26; 2:19–30; Col. 1:7; 4:7–9; 1 Thess. 3:1–2; 2 Tim. 4:9–13; Titus 3:12; Philem. 8–22.

13. Rom. 15:25–27; 1 Cor. 16:1–4; 2 Cor. 8–9; Phil. 4:10–20.

14. Rom. 1:9–10; 15:30–31; Eph. 1:15–18; 3:14–21; 6:18–20; Phil. 1:3–11; Col. 1:3–12; 4:2–4, 12; 1 Thess. 1:2–3; 5:25; 2 Thess. 1:11–12; 3:1–2; Philem. 4–6, 22.

15. Banks, *Community*, 48. "These scattered Christian groups did not express their unity by fashioning a corporate organization through which they could be federated with one another, but rather through a network of personal contacts between people who regarded themselves as members of the same Christian family" (ibid.).

16. Thus Banks, *Community*, 36; followed by O'Brien, *Colossians*, 59–60. Paul, having spoken in Gal. 1:13 of "persecuting the church," goes on to speak in 1:22 of "the churches of Judea."

realms" (Eph. 3:10 NIV; cf. 1:20–23). Similarly, the declaration of Colossians 1:15–20 about Christ's sovereignty over both heaven and earth, and over all rulers and authorities, suggests that "the body, the church" over which he rules (1:18) "is not an earthly phenomenon . . . but a supernatural and heavenly one."[17]

It would therefore be incorrect to say that the singular *ekklēsia* in those texts of Colossians and Ephesians is equivalent to Paul's earlier phrase *all the churches of Christ* (Rom. 16:16)—to say, in other words, that these two letters envisage a worldwide *ekklēsia* where the idea of a gathered church has perforce been left behind. For one thing, Colossians itself speaks of a house-church and a city-church (4:15–16).[18] For another, the concept of the church as a heavenly reality is anticipated in earlier letters.[19] What then is the relationship between the heavenly church and the local church? While the former is no earthly phenomenon, it is ruled by the Lord of both heaven and earth; it embraces all the people of God presently living on earth; the saints who are "blessed in the heavenly realms" are the very ones called upon to live obediently in the world; and the Christ who ascended "in order to fill the universe" has imparted gifts "to equip the saints for the work of ministry" (Eph. 4:10–12). The local *ekklēsia* remains the church, and is meant to evidence all the marks of the church. The people of God in a given city are not a segment of the heavenly church but that church itself in its earthly, local manifestation. Both when they gather together, and when they do not, they participate in the heavenly reality.[20]

That is as profound an expression of community as we shall find in Paul. At the same time he employs terms that express more vividly than does *ekklēsia* his idea of Christian community.

17. O'Brien, *Colossians*, 60; cf. idem, "The Church as a Heavenly and Eschatological Entity," in *The Church in the Bible and the World*, ed. D. A. Carson (Grand Rapids: Baker, 1987), 88–119; Banks, *Community*, 43–48. On the teaching of Colossians and Ephesians about the church's union with the heavenly Christ, and Christ's rule through and for the church, see Andrew T. Lincoln, *Paradise Now and Not Yet* (Cambridge: Cambridge University Press, 1981), 110–68.

18. Cf. Philem. 2 ("the church that meets in your house"), addressed to a Colossian Christian. All three instances of *ekklēsia* in the later Pastoral Epistles (1 Tim. 3:5, 15; 5:16) have the local congregation in view; thus too J. N. D. Kelly, *The Pastoral Epistles* (San Francisco: Harper and Row, 1960), 87–88.

19. Cf. Gal. 4:26 ("the Jerusalem that is above"); 1 Thess. 4:16 ("the dead in Christ"); Phil. 3:20 ("our citizenship is in heaven"). 1 Cor. 12:28, "And in the church God has appointed first apostles, second prophets . . .," appears both (1) to have the church at Corinth primarily in view (cf. 12:27), and (2) to anticipate, with its plural *apostles*, the broader use of Colossians and Ephesians (see Eph. 4:11); cf. Gordon D. Fee, *The First Epistle to the Corinthians* (Grand Rapids: Eerdmans, 1987), 618, n. 13.

20. "Each of the various local churches are tangible expressions of the heavenly church, manifestations in time and space of that which is essentially eternal and infinite in character. . . . Christians belong both to a heavenly church which is permanently in session and to a local church which, though it meets regularly, is intermittent in character. This means that Christians are in a common relationship with Christ not only when they meet together . . . but at all times, wherever they are and whatever they do" (Banks, *Community*, 47; followed by O'Brien, *Colossians*, 60–61).

The Body

Viewed as a heavenly reality, the church is "the body of Christ": "Christ is the head of the church (*ekklēsia*), his body" (*sōma*, Eph. 5:23; cf. 4:15–16; 5:30; Col. 1:18). The same holds true for the church in its local manifestation: "Now you are the body of Christ" (12:27)—"you" being the church at Corinth (1:2).[21]

Like the human organism, the church is a unity in diversity, and a diversity in unity; Paul accentuates now the one, now the other, in the face of a host of pastoral needs. The unity of believers in Christ is for Paul not a goal but a fact: "For we were all baptized with one Spirit into one body" (1 Cor. 12:13). It remains a fact even in view of the church's astonishing diversity: "There is neither Jew nor Greek, there is neither slave nor free, there is neither male nor female; for you are all one in Christ Jesus" (Gal. 3:28 NKJV; cf. Col. 3:11). That believers already belong to one another is foundational for all of Paul's ethical exhortations. Conversely, given a community that is diverse racially (Jew and Gentile), economically (rich and poor), socially (slave and free), sexually (male and female), and spiritually (strong and weak), such exhortations become absolutely essential. It is not at all surprising that Paul must repeatedly address problems that arise on account of one or more of these differences, and urge believers to reject practices that visibly deny or threaten to destroy their unity, and to embrace those that bring their unity to concrete expression. "Make every effort to maintain the unity of the Spirit by the bond of peace. There is one body and one Spirit . . . one Lord, one faith, one baptism; one God and Father of all . . ." (Eph. 4:3–4). "Therefore let each of you put off falsehood and speak truth to his neighbor, because we are members of one another" (4:25; cf. Col. 3:15).[22]

Abuses in the Corinthian assembly, especially in connection with the Lord's Supper, are flagrant violations of the church's unity, in consequence of which God's judgment has already begun to fall (1 Cor. 11:17–34). Yet even in this crisis Paul does not order that the meetings be canceled, which suggests both that he attached tremendous weight to believers' coming together (11:18) as visible evidence of the body's unity, and that corrections to the abuses were most likely to occur in those very gatherings.[23]

The unity of the body does not call for the abolition of differences. Not only would that be impossible; diversity is essential for the body's unity.

21. Cf. the comments on 12:28 in n. 19. Colossians witnesses to both senses of *ekklēsia* (1:18 and 4:15–16 respectively), and correspondingly to both senses of *sōma* (1:18 and 3:15 respectively). On Paul's varied use of "the body of Christ," see chap. 4, pp. 92–93.

22. Ephesians, for example, takes account of four of the differences noted above—the racial (2:11–22), the economic (4:28), the social (6:5–9), and the sexual (5:22–33).

23. Writes Oscar Cullmann, *Early Christian Worship*, trans. A. Stewart Todd and James B. Torrance (London: SCM, 1953), 33: "The Church as the body of this Christ must take shape in the gatherings of the community. The Church is built up in virtue of its coming together."

As we saw in chapter 6, the very differences between the "strong" and the "weak" provide love its greatest opportunity. Using the image of the human organism to combat erroneous notions about spiritual gifts in Corinth, Paul avers that "the body is not made up of one member but of many," and asks, "If all were one member, where would the body be?" (1 Cor. 12:14–20); and he proceeds immediately to emphasize that the diverse parts of the human organism are mutually dependent (12:21–26; for the same sequence, see Rom. 12:4–5). It is precisely in the mutuality of the diverse members that unity is maintained: "in order that there may be no division in the body, but that its members may have equal concern for one another" (1 Cor. 12:25; cf. Eph. 4:11–16, concluding that the proper working of each part contributes to building up the body in love).[24]

The Saints

Paul frequently (about forty times) speaks of the people of God as "the saints," that is, "the holy ones" (*hagioi*), those whom God has set apart to serve him. The church does not include but consists of "the saints": Paul addresses himself "to the church of God in Corinth, to those sanctified (*hēgiasmenois*) in Christ Jesus, called to be saints" (*hagiois*, 1 Cor. 1:2); and "to the church of God in Corinth, together with all the saints [that is, all the other congregations] throughout Achaia" (2 Cor. 1:1).[25]

There is a sense in which "the saints" are an exclusive company: they are distinguished from "the ungodly," from "the unbelievers," from "the people of the world" (1 Cor. 5:9–6:6; 2 Cor. 6:14–18). But Paul lays much greater stress upon their inclusiveness. His repeated references to "all the saints" must be viewed in light of the church's manifold diversity.[26] Essential for establishing and maintaining the togetherness of "the holy ones" (*hagioi*) is "the Holy Spirit" (*pneuma hagion*). The whole church, not just the individual believer, is the Spirit's chosen dwelling-place: "you are God's temple . . . God's Spirit lives in you" (1 Cor. 3:16–17).[27] This holds true both

---

24. The Corinthians "need both unity and diversity. But they cannot have the one without the other" (Fee, *1 Corinthians*, 616). Writes Ernst Käsemann, "On Paul's Anthropology," in *Perspectives on Paul*, trans. Margaret Kohl (Philadelphia: Fortress, 1971), 3, "For Paul, unity in the body of Christ does not mean the sameness of all the members; it means the solidarity which can endure the strain of the differences." To be sure, differences offer potential for endless conflict, but they also hold out hope for a life that is interesting. Would not the "sameness" of all the members be a greater strain, if only from sheer boredom?

25. Cf. 1 Cor. 14:33, "all the congregations of the saints." On "holiness" as both standing and conduct, see chap. 3, pp. 65–66.

26. For "all the saints," see Rom. 16:15; 2 Cor. 1:1; 13:12; Eph. 1:15; 3:8, 18; 6:18; Phil. 1:1; 4:21–22; Col. 1:4; Philem. 5. Cf. 1 Cor. 14:33 ("all the churches of the saints"); 1 Thess. 3:13 (where "the holy ones" include angels). Paul never refers to an individual believer as a "saint" (Phil. 4:21, "every saint," is no exception); they are always "the saints," itself indicative of Paul's accent on community.

27. Each "you" is plural. Writes Herman Ridderbos, *Paul: An Outline of His Theology*, trans. John R. DeWitt (Grand Rapids: Eerdmans, 1975), 221: "The corporate viewpoint is decisive. . . . Being-in-the-Spirit is . . . not in the first place a personal, but an ecclesiological category."

for the *ekklēsia* as a heavenly reality and for its local manifestations: "In [Christ] the whole building [the whole church] is joined together and rises to become a holy (*hagion*) temple in the Lord. And in him you too [the congregations Paul writes] are being built together to become a dwelling in which God lives by his Spirit" (Eph. 2:21–22 NIV).[28] Correspondingly, the fullness of the Spirit is manifested not in purely individual experience but in corporate worship and personal relationships (Eph. 5:18–21 *et seq.*). The directive of 1 Thessalonians 5:26 is therefore appropriate: "Greet all the brothers with a holy (*hagion*) kiss." As a mark of fellowship among believers, this kiss is distinguishable from the erotic kiss and the kiss of friendship, and it is to be offered and received impartially.[29]

The Family

Ephesians speaks of Christians not only as stones in a holy temple, but also as "members of the household of God" (2:19), the language of the family. "God's household" is surnamed "the church of the living God" in 1 Timothy 3:15 (cf. 3:5). As with "church," so "household" (*oikos* or *oikeioi*) in such passages denotes a gathered people, not the place of their gathering.[30] "The God and Father of the Lord Jesus" (2 Cor. 11:31) is also "God and Father" to all who belong to Christ. By virtue of their union with his beloved Son, believers become God's "beloved children" (Eph. 5:1). To be a son or a daughter of God is to enter "the household of faith" (Gal. 6:10), and to become brother or sister to all other members of God's family. Paul habitually speaks of God as "our Father," never as "my Father."[31] By far his favorite term for fellow Christians is "brothers." His letters provide opportunity for exchanges of greeting within the family; the "holy kiss" is a greeting between brothers and sisters.[32]

---

28. Cf. Andrew T. Lincoln, *Ephesians* (Dallas: Word, 1990), 156–58.

29. True to Paul's intent is the NRSV of 1 Thess. 5:26, "Greet all the brothers and sisters with a holy kiss." No less comprehensive is the directive, "Greet one another with a holy kiss" (Rom. 16:16; 1 Cor. 16:20; 2 Cor. 13:12). The purpose of the "kiss of love" (*agapē*, 1 Pet. 5:14) is the same. 1 Thess. 5:26 (*Phillips*) transposes the directive into a modern Western setting: "Give a handshake all round among the brotherhood."

30. *Oikeioi* denotes "members of the household" (BAGD), whether one's own household (1 Tim. 5:8) or God's (Gal. 6:10; Eph. 2:19). *Oikos* means "household, family" (BAGD) in, e.g., 1 Cor. 1:16; 1 Tim. 3:4–5, 15; 2 Tim. 1:16; 4:19. In other places it denotes a dwelling, e.g., one in which the *ekklēsia* gathers (Rom. 16:5; Col. 4:15; Philem. 2).

31. Paul does on occasion speak of "my God" (Rom. 1:8; Phil. 1:3; 4:19). The designation *God our Father* or the equivalent occurs about twenty-five times in Paul's letters (e.g., Rom. 1:7; 1 Cor. 1:3; 1 Thess. 1:3). Of special note are passages in which God is identified as the Father of Jesus and of believers respectively (e.g., 2 Cor. 1:2–3; Gal. 1:1–4; Eph. 1:2–3; Col. 1:2–3).

32. Paul employs the term *brother* (*adelphos*) in this sense some 130 times (H. F. von Soden, *TDNT* 1:145), of which about 70 are the vocative of direct address, as, e.g., in 1 Thess. 1:4, "Brothers beloved by God, we know that he has chosen you." By contrast the term *saints* (*hagioi*) occurs only about forty times. For exchanges of greeting, especially between "brothers" or "all the brothers," see Rom. 16:3–16; 1 Cor. 16:20; Eph. 6:23; Phil. 4:21; Col. 4:15; 1 Thess. 5:26; 2 Tim. 4:21.

In earlier chapters we saw how important to Paul is the institution of the family within the created order. Nonetheless, for him the church as the family of God is by far the greater reality.[33] It is emphatically not the case with Paul that language used literally of one's own family is applied metaphorically to the church: other believers are in fact one's brothers and sisters. This family shall endure when all institutions belonging to the present order will have perished or been transcended (1 Cor. 7:29–31; 13:8–13). All of Paul's instructions about life in the family as a social unit are placed within the framework of his counsel to the church. In this regard, 1 Timothy is especially interesting. Here we find Paul's fullest statement about responsibilities in the domestic sphere, and also a sustained use of the language of the family for the ecclesiastical sphere.[34] The relationship is reciprocal. On the one hand, what God ordains for the home is in many ways analogous to his will for the household of faith (e.g., 3:4–5). The respect that is due the members of one's own family is likewise due one's fellow Christians, with the same attentiveness to diversity: "Do not speak harshly to an older man, but speak to him as to a father, to younger men as brothers, to older women as mothers, to younger women as sisters—with absolute purity" (5:1–2 NRSV; cf. the command that Timothy love his people, 4:12; 6:11).[35] On the other hand, participation in the Christian family is meant to have a transforming effect upon life in one's own family. Let believers "put their religion into practice by caring for their own family" (5:4 NIV); where such care is lacking, the church is to assist—and this, no less than the other, is a ministry within the family (5:3–16). The same reciprocity may be seen in Ephesians. The love that should mark all domestic relationships is likewise due other "members of God's household" (2:19); God's "beloved children" imitate him by loving and forgiving one another (4:32–5:2). Conversely, union with Christ and his Spirit governs all of life within the home (5:18–6:9).

How then does God equip his children for life in the family?

33. Mary Stewart Van Leeuwen, *Gender and Grace* (Downers Grove: InterVarsity, 1990), 175, rightly emphasizes (following Rodney Clapp) that in biblical perspective the church is "first family" and one's own family "second"; and that the former, not the latter, is "the basic institution that undergirds all else" (see further 171–77).

34. Vern S. Poythress, "The Church as Family: Why Male Leadership in the Family Requires Male Leadership in the Church," in *Recovering Biblical Manhood and Womanhood*, ed. John Piper and Wayne Grudem (Wheaton: Crossway, 1991), 233–47, while chiefly concerned with the subject of the subtitle, is a helpful discussion of the whole of 1 Tim., viewed as "a catalog of types of behavior and organization needed in a harmonious family" of either kind (237).

35. "In the intimacy of this spiritual family, people find that they are treating one another in a manner that respects differences of age, sex, and personality. . . . We are to express intimacy and care for one another as we would towards members of our own family, since we are in fact all members of . . . God's household" (Poythress, "The Church as Family," 241, 243).

Gifts to the Community

As God endows his human creatures with native skills, so he imparts to his redeemed people the gifts essential for life in community. These are gifts specifically for "the church" (1 Cor. 12:28), for "the saints" (Eph. 4:12), for persons who have been baptized with the Spirit into the body of Christ (Rom. 12:4–9; 1 Cor. 12:12–27).[36]

The Benevolent God

Like the church itself, the gifts for the church have their source in the triune God. Says 1 Corinthians 12:4–6 (NRSV), "Now there are varieties of gifts (*charismata*), but the same Spirit; and there are varieties of services (*diakoniai*), but the same Lord [that is, Jesus; cf. 12:3; 8:6]; and there are varieties of activities (*energēmata*), but it is the same God [that is, the Father; cf. 8:6] works activates them all in everyone." As the gift (*charisma*) is exercised, the Spirit bestows his grace (*charis*); cf. Rom. 12:6, "We have different gifts (*charismata*), according to the grace (*charis*) given to us." Likewise the term *pneumatikōn* ("spiritual gifts," 1 Cor. 12:1; 14:1) directs attention to the Spirit (*Pneuma*) from whom all such endowments come (12:7–11; cf. Rom. 1:11, "spiritual gift," *charisma pneumatikon*). Christ the Lord engages in ministry (*diakonia*) through his human servants. Similarly, the ascended Christ imparts gifts to "equip the saints for works of service" (*diakonia*, Eph. 4:7–12). By the same token, in all varieties of human activity (*energēma*) "it is the same God who activates (*energōn*) all of them" (1 Cor. 12:6).

The church is therefore utterly dependent upon God. Believers may desire certain gifts (1 Cor. 12:31), but it is the Spirit who decides how and to whom they shall be given (12:11). Such decisions are wed to the Benefactor's extravagance toward his people: taking account of all three passages about spiritual gifts, we find a range of *charismata* that is fully adequate for the needs of the church in its every local manifestation.[37] As each gift is graciously and wisely offered, none is to be despised: in urging the Corinthians to desire "the greater gifts" (12:31), Paul does not imply that they should spurn the implied lesser ones. Nor is there any room for boasting (1 Cor. 4:7), or for despising persons whose gifts differ from one's own (12:14–30).

---

36. James D. G. Dunn, *Jesus and the Spirit* (Philadelphia: Westminster, 1975), 255, writes "that *charisma is not to be confused with human talent and natural ability;* nowhere does charisma have the sense of a human capacity heightened, developed or transformed." Still, a natural talent (e.g., one's native intelligence, or a well-trained voice) may provide a vehicle for the exercise of a charisma.

37. Lists of the gifts and/or their recipients are found in Rom. 12:6–8; 1 Cor. 12:8–10, 28–30; and Eph. 4:11. No list is exhaustive, only representative (cf. Dunn, *Jesus*, 256). There is no exact repetition from one list to another (not even between 1 Cor. 12:8–10 and 12:28–30, each of which totals nine)—a witness to the Spirit's freedom and Paul's flexibility.

The bestowal of the gifts corresponds to the comprehensiveness of redemption. In declaring that "to each one is given the manifestation of the Spirit" (1 Cor. 12:7), or that "to each of us grace (*charis*) was given according to the measure of Christ's gift" (Eph. 4:7), Paul means in part that the triune God shows no "respect of persons." Every believer is a "charismatic"; each member of the body without exception may expect a rich endowment from the Spirit. Gentiles as well as Jews receive gifts; slave as well as free; female as well as male; poor as well as rich; weak as well as strong.[38] The gifts, furthermore, are eschatological blessings, each of them (apostleship alone excepted) granted to sustain the new community until the consummation (1 Cor. 13:8–13).[39]

Exercising the Gifts

While no individual is slighted in the distribution of the *charismata*, these are emphatically not private possessions. "Now to each one is given the manifestation of the Spirit for the common good" (1 Cor. 12:7). Paul places prophecy above tongues, because "the one who speaks in a tongue edifies himself, but the one who prophesies edifies the church" (14:4–5). Christ imparts his gifts "to equip the saints for the work of ministry, for building up the body of Christ" (Eph. 4:12 NRSV). Romans 12:6–8 exhorts readers, not to search for their spiritual gifts but to employ what they already possess for the sake of others. Indeed it is only in the using that the gift becomes an actuality.[40] Moreover, for the growth of the body the concerted exercise of all the gifts is vital (1 Cor. 12:12–27). We shall now consider, if only in the broadest terms, three kinds of *charismata*.

Those of the first kind propagate God's Word. "The higher gifts" (1 Cor. 12:31) are, I believe, those whose immediate purpose is to impart the Word of God. "The utterance of wisdom" and "the utterance of knowledge" appear first in the list of 1 Corinthians 12:8–10. While in this list "prophecy" appears after other kinds of gifts, in 12:28 Paul states that "in the church God has appointed first apostles, second prophets, third teachers."

38. In each of the three letters where Paul discusses spiritual gifts, some or all of these areas of prejudice are in view. E.g., 1 Corinthians 12–14 should be read in light of chaps. 8–10 (the strong and the weak) and 11 (male and female in worship; rich and poor at the Lord's Table); Rom. 12:4–8 in light of chaps. 1–4, 9–11 (Jew and Gentile) and 14–15 (the strong and the weak); and Eph. 4:7–13 in light of chaps. 2–3 (Jew and Gentile) and 5–6 (male and female; slave and master).

39. "The apostolate . . . is distinguished from all the other gifts and ministries because it does not belong to the continuing, repeatedly renewed equipment of the church, but bears a foundational and once-for-all character" (Ridderbos, *Paul*, 448). On the duration of all the other *charismata* till the parousia, see D. A. Carson, *Showing the Spirit: A Theological Exposition of 1 Corinthians 12–14* (Grand Rapids: Baker, 1987), 67–72.

40. This is well emphasized by Dunn throughout his discussion of spiritual gifts (*Jesus*, 199–258). "Charisma is not a possession or an office . . . the exercise of a spiritual gift is itself the charisma" (254). Thus it is not "wisdom" but the actual "utterance of wisdom" that Paul identifies as a gift (1 Cor. 12:8); not "healing" but "gifts of healing" (12:9; "gifts," because manifested in the actual healing of various maladies).

In 14:1, enlarging upon 12:31, he urges readers to seek especially "the gift of prophecy"; and in 14:6 he joins together "revelation," "knowledge," "prophecy," and "teaching."[41] Romans 12:6–8 speaks first of "prophecy," and also of persons who "teach" and "exhort" or "encourage" others. Ephesians 4:11 focuses exclusively on those who minister the Word in some way: apostles, prophets, evangelists, and pastor-teachers.[42] Especially to be honored are the elders "who labor in preaching and teaching" (1 Tim. 5:17).

It is likely that "the utterance of wisdom" unfolds truth about Christ crucified, "the wisdom of God" (1:18–2:16); and that "the utterance of knowledge" provides insight into the character of God, the nature of reality, and believers' responsibility in the world (8:1–13; 13:1–13, both of which affirm that true knowledge manifests itself in love).[43] We may provisionally define prophecy as "spontaneous, Spirit-inspired, intelligible messages, orally delivered in the gathered assembly, intended for the edification or encouragement of the people [1 Cor. 14:3]."[44] The chief task of both apostle (*apostolos*) and evangelist (*euangelistēs*) was to proclaim the gospel (*euangelion*) of Christ for the conversion of nonbelievers and the growth of believers.[45] The above definition of prophecy applies with equal validity to the "teaching" of 1 Corinthians 14:6, 26; the distinctive purpose of the latter is to provide insight into existing apostolic teaching, and it therefore stands very close to the utterances of wisdom and knowledge (12:8; cf. Colossians 3:16, "teaching . . . one another with all wisdom").[46] "Teachers" (1 Cor. 12:28) were appointed to bear, expound and guard the

41. Both "knowledge" and "prophecy" appear in 12:8–10; both "revelation" and "teaching" (but not the other two) recur in 14:26. Such activities "shade too finely into one another for rigid distinctions to be profitable or even accurate" (C. K. Barrett, *1 Corinthians* [New York: Harper and Row, 1968], 317). "Teaching" imparts "knowledge"; "prophecy" can be identified as "revelation" (14:29–31).

42. The principal function of such persons is to propagate the Word of God. This of course does not mean that they were exempt from other kinds of gifts. Paul may well have exercised every gift named in 1 Cor. 12:8–10.

43. However the content of the one utterance differs from the other, by both means the Spirit (12:7) imparts a knowledge of God and Christ that is both cognitive and experiential (Dunn, *Jesus*, 217–21; Fee, *1 Corinthians*, 591–93).

44. Fee, *1 Corinthians*, 595.

45. As a declaration of the full breadth and depth of the person and work of Christ (chaps. 3, 4), the *euangelion* is for believers as well as nonbelievers: cf. J. Knox Chamblin, *Gospel according to Paul* (Ann Arbor: University Microfilms, 1979), 413–17. That proclaiming the gospel to both audiences stood at the heart of Paul's commission is clear from such passages as Rom. 1:14–17; 1 Cor. 1:17–2:5; 9:12–23; Gal. 1:1–17; 1 Thess. 2:2–9; 2 Tim. 1:8–12. The term *euangelistēs* designates heralds of the gospel who are distinct from the apostles (Eph. 4:11): Philip the evangelist (Acts 21:8) is different from Philip the apostle (Acts 1:13); Paul the apostle is never called an evangelist. As a bearer of the *euangelion*, the *euangelistēs* witnesses to both nonbelievers (Acts 8:26–40, Philip and the Ethiopian) and believers (Eph. 4:11–12, of preparing God's people for service; 2 Tim. 4:5, of Timothy's service in the local church).

46. By both prophecy and teaching the church is edified (*oikodomeō*, 14:4; *oikodomē*, 14:3, 5, 26). Dunn (*Jesus*, 237) rightly distinguishes the "non-charismatic sense" of teaching (*didachē*) in Rom. 6:17 from the "charismatic insight" of 1 Cor. 14:6, 26 (as indicated by the terms to which it is joined). The latter furnishes "*a new insight into an old word from God*, into the traditions already accepted by the community . . ." (ibid.).

apostolic tradition; in the language of Ephesians 4:11, "pastor and teacher" better describes Timothy or Titus than does "evangelist" or "prophet."[47]

Gifts of the second kind manifest God's power. In all the *charismata*, supremely in the utterances of the Word, the mighty God is active (1 Cor. 12:6). But in view here are those activities (joined together in 1 Cor. 12:9–10) in which that power is present in a particularly striking way: "gifts of healing," "miraculous powers," and the "faith" in response to which God does great and mighty things—"a faith that can move mountains" (1 Cor. 13:2).[48]

Finally, there are activities that serve God's people. This of course may be said of all the gifts (1 Cor. 12:5), tongues alone excepted. Yet Paul uses such language of selected *charismata*. First Corinthians 12:28 refers to "gifts for helping others" and "gifts of administration." Romans 12:7–8 amplifies the first in speaking of persons who "serve," who "contribute to the needs of others," and who "show mercy"; and echoes the second in speaking of persons who "lead," or further amplifies the first if this verb (*proïstēmi*) means to "give aid."[49]

Testing the Gifts

From one standpoint the gifts may be exercised with utter freedom, in obedience to the Spirit's promptings. At the same time, to claim that the Spirit is at work is not to assure that he is. Thus Paul offers criteria for testing the authenticity and the value of the *charismata*.[50] The first has already

---

47. "Pastors and teachers" describes a dual function. As a commissioned apostle, Paul is also a teacher (*didaskalos*), 1 Tim. 2:7; 2 Tim. 1:11. The apostolic teaching (*didachē* and *didaskalia*) is authoritative for the church. The "word of instruction" (*didachē*) of 1 Cor. 14:6, 26, while not restricted to "teachers" (*didaskaloi*), is based on the apostolic tradition (see n. 46). The principal task of Timothy and Titus is to propagate and safeguard this "sound doctrine" (1 Tim. 1:10–11; 4:6, 16; 6:3; 2 Tim. 2:2; 3:10; 4:3; Titus 1:9; 2:1; cf. Rom. 6:17; 16:17). It is as a pastor-teacher (1 Tim. 4:13–16) that Timothy does "the work of an evangelist" (2 Tim. 4:5). While the functions of prophet and teacher may be joined in one person (Acts 13:1), and while someone may be encouraged by teaching as well as by prophecy (2 Tim. 4:2), instructed by prophecy as well as by teaching (1 Cor. 14:31), and edified by both (1 Cor. 14:3–5, 26), the functions themselves must be carefully distinguished. See Wayne Grudem, *The Gift of Prophecy in the New Testament and Today* (Westchester, Ill: Crossway, 1988), 135–48.

48. "Gifts of healing" (12:9) repeats the *charismata* of 12:4; "the working of miracles" (12:10), the *energēmata* of 12:6. These two gifts are again mentioned in 12:28–30. The latter term "most likely covers all other kinds of supernatural activities beyond the healing of the sick" (Fee, *1 Corinthians*, 594); cf., with reference to Paul, Acts 13:11; 16:18; 19:11–12; 2 Cor. 12:12. Dunn rightly includes "faith" with the other two under the heading "Miracles" (*Jesus*, 209–12).

49. I believe that *proistēmi* in Rom. 12:8 more likely means "rule, direct" (BAGD, *s.v.* 1; NRSV) than "care for, give aid" (BAGD, *s.v.* 2; RSV); cf. the verb's usage in 1 Thess. 5:12. The terms of 1 Cor. 12:29 form a couplet (as do several other terms in 12:8–10 and 12:28–30), suggesting that "administration" pertains, at least in part, to planning and supervising various kinds of "helps." Essentially the same pairing, reflecting a later stage of church order, is found in Phil. 1:1, "together with the overseers (*episkopoi*) and deacons (*diakonoi*)" (cf. 1 Tim. 3:2, 8). See the discussion of "Service" in Dunn, *Jesus*, 248–53.

50. He does so by virtue of his incontestable apostolic authority. Paul's injunction to "test everything" a prophet says (1 Thess. 5:20–21) is itself not subject to testing. "If anybody thinks he is a prophet or spiritually gifted, let him acknowledge that what I am writing to you is the Lord's command" (1 Cor. 14:37 NIV). "Not to submit to what the apostle writes is thus to deny the lordship of Jesus, which is the Christian's central confession as stipulated at the beginning of these three chapters (12:3)" (Carson, *Spirit*, 132).

been mentioned: Is the Christian community edified? We consider two more.[51]

The second test is to ask whether a given exercise accords with apostolic teaching. Especially does this apply to prophetic utterances. In 1 Corinthians 12:10 prophecy is coupled with "the ability to distinguish between spirits." The latter takes account both of the prophecy's source (whether the Spirit of truth or a demonic spirit) and of its human channel.[52] Members of the congregation "should weigh carefully" what the prophets say (14:29).[53] That ability in turn depends upon a grasp of the Word of Christ as imparted to the church through his apostles.

The recorded word of an Old Testament prophet or a New Testament apostle is an authoritative and infallible utterance directly from God, and is therefore not subject to testing. Such prophecy is "Spirit-inspired" (see the definition on p. 210) in a primary sense (sense A). The prophecy of which Paul speaks in 1 Corinthians 14 is an edifying but fallible utterance; it is "Spirit-inspired" (as are all the *charismata*), but in a secondary sense (sense B). Prophecy in sense B may manifest "the Spirit's fire" but is still subject to testing (1 Cor. 14:24–29; 1 Thess. 5:19–22). Prophecy in sense A is Revelation; in sense B, revelation—or, in more traditional terms, illumination or insight.[54] Prophecy in sense A ceases at the close of the apostolic age; prophecy in sense B lasts until Christ returns, when all things "imperfect," prophecy included, will cease (1 Cor. 13:8–12).[55]

As we ponder the contemporary church's appropriation of the above teaching, two points call for emphasis. (1) Both prophecy and teaching may be occasional or customary. A "prophecy" or a "teaching" of the kind mentioned in 1 Corinthians 14:6, 26, may, by the Spirit's prompting, be spontaneously offered by any member of the congregation for the encouragement or enlightenment of the gathered worshipers. A person whose prophetic utterances are both frequent and effective (in the terms of 1 Cor. 14:3) may come to be acknowledged as a "prophet."[56] By the same token, one who has demonstrated, both by habit and by educational achievement, an

51. For the same three, see James D. G. Dunn, *Unity and Diversity in the New Testament* (Philadelphia: Westminster, 1977), 192–94.
52. Cf. 1 Thess. 5:19–22; 1 John 4:1–6; Fee, *1 Corinthians*, 596–97; Dunn, *Jesus*, 233–36.
53. With Carson, *Spirit*, 120, I take "the others" who judge the prophecies to be not just other prophets but the congregation as a whole.
54. Thus does Paul employ the verb *apokalyptō* (reveal) in 1 Cor. 14:30; Eph. 1:17; Phil. 3:15. See Grudem, *Prophecy*, 67–88, 115–34; Carson, *Spirit*, 162–64.
55. See Grudem, *Prophecy*, 227–52. As prophecy in both senses A and B occurs during the apostolic age, it is sometimes hard to tell which sense is intended. It is likely that the prophets of Eph. 2:20; 3:5; and 4:11, joined as they are to the apostles as recipients of revelation (3:5), are to be understood in sense A. Does "prophets" in 1 Cor. 12:28 embrace both senses?
56. "Many have suggested that we need to distinguish between those who prophesy now and then, and those whose gift is so developed, or so deployed, or whose prophecies when evaluated receive such high assessments, that they achieve the semistatus of 'prophets'" (Carson, *Spirit*, 118).

exceptional ability to expound biblical truth, may be recognized and ordained as a "teacher."[57] (2) Both prophecy and teaching, whether occasional or customary, are fallible and therefore subject to testing. Prophetic utterances today, like those in the first-century church, must be weighed carefully on the basis of the apostles' teaching as incorporated into the Scriptures and as faithfully expounded by the church's teachers. And the teaching itself must be constantly judged in the light of that scriptural deposit. Each remains a useful though imperfect channel for the mighty working of God's Spirit.

The third test is to ask whether the alleged *charisma* fosters love in the community. The Spirit who bestows the gifts also cultivates certain "fruit" among his people, the foremost of which is *agapē* (Rom. 5:5; 15:30; Gal. 5:22–23). Each of the nine qualities of Galatians 5:22–23 enhances the effectiveness of the gifts' exercise. For example, love and joy prompt people to contribute generously to those in need (cf. Rom. 12:8; 2 Cor. 8:2–8); and one who teaches needs the whole range of qualities listed here, from "love [and] joy" to "gentleness and self-control." Conversely, it is better to refrain from the gifts altogether than to exercise them without love (1 Cor. 13:1–3).[58] It is most significant that Paul celebrates love precisely amid his discussion of *charismata* (1 Cor. 13): he longs for his readers to pursue both love and the gifts (14:1); but love remains the "far better way" (12:31), a subject to which we shall return.

The Caring Community

This subject has been before us since the beginning of the chapter. In Paul's understanding the *ekklēsia* by its very nature is a caring community, and the singular purpose of the Spirit's *charismata* is that believers build up one another. The offering of one's own body to God (Rom. 12:1–2) takes place in acts of service to other people (12:3–21).[59] This accords with one of our findings in chapter 1, namely, that Paul's greatest anguish and greatest

---

57. The utterances of a prophet remain typically spontaneous: as Fee notes (*1 Corinthians*, 595), the prophecy of 1 Cor. 14 "is *not* the delivery of a previously prepared sermon." The message of a teacher would normally be based on serious study. As in the case of Timothy and Titus, the minister of a local church today is better termed a teacher than a prophet, although his preaching may be expected to include the prophetic elements of 1 Cor. 14:3.

58. In 1 Corinthians 1:4–7 Paul gives thanks for the Corinthians' *charismata*. But thanks for their *agapē* is conspicuous by its absence (contrast Col. 1:4–5)—not surprisingly, in face of the party spirit that was rife in Corinth (1:10–12).

59. "While for us the body is primarily that which marks out our individuality, our separateness, for Paul it primarily represents the means of relationship with one another" (John Ziesler, *Pauline Christianity*, rev. ed. [New York: Oxford University Press, 1990], 59). Robert Wuthnow, "Evangelicals, Liberals, and the Perils of Individualism" (*Perspectives* [May 1991]: 10–13), shows that the community is an essential link between personal spirituality and care for the needy.

joy were prompted by the state of things between the people under his care and the God who had commissioned him.

Caring within the new community is predicated upon mutual empathy. This is the effect of membership within the same family and the same body. God's design is that the parts of the body "may show the same care for one another. If one member suffers, all the members suffer with it; if one member is honored, all the members rejoice with it" (1 Cor. 12:24–26). "Rejoice with those who rejoice, weep with those who weep" (Rom. 12:15).

Support

This may be offered in words. "The one who prophesies speaks to others for their upbuilding and encouragement and consolation" (1 Cor. 14:3; cf. 14:31). As we have seen, any Christian has the capacity, under the Spirit, to sustain others by such an utterance. It may occur in "the gathered assembly," but it may also occur in the course of a personal conversation or a counseling session, through a letter or amid a neighborhood Bible study.[60] Another avenue of verbal support is intercessory prayer, a subject of chapter 10.

Support may also be offered tangibly. Paul joins the appeals to encourage others and to contribute generously to those in need (Rom. 12:8). "Contribute to the needs of the saints, practice hospitality," he goes on to say (12:13).

Healing

God may choose to employ believers, whether through the gifts of faith, healing, and miraculous powers (1 Cor. 12:9–10), or through prayers of intercession, to liberate persons from physical malady or demonic oppression.

God's people are also his channels of consolation to those who grieve (Rom. 12:15; 1 Cor. 12:26), a purpose served by prophetic utterances (1 Cor. 14:3). One's own comfort from God is meant to be shared (2 Cor. 1:3–4).[61] To forgive a person who is overwhelmed by sorrow on account of his sin and his alienation offers both restoration and comfort (2 Cor. 2:5–11).[62]

60. Fee's definition of prophecy (quoted on p. 210) is thus modified. For practical manifestations of this kind of caring, see Lawrence J. Crabb, Jr., and Dan B. Allender, *Encouragement: The Key to Caring* (Grand Rapids: Zondervan, 1984), especially 131–39 ("The Local Church: A Restoring Community").

61. Margaret D. Smith offers a sensitive review of Luci Shaw's book, *God in the Dark: Through Grief and Beyond* (Grand Rapids: Zondervan, 1989), based on journals written during and after her husband's long and losing battle against cancer. "Through the book, [Luci] calls to God, asking ... 'Where are you? I call, but you don't answer. You have left me here, alone'.... Through the book, friends flit in and out like fireflies, giving off brief sparks in the darkness, telling Luci in a thousand thoughtful ways that they love her. But while she appreciates these friends, Luci never seems to connect the two wires: Where is God? and, Here are God's people. If you want to find me, God seems to be telling her secretly, come to my Body, and there you may embrace me" (*The Reformed Journal* [October 1989]:29).

62. In this forgiveness, as in the act of Christ upon which it is based (Eph. 4:32–5:2; Col. 3:13), the offended party absorbs the wrong and prevents it from spreading (cf. chap. 3, pp. 76–77; chap. 4, p. 106).

Healing includes the restoration of the erring (Gal. 6:1–10). A fellow believer has been "caught in a sin" (6:1)—not caught in the act, but over-taken and entrapped by a destructive force (6:8). My "own load" (6:5) in this case is the responsibility to bear the "burden" of the one who has erred (6:2).[63] My deepest motive for doing so is not that he is a sinner but that he is a brother, one who belongs to "the household of faith" (6:10). The "spir-itual" persons whom Paul calls into action are those who live by the Spirit (5:22–25) and who therefore love the brother (and thus "fulfill the law of Christ," 6:2; 5:14, 22) and deal gently with him (6:1; 5:23): that is, they treat him as they would want to be treated when likewise ensnared by sin (6:1b).

A society like ours, with its insistence on personal rights, threatens to deprive us of the community of healing.[64]

Accountability

This dimension of caring, no less than the others, depends upon mutu-ality. "The eye cannot say to the hand, 'I have no need of you,' nor the head to the feet, 'I have no need of you'" (1 Cor. 12:21). "Carry one another's bur-dens," says Galatians 6:2. This is not merely a prescription for dealing with the crisis of 6:1; "burdens" are represented by but not restricted to "sins." Paul has in view an established network of mutual support, based on love for fellow-believers (5:14; 6:10); it does not come into being, rather, it goes into action, when a crisis arises. Moreover, there is no telling how many "works of the flesh" (5:19–21) might be forestalled in a fellowship of mutual accountability. Better to deal with anger than with murder, or with lust than with actual adultery.

Accountability entails a willingness to offer counsel that is based both on apostolic teaching and on love for the brotherhood. This applies both to pastors ("correct, rebuke, encourage—with great patience and careful instruction," 2 Tim. 4:2 NIV) and to God's people generally ("We urge you, brothers, admonish the idle, encourage the fainthearted, help the weak, be patient with them all," 1 Thess. 5:14). It also calls for a willingness to dis-close to other believers (if only to very few) one's besetting sins and strug-gles, such as those considered in chapter 7, and to heed the counsel (as already defined) that is offered in that light ("We ask you, brothers, to respect those who labor among you, who are over you in the Lord and who admonish you," 1 Thess. 5:12).

---

63. See the comments on this passage in chap. 5, pp. 115–16.

64. Reviewing Mary Ann Glendon's book *Rights Talk: The Impoverishment of Political Discourse*, George F. Will writes: "By neglecting the social dimension of personhood and exalting autonomy, rights talk cre-ates a climate of callousness toward those who do not thrive on independence—the very young, the se-verely ill and disabled, the frail elderly. So, for example, a poor and unmarried pregnant woman has a glistening 'privacy right' to seek an abortion, but she has precious little claim on the community's compas-sion" *Newsweek* (23 September 1991), 68.

Two comments are now in order. The first is to remind ourselves that in a caring community, no one person is responsible for bearing every burden or relieving every need; tasks are distributed throughout the *ekklēsia*. Secondly, given the theme of this chapter, let it be emphasized that Paul opposes a self-centered church as vigorously as a self-centered individual. He does urge Christians to "be devoted to one another in brotherly love" (Rom. 12:10); he even exhorts, "Let us do good to all people, especially to those who belong to the family of believers" (Gal. 6:10 NIV). But as this verse shows, love is not to be confined to Christians. There is no such restriction to the command in Romans 13:8–10.[65] Paul's whole ministry bears eloquent testimony to his love for nonbelievers (1 Cor. 9:19–23; 2 Cor. 5:11–15). One reason he insists that Christians love each other is that this constitutes one of the church's most powerful witnesses to the watching world (Phil. 2:12–16). First Corinthians 13, the passage about to be considered, places no limits on the objects of one's love (there is no mention of "church" or "brothers" or "saints") nor on those who are to love (unlike a given *charisma*, "the most excellent way" is for every Christian).[66] Yet in keeping with the subject of the present chapter, we will continue to focus chiefly on relationships among believers.

Loving One Another: 1 Corinthians 13

The foremost "fruit" of the Spirit, love (Gal. 5:22; Col. 3:14), is greater than the Spirit's "gifts." In 1 Corinthians 13:1–3, no fewer than six of the latter are in view: tongues, prophecy, wisdom (the "fathoming of mysteries"), knowledge, faith, and giving. The gifts are of great importance, as the flanking chapters show. Yet, says Paul, to exercise a gift without love is to gain nothing, indeed to be nothing (13:2–3). Love is the "more excellent way," surpassing even "the greater gifts" (12:31). The *charismata* will cease at the consummation of history; but faith, hope, and love will last forever (13:8–13).

Our Longing to Love

First Corinthians 13 is one of the best-loved chapters in the Bible; it is also one of the most elusive. For most of us, the love portrayed here is an aspiration rather than an experience. The appeal of these verses is like that of a lofty mountain. We stand in silent awe before its majesty and long to

---

65. So too John Murray, *The Epistle to the Romans* (Grand Rapids: Eerdmans, 1968), 2:158–64. Here, as in Rom. 12:14–21, Paul makes it "quite clear that the Christian love command does not apply only to intramural relationships" (Victor Paul Furnish, *The Love Command in the New Testament* [Nashville: Abingdon, 1972], 109). Such love embraces the civil magistrates (13:1–7).

66. Leon Morris, *Testaments of Love* (Grand Rapids: Eerdmans, 1981), 240, n. 32, forcefully assaults the idea that 1 Cor. 13 is confined to love within the Christian community.

scale its heights, but then we realize how earthbound we are and how ill-equipped to climb. We know the shape of love; but we also know ourselves and how far short of the actuality we fall. Love itself "never fails" (13:8), but we do, and often.

Significantly, love itself sits for this portrait. Paul does not say that "Christians suffer long and are kind," or that "believers do not envy and do not boast." It makes sense to replace "love" with "Jesus": "Jesus was not proud or rude or self-seeking or easily angered."[67] But when we substitute our own names, we can hardly speak the words; we hold our tongues for shame. We are aware of persons from whom we are alienated, toward whom we feel envy and resentment, whose wrongs toward us we keep recorded with a view to getting even. "We know in part, we prophesy in part"—and we also love in part. It is far easier to write about love than to put it into action.

Yet three times in the opening verses Paul challenges us to "have love." We do not yet possess it, but we desperately want to. Should this not encourage us? Does not that very longing afford a glimpse of love itself, which "always hopes, always perseveres" (13:7)? Is it not a sign of love that we want to be rid of our pride and jealousy and selfish ambition? When we behave rudely, does not the hurt that ensues give evidence of love toward the person we have wronged? If we recognize ourselves to be unloving, we have at least begun to "put childish ways" behind us (13:11).

To be mature in understanding is to know that "perfection" does not come now, but only hereafter (13:10). Paul advances from "childishness" to "childlikeness" by recognizing the imperfection and incompleteness of his present experience (13:11–12). To be childish is to be unloving but think we are loving. But when we know we are unloving but want to be different, we have made some progress. Is it not a relief to learn that perfection is not yet possible? to realize that failures in loving are inevitable? Does not this knowledge free us to be better lovers? "Love is the power to live gladly as imperfect lovers."[68]

The Character of Love

Love is by nature communal; it becomes a reality in relationship to others, whether God or neighbor. Paul focuses on the latter in this chapter: We show love for God by the way we treat other people (13:4–7). Love is therefore a kind of knowledge. In one sense the two are distinguishable. Love is

---

67. See Günther Bornkamm, "The More Excellent Way," in *Early Christian Experience*, trans. Paul L. Hammar (New York: Harper and Row, 1969), 180–93.

68. Lewis B. Smedes, *Love Within Limits: A Realist's View of 1 Corinthians 13* (Grand Rapids: Eerdmans, 1978), 135. Writes Lawrence J. Crabb, Jr., *Understanding People* (Grand Rapids: Zondervan, 1987), 194, "Maturity is less related to perfection than to a growing awareness of imperfection. . . ."

a fruit of the Spirit, knowledge is one of his gifts (13:2; 12:8); love remains (13:13), but knowledge passes away (13:8). At the same time, to love is to know, in the Hebraic sense of deeply personal communion and mutual understanding (cf. 1 Cor. 8:1–3). Our present knowledge both of God and of other people is partial; but we are progressing toward fullness of knowledge: to "know fully, even as I am fully known" is to experience the love that abides forever (13:12–13).

Love is unselfish. It is possible to be relational, even charitable, and yet to remain egocentric (13:3). The *agapē* portrayed in this chapter is a gift-love, not a need-love; it is "not self-seeking" (13:5). Unlike envy, which longs for one's own sake that the other be deprived of something, love wants to give to the other for the sake of the other, in keeping with God's own *agapē* (Rom. 5:8; Eph. 5:2).[69]

Love is combative. When the negative formulations of 1 Corinthians 13: 4b–6a are converted into positive ones, a revealing portrait of pride emerges: "Pride is envious, pride is boastful. . . . It is rude, it is self-seeking, it is easily angered, it keeps a record of wrongs. Pride delights in evil [particularly when a rival is snared by it, Gal. 6:1]." Moreover, the distinction between the *charismata* and *agapē* in 13:1–3 indicates that the Corinthians were employing the gifts competitively, as a means of surpassing or dominating others (cf. 12:14–26). Love itself is "not proud" (13:4). Not only so: by its patience, kindness, trust, tenacity, and joy (the positive formulations of 13:4a, 6b–7) it exerts the power needed for assaulting and reversing all those manifestations of pride, whether in the *charismata* or elsewhere.

The Endurance of Love

At the heart of love is its power to endure. Love "suffers long. . . . [it] bears all things, believes all things, hopes all things, endures all things" (13:4, 7 NKJV). "Love never fails" (13:8), "love remains" (13:13). The explanation for love's endurance is the prospect of the heavenly kingdom (2 Tim. 4:18). Our longing to love other people is part of something larger, namely, hope for "that which is perfect" (13:10), for heaven and for him who dwells there (Rom. 5:2). Our fleeting experiences of *agapē* make us yearn for an *agapē* that is lasting and permanent.

We "now see in a mirror, dimly, but then we will see face to face" (13:12 NRSV). Paul is doubtless thinking principally of the beatific vision of God himself; but integral to that is a fuller and deeper understanding of all who

---

69. "What an envier wants is not, first of all, what another has [that is covetousness]. What an envier [like Cain] wants is for the other not to have it" (Cornelius Plantinga, Jr., "Murder, Envy, and the Harvest Princess," *Christianity Today* [25 November 1991]: 28). For the distinction between the "gift-love" (*agapē*) and the "need-loves" (*storgē, erōs,* and *philia*), see C. S. Lewis, *The Four Loves* (New York: Harcourt Brace Jovanovich, 1960). Still, the distinction between selfish and selfless exercises of love rests far more on the actual marks of love according to 1 Cor. 13 than on the term *agapē* (see Carson, *Spirit,* 64–65).

belong to him. We now see but poor reflections, or, as it were, mere photographs, of each other.[70] But in the heavenly glory we shall see one another face to face. Then we shall be viewing real persons, persons in whom God's image has been fully restored. Then our knowledge of each other will correspond to God's present knowledge of us all. When "the imperfect disappears" and the heavenly kingdom comes, when all our ego-defense mechanisms have been scrapped, when all our barriers have been removed, when all our pretense vanishes, then we shall face one another as heart to heart, and as soul to soul, and shall really know one another for the first time.

On one reading of 1 Corinthians 13:13, love is greater than faith and hope because love, unlike the other two, remains beyond this life into the next. But if, as I believe, Paul is saying that faith and hope also endure into the heavenly kingdom,[71] then he is holding out the prospect of growth in love through eternity. There will still be room for love to trust: love by nature trusts. And there will still be room for love to hope: love by nature hopes—for an ever-increasing mutual experience of *agapē*.

All of this means that we are to relate to people, not just in light of what they are, but in light of what they shall one day become. On the model of Christ's own love for the church (Eph. 5:25–28), love trusts that the good work that God has begun in another Christian will continue until it is perfected (Phil. 1:6). It is almost certain that God will place us at close quarters with persons whom we find it difficult to love. (By the same token, some will think of us as the cross God has given them to bear!) He will do this in order to cultivate in us love's endurance. Do we not require such relationships?—since love by its very nature "bears and endures all things"? Without such demands, love will not grow. If love must be tough, it must also be painful.

For God wants us to be conformed to the image of his Son. And for Paul, that means becoming like "Christ crucified." This means that in our loving, we must be vulnerable to sorrow. "Love anything, and your heart will certainly be wrung and possibly be broken. If you want to make sure of keeping it intact, you must give your heart to no one, not even to an animal. Wrap it carefully round with hobbies and little luxuries; avoid all entanglements; lock it up safe in the casket or coffin of your selfishness. But in that casket—safe, dark, motionless, airless—it will change. It will not be broken; it will become unbreakable, impenetrable, irredeemable. The alternative to tragedy, or at least to the risk of tragedy, is damnation. The only

---

70. Cf. Fee, *1 Corinthians*, 648. George MacDonald, *Phantastes* (Grand Rapids: Eerdmans, 1964), 99, asks, "How many who love never come nearer than to behold each other as in a mirror; seem to know and yet never know the inward life; never enter the other soul; and part at last, with but the vaguest notion of the universe on the borders of which they have been hovering for years?"

71. So also Carson, *Spirit*, 72–76.

place outside Heaven where you can be perfectly safe from all the dangers and perturbations of love is Hell."[72] In hope of heaven we endure the suffering which inevitably marks our present experiences of love. That "hope does not disappoint us, because the love of God has been poured into our hearts by the Holy Spirit" (Rom. 5:2–5).

> *And I pray that you, being rooted and established in love, may have power, together with all the saints, to grasp how wide and long and high and deep is the love of Christ. [Eph. 3:17–18 NIV]*

72. Lewis, *The Four Loves*, 169. Paul views the person "in the consummation only as one dependent on God and unendingly open to him, constantly a recipient who does not have the basis of his life in himself ('faith'), constantly one who . . . waits for God ('hope')," Bornkamm, "The More Excellent Way," 187, on 1 Cor. 13:13.

10

The Church at Worship and at Prayer

As observed in the preceding chapter, the *ekklēsia* is a heavenly reality of which the *ekklēsia* in a given locale is an earthly manifestation. Both when they gather together and when they do not, the people of God participate in that reality. To put the matter another way: Both in the assembly and in their places of responsibility in the world, believers are to conduct themselves as members of the new humanity inaugurated by the risen Christ.[1] We shall now explore the implications of this for the church's worship and prayer.

The Worshiping Community in Ephesians

It is fitting that we begin with the letter in which Paul's twin teaching about the heavenly church and the new humanity comes to its loftiest expression.

The Vertical Dimension of Worship

We have already seen that Ephesians 1:3–14 is an offering of praise.[2] The purpose of the prayer in 1:15–23 is that believers may be enlightened by the Spirit about the work of God the Father in the Lord Jesus Christ, and

1. See pp. 85–89, 202–3.
2. See p. 105.

thereby moved to join Paul in the adoration of the Trinity.[3] Ephesians 2, with its teaching about the saving grace of God, and the uniting of Jew and Gentile in Christ the New Man, provides a means for readers' further enlightenment and a bridge between the prayer of 1:15–23 and that of 3:14–21. Ephesians 3:2–13 expounds the theme introduced in 2:11–22, the new unity of Jew and Gentile in Christ (see 3:6). But already in 3:1 Paul prepares for the prayer that is offered in 3:14–21; which is to say that this prayer is founded upon the exposition of 2:11–22.

Paul writes in 3:14, "For this reason [repeating the phrase of 3:1] I kneel [expressive of earnestness] before the Father. . . ." As in 1:15–23, the prayer rests on the enlightenment that Paul himself has received (3:5) and that he has just imparted (2:11–22; 3:2–13). He now asks that believers, through the empowering Spirit, may likewise be granted understanding of the deep and vast truth of Christ (3:16–19) and thus be moved to praise (3:20–21).[4] Such a prayer is answered in the public assembly (5:19–20), where the fullness of the Spirit (5:18) manifests itself in believers' offerings of praise and thanksgiving to God the Father and the Lord Jesus Christ.[5]

The Horizontal Dimension of Worship

Paul utters the prayer of 1:15–23 out of a deep awareness of Christian community: "your love for all the saints" (1:15); "the riches of his glorious inheritance in the saints" (1:18); "to be head over all things for the church, which is his body, the fullness of him. . ." (1:22–23). Both the theological enlightenment and the adoration that it evokes take place within the *ekklēsia*.

The corporate nature of the understanding is yet plainer in Ephesians 3: "And I pray that you . . . may have power, together with all the saints, to comprehend . . ." (3:17–18), where "all the saints" has especially in view the newly accomplished unity between Jews and Gentiles (2:11–3:13). Believers' grasping the vastness of revealed truth depends on their deliberately seeking light from others who participate in the fellowship of the Trinity and who adhere to the "one faith" (4:4–6). Accordingly, in the public assembly the vertical dimension of worship is inseparable from the horizontal; "Speaking to one another with psalms and hymns and spiritual

---

3. With Andrew T. Lincoln, *Ephesians* (Dallas: Word, 1990), 56–58, I take the *pneuma* of 1:17 to be the Holy Spirit, not the human spirit.

4. Eph. 1–3 has "the overall framework of a long thanksgiving" and is "distinguished by its epistolary use of liturgical forms" (Lincoln, *Ephesians*, xxxvi, xxxvii).

5. Praise is offered both to Christ (5:19) and through him (or "in his name") to God the Father (5:20). Eph. 5:20a, "always giving thanks to God the Father for everything," is qualified by 5:20b, "in the name of our Lord Jesus Christ." There are some things for which I must assuredly not give thanks, such as the brutal murder of a child. We are to thank God for the things that are consistent with his revelation of himself, supremely of his grace and love, in the person and work of Christ (2:4–7; 3:18–19). It may be that I can "give thanks in all circumstances" (1 Thess. 5:18a); but even that formulation is qualified ("for this is the will of God in Christ Jesus for you," 5:18b).

songs, singing and making music in your hearts to the Lord, always giving thanks to God the Father" (5:19–20). In the very adoration of God, the members of the "one body" (4:4) instruct each other. It is in this twofold corporate activity that the "fullness of the Spirit" (5:18) is manifested; individuals experience the fullness precisely in relationship to the Trinity and to other members of the gathered *ekklēsia*.[6]

Life in the World

The prayer of Ephesians 3 implores God to equip the saints for lives of obedience. How deeply they are rooted in Christ's love, and how firmly they have understood it (3:17–19), will be evident in their conduct toward others both within and beyond the church. Here as elsewhere it is the Spirit who enables believers to obey; and he bestows his power (3:16, 18, 20) in the same way that he manifests his fullness—within the communion of the saints.[7]

That prayer paves the way for the second major section of Ephesians, 4:1–6:20. Paul's opening appeal: "As a prisoner in the Lord, therefore, I urge you to live a life worthy of the calling to which you have been called" (4:1, the last eight words being a concise summary of chaps. 1–3).[8] He immediately states one way of doing so: "Be completely humble and gentle; be patient, bearing with one another in love" (4:2 NIV). Having affirmed in the strongest confessional terms the unity of God's people (4:3–6, words both retrospective and prospective), Paul sets forth in the ensuing chapters some practical effects of God's call (cf. 1:4; 2:10). In the passage already considered, he admonishes readers to "be careful how [they] live," to "make the most of their time," and to "understand what is the will of the Lord" (5:15–17) both in the assembly (5:19–20) and in their various places of responsibility (5:21–6:9).

The evidence of Ephesians is confirmed in other letters. One's whole being and all one's time are to be consecrated to God. This means that believers must frequently "come together as a church" for worship (1 Cor. 11:18), to be reminded of the singular purpose of their lives, and to be newly empowered to obey God in the world. It also means that worship is not confined to public assemblies but can find expression wherever Christians live amid whatever they are doing: "So whether you eat or drink or whatever you do, do all things for the glory of God" (1 Cor. 10:31), an

---

6. This strongly suggests that something happens in the gathered church that does not happen, at least to the same degree, when a person watches a televised service alone at home.

7. Peter Richardson, *Paul's Ethic of Freedom* (Philadelphia: Westminster, 1979), 138, rightly says that Eph. offers "a church-centered view of the strength of God." See chap. 9, pp. 213–16, on "the caring community."

8. "The celebration, worship, and prayer [chaps. 1–3] that precede the paraenesis [chaps. 4–6] are likely to move and inspire the readers to the action called for more effectively than if the letter had consisted primarily of a string of exhortations" (Lincoln, *Ephesians*, xlii).

admonition that applies to every exercise of the Spirit's gifts and every effort to love other people, both within and outside the assembly (1 Cor. 11–14). Romans 12:3–21 describes various ways to offer one's body as a "living sacrifice," in an act of "spiritual worship" (12:1–2).[9]

We turn our attention first to worship in the assembly. On that basis we shall consider the priestly service in the world that stands closest to that of the assembly, namely, prayer.

Wholeness in Public Worship

It is perhaps especially hard for Americans, given our history of individualism and our current addiction to self-determination, to appreciate Paul's teaching about the gathered community.[10] For many reasons, our minds urgently need to be renewed in this regard. I mention three: (1) Our growing enslavement to the electronic media jeopardizes personal relationships. "In such a dehumanized society the fellowship of the local church will become increasingly important, whose members meet one another, and talk and listen to one another in person rather than on screen."[11] (2) The fragmentation and dissolution of the American family calls for marshaling all the resources of the family of God, especially for persons who have no other family, who are orphaned or widowed or divorced, who have no children or have never married, or who have experienced abuse and alienation within their own families.[12] (3) The enriching of personal relationships by those two means serves a far higher purpose. Living as we do in "an age of skimmed surfaces, of facile confidence that reality is whatever can be seen and taped and reported,"[13] when "the analyst's couch, the test tube, the questionnaire [and] the computer" are thought to be adequate tools for arriving at truth, our minds and imaginations desperately need to be awakened to the metaphysical and the transcendent.[14] Above all, we need a personal encounter with God himself.

9. On the interlacing of worship in the assembly and in the world, see C. F. D. Moule, *Worship in the New Testament* (London: Lutterworth, 1961), 82–85; and Herman Ridderbos, *Paul: An Outline of His Theology*, trans. John R. DeWitt (Grand Rapids: Eerdmans, 1975), 480–86.

10. In the judgment of Dietrich Bonhoeffer, "It has been granted to America, less than to any nation on earth, to realize the visible unity of the church of God" (quoted by Nathan O. Hatch, *The Reformed Journal* [October 1984]: 11).

11. John R. W. Stott, *Between Two Worlds: The Art of Preaching in the Twentieth Century* (Grand Rapids: Eerdmans, 1982), 69.

12. Vern S. Poythress, "The Church as Family: Why Male Leadership in the Family Requires Male Leadership in the Church," in *Recovering Biblical Manhood and Womanhood*, ed. John Piper and Wayne Grudem (Wheaton: Crossway, 1991), 242–43, laments the absence of a sense of family life in the contemporary American church.

13. George F. Will, *Newsweek* (19 July 1982): 76.

14. Thomas Howard, *The Achievement of C. S. Lewis* (Wheaton: Harold Shaw, 1980), 14. Lewis wrote his books in an effort to awaken the "stultified modern imagination to ancient and eternal blisses and realities" (ibid., 15).

The Ingredients

Our access to the patterns, the varieties, and the development of worship in the Pauline churches is limited. Yet there is much that we can learn. Some of Paul's instructions pertain directly to the conduct of worship (1 Cor. 11, 14; 1 Tim. 2), and most of his letters are written with a view to their being read aloud to Christians assembled for worship (1 Thess. 5:27, "I charge you by the Lord that this letter be read to all the brothers"; cf. Col. 4:16). We approach the subject in the awareness that the ingredients of worship are hard to isolate and classify,[15] and that a given ingredient was not necessarily found in every service, or at every stage of growth, in these communities.

In public worship, as elsewhere, the *charismata* are to be exercised in concert for the common good (1 Cor. 14). This means that an openness to the freedom of the Spirit (as manifested for example in a prophetic utterance or an interpreted tongue) is joined to a respect for the order that God has ordained (as evidenced for example in the leadership of the apostle and the teacher). A one-sided stress on freedom threatens the church with anarchy (1 Cor. 14:40); order without freedom leaves the church with a form of godliness bereft of power (2 Tim. 3:5). "It is precisely in this *harmonious combination of freedom and restriction* that there lies the greatness and uniqueness of the early Christian service of worship."[16] Yet there is no doubt that Paul's chief desire was the unleashing of the Spirit's power in the assembly. Order became necessary so that the power might (so to speak) be harnessed for the greatest good of the community.[17]

A further mark of wholeness in worship is the inseparability of proclamation and praise. Paul breaks into doxology under the impact of his theology (Rom. 11:33–36), and writes theology as an act of adoration (Eph. 1:3–14). The gospel's great indicatives are, by their very nature, ascriptions of praise to the triune God of salvation; and to judge from the letters, the principal way the gathered believers expressed their appreciation of the Word was with utterances of their own, whether in song or spoken word. To state the matter differently, the church's theology must be wed to the church's

---

15. "Prose and poetry, adoration and statement, quotations from recognized liturgical forms and free, original composition, mingle and follow one another so easily in the mind of a Christian thinker that, without some external criterion, one can never be certain how much or how little of 'common prayer' one is overhearing" (C. F. D. Moule, *The Birth of the New Testament*, 3d ed. [San Francisco: Harper and Row, 1982], 35).

16. Oscar Cullmann, *Early Christian Worship*, trans. A. Stewart Todd and James B. Torrance (London: SCM, 1953), 33.

17. Thus there is far greater emphasis on church order in 1 Timothy (one of the last letters) than in 1 Corinthians (one of the earlier ones). But in both places Paul calls on church leaders to direct, not to supplant, congregational participation in worship (Ridderbos, *Paul*, 482–84). In some contemporary churches, by contrast, strengthening and enlarging the organization seems to be thought the way to inject new life into the church.

worship—the theology effectively incorporated into the service of worship to instruct and sustain God's people, and the worship exerting its influence upon the church's theological formulations. Says Helmut Thielicke (following Anselm), "A theological thought can breathe only in the atmosphere of dialogue with God." Says Paul King Jewett (following Augustine), "The matrix of all theology is the worshiping congregation, for it was out of the experience of worship that theology was born."[18]

The Participants

In public worship, all three of the self's relationships are bound together. The communion of saints occurs in their common worship of God; and the individual grows both in self-understanding and in the knowledge of God through fellowship with believers. The worst thing that can befall a person who longs for self-fulfillment is to be deprived of, or willfully to isolate oneself from, the *ekklēsia*.[19] There are two extremes to avoid. One is the idea that fellowship between God and myself is all that I need (a danger inherent in the use of tongues, 1 Cor. 14). I can recall more than one occasion when I have retreated into God's presence to escape a threatening personal relationship. The other extreme is to imagine that the companionship of Christians is adequate to meet my need. I may use a gathering of believers (particularly where there is no mutual accountability) as a means of avoiding a close encounter with God. For Paul, such an "either-or" choice is inconceivable, so fully does he integrate the vertical and the horizontal dimensions of fellowship.[20]

Moreover, worship calls for the active involvement of the whole person. Here, as in other respects, the heart (*kardia*) is the integrating center of the self as a rational, emotional, and volitional being.[21] Reflected in Colossians 3:16 is a gathering in which all three aspects are called into action, with attentiveness moreover to both the horizontal and the vertical dimensions of worship: "Let the word of Christ dwell in you richly [cognitive] as you teach and admonish one another with all wisdom [cognitive and directive], and as you sing psalms, hymns and spiritual songs with gratitude in your hearts [cognitive and affective] to God" (NIV).[22]

18. Helmut Thielicke, *A Little Exercise for Young Theologians*, trans. Charles L. Taylor (Grand Rapids: Eerdmans, 1962), 34. Paul King Jewett, *Election and Predestination* (Grand Rapids: Eerdmans, 1985), 139.
19. John Leith, *From Generation to Generation* (Louisville: Westminster/John Knox, 1990), 47, joins sociologist Daniel Bell in the belief that "religion is a return . . . to the community of the living and the dead and those to be born, not to the self."
20. These two are well integrated in Jerry Bridges, *True Fellowship* (Colorado Springs: NavPress, 1985).
21. Cf. the discussion of the unity and diversity of the human self in chap. 2, pp. 42–46.
22. Cf. the remarks on Col. 3:15–17 in chap. 1, pp. 32–33. William S. Smith, *Musical Aspects of the New Testament* (Amsterdam: Ten Have, 1962), 168–74, observes that in musical praise especially, all dimensions of the self are actively and simultaneously engaged.

Reflecting on the above, many of us have to acknowledge an absence of wholeness in our worship services. One reason for this may be the dominance of certain *charismata* and the omission (if not suppression) of others (1 Cor. 12:14–26). Another may be that either proclamation or praise is not being given its rightful due. Yet another may be an imbalance and one-sidedness in the cultivation of the self's relationships, or the failure of the self to participate as a whole person. I suspect that a main reason is the nature of the gathering itself. For most American Christians at least, the church assembly corresponds to other "assemblies," to a large family reunion, let us say, or to the weekly meeting of the Rotary Club or the Junior League—to our congregating, in other words, with persons like ourselves.

It is when we honor the distinctive character of the *ekklēsia* according to Paul that the assembly holds out greatest hope of wholeness. Christ unites persons who were divided racially, economically, socially, sexually, and theologically. The barriers are huge and the risks are many; but the more that manifold reconciling work finds concrete expression in Christian assemblies, the richer and the more edifying the offerings of proclamation and praise shall be. Moreover, we have seen the importance Paul attaches to the church's witness in the community. When, in a given city, lines that distinguish denominations from each other are raised into walls that separate persons who belong to the one *ekklēsia*, the wholeness of worship is jeopardized.[23]

Proclamation and Praise in the Assembly

We have seen that these two are inseparable. We now look more closely at the setting in which, and the means by which, they come to expression in the Pauline churches.

God-centered Worship

The highest purpose of public worship is to glorify God. This explains the directives of 1 Corinthians 11:2–16. "A man . . . is the image and glory of God, but the woman is the glory of man" (11:7). Honor for creating the man belongs to God alone. But the fashioning of the woman, while no less the activity of God, presupposes the existence of the male and comes about through God's use of his body (11:8, "For man did not come from woman, but woman from man"). Praise, or "credit," for her existence belongs both to God and to the man. Therefore the man's head must not be covered in

---

23. See Eph. 4:1–6. Paul would be utterly dismayed over the proliferation of modern denominations, a usage of "church" that is foreign to his letters (see chap. 9, pp. 200–203). The problem is addressed in Richard F. Lovelace, *Dynamics of Spiritual Life* (Downers Grove: InterVarsity, 1979), 289–336; and John M. Frame, *Evangelical Reunion: Denominations and the Body of Christ* (Grand Rapids: Baker, 1991).

worship, for the man provides the "glass" in which the glory of God is reflected (2 Cor. 3:18). But the woman's head must be covered (11:5); for she is the glory of man, and it is God alone who is to be glorified in the public assembly ("For this reason," 11:10, harking back to v. 7).[24]

That purpose is served by both proclamation and praise. The declaration of the Word of God is an offering of worship by the one who speaks, and a basis for worship on the part of those who listen.[25] God may mediate his Word through the reading of the (Old Testament) Scriptures (1 Tim. 4:13a; cf. 2 Tim. 3:16–17) or an apostolic letter (2 Thess. 3:14), or through an exposition by the pastor-teacher (1 Tim. 4:13b; 2 Tim. 4:2).[26] He may also choose to speak through a spontaneous utterance from within the congregation, whether spoken or sung, to "teach and admonish" those assembled (Col. 3:16) by means of "some revelation or knowledge or prophecy or teaching" (1 Cor. 14:6).[27]

Worship centers also upon the Son of God. It became common for Christians to congregate on the first day of the week in honor of his resurrection (1 Cor. 16:2; cf. Acts 20:7). "The word of [or about] Christ" was proclaimed as a source of wisdom and a basis for praise (Col. 3:16); songs of adoration were offered to him (Eph. 5:19). Confessional statements and hymns were christological in character.[28] Persons baptized into Christ (Rom. 6:3; 1 Cor. 12:13) exclaimed, "Jesus is Lord!" (Rom. 10:9; 1 Cor. 12:3).[29] "The Lord's Supper," celebrated in remembrance of him, joined the visible Word of Christ to the verbal, and anticipated his return (1 Cor. 11:17–34).[30]

24. For this interpretation, see C. K. Barrett, *The First Epistle to the Corinthians* (New York: Harper and Row, 1968), 253–54 (following Morna D. Hooker).

25. "Word and worship belong indissolubly to each other. . . . [P]reaching is making known the Name of the Lord, and worship is praising the Name of the Lord made known. . . . Our worship is poor because our knowledge of God is poor, and our knowledge of God is poor because our preaching is poor" (Stott, *Between Two Worlds*, 82, 83).

26. Lincoln calls the body of Ephesians "the written equivalent of a sermon or homily" (*Ephesians*, xxxix).

27. On the varieties of proclamation, see Ridderbos, *Paul*, 482–84; James D. G. Dunn, *Jesus and the Spirit* (Philadelphia: Westminster, 1975), 225–48. Women as well as men have the right to speak in the ways indicated in 1 Cor. 14:6, 26. The "sign of authority" (*exousia*) on the woman's head (1 Cor. 11:10), which veils the glory of the male, is primarily an emblem of her right to pray and prophesy (11:5): it "represents the new authority given to the woman under the new dispensation to do things which formerly had not been permitted her" (Barrett, *1 Corinthians*, 255).

28. See Rom. 1:3–4; 4:24–25; 10:9–10; 1 Cor. 11:23–26; 15:3–7; Eph. 5:14; Phil. 2:6–11; Col. 1:15–20; 1 Tim. 2:5–6; 3:16; and the discussions in A. M. Hunter, *Paul and His Predecessors*, rev. ed. (Philadelphia: Westminster, 1961), 15–44; and Vernon H. Neufeld, *The Earliest Christian Confessions* (Leiden: Brill, 1963), 42–68. Also noteworthy is the christological emphasis in certain "trustworthy sayings" of the Pastoral Epistles (namely, 1 Tim. 1:15; 2 Tim. 2:11–13; and Titus 3:4–8); see George W. Knight III, *The Faithful Sayings in the Pastoral Letters* (Kampen: Kok, 1968).

29. "Baptism is the most natural setting" for such early Christian confessions as those of Acts 8:37 and 1 Cor. 12:3 (Moule, *Birth*, 40). With Lincoln (*Ephesians*, 318–19, 331–32), I take Eph. 5:14b ("Wake up, O sleeper, rise from the dead, and Christ will shine on you") to be lines from a baptismal hymn.

30. See chap. 12. 1 Cor. 16:22 ("Come, O Lord!") may reflect a eucharistic setting (cf. 11:26, "you proclaim the Lord's death until he comes"): see Gordon D. Fee, *The First Epistle to the Corinthians* (Grand Rapids: Eerdmans, 1987), 837–39.

Christ is the mediator of worship as well as its object. Paul typically speaks of addressing God the Father through Jesus Christ (2 Cor. 1:20; Eph. 5:20; Col. 3:17).[31] Christ's mediatorial work in this respect is integral to his saving work generally: "there is one God and one mediator between God and men, the man Christ Jesus, who gave himself as a ransom for all" (1 Tim. 2:5); "we have peace with God through our Lord Jesus Christ, through whom we have obtained access by faith into this grace in which we stand" (Rom. 5:1–2; cf. Eph. 2:18). In Romans 7:25a, "Thanks be to God through Jesus Christ our Lord!" the latter phrase embraces both the thanksgiving and the rescuing work (7:24b) that calls it forth. It is only "in the name of the Lord Jesus" (Col. 3:17)—that is, on the basis of his achievement and authority—that human beings may come into God's presence.[32]

The Holy Spirit provides the setting and the impetus for worship. A "demonstration of the Spirit's power" is essential for proclaiming the gospel effectively; the "joy of the Holy Spirit" is the effect of receiving it (1 Cor. 2:4–5; 1 Thess. 1:5–6). By the Spirit a person is united to Christ the Redeemer and enabled to call God "Father" (Rom. 8:15–16; Gal. 4:6–7). It is in the "fellowship of the Holy Spirit" that believers experience "the grace of the Lord Jesus Christ" and "the love of God" (2 Cor. 13:14). Accordingly, it is "by the Spirit of God" that Christians worship (Phil. 3:3).[33] By the Spirit they exclaim "Jesus is Lord" (1 Cor. 12:3). In the "fullness of the Spirit," and "speaking to one another in psalms and hymns and songs inspired by the Spirit," they adore the Father and the Son (Eph. 5:18–20).[34]

Responses to God

We begin with the congregational "Amen" (*amēn*). The Hebrew term here transliterated was used in the Old Testament to voice adoration of God, or submission to his Word, or a longing that his promises be fulfilled.[35] Paul's usage corresponds to the first: "how can one . . . say 'Amen' to your thanksgiving . . ." (1 Cor. 14:16); "For no matter how many promises God has made, they are 'Yes' in Christ. And so through him the 'Amen' is spoken by us to the glory of God" (2 Cor. 1:20 NIV). This "Amen" is no

31. For prayers directed to Jesus, see, e.g., 1 Cor. 16:22 ("Come, O Lord!"); 2 Cor. 12:8 ("Three times I pleaded with the Lord"); and 1 Tim. 1:12 ("I thank Christ Jesus our Lord"). A benediction offers a prayer indirectly (e.g., "May the grace of the Lord Jesus Christ . . . be with you all," 2 Cor. 13:14).

32. "The whole content of salvation revealed in Jesus is comprised in his name" (Peter T. O'Brien, *Colossians, Philemon* [Waco: Word, 1982], 211). Cf. 1 Cor. 6:11; Eph. 5:20.

33. This reading, or "who worship in the Spirit of God" (NRSV), is much more likely than "who worship God in spirit" (NRSV mg.). See Peter T. O'Brien, *Philippians* (Grand Rapids: Eerdmans, 1991), 346, 360.

34. This translation of Eph. 5:19 comes from Lincoln (*Ephesians*, 337), who (in my judgment) rightly says that *pneumatikais* (spiritual) denotes the Holy Spirit and modifies "psalms and hymns" as well as "songs" (ibid., 346). The Pauline pattern is to pray and praise by or in the Spirit; never does he speak of prayer or praise directed specifically to the Spirit. See A. W. Wainwright, *The Trinity in the New Testament* (London: SPCK, 1962), 227–28.

35. For the references see Alfred Jepsen, *TDOT* 1:320–22.

less communal than that of 1 Corinthians 14; "by us" embraces the readers who have received the message preached by Paul and his colleagues (1:19), who "stand firm in Christ" (1:21), and who now thank God for salvation in his Son.[36]

Paul's letters contain confessions of faith and creedal formulations, prayers and petitions, doxologies and benedictions, of the sort we would have heard in an early Christian gathering. Such utterances might take the form of prose or poetry, of speech or song. They might be well-established ingredients of the church's liturgy or spontaneous compositions. They both instructed believers and helped them to articulate their praise.[37]

"A tongue" (1 Cor. 14:26) is directed to God: "For anyone who speaks in a tongue does not speak to men but to God. Indeed, no one understands him; he utters mysteries with his spirit" (14:2 NIV).[38] Though the utterance is unintelligible to others and one's own mind is unfruitful, real prayer is nonetheless occurring (14:14–19).[39] It is, moreover, a prayer of adoration and thanks ("you are praising God with your spirit . . . your thanksgiving," 14:16), one which might be spoken or sung ("I will pray with my spirit . . . I will sing with my spirit," 14:15). Because it is both unintelligible and potentially beneficial to others, the tongue must be joined in the assembly to the "interpretation of tongues" (14:5, 26–28). Thus translated and explained, the utterance becomes a vehicle of corporate praise and thanksgiving, by which means the participants are edified (14:4–5, 16–17).[40]

36. The "Amen" of 2 Cor. 1:20 may well echo that of 1 Cor. 14:16. In 2 Cor. 1:21b–22 (beginning "He anointed us") Paul reverts to the apostolic mission of 1:19. On these points, see Ralph P. Martin, *2 Corinthians* (Waco: Word, 1986), 27–28. In the NT Epistles the "Amen" invariably comes at the end of a statement; in the Gospels, always at the beginning and always on the lips of Jesus. The placement in the Gospels corresponds to the *Niphal* stem of the Hebrew verb *aman*, "prove oneself reliable, have stability," and denotes the trustworthiness of what Jesus is about to say. The epistolary usage corresponds to the *Hiphil*, "view something or someone as reliable, have faith in," and affirms one's trust in what has just been said.

37. On the matters summarized in this paragraph, see Moule, *Birth*, 28–43; Cullmann, *Worship*, 12–26; Ralph P. Martin, *Worship in the Early Church* (London: Marshall, Morgan and Scott, 1974), 28–76. For examples of confessional and creedal material, see Rom. 1:3–4; Eph. 4:4–6; Phil. 2:6–11; Col. 1:15–20; 1 Tim. 3:16. Consonant with the letters' being read during the assembly, is Paul's placement of benedictions and doxologies at the beginning ("Grace and peace to you . . . " 1 Cor. 1:3 *et passim*) and end (e.g., Rom. 16:25–27; 1 Cor. 16:23; 2 Cor. 13:14). For prayers and songs in the assembly, see 1 Cor. 11:3–10; 14:13–17, 26; Eph. 5:19; Col. 3:16; 1 Tim. 2:1–8; Smith, *Musical Aspects*, 22–95, 162–80; 238–39; Dunn, *Jesus*, 238–42.

38. NIV's marginal reading at 14:2 has "by the Spirit" in place of "with his spirit." The textual reading is the more likely, in view of 14:14, "For if I pray in a tongue, my spirit prays. . . " Yet the person prays because the Spirit prays (Rom. 8:26–27), and tongues is one of the Spirit's gifts (1 Cor. 12:10–11).

39. "My spirit prays . . . I will pray with my spirit" (14:14–15); cf. chap. 2, p. 48

40. See Dunn, *Jesus*, 246–48. Such an utterance is granted by the Spirit for edifying God's people, both oneself and others. Yet it remains a fallible utterance, like prophecy (chap. 9, pp. 208–13). The same is true of prayers in one's native language: no prayer can be offered without the interceding Spirit (as we shall presently see), but who would claim ever to have composed an infallible prayer?

The Cure of Souls

By the propagation of the Word of God, believers are edified intellectually, emotionally, and volitionally. The pulpit affords the pastor one of
the best opportunities for pastoral counseling. "The sermon for Protes-
tants traditionally is the primary means by which God's grace is mediated to troubled human souls. . . . Great preaching is always pastoral."[41]
God's people will not be made whole by sensitivity groups that seek to
clarify values lying deep within their own psyches, and that confirm
them in whatever convictions they sincerely hold. It will happen instead
by the proclamation of the Word of power mediating God's saving righteousness to them (Rom. 1:16–17) and challenging them to grow in faith,
hope, and love (1 Thess. 1:2–10); and it will happen by prophetic utterances prompted by the Spirit to strengthen, encourage, and comfort them
(1 Cor. 14:3).[42]

Two other cardinal aspects of worship serve the same purpose. One is
the Lord's Supper, a subject reserved for later. The other is corporate praise
and thanksgiving. The tongue of praise refreshes and restores both the person who speaks and those who, through interpretation, enter into what is
said (14:4–5, 16–17). It is hard to imagine a more therapeutic and cathartic
exercise than the offering of "psalms, hymns and spiritual songs" to God
from the heart in the company of other believers.[43]

The cure of souls extends to the watching world. "The assembled community is . . . the organ which Christ employs in order to show forth his
body as the Church."[44] First Corinthians 14:20–25 speaks of proclamation to
"unbelievers" who are present in the Christian assembly. Tongues are quite
unintelligible to outsiders, and likely to drive them away from the church
(14:23); yet tongues are "a sign . . . for unbelievers" (14:22). Prophecy, on the
other hand, is good for unbelievers in that it brings conviction of sin and
reverence for God (14:24–25); yet prophecy is a sign "for believers" (14:22).
What does Paul mean?

The use of Isaiah 28 in 14:21 provides a clue. Since Judah has ridiculed
and rejected Isaiah's message as nonsensical, God will respond in kind.
Through the Assyrians he will give them a message they are sure to find

41. Leith, *Generation*, 154. Stott calls the Word of God the food with which Christ nourishes his church
(*Between Two Worlds*, 109), and the medicine with which he heals it (ibid., 20, quoting Chrysostom).

42. These comments should be taken together with those concerning psychotherapy in chap. 7, p. 168.

43. On praise as "inner health made audible," and as joy completed, see C. S. Lewis, *Reflections on the
Psalms* (New York: Harcourt Brace, 1958), 90–98.

44. Cullmann, *Worship*, 34. "God means the congregation to be a visual aid to the world" (Stott, *Between Two Worlds*, 78). Leith (following William Temple) speaks of the whole congregation as the bearer of
the gospel (*Generation*, 34–35).

unintelligible (28:11).[45] As the "strange tongues" of the Assyrians signaled God's judgment on Judah, so in Corinth tongues are "a sign for unbelievers" (14:22a)—a sign of judgment. If an unbeliever hears nothing but tongues, he is sure to remain an outsider under God's wrath. Prophecy, on the other hand, is "a sign for believers" (14:22b). This too is a sign of judgment: the tongue judged by being unintelligible, prophecy does so by being intelligible. But the judgment of prophecy, unlike that of tongues, is intended to save (1 Cor. 11:31–32; 2 Cor. 7:10). While the passage is not concerned with persons who are already Christians, it does refer to a person who is becoming one, and doing so through prophecy: "he will be convinced by all that he is a sinner and will be judged by all, and the secrets of his heart will be laid bare. So he will fall down and worship God, exclaiming, 'God is really among you!'" (14:24–25 NIV). Such conviction may come, of course, to persons who are already Christians: "Do not despise prophesying," says 1 Thessalonians 5:20. The temptation is to despise prophecy, not because it is strange but because it is convicting. God's Word sometimes cures by stroking the heart, at other times by striking it.[46] "'Twas grace that taught my heart to fear, and grace my fears relieved."[47]

Prayers of Intercession

"Prayer is at the heart of Paul's thinking and practice. . . . The apostle demonstrates that prayer and theology belong together."[48] Moreover, as we have seen, Paul demonstrates that worship in the assembly has its counterpart in the world. Particularly is this evident in his references to prayers of intercession: for these are offered both in the assembly and at all other times; they are filled with praise and thanksgiving to God; and they are by nature a communal activity.[49] However, another kind of intercession must first be considered.

45. 1 Cor. 14:21 does not fully agree with the MT (or the LXX) of Isa. 28:11–12. In the MT the judgment is the effect of failing to listen to God's Word; in Paul failing to understand God's Word is the consequence of the judgment. The kinship between the MT and Paul is that unintelligible speech is the instrument of God's judgment.

46. Stott, *Between Two Worlds*, 248 (following Richard Baxter).

47. John Newton, "Amazing Grace" (1779). Wrote Francis Scott Key ("Lord, with glowing heart I'd praise thee," 1817): "Praise the grace whose threats alarmed thee, roused thee from thy fatal ease; praise the grace whose promise warmed thee, praise the grace that whispered peace."

48. David G. Peterson, "Prayer in Paul's Writings," in *Teach Us to Pray*, ed. D. A. Carson (Grand Rapids: Baker, 1990), 84. Paul would agree with the late rabbi Abraham Joshua Heschel that "talking *about* God, which is what theologians do, was idle chatter unless one first learned to talk *to* God" (Kenneth L. Woodward, *Newsweek* [6 January 1992]: 39). Like other dimensions of life in community, prayer is related to every subject thus far considered in this book; cf. the opening paragraph of chap. 9.

49. In keeping with our findings in chap 1, Paul's prayers for himself are offered for the sake of the community: "I pray that now at last by God's will the way may be opened for me to come to you" (Rom. 1:10 NIV; cf. 1:14–15).

The Divine Intercessors

"Christ Jesus, who died—more than that, who was raised to life—is at the right hand of God and is also interceding for us" (Rom. 8:34 NIV). He who intercedes is the very One who bore his people's sorrow and suffering and sin, and who is therefore able to identify in the closest way with the prayers they offer. He is moreover the One who, by virtue of his triumph over Sin and Death, prays with the highest authority. Who can imagine what sort of translation and interpretation of believers' prayers is involved in the Son's intercessions on their behalf?

The intercessory work of the Holy Spirit is the subject of Romans 8:26–27. In the first place, the Spirit sustains his people: "In the same way the Spirit helps us in our weakness." It is not merely energy or will power that he supplies: "We do not know what we ought to pray" (8:26). The statement is unqualified; our helplessness is complete. "The best disposition for praying is that of being desolate, forsaken, stripped of everything," said Augustine.[50] This includes being stripped of the knowledge of that for which we must pray. Even the believers' initial and most fundamental response is impossible without the Spirit: "by him [the Spirit of sonship] we cry, '*Abba*, Father'" (8:15).[51] We do not merely speak the word *Father*: we shout it (the verb is *krazō*), as persons longing to be freed from the spirit of bondage (8:15a). While we cannot do so except by the Spirit, it is nonetheless we who cry. Recognizing the Spirit's intercession provides the greatest incentive to pray with boldness.

Secondly, the Spirit struggles on believers' behalf: "the Spirit himself intercedes for us with unuttered groanings" (8:26b). The groanings are his, corresponding to those of believers and indeed of the whole creation (8:22–23).[52] The Spirit who is utterly serene within the fellowship of the Holy Trinity is, at the same time, the One who indwells believers and identifies with them in the closest way (8:9, 16); is thus acutely aware of their longing for the end of suffering and sorrow and the struggle against Sin (7:14–25; 8:35–39); and therefore enters into their longing with a struggle of his own, appealing thereby to God the Father for the hastening of the consummation.

Finally, the Spirit is a sovereign intercessor: "And God, who searches the heart, knows what is the mind of the Spirit, because the Spirit intercedes for the saints according to the will of God" (8:27 NRSV). The Spirit of

50. Quoted in Donald G. Bloesch, *The Struggle of Prayer* (San Francisco: Harper and Row, 1980), 7.

51. As preparation for our doing so, the Spirit himself utters "*Abba*" on our behalf (Gal. 4:6). "The essence of prayer is not a mystical lifting up of the mind to God but the descent of the Spirit into our hearts" (Bloesch, *Prayer*, 6).

52. C. E. B. Cranfield, *The Epistle to the Romans*, vol. 1 (Edinburgh: T. & T. Clark, 1975), 423, calls attention to the *hōsautōs* (in the same way) at the beginning of 8:26, joining the Spirit's own "groans" (*stenagmois*, 8:26) to those of the creation (*systenazei*, 8:22) and of believers (*stenazomen*, 8:23).

God knows the will of God fully and flawlessly and prays accordingly. The New English Bible may be correct in making the Spirit the subject of both 8:27b and 28: "he [the Spirit] pleads for God's people in God's own way; and in everything, as we know, he co-operates for good with those who love God and are called according to his purpose."[53] But however 8:28 is translated, verses 28–30 flow out of verses 26–27. The Spirit's intercession is essential for the achieving of God's saving purpose. It is the Spirit who prays that Christians may be fully conformed to the image of God's Son; and it is the Spirit who prays that the plan of God conceived before the foundation of the world, and carried forward in calling and justification, may hasten to its completion in the glorification of the saints (8:29–30).[54]

Flanking our prayers is the joint activity of the indwelling Spirit and the exalted Christ. With this encouragement we turn to believers' own responsibility in intercession.

Believers' Prayers for One Another[55]

In eight of his thirteen letters, Paul expressly asks readers to pray for him and his colleagues. One such request is general, "Brothers, pray for us" (1 Thess. 5:25); all the others are specific. The fact that similar requests are made of six churches (seven if we count the church in Laodicea), together with the individual Philemon, indicates that there is value in the quantity as well as the quality of prayer on another's behalf. That the prayers might be intelligent and focused, Paul informs readers of his circumstances both directly (Rom. 15:23–33) and indirectly (Col. 4:7–9; Eph. 6:19–22). The burden of his requests is that the gospel might progress through his apostolic labors, and that opposition both human and demonic might be overcome. There is no contradiction in his mind between confidence that the sovereign God will fulfill his saving purpose despite all obstacles, and appeals for prayer on behalf of his mission. God ordains prayer as the instrument of his sovereignty, and prayer by its

53. Favoring the NEB is the kinship among the compound verbs *symmartyrei* (8:16, of the Spirit's witness), *synantilambanetai* (8:26, of the Spirit's help), and *synergei* (8:28, "co-operates"). Note also the kinship between the phrases *kata Theon* (according to God [i.e., according to God's will], v. 27) and *kata prothesin* (according to [God's] purpose, v. 28). In the NIV "God" is the subject in 8:28; in the NKJV, "all things."

54. The answer to the question "What is prayer?" in the Westminster *Shorter Catechism*: "Prayer is an offering up of our desires unto God, for things agreeable to his will, in the name of Christ, with confession of our sins, and thankful acknowledgment of his mercies." The *Larger Catechism* answers, "Prayer is an offering up of our desires unto God, in the name of Christ, by the help of his Spirit, with confession of our sins, and thankful acknowledgment of his mercies." These answers should be combined; for the first says nothing about the Spirit and the second nothing about praying in accord with God's will. Rom. 8 teaches that our doing the latter requires the Spirit's help.

55. Gordon P. Wiles, *Paul's Intercessory Prayers: The Significance of the Intercessory Prayer Passages in the Letters of St Paul* (Cambridge: Cambridge University Press, 1974), is a useful study but is limited to seven letters (all but Ephesians, Colossians, 2 Thessalonians, and the Pastorals).

very nature depends upon God.[56] "On [God] we have set our hope that he will continue to deliver us, as you help us by your prayers" (2 Cor. 1:10–11 NIV). "Pray for us that the word of the Lord may spread rapidly and be honored... and that we may be rescued from wicked and evil persons..." (2 Thess. 3:1–2). The prayer in the Spirit joins "the sword of the Spirit" in combating "the spiritual forces of evil in the heavenly realms" (Eph. 6:10–20).[57]

The epistles speak more often of Paul's prayers for his readers than of theirs for him.[58] He does not merely tell readers that he is praying for them, he invariably tells them what. The prayer is sometimes incorporated into the letter (e.g., Eph. 3:14–21). Although we can only estimate the size of the various churches, it is probable that Paul prayed frequently and intelligently for hundreds of people. For he prayed both for churches as a whole and (to judge from his greetings especially) for many individuals in the churches.[59] Evidence of readers' spiritual growth explains the thanksgiving with which several letters begin. "We always thank God for all of you, mentioning you in our prayers. We continually remember before our God and Father your work produced by faith, your labor prompted by love, and your endurance inspired by hope in our Lord Jesus Christ" (1 Thess. 1:2–3 NIV).[60] He prays that such growth will continue. "We have not stopped praying for you and asking God to fill you with the knowledge of his will through all spiritual wisdom and understanding. And we pray this in order that you may live a life worthy of the Lord and may please him in every way: bearing fruit in every good work, growing in the knowledge of God..." (Col. 1:9–11 NIV).[61] In keeping with his requests for

56. "I pray that now at last by God's will the way may be opened for me to come to you" (Rom. 1:10); "Pray that I may be rescued... so that by God's will I may come to you... (Rom. 15:31–32). "Prayer frees us to be controlled by God" (Richard J. Foster, *Freedom of Simplicity* [San Francisco: Harper and Row, 1981], 58); see idem, *Prayer: Finding the Heart's True Home* (San Francisco: Harper, 1992), for an excellent treatment of the various kinds of prayer. On the relation between God's sovereignty and the response of faith (of which prayer is one expression), see pp. 64–66, 95–97.

57. On prayer in this passage see chap. 7, pp. 78–79. For other such requests see Rom. 15:30–32; Phil. 1:19; Col. 4:2–3; Philem. 22. "Thus there is no escaping the centrality of intercessory prayer to Paul's theology of mission" (Peterson, "Prayer," 100).

58. References to Paul's prayers for other believers are found in ten of the thirteen letters: see, e.g., Rom. 1:9–10; 1 Cor. 1:4; 2 Cor. 13:9; Eph. 1:16–19; Phil. 1:3–11; Col. 1: 3–12; 1 Thess. 3:9–13; 2 Thess. 1:3, 11–12; 2 Tim. 1:3; Philem. 4.

59. "God... is my witness that without ceasing I remember you always in my prayers" (Rom. 1:9–10 NRSV; cf. the long list of greetings in 16:3–16). Perhaps significantly, the two individuals for whom Paul expressly says he is praying are leaders in the church: "I always thank my God as I remember you in my prayers" (Philem. 4); "I constantly remember you in my prayers" (2 Tim. 1:3).

60. Similarly in Rom. 1:8; 2 Thess. 1:3; Col. 1:3–5; 2 Tim. 1:3–5; Philem. 4–5. 1 Cor. 1:4–9 gives thanks for evidence of the *charismata* but not for the cardinal virtues of 13:13 (which are woefully lacking at Corinth). The opening thanksgiving is altogether absent from Gal. For a thorough treatment of the subject, see Peter T. O'Brien, *Introductory Thanksgivings in the Letters of Paul* (Leiden: Brill, 1977).

61. Cf. 2 Cor. 13:7–9; Eph. 1:16–17; 3:14–21; Phil. 1:9–11; 1 Thess. 3:10–13. Paul's own prayers are taken up by others: Col. 4:12 (Epaphras's prayer for the Colossians); 1 Cor. 7:5 (prayers by the husband and the wife, focusing especially, to judge from the immediate context, on the sexual dimension of their marriage).

prayer, Paul acknowledges believers' participation in his ministry: "I thank my God every time I remember you. In my every prayer for all of you, I always pray with joy because of your participation in the gospel from the first day until now . . ." (Phil. 1:3–5); one reason for his joy is knowledge of the blessings God will grant them in response to their obedience (4:10–20).

Yet intercessory prayers are not restricted to believers.

Prayers for the World

For the sake of the world, Paul requests prayer for the progress of the gospel, urges the Colossians to devote themselves to prayer (Col. 4:2–6), and prays that Philemon will actively share his faith (Philem. 6). The ordering of public worship in 1 Timothy 2 begins, significantly, with prayers of intercession for the nonbelieving world: "First of all, then, I urge that supplications, prayers, intercessions, and thanksgivings, be made for everyone . . ." (2:1 NRSV).[62] Attention is especially focused on "kings and all those in authority" (2:2a), because their maintaining peace (2:2b) will expedite the spread of the gospel to "all men" (2:4–7).[63] A further effect of such order is that believers "may live peaceful and quiet lives in all godliness and dignity" (2:2b)—a real, if only a faint, foretaste of a restored universe. For both reasons, the intercession "is good, and pleasing to God our Savior" (2:3).

I offer three concluding observations. (1) Intercession enriches our three relationships. It makes us attentive to other people, both within and beyond the church. Moreover, our attention is drawn to God (the prayer is offered to the Father through his Son by the Spirit) and to the relationship of others to him. And nothing edifies the self so much as getting the mind off the self. (2) Effectively praying that way entails struggle: there is unrelenting opposition from "the world, the flesh and the devil"; and answers do not always come swiftly.[64] (3) Paul's teaching on prophecy is pertinent;

---

62. This is the more significant, given the emphasis in 1 Tim. 1 (to which chap. 2 is joined by its opening "then") on the dangers posed by false teachers (1:3–7) and on Timothy's charge to uphold sound doctrine (1:18–19). It is not necessary to attempt precise distinctions among the four terms of 2:1. The cluster accentuates the centrality of prayer, especially the prayer of intercession; cf. J. N. D. Kelly, *The Pastoral Epistles* (San Francisco: Harper and Row, 1960), 60. The focus of the intercession discourages self-centeredness in the assembly.

63. One cause for "thanksgiving" (2:1) is that human beings are "saved and . . . come to a knowledge of the truth" (2:4). Cf. 2 Cor. 4:15, "so that the grace that is reaching more and more people may cause thanksgiving to overflow to the glory of God" (NIV).

64. Cf. Rom. 15:30–31 ("I urge you . . . to join me in my struggle by praying to God for me. . . . that I may be rescued . . ."); Col. 4:2 ("Devote yourselves to prayer, being watchful [i.e., vigilant; the verb is *grē-goreō*] . . ."), 12 (Epaphras "is always wrestling in his prayers on your behalf"). Especially to be commended in this regard is Bloesch, *The Struggle of Prayer*. One of my colleagues prayed for two years before the girl he loved consented to marry him: see Douglas F. Kelly, *If God Already Knows, Why Pray?* (Brentwood, Tenn.: Wolgemuth and Hyatt, 1989), 1–2.

the Spirit who prompts us to speak to another's need (1 Cor. 14:3) also prompts us to pray.[65]

The Prayer of Anxiety

Philippians 4:6–7 enlarges our understanding both of worship and of intercession according to Paul, but also accentuates an aspect of prayer not yet considered.

The Worry

"Do not be anxious about anything but in everything by prayer and entreaty with thanksgiving let your requests be made known to God," says Philippians 4:6. The opening imperative is more accurately rendered "Stop worrying." Paul urges his readers to break an established pattern.[66] The same verb is used of Timothy in 2:20. There it has a positive connotation ("a genuine interest in your welfare"), here the negative one of "anxious harassing care."[67] The language is as comprehensive as it can be: "not . . . about anything, but in everything. . . ." No anxiety, real or potential, is excluded. Appropriating this verse means recognizing the presence of anxiety in our lives, however unreasonable or embarrassing it may appear to be. Nothing is gained by ignoring it or trying to suppress it.

Paul does not exhort us to get rid of anxiety before we pray. Prayer itself is the therapy. God provides prayer as a channel for expressing our anxiety; the worry itself is lifted to God in prayer (cf. 1 Pet. 5:7). Paul is not saying, "The Lord is near [4:5b], there is therefore no need to be anxious"; but rather, "The Lord is near, therefore offer your anxiety to him." This verse is disobeyed, not by being afflicted with worry but by refusing to present it to God.

The surrounding verses point to some causes of worry. On the negative side, it may be that the way of thinking and living described in 4:8–9 (and expounded elsewhere by Paul) has been violated. A person who aspires to grow in holiness yet feeds on a steady diet of R-rated movies can expect to be anxious. On the positive side, a believer who seeks to follow Christ's example (2:6–11) and who becomes enslaved to other persons for his sake (as did Timothy and Epaphroditus, 2:19–30) can hardly help being anxious

65. For example, one may suddenly and inexplicably sense a need to pray for someone in another place, and later learn that the person faced a grave peril at that very hour. See the earlier comments on Rom. 8:26–27; and Wayne Grudem, *The Gift of Prophecy in the New Testament and Today* (Westchester, Ill: Crossway, 1988), 132–34, as well as the discussion of prophecy in chap. 9.

66. "The negative *mē[den]* with the present imperative, *merimnate*, assumes that the Philippians had been anxious, and they are now urged to stop being so" (O'Brien, *Philippians*, 491).

67. Gerald F. Hawthorne, *Philippians* (Waco: Word, 1983), 183, who thinks the term speaks "especially about things over which one has no control."

about such a relational problem as is described in 4:2–3.[68] To let one's "gentleness be known to all" (4:5) is to be obedient to the commands of 2:1–5; gentleness is "a quality . . . that keeps one from insisting on his full rights."[69] Does not such a forbearing spirit entail absorbing the wrongs of others, and holding in one's resentment? Would not this cause untold psychic damage, were there not the outlet of prayer?

The Worship

The "prayer and entreaty" of anxiety is to be offered "with thanksgiving" (4:6). It may be legitimate to link the latter directly to the former, for example, to give thanks for a person's life even as we voice anxiety over his terminal cancer. Yet in this passage the impetus for the thanksgiving is christological. We approach God on the basis of our union with Christ (2:1), a bond that nothing can sever (1:20–23). He and the righteousness he embodies (3:9) account for the inscription of our names in "the book of life" (4:3) and our hope of heaven (3:14, 20–21).

In the light of those great indicatives, there are certain imperatives. We noted earlier that the phrase *in Christ* usually speaks of believers' corporate life in Christ, and "in the Lord" of the implications for their conduct.[70] Attentiveness to the three instances of the latter phrase in 4:1–5 is an important aspect of appropriating 4:6–7 itself. To "stand firm in the Lord" (4:1) is one way to quell anxiety. One key to giving thanks "in everything" (4:6) is to "rejoice in the Lord always" (4:4).[71] Amid the very experience of worry, we are united to Christ, the very place of joy. "The Lord is near" (4:5) has both spatial and temporal dimensions. Being "in Christ" assures us of his presence with us (even when we feel that he is distant), though this is a reality that transcends purely spatial categories. The eager expectation of Christ's return (3:20–21) gives us hope amid pressures and anxieties.[72]

Where the anxiety results from personal sin, the worship will include an acknowledgment of guilt and a renewed appropriation of Christ's saving work on one's behalf (Phil. 3:2–11).

The Father makes his presence known to those who cast their anxiety upon him: "And the peace of God, which surpasses all understanding, will stand guard over your hearts and your minds in Christ Jesus" (4:7). It is to just such people that God delights to reveal himself (Ps. 51:17; Isa. 57:15). It

68. This suggests that there may not be so great a difference between the "concern" of 2:20 and the "worry" of 4:6 as first appears.

69. Hawthorne, *Philippians*, 182. On Christ's relinquishing of rights, see the comments on Phil. 2:1–11 in chap. 5, pp. 121–22.

70. This distinction was noted in chap. 7, p. 156. Note the use of "in the Lord" in Paul's appeal to Euodia and Syntyche, 4:2.

71. The adverb is not *aei* (always, constantly), but *pantote* (at all times, in all circumstances).

72. On the interlacing of the spatial and the temporal in 4:5b, see O'Brien, *Philippians*, 488–90.

is not cognitive knowledge about peace that he grants (*savoir*), but experiential knowledge of his peace (*connaître*)—knowledge that affects the mind more deeply than does the other kind (cf. Eph. 3:18–19; Phil. 3:10). We are confirmed in our belief that prayer is the avenue of anxiety, not its aftermath: "the peace of God" is the consequence of prayer rather than its basis. Nothing is said about removing the cause of the anxiety; God's peace provides a garrison amid that very circumstance (cf. 1 Cor. 10:13, "a way out so that you can bear up under it").

The Work

Prayer entails struggle, as already noted. The "requests" and "petitions" (4:6) are not always easily offered; my own prayers are exceedingly laborious at times. Nor are they always immediately answered, nor is every anxiety instantly lifted. For such reasons, the presence of anxiety calls for drawing upon the resources of the Christian community, and asking others who are united with us "in Christ" to pray for us. This is one way in which believers may bear one another's burdens (Gal. 6:1–5) and demonstrate the "tenderness and compassion" to which Paul summons them in Philippians 2:1–4. Corporate prayer is implied in the plural verbs of 4:6–7. This is one way in which the "loyal yokefellow" and others can help Euodia and Syntyche (4:2–3).

There is also a work that accompanies prayer. The teaching of Philippians 4:6–7 is followed immediately by a twofold command to ponder certain qualities (4:8) and to pursue certain practices (4:9). Neither the prayer nor the contemplation is an end in itself, but preparation for purposeful activity in the world. Obedience to 4:8–9 is both an expression of gratitude for the peace of God (4:7) and a means of overcoming at least some causes of anxiety. Significantly, the promise of 4:9b—"And the God of peace will be with you"—follows the command to live a holy life. The statement is doubtless meant to encourage the Philippians to follow Paul's example, including his practice of prayer (4:9a). Yet it remains a promise whose fulfillment is, in some sense, consequent upon believers' conduct. Here, as in verses 6–7, the presence of God provides the strongest incentive to obedience.

This joining of prayer to life in Christ and in the world brings to mind those major chords of Ephesians with which the chapter began.

> *Now to him who is able to do immeasurably more than all we ask or imagine, according to his power that is at work within us, to him be glory in the church and in Christ Jesus throughout all generations, for ever and ever! Amen. [Eph. 3:20–21 NIV]*

11

The Christian Hope

Faith, hope, and love are indissolubly joined together, both now and in the life to come.[1] Of the three, the greatest is love (1 Cor. 13:13). Love arises from faith (1 Tim. 1:5) and brings faith to concrete expression (Gal. 5:6). Yet there is a sense in which both love and faith depend on hope: "we have heard of your faith in Christ Jesus and of the love that you have for all the saints, because of the hope that is stored up for you in heaven . . ." (Col. 1:4–5). For Paul "the attitude of faith is one which looks at the earthly in the light of the heavenly."[2]

That hope is "stored up in heaven," because that is where Christ presently reigns (Col. 3:1–3): he accounts for the hope, together with the faith and love that spring from it. To be separate from Christ is to be "without hope" (Eph. 2:12); he becomes the embodiment of hope for those united to him. Paul's view of the future is thoroughly christological.[3]

The Historical Perspective

Before we turn to those events in which believers' patience is rewarded and their hope fulfilled, we consider from what standpoint Paul instructs them to view what is yet to be.

1. See Rom. 5:1–5; 1 Cor. 13:13; Gal. 5:5–6; Col. 1:4–5; 1 Thess. 1:3; 5:8.
2. Andrew T. Lincoln, *Paradise Now and Not Yet* (Cambridge: Cambridge University Press, 1981), 191. See, e.g., 2 Cor. 4:17–18; Col. 3:1–4.
3. He is "our hope" (1 Tim. 1:1) and "the hope of glory" (Col. 1:27); present endurance is "inspired by hope in our Lord Jesus Christ" (1 Thess. 1:3). The christological character of Paul's hope is well emphasized by Lincoln, *Paradise*, 169–95.

Salvation Already and Not Yet

Salvation embraces the past, the present, and the future.[4] "Christ Jesus came into the world to save sinners" (1 Tim. 1:15). In his death and resurrection he achieved a decisive victory over Sin and its agencies, by virtue of which salvation can now be experienced: "by grace you have been saved" (Eph. 2:5, 8). We may therefore be confident that God's saving purpose will reach its appointed goal. As persons taught by the grace manifested in Christ's first advent, "we wait for the blessed hope" of his return (Titus 2:11–13). Those already justified by God's grace have "the hope of eternal life" (Titus 3:5–7). D-Day has occurred, V-Day is assured. God "has saved us" through "our Savior Christ Jesus, who abolished death and brought life and immortality to light through the gospel" (2 Tim. 1:9–10); therefore, says Paul, "the Lord will rescue me from every evil work and will save me for his heavenly kingdom" (2 Tim. 4:18). The same holds true for those under Paul's care: "He who began a good work in you will bring it to completion on the day of Christ Jesus" (Phil. 1:6; cf. 1 Cor. 1:7–9). It is "in this hope" that we were saved in the first place: what we have already experienced of liberation from Sin and of life in God's family makes us "groan inwardly as we eagerly await our adoption . . . the redemption of our bodies" (Rom. 8:23–24). Therefore the cry "Come, O Lord!" (1 Cor. 16:22) became a common feature of Christian worship.[5]

As the decisive shift in history has already occurred (1 Cor. 10:11; Gal. 4:4), there is the closest logical connection between Christ's first advent and his return; the latter is perpetually imminent. When writing 1 Thessalonians Paul naturally associates himself with the living: "we who are alive, who are left . . . we who are alive and are left" (4:15, 17). When writing 2 Timothy some fifteen years later, he expects to die before Christ returns. Yet he has not become disillusioned; his hope for the consummation is undiminished (4:1–8). He still longs for Christ's appearing (4:8), and it may well be that he now applies to himself what he wrote about the Christian dead in 1 Thessalonians 4–5. For Paul the great overriding reality is the certainty that Christ will return; when it happens is for the sovereign God to determine. In 1 Timothy (written near the time of 2 Timothy) Paul charges Timothy to be faithful "until the appearing of our Lord Jesus Christ, which God will bring about in his own time—God, the blessed and only Ruler . . ." (6:14–15 NIV).[6]

---

4. For salvation as a past event, a present experience, and a future hope in Paul, see E. M. B. Green, *The Meaning of Salvation* (London: Hodder and Stoughton, 1965), 152–89.

5. See Gordon D. Fee, *The First Epistle to the Corinthians* (Grand Rapids: Eerdmans, 1987), 838–39.

6. The delay of Christ's return "does not appear to have occasioned any material change in [Paul's] theology in general or his eschatology in particular. The apostolic doctrine of the Parousia is independent of its timing" (F. F. Bruce, *1 and 2 Thessalonians* [Waco: Word, 1982], xxxviii).

The Personal and the Historical

By this stage of our study we ought to be fully convinced that salvation according to Paul is deeply and thoroughly personal. Yet as we began to see at the close of chapter 1, this same salvation embraces all of history and all of creation. The all-encompassing character of God's saving plan challenges the strong tendency in much modern thought to view salvation (of whatever sort) in purely subjective and individualistic terms.[7] Yet for Paul it is precisely a salvation that is cosmic in scope that offers fulfillment at the personal level. The Redeemer of individuals is also the Lord of creation and history. Through the death and resurrection of his Son, God the Father both reconciles to himself "all things, whether things on earth or things in heaven," and liberates believers from the dominion of darkness and ushers them into the kingdom of light: in both respects, Christ is "the hope of glory" (Col. 1:12–27). Integral to God's plan "to gather together in Christ all things in heaven and on earth," is the glorification of his people (Eph. 1:3–23). Loosed from God's purpose for history and the universe, the life of the individual becomes meaningless.[8]

Suffering and Glory

Just as Christ's suffering and death were essential for his victory over Sin and death, so it is for those who belong to him: "we suffer with him in order that we may also be glorified with him" (Rom. 8:17); "If we died with him, we will also live with him; if we endure, we will also reign with him" (2 Tim. 2:11–12). Moreover, the saints' glorious inheritance belongs not to the present order of existence but to a transformed universe and a renewed creation (Eph. 1:10, 18; Col. 1:20).

Persons united to Christ already experience "righteousness and peace and joy in the Holy Spirit" (Rom. 14:17). Still, says Paul, "If in this life only we have hope in Christ, we are of all people the most to be pitied" (1 Cor. 15:19). For "the present form of this world is passing away" (1 Cor. 7:31), and Paul's gospel promises wholeness of life in an imperishable order. If this were an illusory hope, why should Paul aspire to the fellowship of Christ's sufferings (Phil. 3:10)? How could one understand, let alone

---

7. C. S. Lewis speaks of "that great movement of internalisation, and that consequent aggrandisement of man and desiccation of the outer universe, in which the psychological history of the West has so largely consisted" (*The Discarded Image* [Cambridge: Cambridge University Press, 1964], 42).

8. Writes R. P. Martin, *Carmen Christi* (Cambridge: Cambridge University Press, 1967), 311: "The questions that lie aback the fears and uncertainties of the ancient world still persist in a modern scientific age. Are we at the mercy of blind cosmic forces, impersonal and inevitable? Has life a meaning outside of this world? Is the universe friendly? And if there is a God behind and above the phenomena, does He live and rule in love and concern for His creatures? . . . [Phil. 2:6–11] proclaims that the humiliated and obedient Christ is Lord of all spirit powers. Life, therefore, is under His rule and derives its purpose from the meaning which His incarnate existence gives to it."

endure, present sorrow and suffering and struggle against Sin, if the only prospect were more of the same, ended only by death and oblivion? "If the dead are not raised, 'Let us eat and drink, for tomorrow we die'" (1 Cor. 15:32).[9] As it is, we can "boast in our sufferings, because we know that suffering produces . . . hope," a hope that "does not disappoint us" because of what God has already accomplished (Rom. 5:3–11). Present endurance is "inspired by hope in our Lord Jesus Christ" (1 Thess. 1:3 NIV), by the confidence that he will bring his saving work to completion (cf. 1:10). "The hope of salvation" equips us to be "alert and self-controlled" amid spiritual battle (1 Thess. 5:4–11). Knowing that "our salvation is nearer now than when we first believed," we can more resolutely "put off the deeds of darkness" (Rom. 13:11–14). Hope for an amelioration of one's lot within the present order is therapeutic enough. Well-founded hope of a qualitatively different order of life beyond the present enables one to cope with present distresses more effectively: "May the God of hope fill you with all joy and peace as you trust in him, so that you may overflow with hope by the power of the Holy Spirit" (Rom. 15:13 NIV).

We are now ready to consider the great events in which salvation in Christ reaches its appointed goal.

The Return of Christ

In one of his earliest letters Paul affirms his belief in this event: "For the Lord himself will descend from heaven" (1 Thess. 4:16). Over the years the apostle's understanding of Christ's present work in his church steadily deepens, as is especially evident in Ephesians. Yet he never abandons the other conviction; indeed, it comes to its most theologically potent expression in one of his last epistles: "we wait for the blessed hope—the glorious appearing of our great God and Savior, Jesus Christ" (Titus 2:13 NIV).[10]

This event marks the full disclosure of Christ (1 Cor. 1:7, *apokalypsis*). We await "the manifestation (*epiphaneia*) of the glory" (*doxa*) of Christ—a more adequate translation of Titus 2:13 than the above.[11] Paul's favorite term for the event is *parousia*, "presence"—in this case, Christ's "coming."[12] In accord with ancient usage, *parousia* signals the majesty of Christ and the

9. Writes Herman Ridderbos, *Paul: An Outline of His Theology*, trans. John R. DeWitt (Grand Rapids: Eerdmans, 1975), 540: "Without the hope of the resurrection at Christ's parousia the Christian life and the Christian life-struggle lose their meaning."

10. Eph. too awaits the consummation of God's saving purpose: 1:14; 2:7; 4:30; 5:5, 27; 6:8, 13.

11. Thus J. N. D. Kelly, *The Pastoral Epistles* (San Francisco: Harper and Row, 1960), 246; Donald Guthrie, *The Pastoral Epistles* (Grand Rapids: Eerdmans, 1957), 199. Cf. the references to the "glory (*doxa*) of Christ [or the Lord]" in 2 Cor. 3:18; 4:4–6; 8:19, 23; 2 Thess. 2:14. "Manifestation" (*epiphaneia*) is also used of Christ's return in 2 Thess. 2:8; 1 Tim. 6:14; 2 Tim. 4:1, 8 (in 1:10 the term is used of his first advent).

12. BAGD, *s.v.*, 2. Paul uses the term of Christ's return in 1 Cor. 15:23; 1 Thess. 2:19; 3:13; 4:15; 5:23; 2 Thess. 2:1, 8.

splendor of his appearing.[13] In testimony to his grandeur, he is attended by an angelic host under command of "the archangel."[14] "The clouds" (1 Thess. 4:17) signal his deity and reflect his glory.[15] Upon his descent, he summons his people from among the living and the dead, whereupon they "appear with him in glory" (Col. 3:4). Their lowly bodies now transformed into the likeness of Christ's own glorious body, their very appearance magnifies the One who has saved them. Having been caught up in the clouds to accord the King the proper welcome, they attend him for the final stage of his triumphal procession to earth.[16]

Paul's teaching about Christ's return is thoroughly pastoral. On the one hand it offers hope in the face of suffering and sorrow. Christ will come to judge those who oppress the church (2 Thess. 1:4–10). At his return, the "dead in Christ" will be accorded a place of singular honor (1 Thess. 4:14–18, concluding, "Therefore encourage each other with these words"). On the other hand, this event provides an incentive for holy living. "The day of the Lord will come like a thief in the night"—suddenly and unexpectedly (1 Thess. 5:2–3). Christians, however, should not be caught by surprise, for they have been enlightened about and incorporated into God's saving purpose (5:4–5). For that very reason, their lives must be "blameless and holy" (3:13; cf. 4:1–8). The same grace that offers "the blessed hope" of Christ's return "teaches us to say 'No' to ungodliness and worldly passions, and to live self-controlled, upright and godly lives in the present age" (Titus 2:11–13 NIV). The perpetual imminence of Christ's coming discourages idleness and complacency; conversely, the call to holiness in one's place of responsibility combats an unhealthy "rapture fever" (1 Thess. 5:6–23; 2 Thess. 3:6–13). According to Paul the best preparation for the coming of Christ the Lord is daily obedience to his commands.[17]

13. For *parousia* with reference to visits from rulers and gods, see Albrecht Oepke, *TDNT* 5:859–60. The term "denoted the ceremonial arrival of a ruler to a city where he is greeted with honours of one kind and another; the parousia was more than the physical act of arrival; it included the attendant ceremonies in which the ruler was honoured" (Ernest Best, *The First and Second Epistles to the Thessalonians* [New York: Harper and Row, 1972], 353), connotations Best believes to be in view in Paul's usage (ibid., 353–54).

14. "The voice of the archangel" (1 Thess. 4:16) implies an angelic host. Jesus is to be revealed "with his powerful angels" (2 Thess. 1:7). The "holy ones" who attend Christ (1 Thess. 3:13) are, or at least include, the angels (cf. Luke 9:26).

15. On these associations, see Albrecht Oepke, *nephelē* (cloud), *TDNT* 4:902–10.

16. 1 Thess. 4:16–17 (where *apantēsis*, meeting, reflects a "custom of antiquity whereby a public welcome was accorded by a city to important visitors," Erik Peterson, *TDNT* 1:380); 1 Cor. 15:51–53; Phil. 3:20–21; 2 Thess. 1:9–10 (where the "holy ones" [*hagioi*] are "those who have believed"; thus also Best, *1 and 2 Thessalonians*, 265). There is no basis in Paul's letters for the idea that Jesus will first return for his saints and only later with his saints. Believers both living and dead are "caught up" (that is, "raptured") in order to attend Christ for the final stage of his triumphal descent; see Robert H. Gundry, *The Church and the Tribulation* (Grand Rapids: Zondervan, 1973), 103–5.

17. Screwtape advises Wormwood, "He [God, the Enemy] wants men to be concerned with what they do; our business is to keep them thinking about what will happen to them" (C. S. Lewis, *The Screwtape Letters* [New York: Macmillan, 1953], 34).

For he is our Judge, to whom we must give an account of our conduct (2 Cor. 5:9–10).

The Resurrection of the Body

The "already" of believers' newness of life in Christ anticipates, but never supplants or swallows up, the "not yet" of the resurrection of the body upon Christ's return.[18] As surely as the *sarx* (flesh), the instrument of Sin, is appointed for destruction, the *sōma* (body) is destined for resurrection. Believers are saved from the *sarx*, but in the *sōma*.[19] For the present order of existence it is a "psychical (*psychikon*) body," a *sōma* animated by *psychē*; it shall be raised a "spiritual (*pneumatikon*) body," a body animated and dominated by the Spirit (*Pneuma*) of God (Rom. 8:10–11; 1 Cor. 15:44). The former marks one's solidarity with Adam, the latter one's incorporation into the last Adam and participation in the new humanity inaugurated at his resurrection from the dead (1 Cor. 15:20–23, 45–49).[20]

Paul's confidence that believers will be raised rests upon the fact of Christ's own resurrection: "God both raised the Lord and will raise us by his power" (1 Cor. 6:14).[21] Moreover, "as is the man from heaven, so also are they who are of heaven" (1 Cor. 15:48). One respect in which Christ's people shall be conformed to his image (15:49) is to receive a resurrection body like his: "Our citizenship is in heaven, and from there we eagerly await a Savior, the Lord Jesus Christ, who will transform the body of our lowliness that it may become like the body of his glory" (Phil. 3:20–21). In the first place, it is indeed a body that is to be given. Like Jesus' own (Luke 24:39), it shall be fully substantial. It is not an "embodied spirit" that is raised, but a "spiritual body" (1 Cor. 15:44, where, as noted, the adjective signals not immateriality but the work of the Spirit). Secondly, a transformation occurs. The body that belongs to the present order—the "psychical body," "the body of our lowliness"—must be changed if it is to enter the heavenly order (1 Cor. 15:50–54; Phil. 3:21).[22] Thirdly, there is continuity: "we will all be changed," but it is we who are changed (1 Cor. 15:51–52).

---

18. Rom. 6:1–14; 8:1–39; Eph. 1:3–14; Col. 3:1–4; chap. 4, pp. 88–89.

19. Cf. chap. 6, p. 132. There are instances of *sarx* as equivalent to *sōma* (e.g., 2 Cor. 4:10–11; cf. Eduard Schweizer, *TDNT* 7:125–26). Yet never does Paul speak of the raising of the *sarx* from the dead. As Sin's instrument, it is good for nothing but annihilation (1 Cor. 5:5). Yet "even when it is not used in the sense of sinful existence, [*sarx*] always has the meaning of that which is only temporal. It denotes man in his weakness and mortality" (Ridderbos, *Paul*, 548). "Flesh and blood," human life within a perishable order, is not fit for the imperishable order of heaven (1 Cor. 15:50–54); cf. ibid., 545–48. To be sure, the *sōma* as Sin's possession must be destroyed (Rom. 6:6); yet the *sōma* itself is not thereby destroyed but handed over to a new Master (6:11–14). God cares for the *sōma* thus liberated and will surely raise it up (1 Cor. 6:13–14).

20. Cf. the discussion in chap. 4, pp. 85–89.

21. Also Rom. 6:4–10; 1 Cor. 15:3–28; 2 Cor. 4:14; 1 Thess. 4:14; and our discussion on pp. 79–83.

22. What is at most implied in 1 Thess. 4:16–17 is expressly stated in (the later) 1 Cor. 15:51, "We will not all sleep, but we will all [i.e., the living as well as the dead] be changed."

Just as the risen Christ was the very Christ who had died (1 Cor. 15:3–8), so too the Christian does not become another person but the same person in a transformed and glorified state. Paul likens the experience not to replacing one garment by another, but to putting one garment over another: "the perishable must clothe itself with the imperishable, and the mortal with immortality" (1 Cor. 15:53–54 NIV; cf. 2 Cor. 5:4).[23]

Believers who die before Christ returns have not been annihilated or separated from the love of God (Rom. 8:38–39). They are "the dead in Christ," still under his sovereign care and destined for a place of honor in the resurrection (1 Thess. 4:13–16). Second Corinthians affirms not only that deceased believers are with Christ, but that they are conscious of being in his presence and capable of serving him; so that Paul, not surprisingly, prefers "to be away from the body and at home with the Lord" (5:6–9). At the same time the prospect of dying fills Paul with dread, for death causes the disintegration of the self and ushers one into a bodiless existence (2 Cor. 5:1–4).[24] He therefore looks beyond the intermediate state to the day when he shall receive his "eternal house," his resurrection body (5:1–2)—that is, to the day of Christ's *parousia*, when (as he has said in 1 Cor. 15:52) "the trumpet will sound [and] the dead will be raised imperishable." On that day the soul will be reunited with the body, and the self reintegrated.[25] With this "redemption of the body" (Rom. 8:23), death is finally destroyed (1 Cor. 15:26, 54–57), the rule of Sin eradicated, and the mortal "swallowed up by life" (2 Cor. 5:4).

The Final Judgment

Upon his triumphant return to earth, Christ the King will execute the judgment entrusted to him by God the Father. On that day "God will

23. The Westminster *Confession of Faith* affirms that "all the dead shall be raised up with their self-same bodies, and none other, although with different qualities" (34.3). The acorn that perishes comes to life as a full-grown oak tree; at the same time, an acorn is transformed into an oak, not an elm, and the full-grown oak is already present in the acorn. Such an analogy is suggested by 1 Cor. 15:36–38. Yet "the continuity and identity is . . . not to be sought in something that passes from the old body into the new body, but in the miraculous power of God [15:38]. . . . [T]he secret of the continuity does not lie in the human 'being,' but in the Spirit" (Ridderbos, *Paul*, 550, 551).

24. See the discussion in chap. 2, pp. 54–55. On this tension between Paul's desire and dread, see George E. Ladd, *A Theology of the New Testament* (Grand Rapids: Eerdmans, 1974), 552–54. Ridderbos, *Paul*, 507–8, rightly urges caution when speaking of life with Christ in the intermediate state. Paul nowhere describes it, and for us it is "an inconceivable mode of existence" (ibid., 507).

25. 1 Thess. 4:14, 16, "God will bring with Jesus those who have fallen asleep in him . . . the dead in Christ will rise first," may suggest such a reunion. In 2 Cor. 5 Paul expresses the longing that Christ return before his death, so that he will not have to be "unclothed" (by the death of his present body, his "earthly tent") but can instead be immediately "clothed with his heavenly dwelling" (5:4; cf. 1 Cor. 15:53–54). On 2 Cor. 5 as a development of, not a departure from, 1 Cor. 15, see Lincoln, *Paradise*, 60–71. Attentiveness to both immediate and ultimate prospects is also found in Phil.: "For to me to live is Christ and to die is gain. . . . I desire to depart and be with Christ, for that is better by far" (1:21, 23); "we eagerly await a Savior from [heaven, who] . . . will transform the bodies of our lowliness" (3:20–21).

judge the secrets of mankind through Jesus Christ" (Rom. 2:16).[26] The passage which that verse climaxes (Rom. 2:1–16) foretells a judgment embracing all humanity, believers and nonbelievers alike. Later in Romans, Paul speaks to the same effect: "Every knee will bow to me; every tongue will confess to God" (14:11). The judgment awaiting Christians is the special focus of such texts as 1 Corinthians 3:11–15 (those judged have built on the foundation which is Christ) and 2 Corinthians 5:10 (note the repeated "we" in 5:6–10). It is fitting that the judgment follows upon the resurrection of the body; for persons are to give an account "for the things done while in the body" (2 Cor. 5:10) before the dissolution brought on by death. In Paul's teaching about the resurrection (as considered above), it is specifically the experience of Christians that is in view; but his references to a universal judgment imply his belief in the bodily resurrection of non-Christians as well.[27]

The last judgment is a time of disclosure. Each person's "work will be made manifest, for the Day will disclose it" (1 Cor. 3:13). Christ "will bring to light what is hidden in darkness and will expose the motives of men's hearts" (1 Cor. 4:5 NIV; cf. Rom. 2:16). One effect of this is the attendant revelation of God's righteous judgment upon "those who are self-seeking, who disobey the truth and obey unrighteousness" (Rom. 2:8). The day of judgment is also "the day of God's wrath" (2:5), for which the prior manifestations of his wrath "against all ungodliness and unrighteousness of men" (1:18–32) have prepared.[28] By the might of his Word and the splendor of his *parousia*, the Lord Jesus will destroy the last and worst embodiment of the spirit of lawlessness (2 Thess. 2:6–9).[29] By the fire of his judgment and the majesty of his power, he will punish those who oppress God's people, "who do not know God and who do not obey the gospel of our Lord Jesus" (2 Thess. 1:6–9), "who did not believe the truth but took pleasure in unrighteousness" (2:11–12).

26. Since Christ acts as God's representative, we may take Rom. 14:10–11 ("God's judgment seat") and 2 Cor. 5:10 ("the judgment seat of Christ") as twin references to the same event. Language used in the OT of Yahweh's judgment is now applied to Christ (2 Thess. 1:9–10; 2:8).

27. Ridderbos, *Paul*, 555, notes that 2 Thess. 1:8–10 appears to speak only of unbelievers alive when Christ returns, but goes on to say that "the thought of a general resurrection of the dead seems most to correspond to the nature of the judgment that is to take place with the parousia and is also in harmony with what is communicated to us in Acts 24:15 as a pronouncement of Paul ['there will be a resurrection of both righteous and unrighteous']. Against the view that 1 Cor. 15:23–25 envisages two resurrections separated by a millennial kingdom, see Murray J. Harris, *Raised Immortal: Resurrection and Immortality in the New Testament* (Grand Rapids: Eerdmans, 1985), 179–80; Geerhardus Vos, *The Pauline Eschatology* (Grand Rapids: Eerdmans, 1961), 226–60; Ridderbos, *Paul*, 556–59.

28. See chap. 2, pp. 56–57. Speaking of the Jews who "killed the Lord Jesus and the prophets and also drove us out," Paul declares that "the wrath of God has come upon them at last" (1 Thess. 2:15–16 NIV), referring to the forthcoming destruction of Jerusalem (A.D. 70), an especially poignant anticipatory manifestation of "the coming wrath" (1:10). See F. F. Bruce, *1 and 2 Thessalonians* (Waco: Word, 1982), 46–49.

29. On this passage in its biblical context, see Vos, *Eschatology*, 94–135.

It is precisely in face of God's wrath that God's saving righteousness is revealed, both in the cross and in the gospel (Rom. 1:16–18; 3:21–26).[30] "For God did not appoint us to wrath but to the obtaining of salvation through our Lord Jesus Christ" (1 Thess. 5:9). Believers' final rescue from "the coming wrath" (1 Thess. 1:10) occurs at the last judgment. As those who witness the disclosure of their innermost secrets (Rom. 2:16) and the destruction of many of their achievements (1 Cor. 3:10–15), Christ's people will urgently need saving on that day. Before the terrors of judgment, they will find refuge in the Judge himself ("how much more shall we be saved from God's wrath through him," Rom. 5:9), cling to his gift of righteousness ("the righteousness for which we hope," Gal. 5:5), and gladly hear his pronouncement of acquittal ("there is . . . no condemnation for those who are in Christ Jesus," Rom. 8:1). In short, at the last judgment the people of God will have greater cause than ever before to celebrate the wonders of grace; which helps to explain why the final judgment is a theme of the good news according to Paul (Rom. 2:16).[31] As the Thessalonians have embraced the gospel (1 Thess. 1:10; 5:10), their anxiety arises, not over the imminence of the *parousia* but over its delay.

Yet it is not merely evil which the last judgment brings to light. God "will expose the motives of men's hearts. At that time each will receive his praise from God" (1 Cor. 4:5 NIV). Christians whose work survives the fiery test will be rewarded (1 Cor. 3:12–14). Each will receive "the due recompense for the things done in the body, whether good or bad" (2 Cor. 5:10); "the good that each one has done, whether he be slave or free, will receive its due reward from the Lord" (Eph. 6:8). Such statements call for three comments.

1. As "the farmer who does the work should have the first share of the crops" (2 Tim. 2:6), so too there is continuity between the "sowing" of one's present obedience and the "harvest" of eternal life (Gal. 6:8b–9).[32] The proper reward for being in love is marriage, granted for the sake of deepening the partners' love for each other. Correspondingly, the appropriate reward for present service to God is opportunity for further service in the heavenly kingdom—service purged of tedium and pain.[33]

---

30. See chap. 3, pp. 73–76.

31. For this reading of the verse, see Gerhard Friedrich, *TDNT* 2:730; J. Knox Chamblin, *Gospel according to Paul* (Ann Arbor: University Microfilms, 1979), 173–77, 322–28; and NIV (as opposed to KJV). In 2 Thess. 1:8, on the other hand, the gospel is a standard of judgment (cf. 2 Cor. 2:14–17; Chamblin, ibid., 452).

32. The principle "you reap whatever you sow" (Gal. 6:7 NRSV) holds true for wicked works as well: the "harvest" of final punishment is already contained in the "sowing" of sinful practices: Gal. 6:8; Rom. 1:24–28 ("Men . . . received in themselves the due penalty for their perversion," v. 27 NIV).

33. Harris's observation is pertinent: "With a transformed body that is invariably under the sway of the creator Spirit, the believer will have permanent invigoration, unsurpassed beauty, and endless energy" (*Raised Immortal*, 124).

2. Every good work that a Christian accomplishes fulfills God's sovereign purpose and brings God's power to expression. "We are God's workmanship, created in Christ Jesus to do good works, which God prepared in advance for us to do" (Eph. 2:10 NIV). "Continue to work out your salvation with fear and trembling, for it is God who works in you to will and to act according to his good purpose" (Phil. 2:12–13 NIV).[34] Instructive in this regard is Paul's reference to "the crown of righteousness, which the Lord, the righteous Judge, will award to me [and others] on that day" (2 Tim. 4:8). The crown of righteousness points to righteousness itself. For Paul, the justification of the ungodly depends wholly upon the gift of God's righteousness (Rom. 3:21–5:21). Not only so: "the fruit that consists in right conduct" whereby believers will show themselves "pure and blameless for the day of Christ," comes about "through Jesus Christ" (Phil. 1:10–11) no less than does the righteousness by which they are justified (3:9).[35] The crown of righteousness magnifies the God who bestows it. Augustine was right: "thy merits are the gifts of God."[36]

3. In accord with the focus of his whole ministry, the reward that Paul anticipates most eagerly is the completion of God's work in the persons under his apostolic care. "For what is our hope, or joy or crown of boasting before our Lord Jesus at his coming? Is it not you? Yes, you are our glory and joy!" (1 Thess. 2:19–20 NRSV).[37] His hope for "an imperishable crown" (1 Cor. 9:25) is expressed in a passage about his apostolic ministry (9:14–27). Such references confirm the other two observations: for all those who embrace Paul's gospel are trophies of God's grace (Gal. 1:6); and the joy awaiting Paul at the end is but a fuller expression of the joy he now experiences over God's manifest work in his chosen people.[38]

The Hope of Glory

"We rejoice in the hope of the glory of God," says Paul (Rom. 5:2). As employed by Paul the word glory (*doxa*) embraces three ideas. The first is

34. On the compatibility between divine power and human exertions, see chaps. 3, pp. 64–66; 7, p. 176.

35. In rendering *karpon dikaiosynēs* (Phil. 1:11) "the fruit that consists in right conduct," I follow Moisés Silva, *Philippians* (Chicago: Moody, 1988), 60–61.

36. Augustine, "On the Proceedings of Pelagius," trans. B. Holmes, in *Nicene and Post-Nicene Fathers*, ed. Philip Schaff, 1st series (1888; reprint, Grand Rapids: Eerdmans, 1956), 5:199, in comments on 2 Tim. 4:8. He adds that "the crown could not have been given to the man who is worthy of it, unless grace had been first bestowed on him whilst unworthy of it" (ibid.).

37. See the comments on Paul's apostolic struggle and joy in chap. 1, pp. 20–22. Especially striking is Eph. 3:13, "I ask you . . . not to be discouraged because of my sufferings on your behalf, which are your glory" (cf. Col. 1:24).

38. Paul calls the Philippians "my joy and crown" (4:1), both in anticipation of Christ's return (3:20–21) and in view of the good work God has already begun in them (1:3–6). Anticipating the reward of the lasting crown (1 Cor. 9:25) is Paul's present reward (9:17–18), which consists both in offering the gospel "free of charge" (in keeping with the grace of the message itself) and in witnessing its power to transform people (cf. 1 Thess. 1:2–10).

light: "There is one glory of the sun, and another glory of the moon, and another glory of the stars; and star differs from star in glory" (1 Cor. 15:41), that is, in its degree of brilliance.[39] The second is weight: the Hebrew noun *kavōd*, "glory," is related to the verb *kavēd*, "to be heavy, weighty"; 2 Corinthians 4:17 speaks of the "weight of glory."[40] The third is honor: the long hair which is "dishonorable" for a man is a woman's "glory" (1 Cor. 11:14–15); the body "is sown in dishonor [but] raised in glory" (15:43).[41] Paul's interlacing of the three will become apparent as we proceed.

In Paul's teaching, moreover, the hope of glory is related in the closest way to the restoring of the divine image; the fulfillment of the one coincides with the realization of the other. "And all of us, with unveiled faces, seeing the glory (*doxa*) of the Lord as though reflected in a mirror, are being transformed into the same image (*eikōn*) from one degree of glory (*doxa*) to another" (2 Cor. 3:18 NRSV). "For those whom God foreknew he also predestined to be conformed to the image (*eikōn*) of his Son, in order that he might be the firstborn among many brothers. And those whom he predestined . . . he also glorified (*doxazō*)" (Rom. 8:29–30). It is Christ, the image of God, in whose face the glory of God is revealed (2 Cor. 4:4–6). Christ, the One into whose image believers are to be conformed, is their "hope of glory" (Col. 1:27). We will thus consider these two themes together.

Hope for the God of Glory

That for which Paul longs most deeply is not the fully restored image of God or the fully revealed glory of God, but him who is the habitation of both. "For to me to live is Christ and to die is gain. . . . I desire to depart and to be with Christ, for that is better by far" (Phil. 1:21, 23). It is his aspiration to know Christ that impels him toward the heavenly goal (3:10–14); it is Christ himself whose return he eagerly awaits (3:21). The resurrection of the body is a means to a higher end—being "with the Lord forever" (1 Thess. 4:16–17). The principal, though not the exclusive, focus of 1 Corinthians 13:12 ("then we shall see face to face . . . then I shall know fully") is the deeper communion with God and Christ that the consummation brings.[42]

One day Christians will be able to tolerate the now "unapproachable light" of God's dwelling-place (1 Tim. 6:16) and to experience to a far greater degree "the light of the knowledge of the glory of God in the face of Christ" (2 Cor. 4:6). With that will come a greater desire, together with a greater freedom, to "give glory to God" (Rom. 4:20)—that is, to ascribe to

---

39. BAGD, *s.v. doxa*, 1. "brightness, splendor, radiance."
40. On *kavōd* in the Hebrew OT, see Gerhard Kittel, *TDNT* 2:238–42.
41. BAGD, *s.v. doxa*, 3. "fame, renown, honor."
42. The verse also has in view the communion of saints; see chap. 9, 218–19.

him the honor due his holy Name.[43] The opening answer of the Westminster *Shorter Catechism* is that "man's chief end is to glorify God, and to enjoy him forever." As joy spontaneously overflows into praise, and as praise completes joy, we shall discover that glorifying and enjoying God are two aspects of the same experience.[44]

We can now anticipate that experience to some degree, both as we gather for worship and as we fulfill our responsibilities in the world.[45] Recognizing that we presently live in a perishable order, and that all our exertions are tainted by fallenness, we shall not entertain unduly high expectations for ourselves or for others. To expect our present worship and service to be "heavenly" is to place ourselves under intolerable pressure and to assure a more flawed result than would otherwise be the case. Yet as we have seen, there is direct continuity between our present activity and that of heaven. We are like players in spring training, preparing for the regular season; and the work of March often determines where the team stands in September. Endeavors to make present worship God-centered will prove to be the best preparation for the worship of heaven. And the best practice for the service of heaven is obedience to such commands as 1 Corinthians 6:20 ("honor [*doxazō*] God with your body") and 10:31 ("So whether you eat or drink or whatever you do, do all things for the glory [*doxa*] of God").

Hope for the Glory of God

From first to last, the glory belongs to God. Yet as with his righteousness (*dikaiosynē*) and his love (*agapē*), so the glory (*doxa*) that God possesses is a glory that he bestows. "He is . . . a God whose characteristic way of revealing his transcendence is by sharing it."[46] The *locus* for all these gifts is the person of Christ, the Father's supreme gift.[47]

The hope of beholding God's glory is thus joined to the hope of receiving it: "we rejoice in our hope of sharing the glory of God" (Rom. 5:2 RSV). What believers have already experienced of liberation from depravity and bondage makes them long for the completion of God's saving work: "For those

43. The expression *to give glory* (*doxan didonai*) "does not imply the adding of something not already present; it is rather predication in the sense of active acknowledgment [e.g., Rom. 4:20] or in doxologies as the extolling of what is [e.g., Rom. 11:36; 16:27; Eph. 3:21; Phil. 4:20; 1 Tim. 1:17]" (Kittel, *TDNT* 2:248).

44. "If it were possible for a created soul fully . . . to 'appreciate,' that is to love and delight in, the worthiest object of all, and simultaneously at every moment to give this delight perfect expression, then that soul would be in supreme blessedness" (C. S. Lewis, *Reflections on the Psalms* [New York: Harcourt Brace, 1958], 96). In face of heaven's music (to praise God) and silence (to contemplate God), hell resolves to fill the whole universe with nothing but noise (Lewis, *The Screwtape Letters*, 113–14).

45. See chap. 10, pp. 221–24.

46. Frances Young and David F. Ford, *Meaning and Truth in 2 Corinthians* (Grand Rapids: Eerdmans, 1987), 244, with special reference to 2 Cor. 3–4.

47. See, e.g., Rom. 3:21–26; 5:1–21; 2 Cor. 3–4, 8–9 (concluding "Thanks be to God for his indescribable gift!" 9:15); Gal. 4:4–5.

whom God foreknew he also predestined to be conformed to the image of his Son. . . . And those whom he predestined he also called; and those whom he called, he also justified; and those whom he justified, he also glorified" (Rom. 8:29–30).[48] The "wisdom of God," which decrees that the sole basis for boasting in the divine presence is the crucified "Lord of glory (*doxa*)" (1 Cor. 2:8, with 1:18–31), also ordains the glorification of those who belong to Christ (2:7, "God's secret wisdom . . . which God destined for our glory [*doxa*] before time began"). In the end, God honors those who pledge their allegiance and offer their praise to his Son.

Paul closely joins "rejoicing in hope of the glory of God" to "rejoicing in our sufferings" (Rom. 5:2–3). Present trials are related to future glory in two ways. On the one hand, the hope of heaven enables us to persevere amid the innumerable tribulations associated with this perishable order, as we saw earlier in the chapter. We "rejoice in our sufferings, because we know that suffering [eventually produces] hope [which] does not disappoint us" (5:3–5). On the other hand, the hope that equips us to endure is itself a product of affliction: "suffering produces endurance, and endurance character, and character hope" (Rom. 5:3–4). To seek at all costs to avoid pain and to maintain comfort risks the dimming of our hope. Not only so: the realization of hope is itself the product of suffering. Paul declares in 2 Corinthians 4:17 that "our light and momentary affliction is achieving for us an eternal glory that far outweighs it."[49] The same dual emphasis recurs in Romans 8: present sufferings that are "not worth comparing with the glory that is to be disclosed to us," are likened to an expectant mother's labor pains—pains that both forecast the birth and help to bring the child into the world (8:17–25).

Hope for the Glorious Inheritance

The whole of creation is destined to share in the glory awaiting God's people: "The creation itself will be liberated from bondage to decay into the liberty of the glory of the children of God" (Rom. 8:21). "The heavens and the earth," both affected by the fall,[50] will one day be reconciled to God by virtue of Christ's saving work (Col. 1:19). Paul is assured of being brought safely to the "heavenly kingdom" (2 Tim. 4:18). But in the end, at his return,

---

48. Paul's use of the aorist (past) tense for the verb *glorify* as for the others expresses both certainty (that God will bring his saving purpose to its appointed goal) and eagerness (that the consummation come speedily).

49. By the same token 2 Cor. 12:1–10 teaches that a life dominated by "weaknesses, insults, hardships, persecutions and calamities" is better preparation for future glory than is preoccupation with prior revelations of the glory.

50. As a habitation of hostile powers (Eph. 1:21; 3:10; 6:12; Col. 1:16), "heaven" is embraced by "the present evil age," a point well made by Lincoln, *Paradise*, 170–74.

Christ "will bring the glory of heaven to earth"[51] and restore harmony to a fragmented cosmos (Eph. 1:10).

As Adam inherited a garden in which to live and over which to rule (Gen. 1–2), so Christ the last Adam and those who belong to him will one day inhabit, and rule over, a transformed creation—one as fully material as are the bodies of those who inhabit it, one in which the first paradise is not merely regained but surpassed.[52] Here Christ's people will "reign with him" (2 Tim. 2:12; cf. Rom. 5:17). Here, under the rule of the last Adam, to whom God the Father entrusts dominion over the new creation (1 Cor. 15:20–28), the people of God will at last rightly fulfill the mandate of Gen. 1:28.[53] Here the "good works, which God prepared in advance for us to do" (Eph. 2:10), will attain a quality without precedent; here the purpose of God for the bride of Christ will have reached its appointed goal.[54] For now the creation longs for the proper mastery; but when God's people have themselves been redeemed in the resurrection of the body, they will help to liberate the creation from its own bondage. No wonder "the creation with fervent expectation eagerly awaits the revealing of the children of God" (Rom. 8:19–23).[55]

Many of the trials of which we spoke are associated with daily responsibilities in the home and in the workplace. This is especially true for Christians. As creatures they experience the drudgery and anguish that come from laboring in a fallen world (Gen. 3:16–19). As slaves of Christ they are bound to honor him in their every action (1 Cor. 10:31), which inevitably brings them into conflict with the values and habits of "a crooked and depraved generation" (Phil. 2:15). It is therefore to be expected that Christians will "grow weary in well doing" (Gal. 6:9). Yet it is just here that we are being transformed into Christ's image "from one degree of glory to another" (2 Cor. 3:18). "Let us bear the image of the man of heaven" (1 Cor. 15:49 NRSV mg.), exhorts Paul, by which he means that we should give ourselves unstintingly and unreservedly to the work of the Lord (15:58). The charge to "put on the new man, created in God's likeness, in true righteousness and holiness," is obeyed amid a host of relational and vocational responsibilities (Eph. 4:24–32). Such work is emphatically "not in vain," for

---

51. Lincoln, *Paradise*, 188; cf. 195.

52. Cf. Lincoln, *Paradise*, 190. Those who live in this "new creation" (cf. 2 Cor. 5:17) will not have "psychical bodies" like that of Adam before the fall but the "spiritual bodies" promised to those who belong to the last Adam (1 Cor. 15:42–49).

53. Note the reference to Ps. 8:6 in 1 Cor. 15:27, as well as Eph. 1:22 (cf. Harris, *Raised Immortal*, 168–71). 1 Cor. 15:28 marks not the end of Christ's kingly power but the full realization of God's dominion over all things (cf. Ridderbos, *Paul*, 559–62).

54. See the remarks in chap. 3, pp. 62–63.

55. "As (the rest of) creation in the beginning had its role in relation to man, the crown and steward of creation (Gen 1:26–30; 2:19), so creation's rediscovery of its role depends on the restoration of man to his intended glory as the image of God" (James D. G. Dunn, *Romans* [Dallas: Word, 1988], 487).

it is the very path to glorification and the reception of the heavenly reward (1 Cor. 15:58b; Gal. 6:9). When the present labors of Christ's people are consummated in their exercise of responsible dominion over a renewed creation, then and there the image of God shall be fully restored and the glorification of his people completed (Rom. 8:18–25).[56]

There were two groups of people in one building. The first group thought they were occupying a resort hotel; the second thought it was a prison. The first group complained incessantly about the accommodations, the food and the service; the second discovered that things were not nearly so bad as they had anticipated. If we imagine that this perishable order of existence can provide us with paradise, we are doomed to disappointment and disillusionment. But if we view our present sufferings and the daily demands of our work as essential ingredients of life in a penitentiary designed to prepare us for the life everlasting, our expectations will not be unduly high and we can go on our way rejoicing.[57]

Hope for the Glorified Body

The body that is joined to Christ shall be "raised in glory" (1 Cor. 15:43). To be exact, believers are to be granted bodies "like [Jesus'] glorious body" (Phil. 3:21). We have spoken of the nature of the resurrected body. In keeping with our present theme of *doxa*, let us further observe that this body can be expected to be weighty and to be radiant; and that the very existence of such a body demonstrates that God honors those united to his Son. At the moment the body of the believer is raised in glory, he or she will at last fully bear the image of the man from heaven (1 Cor. 15:42–49).[58] It is noteworthy that the two instances of the adjective *conformed* (*summorphos*) in Paul occur in Romans 8:29 ("conformed to the image [*eikōn*] of [God's] Son") and in Philippians 3:21 ("conformed to the body [*sōma*] of [Christ's] glory [*doxa*].")

Paul incorporates the transformation of the individual into a deeper and broader hope. The continuity between the perishable body and the imperishable (1 Cor. 15:51–54) already points to the recognition of others,

---

56. Jacques Ellul, *The Meaning of the City*, trans. Dennis Pardee (Grand Rapids: Eerdmans, 1970), 176, speaking of Eph. 1:10, foresees a day when, "in a brilliant transfiguration," all of man's achievements, "both his technical failures and the marvels of his cleverness," will be "'recapitulated' in Christ, summed up in him, taken over by him." (The verb used in Eph. 1:10, *anakephalaioō*, may be rendered "sum up" or "recapitulate": BAGD, *s.v.*) On this perfecting of the image of God in relation to nature (as well as in relation to God and to other people), see Anthony A. Hoekema, *Created in God's Image* (Grand Rapids: Eerdmans, 1986), 91–96.

57. These remarks augment those on suffering in chap. 7, pp. 169–70.

58. The continuity of the person ("we shall be changed," 1 Cor. 15:51–52), together with believers' worship of Christ, forestalls any notion of "a mystical absorption of individual personalities into the one Person, or a pantheistic absorption of the many into the One" (so rightly Harris, *Raised Immortal*, 127). So it has been from the beginning for those "in Christ" (cf. chap. 4. pp. 90–91).

and the renewal of fellowship, in heaven. Paul places before us a yet grander prospect: the glorification of the whole body of Christ and the manifestation of the fully restored image of God in the new humanity— twin expressions of one great reality. One day Christ will present to himself "a church gloriously radiant . . . holy and blameless" (Eph. 5:26–27). On that same day and in that very place the "new man," whom Christ died to create, will reach maturity (Eph. 2:15; 4:13–15), and the whole company of those incorporated into the last Adam will corporately bear his image (1 Cor. 15:21–22, 45–49). In summoning believers to works of service for building up (*oikodomē*) the body of Christ (Eph. 4:12), Paul has in view neither individuals' growth in piety nor the increase of the church's numbers (though he favors both), but the qualitative growth of the whole church to "the mature person, to the measure of the stature of the fullness of Christ" (4:13).[59]

The hope expressed in 1 Corinthians 13:12 ("then we shall see face to face . . . then I shall know fully") embraces both God and those who have been adopted into God's family through union with Christ. We already know that God typically mediates knowledge of himself through other members of the body of Christ. In that day we shall likewise discover that God discloses his glory to us through other members of the glorified humanity. "The Glory flows into everyone, and back from everyone: like light and mirrors. But the light's the thing."[60]

The life everlasting will afford us endless opportunities for growth in the communion of saints.[61] As observed earlier, we now see but poor reflections, or as it were, mere photographs of one another. Freedom and intimacy are disconcertingly elusive even in the most mature relationships.

> So our person is, as it were, bound up with our destiny. Something of it is revealed at every turning-point in our lives. . . . But to the end the revelation remains incomplete. The person is still unseen; what we see is but the reflections of it in the manifestations of the body and the mind. It eludes all our attempts to lay hold on it in order to dissect it. . . . It is a mysterious spiritual reality, mysteriously linked to God, mysteriously linked with our fellows. We are aware of these links at those privileged moments when there springs

---

59. This translation of 4:13 comes from Andrew T. Lincoln, *Ephesians* (Dallas: Word, 1990), 256. "The Church in this state is seen as a corporate entity, not as disparate individuals [as was true in Col. 1:28]" (ibid.). On this use of *oikodomē*, see Ralph P. Martin, "Patterns of Worship in New Testament Churches," *JSNT* 37 (October 1989): 72–73 (following Philipp Vielhauer).

60. C. S. Lewis, *The Great Divorce* (London: Bles, 1946), 75–76. In keeping with Paul's understanding of *doxa*, Lewis depicts the inhabitants of heaven as the Shining Ones and the Solid People (weightier than they were on earth), all equally honorable and famous. Hell, by contrast, is dark and dreary, occupied by Ghosts and Shades (beings less solid than they were on earth), forever resistant to being honored by God.

61. For a fascinating treatment of this subject, see Peter J. Kreeft, *Everything You Ever Wanted to Know About Heaven . . . But Never Dreamed of Asking* (San Francisco: Ignatius, 1990), 51–83.

up a fresh current of life, bursting the fatal fetters of the personage, asserting its freedom and breaking out into love.[62]

But in that day when sin is abolished, and with it our alienation from God and from each other, we shall become capable of relating to one another with far greater freedom and intimacy than is now possible or tolerable or even imaginable. In that day *agapē* will be more than a concept and an ideal; it shall have become our normal way of relating to one another, our daily routine. That which we now "know in part" (both in our thinking and in our experience) we shall then know in its fullness. We shall find joy in heaven by being called out of ourselves, to find full selfhood through utter self-abandonment. Such a prospect we can but dimly perceive, since such self-giving is now frustratingly elusive and invariably mixed with selfish motives. But in heaven we shall understand (both as *savoir* and as *connaître*) that "self exists to be abdicated and, by that abdication, becomes the more truly self, to be thereupon yet the more abdicated, and so forever."[63]

All of us have difficulty getting along with other people: perhaps we find them frightening or offensive or tedious. When someone so affects me, it helps me to realize that some people view me in the same ways. It also helps to think of that person in light of things to come, as a person clothed with God's glory or forever removed from it.

It is a serious thing to remember that the dullest and most uninteresting person you can talk to, may one day be a creature which, if you saw it now, you would be strongly tempted to worship, or else a horror and a corruption such as you now meet, if at all, only in a nightmare. . . . It is in the light of these overwhelming possibilities, that we should conduct all our dealings with one another. . . . There are no *ordinary* people. You have never talked to a mere mortal. Nations, cultures, arts, civilisations—these are mortal. . . . But it is immortals whom we joke with, work with, marry, snub, and exploit—immortal horrors or everlasting splendors. . . . Next to the Blessed Sacrament itself, your neighbour is the holiest object presented to your senses. If he is your Christian neighbour he is holy in almost the same way, for in him also Christ . . . the glorifier and the glorified, Glory Himself, is truly hidden.[64]

The subject of our concluding chapter is thus introduced.

Finish, then, Thy new creation;
Pure and spotless let us be;

62. Paul Tournier, *The Meaning of Persons*, trans. Edwin Hudson (New York: Harper and Row, 1957), 233–34. See my remarks on "the endurance of love" in chap. 9, pp. 218–20.
63. C. S. Lewis, *The Problem of Pain* (New York: Macmillan, 1955), 140.
64. C. S. Lewis, "The Weight of Glory," in *They Asked for a Paper* (London: Bles, 1962), 210–11.

Let us see Thy great salvation
Perfectly restored in Thee;
Changed from glory into glory,
Till in heaven we take our place,
Till we cast our crowns before Thee,
Lost in wonder, love, and praise.[65]

65. Charles Wesley, "Love Divine, All Loves Excelling" (1747).

12

The Family Celebration

Let us come, finally, to the Lord's table. I wish that it were possible for us, writer and readers together, to do so in fact. We can at least think together about the event; there is in my judgment no better way to conclude our study.

The Disclosure of God

Here, as in every other respect, Paul is God-centered. It is "the church of God" that gathers for the meal (1 Cor. 11:22), the church that God creates and possesses (3:9). It is "the Lord's table" around which believers gather (10:21), "the Lord's Supper" that they eat (11:20), "the Lord Jesus" who inaugurates the event (11:23) and fills it with meaning (11:24–26).[1]

"God, as it were, focuses His entire being at particular points of intense light and heat, that we may see, and feel, and appropriate."[2] The Eucharist is one such point. Here Christ himself is present in a singular way. Here the Word of Christ is declared both verbally and visibly. "For as often as you eat this bread and drink the cup, you proclaim the Lord's death until he comes" (1 Cor. 11:26). The verbal word (starting with this passage) inter-

---

1. Paul received this account from Jesus (the source of the tradition) through some such person as Peter (cf. Gal. 1:18). See I. Howard Marshall, *Last Supper and Lord's Supper* (Grand Rapids: Eerdmans, 1980), 32; Gordon D. Fee, *The First Epistle to the Corinthians* (Grand Rapids: Eerdmans, 1987), 548–49.
2. C. F. D. Moule, *Worship in the New Testament* (London: Lutterworth, 1961), 83.

prets the visible; the visible dramatizes the verbal. By both means attention is drawn to Christ crucified.[3]

The Lord's Supper does not enact a sacrifice but remembers that "Christ, our Passover lamb, was sacrificed" (1 Cor. 5:7).[4] We recall the night on which Jesus was "handed over" (11:23)—betrayed by Judas and delivered over by God the Father to death.[5] In obedience to Jesus' command, we remember the death itself: "This is my body, which is for you. . . . This cup is the new covenant in my blood . . ." (11:24–25). To aid us in both the remembrance and the proclamation, we invoke Paul's manifold teaching about the cross, from the confession of 1 Corinthians 15:3 to the exposition of Romans 3:21–26.[6]

In the very disclosure of these great spiritual realities, we encounter unfathomable mystery. To be sure, Paul adamantly opposes the notion of "mystery" as esoteric wisdom reserved for the spiritually advanced. For him mystery (*mystērion*) is an *uncovered* secret: God's wisdom, formerly hidden, is now to be made known; "the mystery of the gospel" and "the mystery of Christ" are to be universally proclaimed; and all God's people, not just a chosen few, are promised instruction in "the deep things of God" by the Spirit of wisdom.[7] Yet significantly, Paul retains the word *mystery* (*mystērion*). In being revealed the mystery does not cease to be a mystery: "Its concealment is always manifest with its proclamation."[8] This is true for the cross as for the rest of Paul's gospel. We believe that "the Lord of glory" was crucified (1 Cor. 2:8), yet we cannot comprehend how that could happen.[9] We believe that "God made him who knew no sin to be sin for us" (2 Cor. 5:21), and that "Christ redeemed us from the curse of the law by becoming a curse for us" (Gal. 3:13). Such truth overwhelms us, not because it is com-

3. For the interaction of the verbal and the visible in the Jewish Passover, see Exod. 12:26–27; 13:7–8. "Both Word and sacrament bear witness to Christ. Both promise salvation in Christ. Both quicken our faith in Christ. Both enable us to feed on Christ in our hearts" (John R. W. Stott, *Between Two Worlds* [Grand Rapids: Eerdmans, 1982], 114).

4. "Like the Passover, the Holy Communion is the memorial of an atoning sacrifice, but is not itself an expiatory offering" (E. M. B. Green, "Eucharistic Sacrifice in the New Testament and the Early Fathers," in *Eucharistic Sacrifice*, ed. J. I. Packer [London: Church Book Room Press, 1962], 64). So also Marshall, *Lord's Supper*, 147–50.

5. As the subject of the action denoted by the verb (*paradidōmi*) is not stated, this dual understanding is at least possible. The same verb is used of God's handing his Son over, and Christ's handing himself over, to death (Rom. 4:25; 8:32; Gal. 2:20; Eph. 5:25). Cf. C. K. Barrett, *The First Epistle to the Corinthians* (New York: Harper and Row, 1968), 266.

6. For Paul's teaching on the cross, see chap. 3, pp. 70–79.

7. See the use of *mystērion* in Rom. 11:25; 16:25; 1 Cor. 2:1 (if the true reading), 7 (with 2:6–16); 4:1; 15:51; Eph. 1:9; 3:3–4, 9; 6:19; Col. 1:26–27; 2:2; 4:3; 1 Tim. 3:16.

8. Günther Bornkamm, *TDNT* 4:822, on Paul's use of *mystērion*.

9. The declaration that "in Christ all the fullness of the Deity lives in bodily form" (Col. 2:9; 1:19) both teaches us that Christ discloses God (cf. 1:15a) and confronts us with the wonder of the God-Man (cf. 1 Tim. 3:16), a wonder that becomes yet deeper when we consider that in Christ "all things [in heaven and on earth] hold together" even while he is "making peace through his blood, shed on the cross" (Col. 1:16–17, 20; cf. Heb. 1:2–3).

plicated but because it is far too marvelous for finite minds to fathom.[10] It is simultaneously illuminating and incomprehensible. So we both rejoice in the knowledge of sins forgiven through Christ's redemptive blood, and bow in wonder before the impenetrable mystery of grace (Eph. 1:7).

The mystery deepens with the realization that the Christ whom we remember is present at our gathering. He presides over this meal as surely as he did over the Last Supper. This meal, no less than those beside the sea (John 21) and at Emmaus (Luke 24), is one of communion with the risen Lord. The Eucharist offers not just tokens of Christ's presence but Christ himself: "Christ himself is the matter of the Supper."[11] His spiritual presence is just as real as the physical presence of the bread and cup.[12] Christ is continually present with his people, but in this meal our life "in Christ" is experienced and celebrated to an exceptional degree.[13]

The presence of Christ in the congregation is "an earnest of his coming at the End. . . . The eucharistic meal of the community . . . occupies its appointed place between Christ's resurrection meal and the expected eschatological meal."[14] In the Lord's Supper we "proclaim the Lord's death until he comes" (1 Cor. 11:26). The messianic banquet at the consummation of history will celebrate Christ's final defeat of Sin and all its agencies (1 Cor. 15:20–28). Thus the community that gathers to remember Christ's victory in the decisive battle at the cross, and to enjoy the company of the king, also longs for the end of the war: "Come, O Lord!" (1 Cor. 16:22).[15]

It would be wrong, in my judgment, to infer from 1 Corinthians 11:26 (together with Mark 14:25) that the Lord's Supper will terminate with Christ's return, or (alternatively) to assume that the messianic banquet is a single event. It would be consistent with Paul's accent on the cross for the Lord's Supper to occupy a central place in heaven's perpetual worship of Christ. Such a celebration would be consistent too with the perpetuity of

---

10. "The modern mind always mixes up two different ideas: mystery in the sense of what is marvellous, and mystery in the sense of what is complicated" (G. K. Chesterton, *The Penguin Complete Father Brown* [New York: Penguin, 1981], 99).

11. John Calvin, *Institutes of the Christian Religion*, ed. John T. McNeill, trans. Ford Lewis Battles (Philadelphia: Westminster, 1960), 1405; cf. 1370–71.

12. Ibid., 1362–63. Cf. Westminster *Confession of Faith*, 31.7.

13. "The analogy has been used of a child who is conscious of the love which his father has for him and which is the constant atmosphere in the home; yet there can be occasions when the father takes the child in his arms and expresses his love for him in a special way. The love is real and constant all the time, but it needs to be given special expression from time to time in a way that would lose its value and effect if it were continual" (Marshall, *Lord's Supper*, 152).

14. Oscar Cullmann, *Early Christian Worship*, trans. A. Stewart Todd and James B. Torrance (London: SCM, 1953), 14, 16.

15. 1 Cor. 16:19–24 accords well with a eucharistic setting, though it need not have this reference exclusively. The "coming" of 16:22 is Christ's return (cf. 11:26), rather than his self-manifestation in the eucharist or another Christian gathering. See the discussions in Gordon P. Wiles, *Paul's Intercessory Prayers: The Significance of the Intercessory Prayer Passages in the Letters of St Paul* (Cambridge: Cambridge University Press, 1974), 150–54; Marshall, *Lord's Supper*, 116–17; Fee, *1 Corinthians*, 837–39.

faith, hope and love, and with the deeper experience of knowing God and his people which heaven affords (1 Cor. 13:12–13).[16]

Receiving God's Provision

By that disclosure of God we see ourselves in a clearer light. Paul exhorts each individual to engage in self-examination before receiving the bread and the cup, lest one partake "in an unworthy manner" and be "guilty of sinning against the body and blood of the Lord" (1 Cor. 11:27–28). The very reason Paul includes the tradition about the Supper is to address manifold sin within the Corinthian church—particularly pride and the self-centeredness and self-confidence that it breeds. Some regarded the sacraments as talismans that would protect them whatever their behavior (10:1–13). Some considered themselves strong enough to participate in the Lord's Supper together with pagan feasts without endangering themselves (10:14–24). Some used the common meal (to which the Eucharist was joined) to show they were socially and economically superior to others (11:17–34).

We may well be guilty of those very sins. Yet we may have become accustomed to thinking in terms of "problems" rather than "sins," and to blaming parents or government or our socioeconomic condition for those problems. Perhaps we have also been influenced by a kindred current of thought, namely, that God is responsible for seeing that our needs are satisfied and our problems solved, and shall answer to us should he fail to do so.[17] The Supper calls us—the very people of God—to a renewed sense of personal sin and to the realization that we are answerable to God, not he to us. One reason "mystery is the vital element of Dogmatics,"[18] including a theology of the Eucharist, is that it combats human arrogance and shows us that the Christ of the Supper cannot be brought under our control, intellectually or otherwise. "On the contrary, not the Lord, but the human being and human behavior are seized and impounded in the eucharist, being put under Christ's reign—and judgment [1 Cor. 11:29–32]."[19]

Such an awareness prepares us to receive the grace of the sacrament. We are reminded that Christ gave his body for us (1 Cor. 11:24), and that

16. On the Lord's Supper as an anticipation of the heavenly banquet, see Marshall, *Lord's Supper*, 79–80, 152–53, 157.

17. On these marks of the "modern view" of reality, see C. S. Lewis, "Christian Apologetics," in *God in the Dock*, ed. Walter Hooper (Grand Rapids: Eerdmans, 1970), 94–96; "God in the Dock," ibid., 240–44.

18. Herman Bavinck, quoted in John R. DeWitt, *What Is the Reformed Faith?* (Edinburgh: Banner of Truth, 1981), 10.

19. Peter Lampe, "The Corinthian Eucharistic Dinner Party: Exegesis of a Cultural Context (1 Cor. 11:17–34)," *Affirmation* 4 (Fall 1991): 11. "Christ's real presence in the eucharist is not at our disposal. . . . The Lord is sovereign and not domesticated in human sacramental acts" (ibid.). On Christ as One who cannot be owned or managed, see Thomas Howard, *Christ the Tiger* (New York: Lippincott, 1967), 154–55.

the forgiveness promised in the new covenant becomes ours through his blood (1 Cor. 11:25).[20] To participate in the body and blood of Christ (1 Cor. 10:16) is personally to appropriate the saving benefits of his death, to claim by faith (exercised in receiving the elements) that his blood has covered my sin, has cleansed me from my guilt, has averted the wrath of God, has secured my acquittal before God the Judge, and has redeemed me from slavery to Sin. Behaving "unworthily" is to receive the meal without deep awareness of my personal need and of Christ's mercy on my behalf. Those who are acutely aware of their guilt and who pray accordingly ("We are not worthy so much as to gather up the crumbs under Thy table") are the very ones for whom the table is spread.[21] The greatest sin is to spurn God's grace here offered, to ignore or resist the gospel here verbally and visibly declared, to boast in anything other than the cross (Gal. 6:14), to withhold love from the Lord who has sacrificed himself (1 Cor. 16:22).[22] "Self-righteousness (instead of looking to the cross for justification), self-indulgence (instead of taking up the cross to follow Christ), self-advertisement (instead of preaching Christ crucified) and self-glorification (instead of glorying in the cross)—these are the distortions which make us 'enemies' of Christ's cross [Phil. 3:18]."[23]

As "the table of demons" entails contact with the demons themselves, so in contrast "the Lord's table" offers intimate communion with the Lord himself (1 Cor. 10:18–22). The Christ who presides over the meal gives of himself in the meal. "Just as bread and wine sustain physical life, so are souls fed by Christ."[24] "Feed on [Christ] in your heart by faith with thanksgiving," is the invitation of *The Book of Common Prayer*. That this happens we confidently say; how it happens we cannot fathom. John Calvin said of the matter: "If anyone should ask me how this takes place, I shall not be ashamed to confess that it is a secret too lofty for either my mind to comprehend or my words to declare. And, to speak more plainly, I rather experience than understand it."[25]

We experience this grace in face both of our culpability, our sin and guilt, and of our inability, our spiritual and emotional impotence. The feast offers not only "solace for sinners" but also "medicine for the sick [and]

20. See also Exod. 24:7–8; Jer. 31:31–34; Matt. 26:28; Eph. 1:7. Here, as in the Bible generally, "a covenant is a bond-in-blood sovereignly administered"(O. Palmer Robertson, *The Christ of the Covenants* [Phillipsburg, N.J.: Presbyterian and Reformed, 1980], 15).

21. The quotation comes from "The Order for the Administration of the Lord's Supper" in *The Book of Common Prayer*.

22. The link between 1 Cor. 16:19–24 and 11:17–34 has already been noted. On the place of the "anathema" in this context, see Wiles, *Prayers*, 150–54. It is to be noted that the warning of judgment is followed by the offer of the Lord's grace (16:23) and the apostle's love (16:24).

23. John R. W. Stott, *The Cross of Christ* (Downers Grove: InterVarsity, 1986), 351.

24. Calvin, *Institutes*, 1361.

25. *Institutes*, 1403. Souls are fed by "the secret working of the Spirit" (ibid.).

alms to the poor."[26] Many who come to this table are acutely aware both of Sin's grip upon them and of their powerlessness to break it. All that is required of such people is the capacity to cling to the mighty grace of Christ the Lord (2 Cor. 12:9–10).[27]

Furthermore, we are healed and restored as whole persons.[28] To aid our encounter with the "immense invisibles," God activates all five senses. We see the elements; we hear the Word of the cross; we hold the loaf and the cup; we smell and taste them both. The gospel, as proclaimed both verbally and visibly, is "the power of God for salvation," for wholeness in every sense of the word (Rom. 1:16). The heart in all its dimensions is nourished. Our reason is renewed by ever deeper exploration into the meaning of Jesus' death. Communion with Christ contributes to our mental health.[29] Our emotions are stirred by the great indicatives of the cross. Appropriating its saving benefits liberates us from paralyzing guilt; feeding upon Christ provides healing for deep emotional wounds. Our wills are activated. Contemplation of Christ's sacrifice moves us to a sacrifice of our own (Rom. 12:1). As sin is brought to light, we purpose "to lead a new life, following the commandments of God, and walking from henceforth in his holy ways."[30]

Yet despite our repeated appropriation of sacramental grace, we remain fallen and fallible beings. In directing our attention to Christ's return (1 Cor. 11:26), to the day when the imperfect disappears and all is perfected (13:10), the Supper rekindles our hope. The fact that our hearts are feeding on Christ at the very moment our bodies are being nourished by the bread and the cup points to the day when the disintegration of death is reversed, the soul reunited with the body, and the person made whole for the celebration of the heavenly banquet for all eternity.[31]

---

26. Ibid., 1419. Thomas à Kempis calls this sacrament "the health of soul and body, the remedy for every sickness of the spirit. By it my faults are cured, my passions curbed, temptations overcome or weakened. Grace is outpoured in richer measure, virtue that has taken root is strengthened; faith is increased, hope made strong, love kindled to envelop all my being" (*The Imitation of Christ*, trans. Betty I. Knott [London: Collins, 1963], 223). The whole of book 4 ("A Reverent Recommendation to Holy Communion," 213–50) may be read with great profit.

27. Richard E. Ecker, "Whatever Happened to Grace?" *Perspectives* (March 1992): 12–14, respects the distinction between culpability and capability, and observes that the help offered the physically disabled is often denied the emotionally disabled. He considers that "the need for emotional rehabilitation is the most compelling unmet human need in our culture today" (14). He quotes an unnamed pastoral counselor: "I have talked with a lot of hurting people over the years. With few exceptions, they were solidly in touch with the extent of their sins. Where they needed help was getting in touch with the grace of God" (14).

28. See Anthony A. Hoekema, *Created in God's Image* (Grand Rapids: Eerdmans, 1986), 203–26, for strong emphasis on the human being as a psychosomatic unity. Cf. chap. 2, pp. 42–46.

29. One practical effect of a unitary view of the self is to recognize that "in live human beings, spiritual and mental health are inextricably interwoven" (Howard Clinebell, quoted in Hoekema, *Created in God's Image*, 226).

30. From "The Order for the Administration of the Lord's Supper," in *The Book of Common Prayer*.

31. On the planet Venus, Professor Ransom came to perceive more clearly "that unhappy division between soul and body which resulted from the Fall. Even on earth the sacraments existed as a permanent reminder that the division was neither wholesome nor final" (C. S. Lewis, *Perelandra* [New York: Macmillan, 1968], 144).

The Communion of Saints

We do not partake of this meal as isolated individuals. How absurd to imagine going into your kitchen, cutting yourself a piece of bread and pouring yourself a glass of wine, consuming them and then announcing that you have just celebrated the Holy Communion. This very name signals fellowship both with the Holy Trinity and with the people of God. As the bread and the cup are tangible reminders of Christ's atoning sacrifice, the gathered body of Christ bears visible witness to the effects of his saving work. "And is not the bread that we break a participation in the body of Christ? Because there is one loaf, we, who are many, are one body, for we all partake of the one loaf" (1 Cor. 10:16–17 NIV).[32]

The cardinal Christian virtues here work in concert. Faith clings to Christ and appropriates his salvation (1 Cor. 11:24–25). Hope eagerly awaits his return (11:26; 16:22a). Love is directed both to Christ (1 Cor. 16:22) and to his people (16:24; chap. 13). "We cannot love Christ without loving him in the brethren."[33]

Paul is appalled that the gathering in which believers' unity should be most pronounced is marked by division and dominated by pride rather than love (1 Cor. 11:17–22, 33–34).[34] His warning not to receive the meal "in an unworthy manner" (11:27) directly addresses the issue: "For the one who eats and drinks without recognizing the body of the Lord eats and drinks judgment upon himself" (11:29). Given the repeated references to both body and blood, and to both eating and drinking, in the surrounding verses (11:23–28, 30), it is in my judgment highly probable that verse 29 speaks of "recognizing the body of the Lord," which is the church.[35] Contemplation of the cross, and present communion with Christ, calls believers to behavior like that of the Christ under whose grace and judgment they gather.[36] In remembering the One who emptied himself and became obedient to death, let them (especially the noble and the mighty) likewise humble themselves before other members of the body (Phil. 2:1–11), if only in so small a way as waiting for one another and dining together (1 Cor.

---

32. The "body of Christ," remembered in the Supper (11:24), provided one impetus for Paul's understanding of the church as "the body of Christ" (10:16–17; 12:12–27; Marshall, *Lord's Supper*, 154–55).

33. Calvin, *Institutes*, 1415. He notes that Augustine "frequently calls this Sacrament 'the bond of love'" (ibid.).

34. On (1) the social conditions behind the conflicts of 1 Cor. 11, (2) the joining of the Eucharist to an ordinary fellowship meal, and (3) the frequency of such celebrations, see, e.g., Lampe, "The Corinthian Eucharistic Dinner Party," 1–8; Moule, *Worship*, 18–29; Marshall, *Lord's Supper*, 108–111, 144–46.

35. For this understanding of "body" in 11:29, see especially Fee, *1 Corinthians*, 559–64. Cf. A. J. B. Higgins, *The Lord's Supper in the New Testament* (London: SCM, 1952), 72–73. Moule sees a dual reference: "the body of Christ surrendered for us and that body, which is the Church, which was thereby created" (*Worship*, 37); similarly Günther Bornkamm, "Lord's Supper and Church in Paul," in *Early Christian Experience*, trans. Paul L. Hammer (New York: Harper and Row, 1969), 148–49.

36. A point well made by Lampe, "The Corinthian Eucharistic Dinner Party," 10–11. The Supper "effects an actual participation in Christ's sacrificed life" (Moule, *Worship*, 35).

11:33). In being newly reconciled to God by confession of sin and appropriation of Christ's atoning work (2 Cor. 5:14–21), let them seek reconciliation with believers too (1 Cor. 16:20, "Greet one another with a holy kiss").[37] *The Book of Common Prayer* summons to the table persons who are "in love and charity with [their] neighbors," and who also "repent of [their] sins . . . and intend to lead a new life." It may be that we need to repent our lack of charity and to take action to heal a broken relationship. What better place than the Supper for Christians to offer and receive forgiveness?

The risen Christ manifests himself to us and nourishes us through other believers around the table. I was recently asked to lead a worship service for a church whose pastor (a friend and former student of mine) had been killed in an automobile accident less than a week earlier. We gathered as a shocked and shattered and deeply saddened people. In God's providence the Lord's Supper was already scheduled for this Lord's Day. Christ consoled and healed and restored us both by his own presence and through other members of his body (cf. 2 Cor. 1:3–7).

We commune with God and with one another in light of the manifold "hope of glory," a prospect that fills us both with wonder (it is one ingredient in the "mystery" of the meal) and with longing (1 Cor. 16:22). "On a transformed earth, where perfect communion with God will have become a reality through a transformation of the body, Jesus will again, as now at the Lord's Supper, act as *paterfamilias* and break the blessed bread and offer them the cup of thanksgiving—he himself being once more the giver and the server, and his own the recipients, who in eating and drinking receive the salvation gift of God: eternal life."[38]

The Peace of God, which passeth all understanding, keep your hearts and minds in the knowledge and love of God, and of his Son Jesus Christ our Lord: And the Blessing of God Almighty, the Father, the Son, and the Holy Spirit, be amongst you, and remain with you always. Amen.[39]

---

37. The applicability of this passage to a eucharistic setting has already been noted. "The exchange of mutual greetings would be sealed by the rite of the holy kiss [later called "the kiss of peace"], in itself part of the communion rite, and an act of reconciliation" (Wiles, *Prayers*, 151). Viewed as a liturgical introduction to the Supper itself, 1 Cor. 16:19–24 "signifies that before the meal a complete brotherhood should be established" (Cullmann, *Worship*, 20).

38. Joachim Jeremias, *The Eucharistic Words of Jesus*, trans. Norman Perrin (New York: Scribners, 1966), 218.

39. The concluding blessing in "The Order for the Administration of the Lord's Supper," *The Book of Common Prayer*.

Subject Index

Person Index

Allender, Dan B., 214n
Anselm, 69n, 226
Arnold, Clinton E., 83n, 178n
Augustine, 105n, 226, 233, 250, 265n
Aune, David E., 18n

Banks, Robert, 200n, 202n, 203n
Barrett, C. K., 19n, 25n, 53n, 88n, 142n, 164n, 173n, 185n, 187n, 191n, 210n, 228n, 260n
Barth, Karl, 128n
Bavinck, Herman, 104n, 141n, 262n
Baxter, Richard, 232n
Beare, F. W., 163n
Behm, Johannes, 43n, 44n, 47n, 51n, 52n
Bell, Daniel, 226n
Bellah, Robert, 199n
Bennett, Arthur, 129n, 179n, 198n
Bernard of Clairvaux, 106n
Berne, Eric, 148n
Bertram, Georg, 114n
Best, Ernest, 46n, 62n, 90n, 91n, 197n, 245n
Black, David Alan, 181n, 182n, 188n
Bloesch, Donald G., 58n, 233n, 236n
Bloom, Allan, 28n, 33n
Bonhoeffer, Dietrich, 163, 224n

Boogaart, Thomas, 93n
Bornkamm, Günther, 49n, 50n, 52n, 53n, 55n, 96n, 172, 173, 190n, 217n, 220n, 260n, 265n
Brady, Nicholas, 153n
Bridges, Jerry, 153n, 159n, 160n, 226n
Brown, Colin, 158n
Bruce, F. F., 24n, 27n, 29n, 41n, 50n, 54n, 68n, 73n, 78n, 93n, 101n, 133n, 134n, 137n, 140n, 141n, 164n, 177n, 184n, 189n, 197n, 242n, 248n
Brunner, Emil, 58n
Buckley, William F., Jr., 57n
Budry, Edmond, 83n
Bultmann, Rudolf, 37–38, 45n, 47n, 49n, 56n, 113n, 172n

Caird, G. B., 44n, 83n
Calvin, John, 37–38, 58n, 105n, 106n, 150n, 151n, 261n, 263, 265n
Capon, Robert Farrar, 22n, 112n
Carson, D. A., 185n, 193n, 209n, 211n, 212n, 218n, 219
Chadwick, Henry, 138n
Chamblin, J. Knox, 18n, 26n, 27n, 33n, 35n, 79n, 101n, 210n, 249n
Chesterton, G. K., 125n, 261n

Chilton, Bruce, 27n
Chrysostom, 231n
Clinebell, Howard, 264n
Coenen, Lothar, 200n
Cole-Whittaker, Terry, 106n
Colson, Charles, 127n, 199n
Conzelmann, Hans, 26n, 49n
Cooper, John W., 42n
Covey, Stephen R., 159n
Crabb, Lawrence J., Jr., 13n, 19n, 29n, 35n, 108n, 154n, 168n, 214n, 217n
Cranfield, C. E. B., 50n, 123n, 133n, 142n, 143n, 171n, 173n, 176n, 233n
Cullmann, Oscar, 204n, 225n, 230n, 231n, 261n, 266n

Davies, W. D., 91n
de Witt, John R., 262n
deLacey, D. R., 151n
Demmler, Dieter W., 96n
Denney, James, 78n
Dickens, Charles, 193n
Dobson, James, 147
Dodd, C. H., 47n, 113n, 114n, 131n, 174n, 191n
Dunn, James D. G., 18n, 31n, 38n, 41n, 44n, 45n, 50n, 52n, 53n, 55n, 56n, 57n, 68n, 69n, 70n, 72n, 74n, 75n, 77n, 79n, 87n, 88n, 95n, 99n, 103n, 123n, 125n, 126n, 142n, 145n, 156n, 174n, 175n, 176n, 208n,

271